Shojo Beat

BABY & Me

Vol. 6

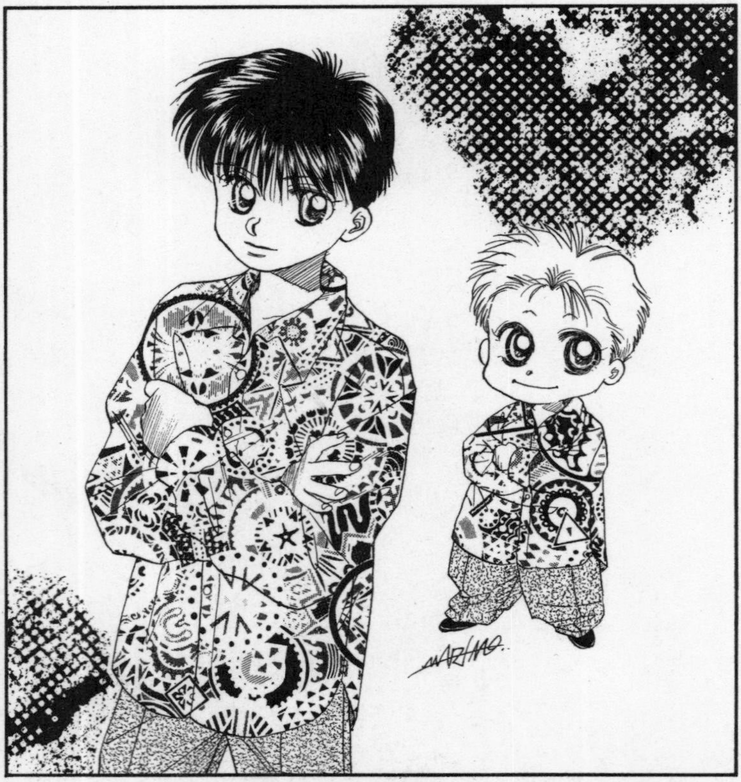

Story & Art by Marimo Ragawa

BABY & ME **Table of Contents**

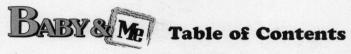

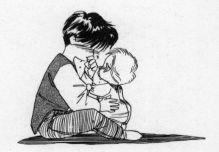

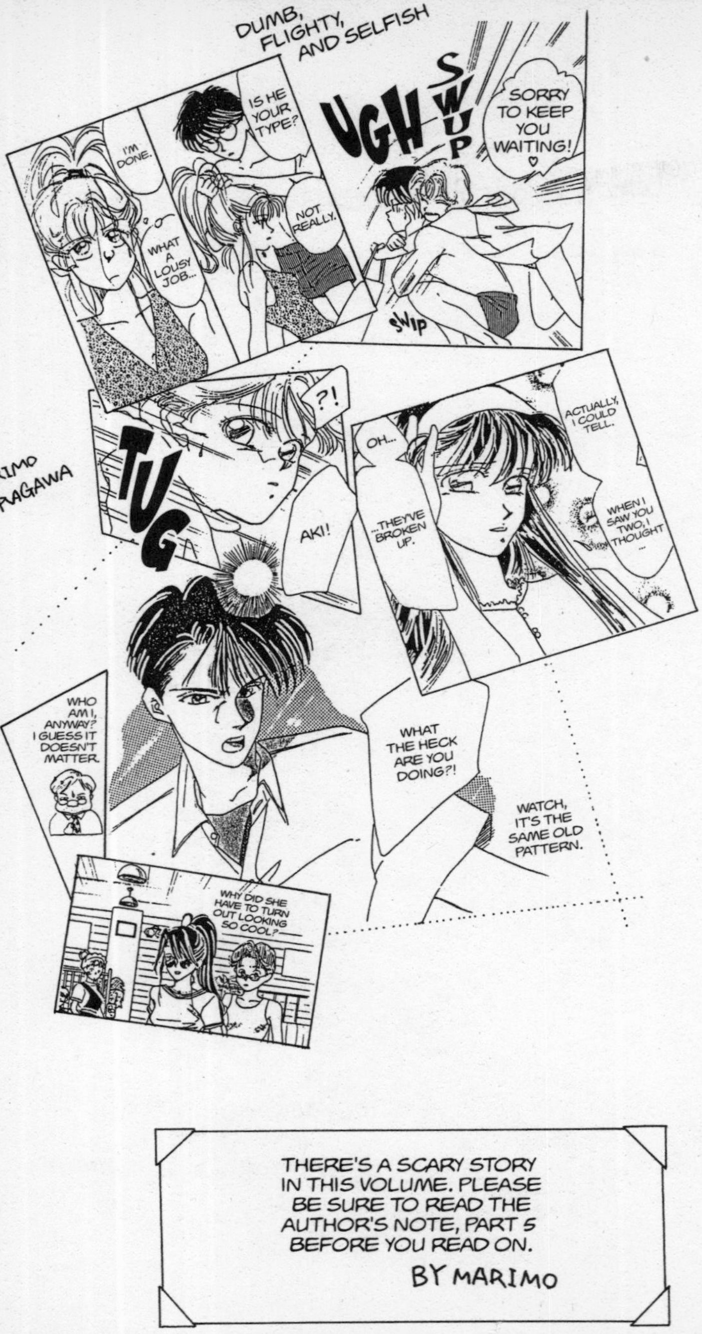
DUMB, FLIGHTY, AND SELFISH
SORRY TO KEEP YOU WAITING!
SWUP
UGH
IS HE YOUR TYPE?
NOT REALLY.
I'M DONE.
WHAT A LOUSY JOB...
SWIP
ACTUALLY, I COULD TELL.
WHEN I SAW YOU TWO, I THOUGHT ...
OH...
...THEY'VE BROKEN UP.
?!
AKI!
TUG
MARIMO RAGAWA
WHAT THE HECK ARE YOU DOING?!
WATCH, IT'S THE SAME OLD PATTERN.
WHO AM I, ANYWAY? I GUESS IT DOESN'T MATTER.
WHY DID SHE HAVE TO TURN OUT LOOKING SO COOL?

THERE'S A SCARY STORY IN THIS VOLUME. PLEASE BE SURE TO READ THE AUTHOR'S NOTE, PART 5 BEFORE YOU READ ON.

BY MARIMO

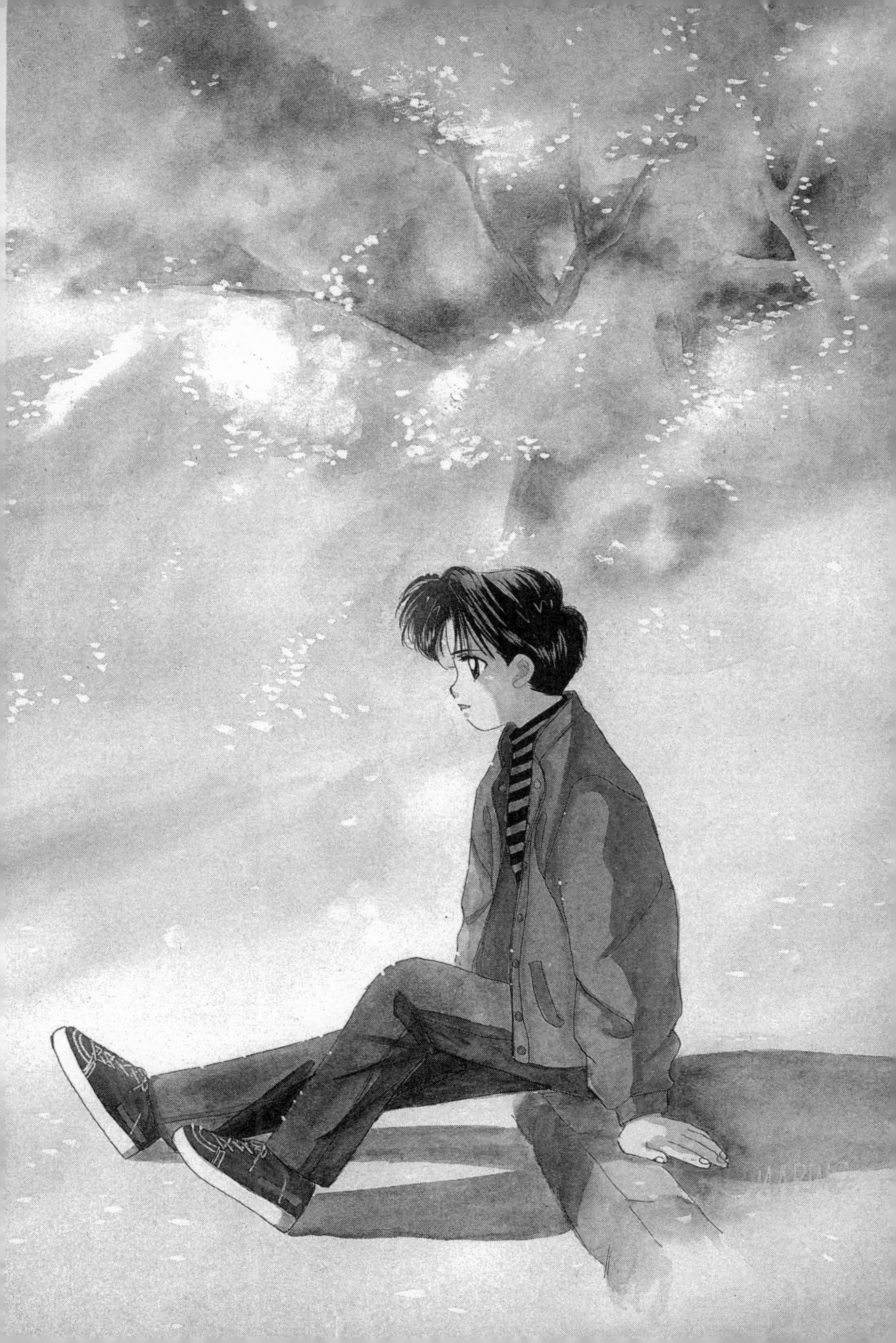

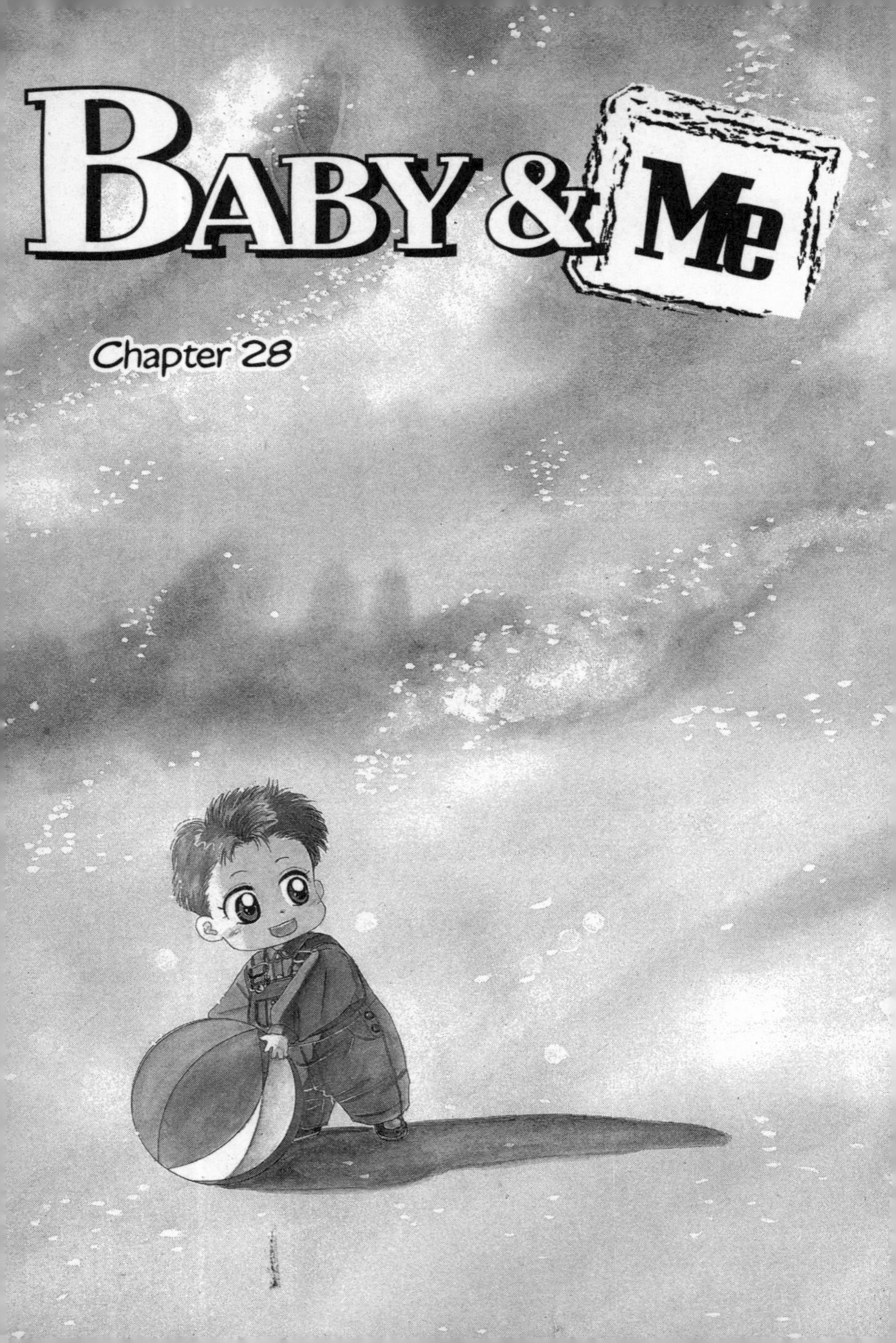
BABY & ME
Chapter 28

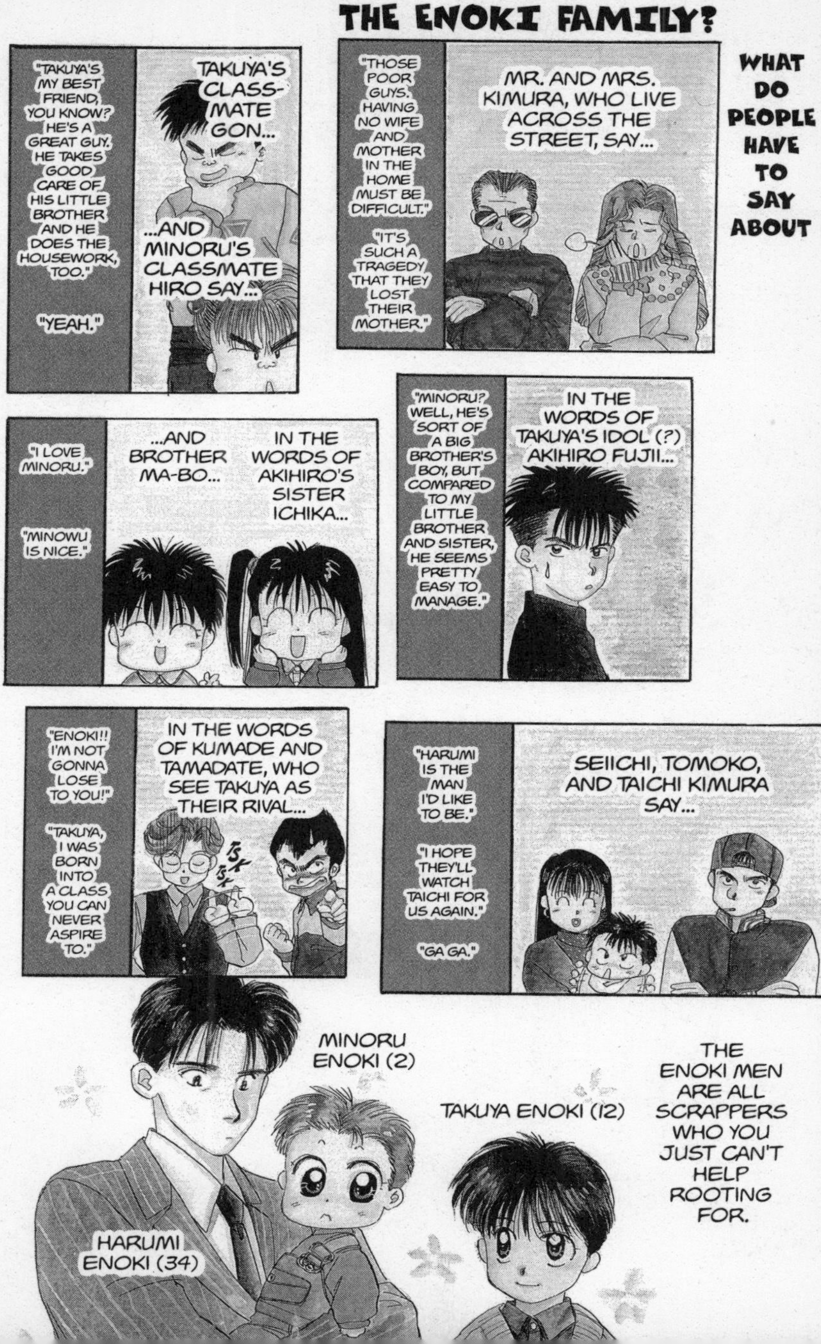
THE ENOKI FAMILY?
WHAT DO PEOPLE HAVE TO SAY ABOUT
MR. AND MRS. KIMURA, WHO LIVE ACROSS THE STREET, SAY...
"THOSE POOR GUYS. HAVING NO WIFE AND MOTHER IN THE HOME MUST BE DIFFICULT."
"IT'S SUCH A TRAGEDY THAT THEY LOST THEIR MOTHER."
TAKUYA'S CLASS-MATE GON...
...AND MINORU'S CLASSMATE HIRO SAY...
"TAKUYA'S MY BEST FRIEND, YOU KNOW? HE'S A GREAT GUY. HE TAKES GOOD CARE OF HIS LITTLE BROTHER AND HE DOES THE HOUSEWORK, TOO."
"YEAH."
IN THE WORDS OF TAKUYA'S IDOL (?) AKIHIRO FUJII...
"MINORU? WELL, HE'S SORT OF A BIG BROTHER'S BOY, BUT COMPARED TO MY LITTLE BROTHER AND SISTER, HE SEEMS PRETTY EASY TO MANAGE."
IN THE WORDS OF AKIHIRO'S SISTER ICHIKA...
...AND BROTHER MA-BO...
"I LOVE MINORU."
"MINOWU IS NICE."
SEIICHI, TOMOKO, AND TAICHI KIMURA SAY...
"HARUMI IS THE MAN I'D LIKE TO BE."
"I HOPE THEY'LL WATCH TAICHI FOR US AGAIN."
"GA GA."
IN THE WORDS OF KUMADE AND TAMADATE, WHO SEE TAKUYA AS THEIR RIVAL...
"ENOKI!! I'M NOT GONNA LOSE TO YOU!"
"TAKUYA, I WAS BORN INTO A CLASS YOU CAN NEVER ASPIRE TO."
TSK TSK
THE ENOKI MEN ARE ALL SCRAPPERS WHO YOU JUST CAN'T HELP ROOTING FOR.
TAKUYA ENOKI (12)
MINORU ENOKI (2)
HARUMI ENOKI (34)

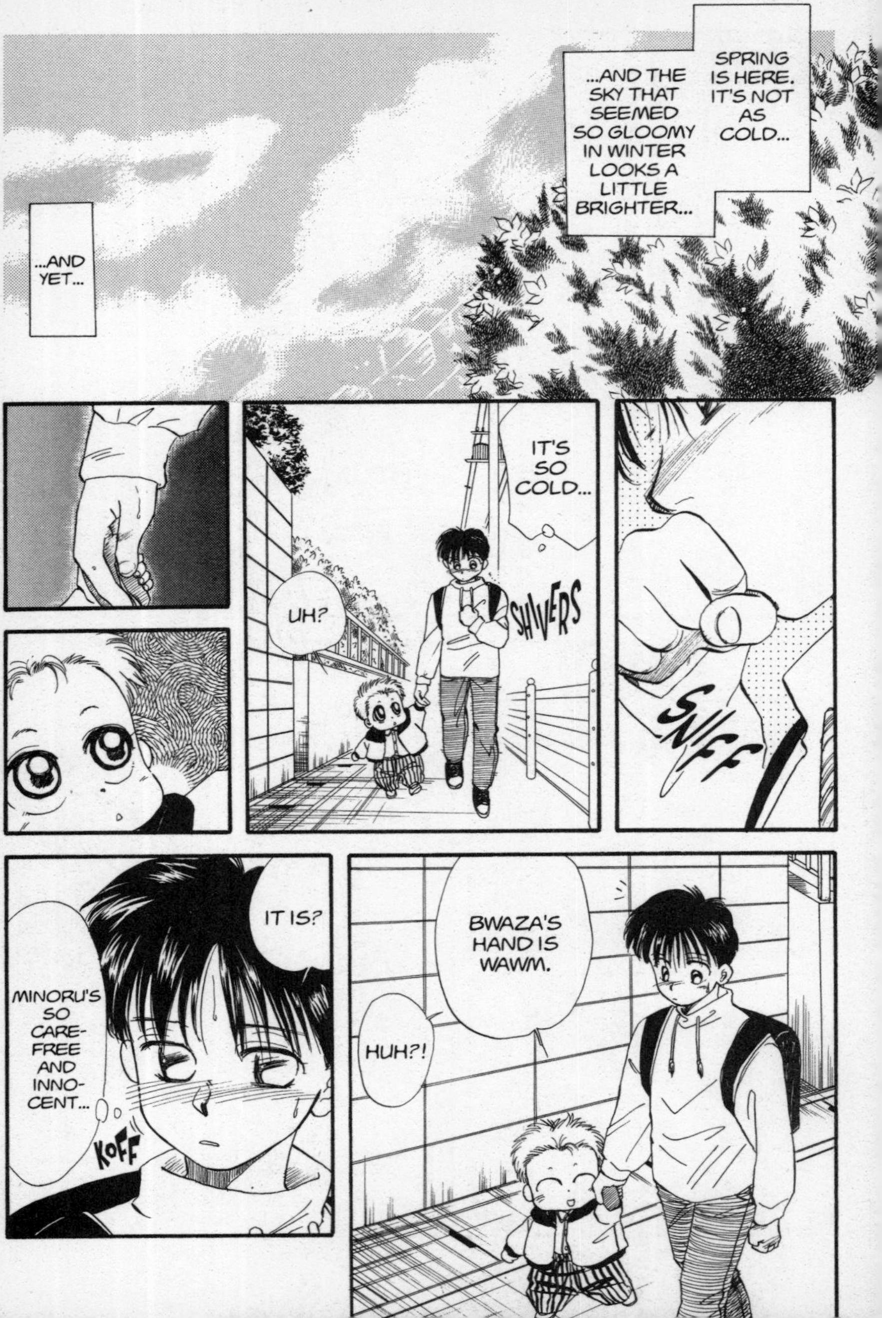
SPRING IS HERE. IT'S NOT AS COLD...
...AND THE SKY THAT SEEMED SO GLOOMY IN WINTER LOOKS A LITTLE BRIGHTER...
...AND YET...
SNIFF
IT'S SO COLD...
SHIVERS
UH?
BWAZA'S HAND IS WAWM.
HUH?!
IT IS?
MINORU'S SO CARE-FREE AND INNO-CENT...
KOFF

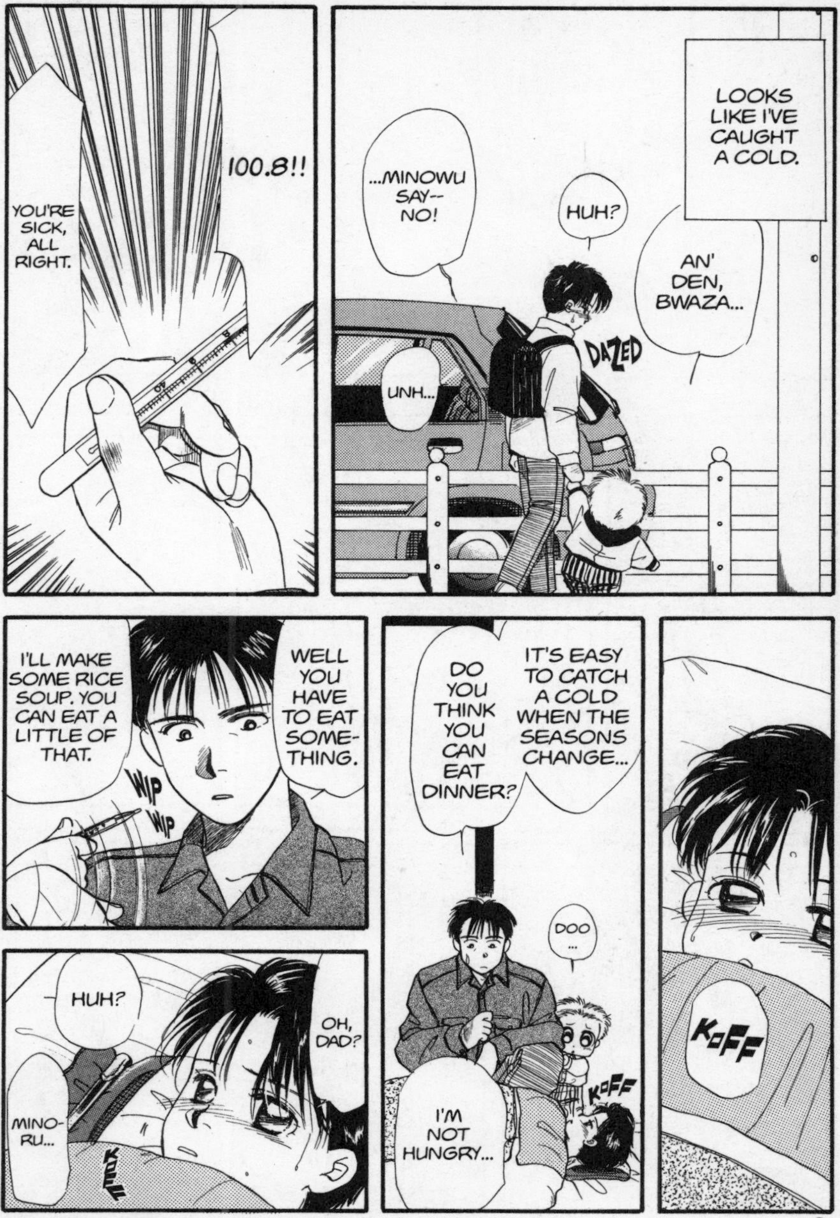
LOOKS LIKE I'VE CAUGHT A COLD.
AN' DEN, BWAZA...
HUH?
DAZED
...MINOWU SAY-- NO!
UNH...
100.8!!
YOU'RE SICK, ALL RIGHT.
KOFF
IT'S EASY TO CATCH A COLD WHEN THE SEASONS CHANGE...
DO YOU THINK YOU CAN EAT DINNER?
DOO...
KOFF
I'M NOT HUNGRY...
WELL YOU HAVE TO EAT SOMETHING.
I'LL MAKE SOME RICE SOUP. YOU CAN EAT A LITTLE OF THAT.
WIP WIP
OH, DAD?
HUH?
MINO-RU...
KOFF

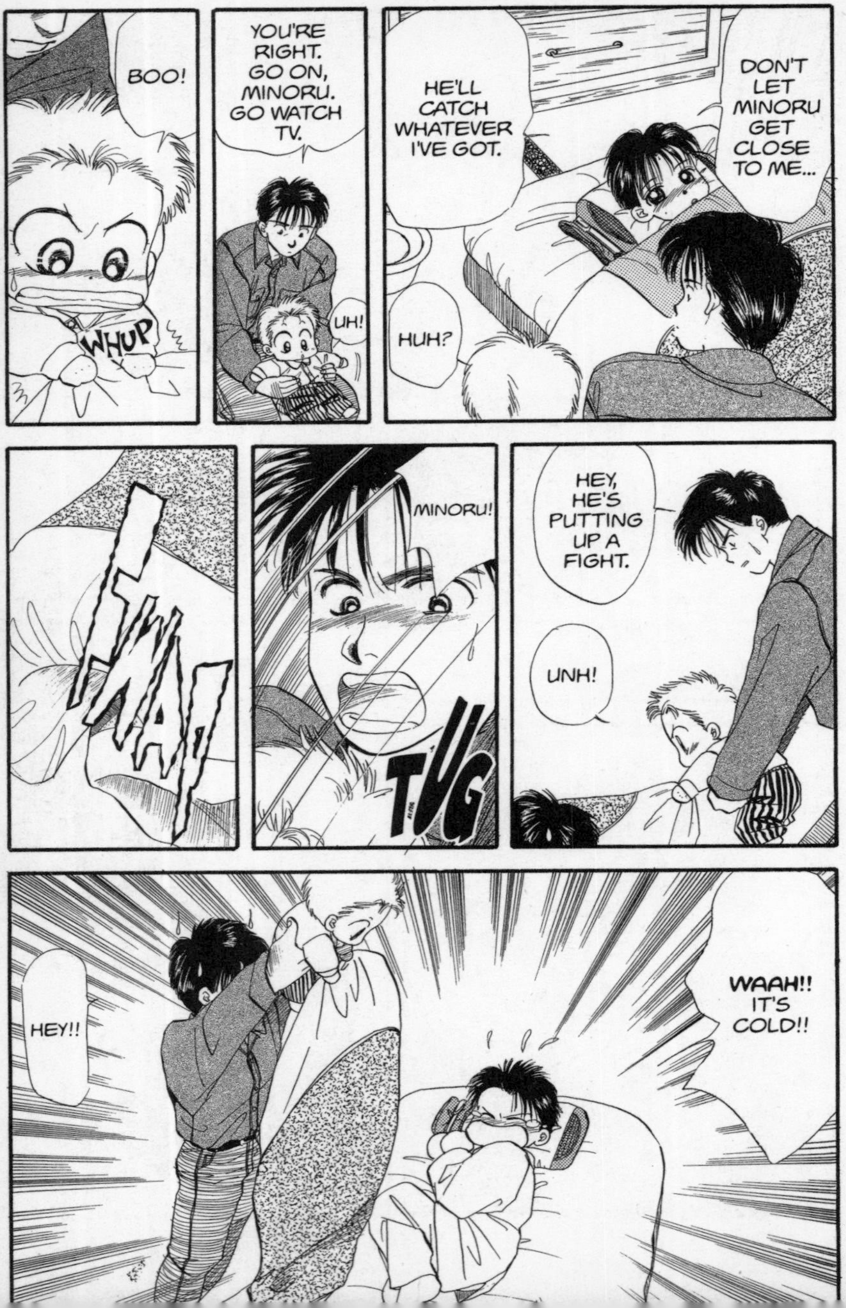
DON'T LET MINORU GET CLOSE TO ME...
HE'LL CATCH WHATEVER I'VE GOT.
HUH?
YOU'RE RIGHT. GO ON, MINORU. GO WATCH TV.
UH!
BOO!
WHUP
HEY, HE'S PUTTING UP A FIGHT.
UNH!
MINORU!
TUG
WAA!
WAAH!! IT'S COLD!!
HEY!!

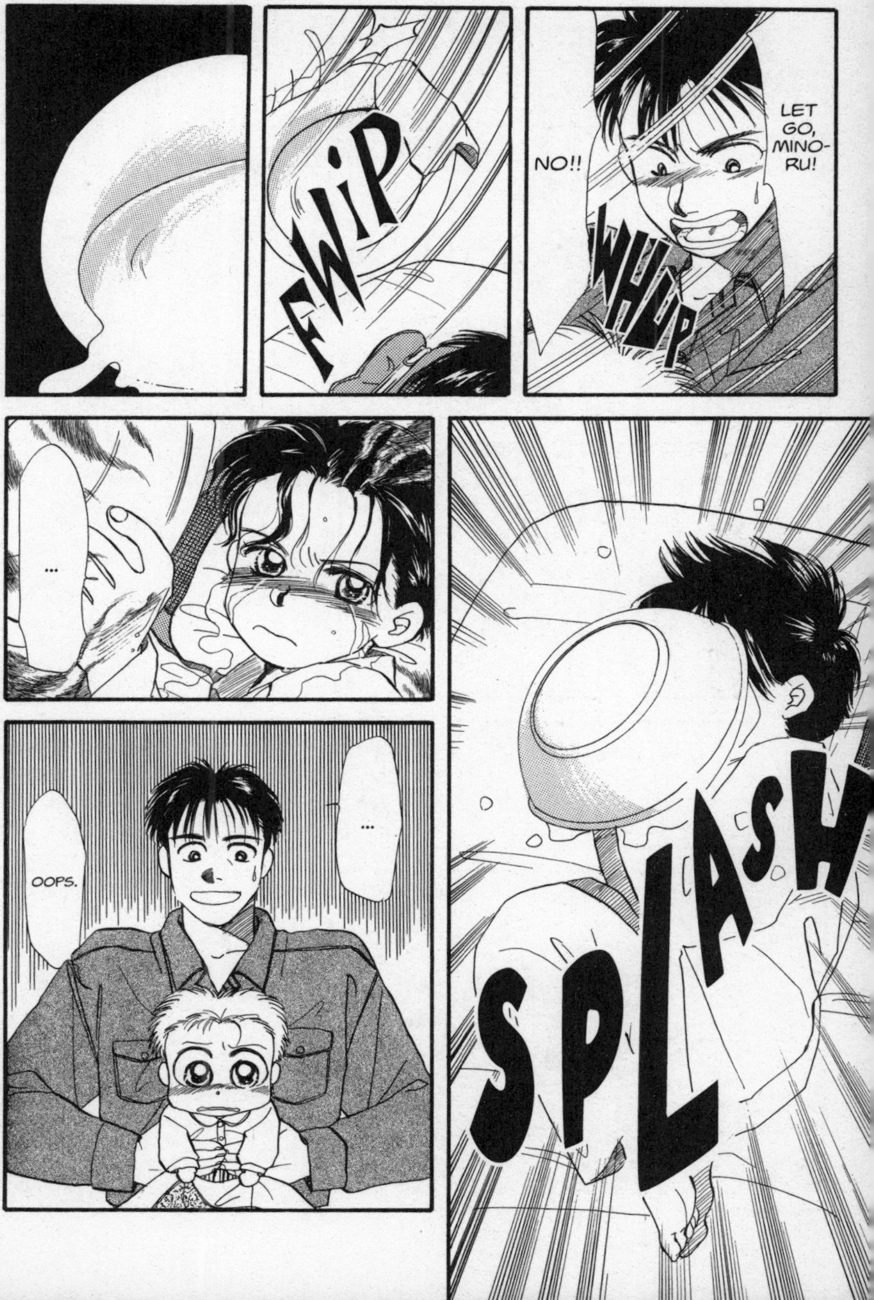
LET GO, MINO-RU!
NO!!
WHUP
FWIP
SPLASH
...
...
OOPS.

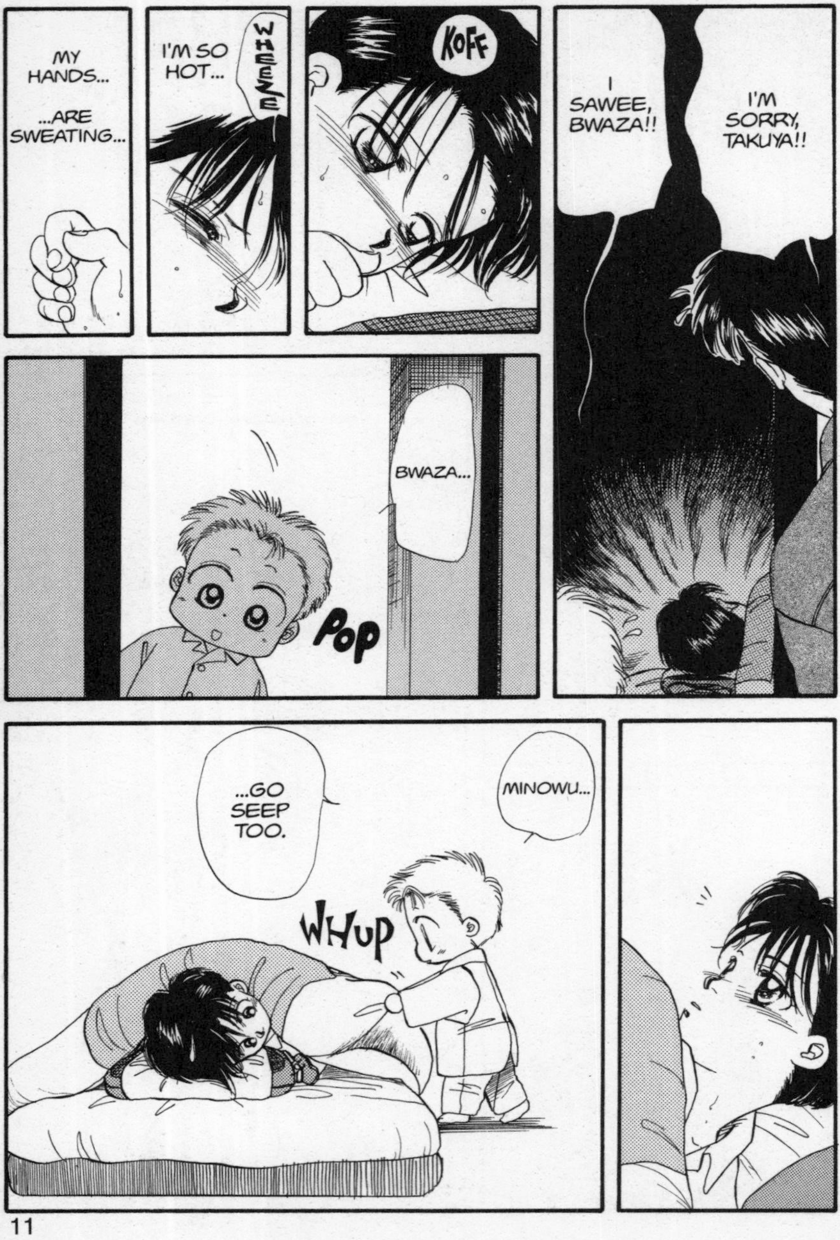
I'M SORRY, TAKUYA!!
I SAWEE, BWAZA!!
KOFF
WHEEZE
I'M SO HOT...
MY HANDS...
...ARE SWEATING...
BWAZA...
POP
MINOWU...
...GO SEEP TOO.
WHUP

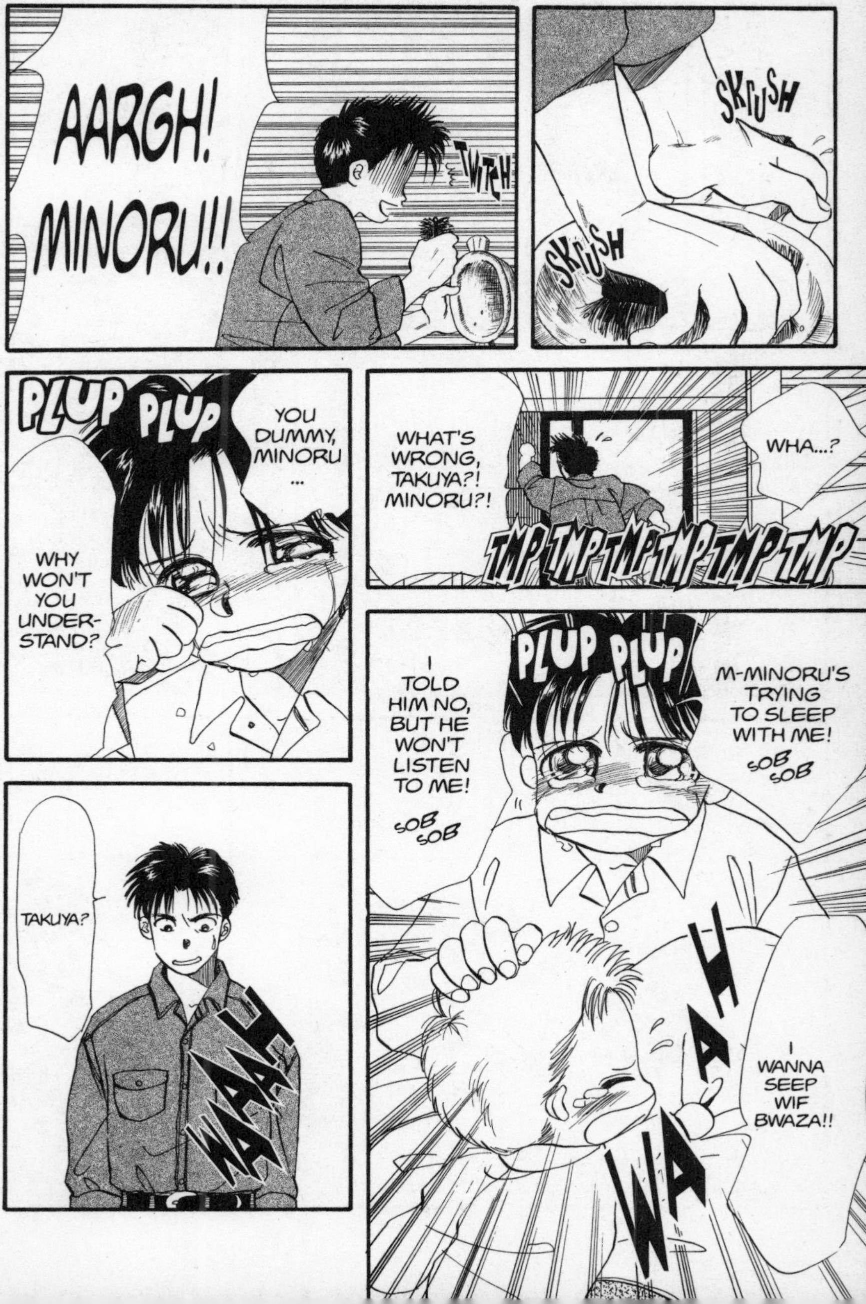
SKRUSH
SKRUSH
AARGH! MINORU!!
TWITCH
WHA...?
WHAT'S WRONG, TAKUYA?! MINORU?!
TMP TMP TMP TMP TMP TMP TMP
PLUP PLUP
YOU DUMMY, MINORU ...
WHY WON'T YOU UNDERSTAND?
PLUP PLUP
M-MINORU'S TRYING TO SLEEP WITH ME!
SOB SOB
I TOLD HIM NO, BUT HE WON'T LISTEN TO ME!
SOB SOB
I WANNA SEEP WIF BWAZA!!
WAH
WAH
TAKUYA?
WAAH!

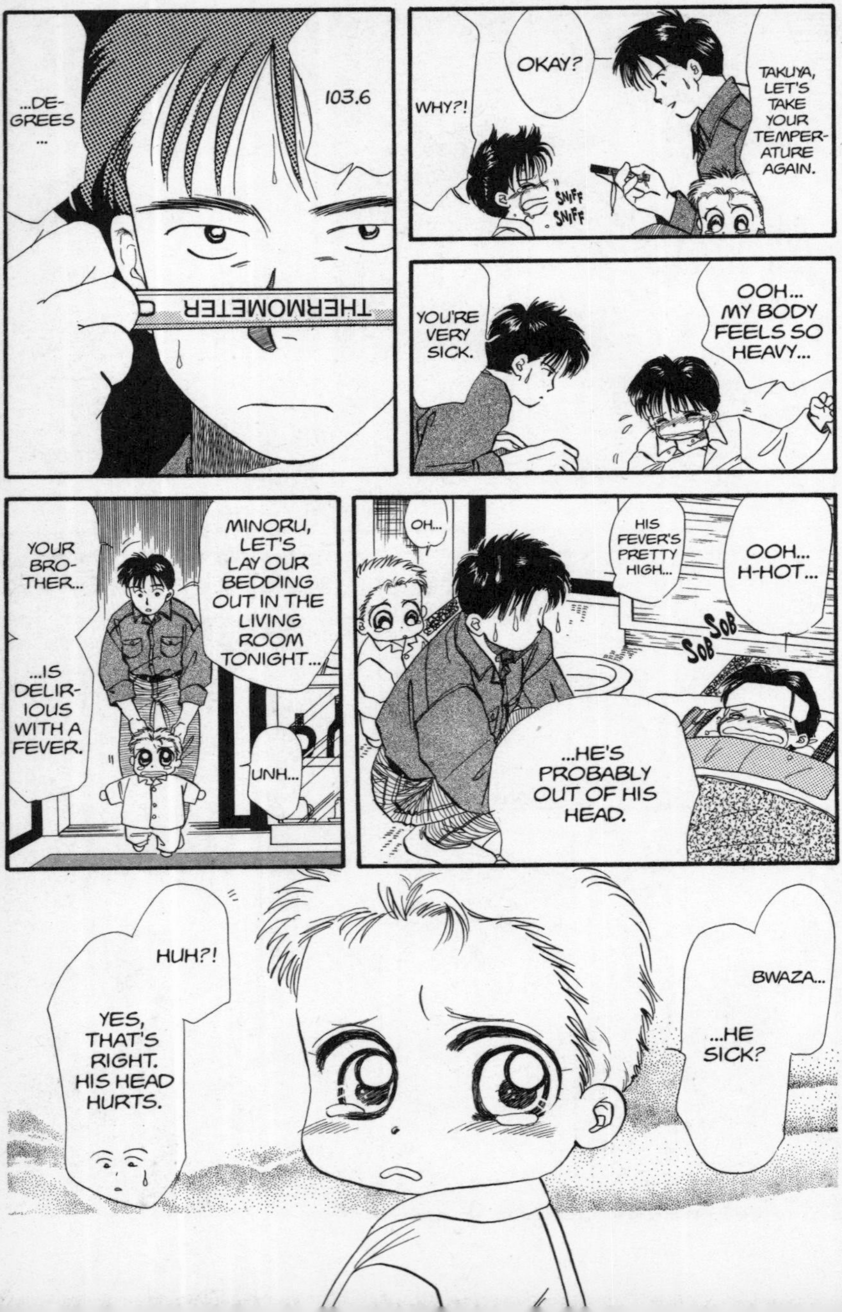
TAKUYA, LET'S TAKE YOUR TEMPERATURE AGAIN.
OKAY?
WHY?!
SNIFF SNIFF
OOH... MY BODY FEELS SO HEAVY...
YOU'RE VERY SICK.
103.6
...DEGREES...
THERMOMETER
OOH... H-HOT...
HIS FEVER'S PRETTY HIGH...
OH...
SOB SOB
...HE'S PROBABLY OUT OF HIS HEAD.
MINORU, LET'S LAY OUR BEDDING OUT IN THE LIVING ROOM TONIGHT...
YOUR BROTHER...
...IS DELIRIOUS WITH A FEVER.
UNH...
BWAZA...
...HE SICK?
HUH?!
YES, THAT'S RIGHT. HIS HEAD HURTS.

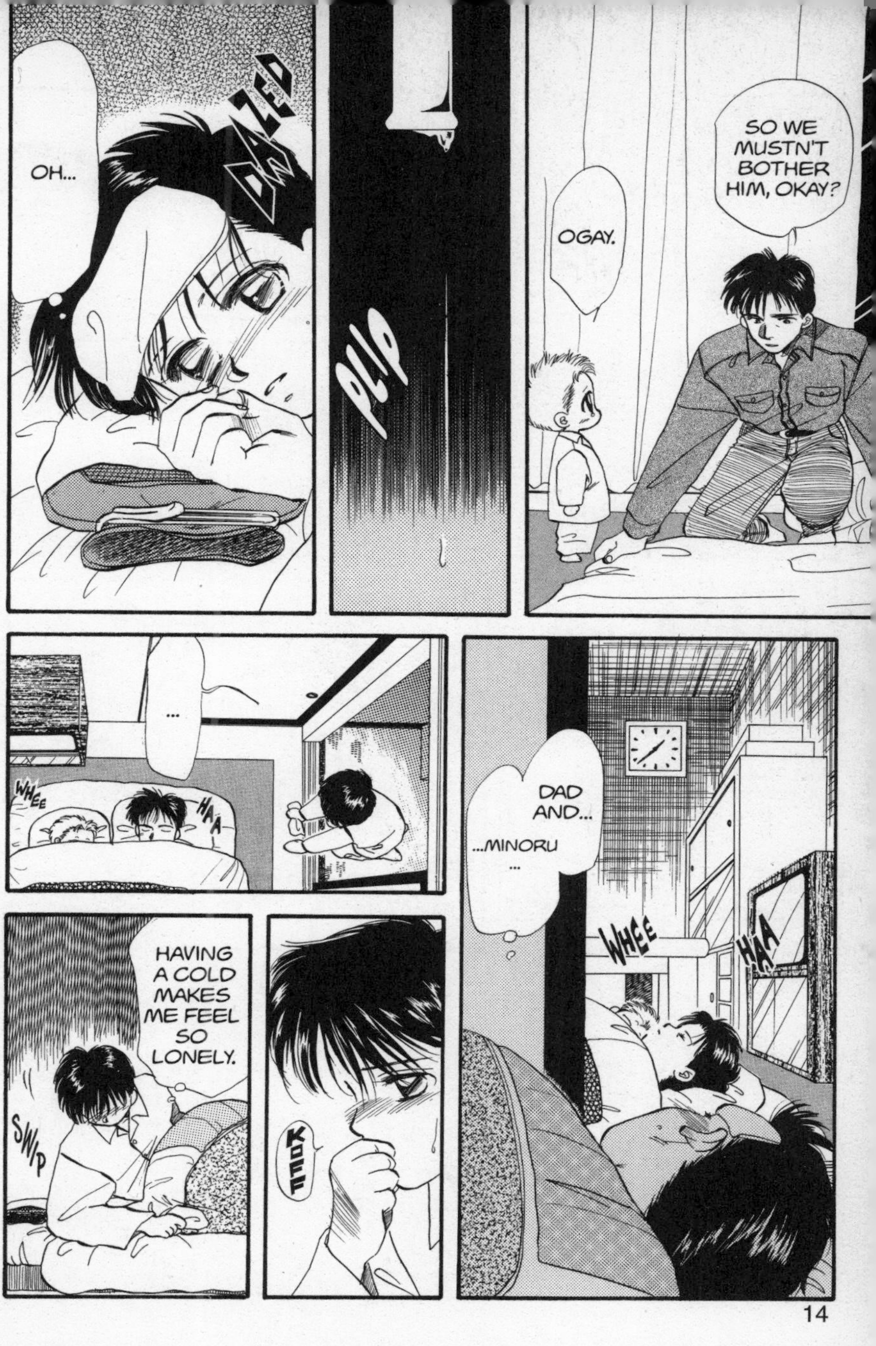
SO WE MUSTN'T BOTHER HIM, OKAY?
OGAY.
PLIP
DAZED
OH...
DAD AND...
...MINORU ...
WHEE
HAA
...
WHEE
HAA
KOFF
HAVING A COLD MAKES ME FEEL SO LONELY.
SWIP

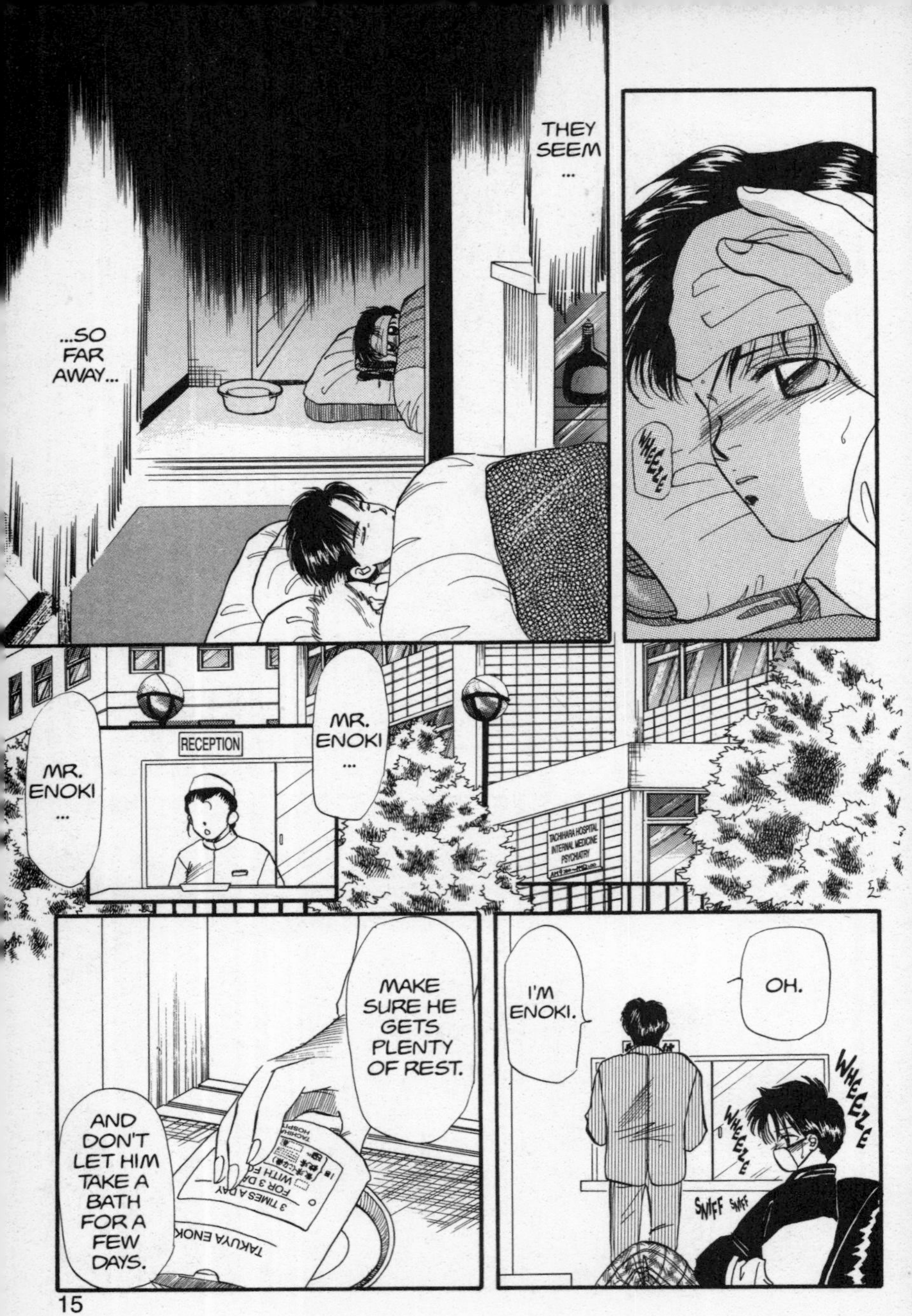
WHEEZE
THEY SEEM ...
...SO FAR AWAY...
MR. ENOKI ...
RECEPTION
MR. ENOKI ...
TACHIHARA HOSPITAL
INTERNAL MEDICINE
PSYCHIATRY
OH.
I'M ENOKI.
WHEEZE
WHEEZE
SNIFF SNIFF
MAKE SURE HE GETS PLENTY OF REST.
AND DON'T LET HIM TAKE A BATH FOR A FEW DAYS.
3 TIMES A DAY

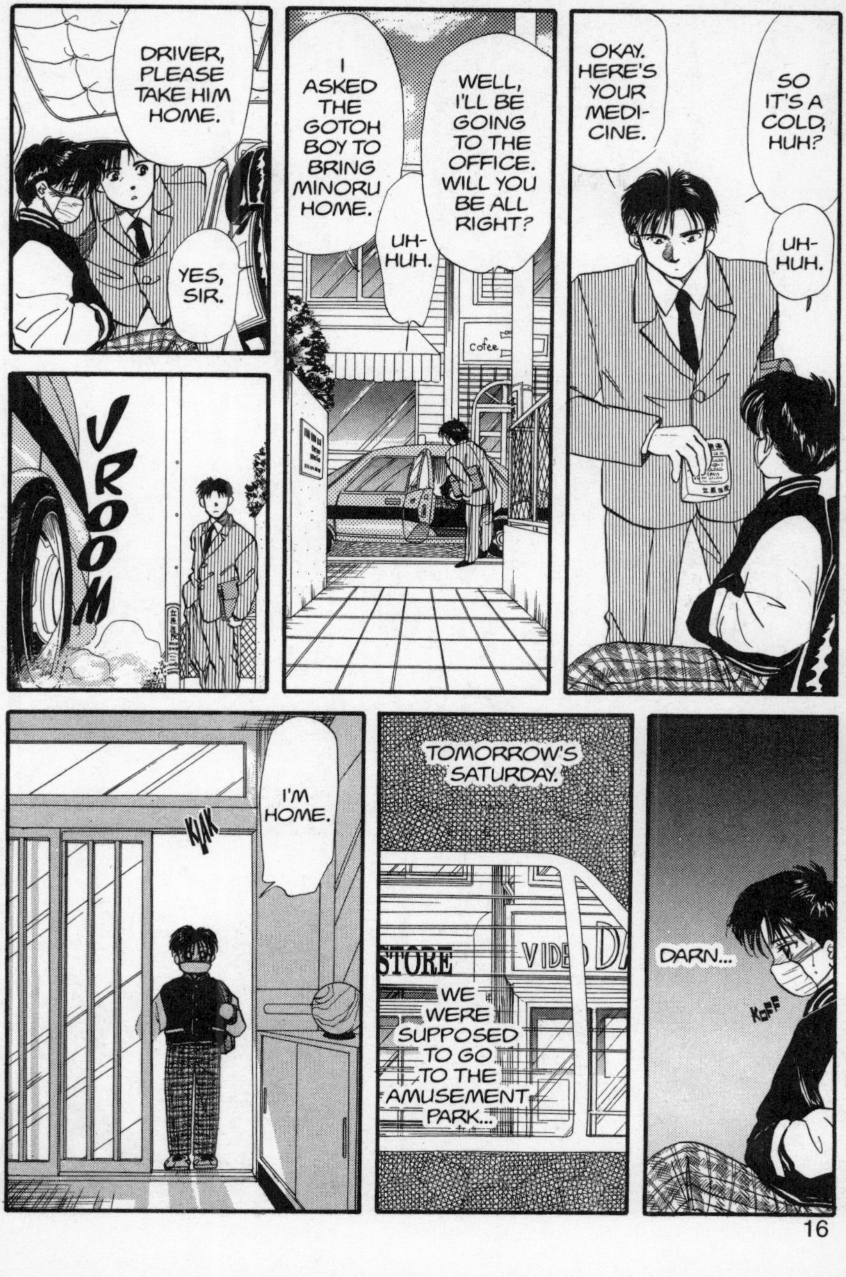
SO IT'S A COLD, HUH?
OKAY. HERE'S YOUR MEDI-CINE.
UH-HUH.
WELL, I'LL BE GOING TO THE OFFICE. WILL YOU BE ALL RIGHT?
I ASKED THE GOTOH BOY TO BRING MINORU HOME.
UH-HUH.
cofee
DRIVER, PLEASE TAKE HIM HOME.
YES, SIR.
VROOM
DARN...
KOFF
TOMORROW'S SATURDAY.
STORE
VIDEO
WE WERE SUPPOSED TO GO TO THE AMUSEMENT PARK...
KLAK
I'M HOME.

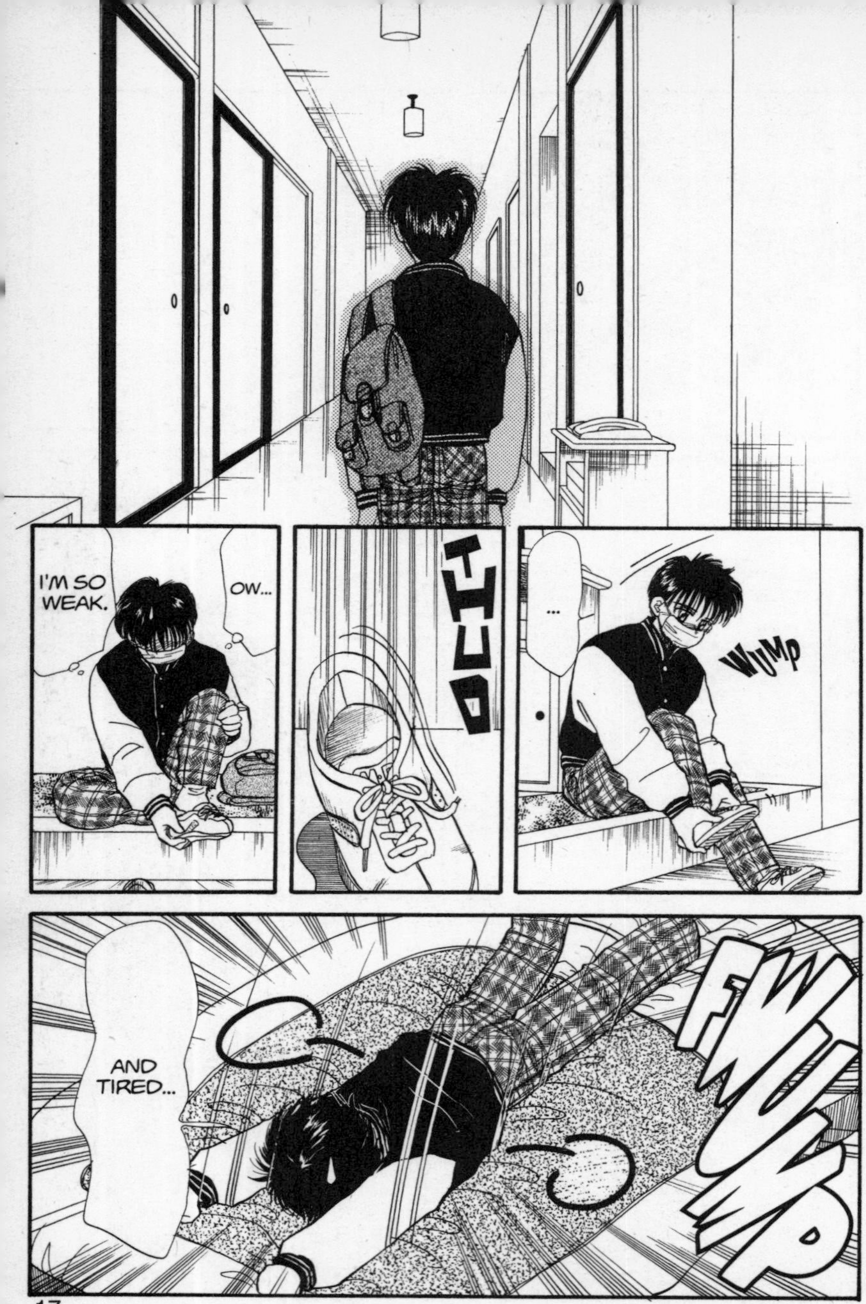
...
WUMP
THUD
OW...
I'M SO WEAK.
AND TIRED...
FWUMP

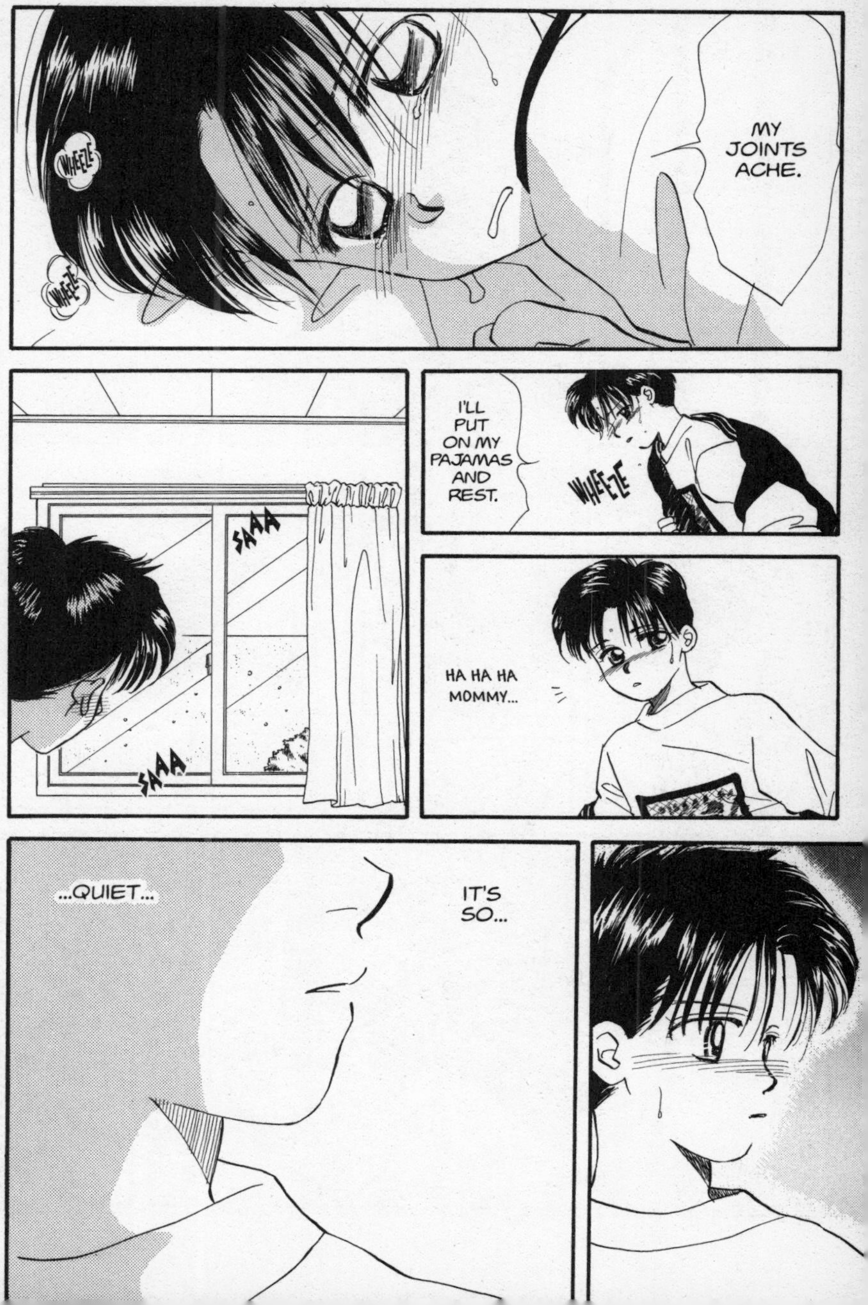
MY JOINTS ACHE.
WHEEZE
WHEEZE
I'LL PUT ON MY PAJAMAS AND REST.
WHEEZE
HA HA HA MOMMY...
SAAA
SAAA
IT'S SO...
...QUIET...

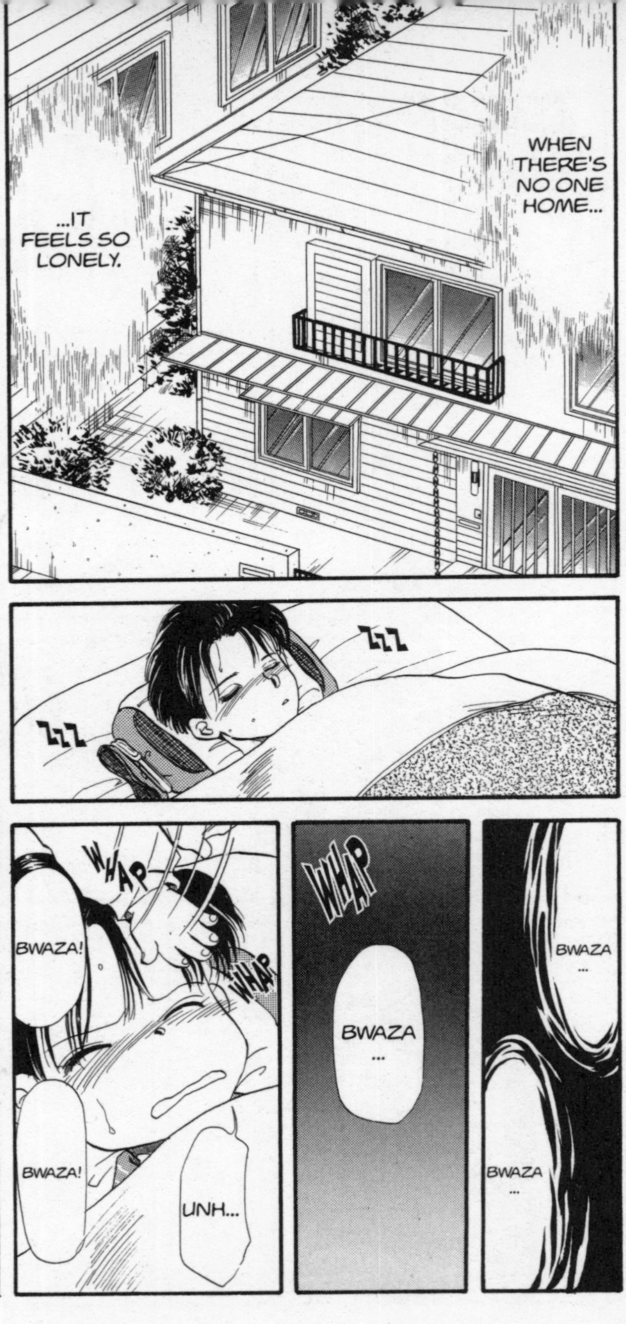
WHEN THERE'S NO ONE HOME...
...IT FEELS SO LONELY.
ZZZ
ZZZ
BWAZA ...
BWAZA ...
WHAP
BWAZA ...
WHAP
BWAZA!
WHAP
BWAZA!
UNH...

Author's Note, Part 1

Hello, this is Ragawa. This is volume 6 of *Baby and Me*, so let's get started!! The subject this time is my excuses. Your letters always encourage me. Sometimes, you're confused by something and want me to clarify it. I'm happy to do so, but sometimes my explanations may sound like excuses. This continues in Part 2.

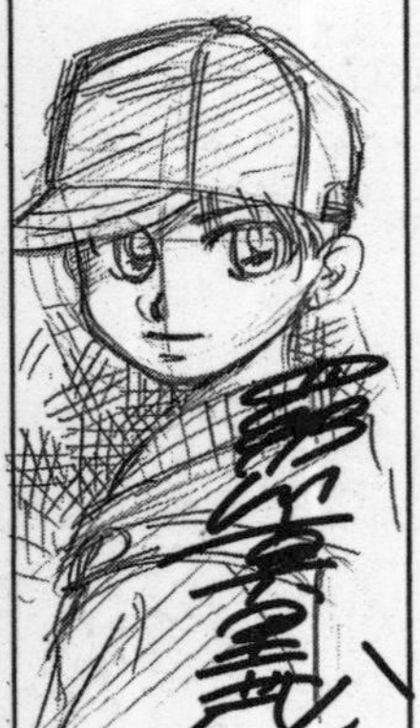

The Kenji Kurita character that appears in Chapter 31 is one of my favorites, and was popular with my assistants. But for some reason, the readers didn't like him...

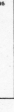

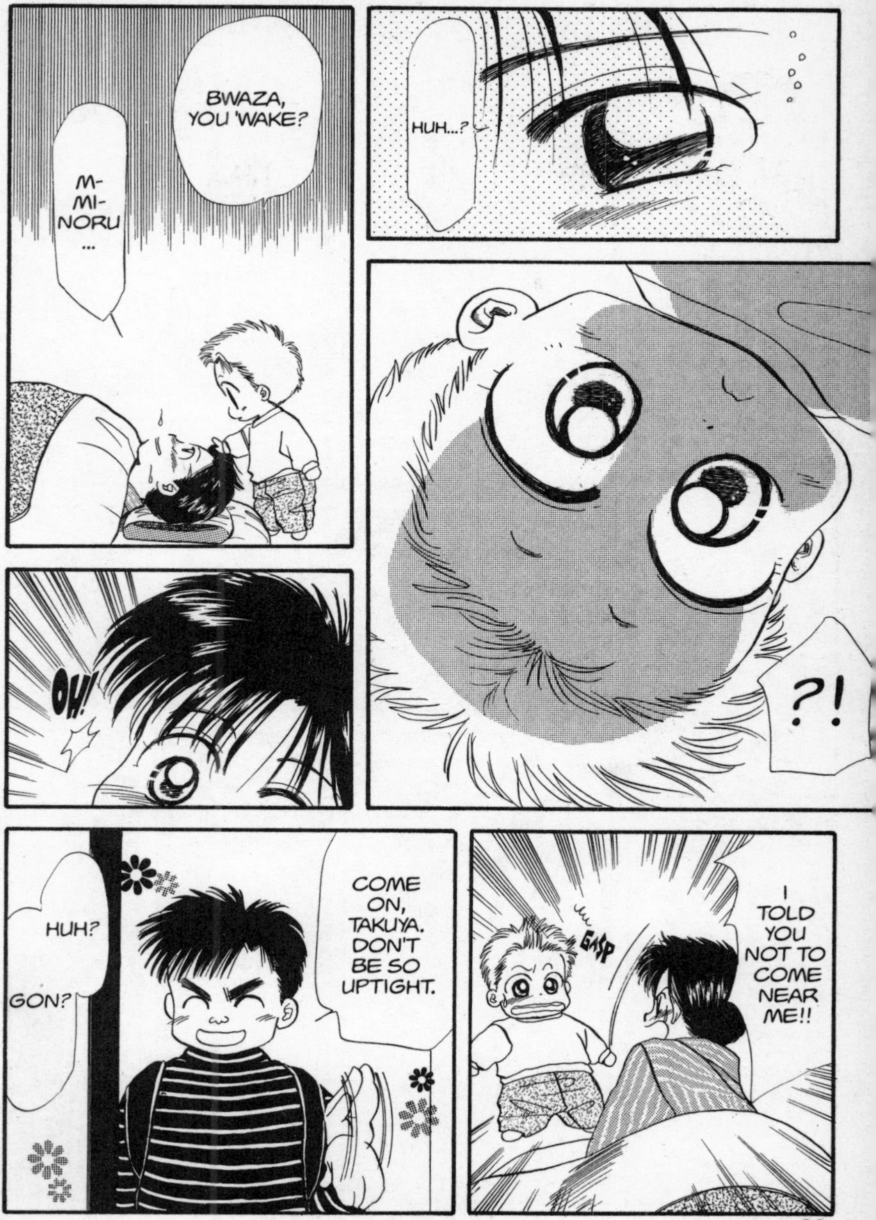
HUH...?
BWAZA, YOU 'WAKE?
M-MI-NORU ...
?!
OH!
I TOLD YOU NOT TO COME NEAR ME!!
GASP
COME ON, TAKUYA. DON'T BE SO UPTIGHT.
HUH?
GON?

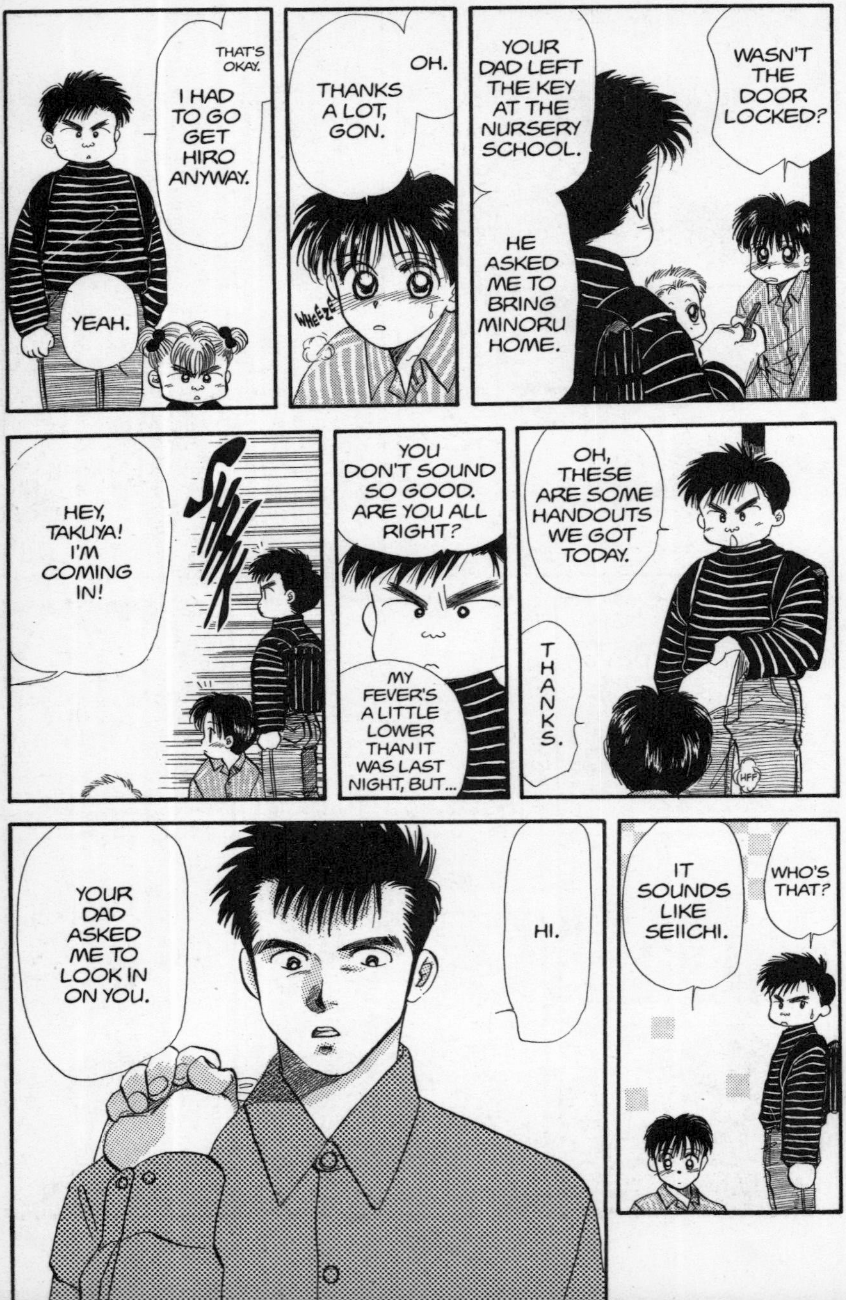
WASN'T THE DOOR LOCKED?
YOUR DAD LEFT THE KEY AT THE NURSERY SCHOOL.
HE ASKED ME TO BRING MINORU HOME.
OH. THANKS A LOT, GON.
WHEEZE
THAT'S OKAY.
I HAD TO GO GET HIRO ANYWAY.
YEAH.
OH, THESE ARE SOME HANDOUTS WE GOT TODAY.
THANKS.
HFF
YOU DON'T SOUND SO GOOD. ARE YOU ALL RIGHT?
MY FEVER'S A LITTLE LOWER THAN IT WAS LAST NIGHT, BUT...
HEY, TAKUYA! I'M COMING IN!
WHO'S THAT?
IT SOUNDS LIKE SEIICHI.
HI.
YOUR DAD ASKED ME TO LOOK IN ON YOU.

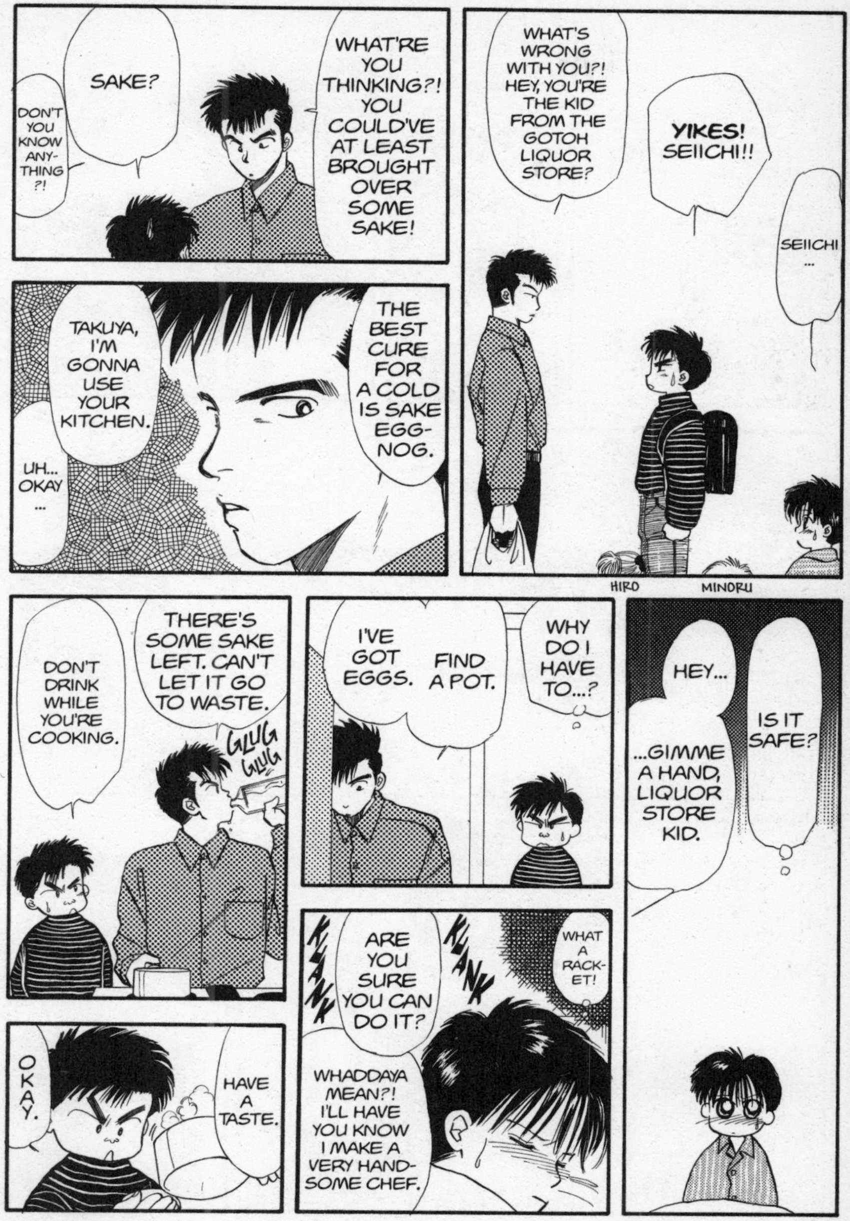
YIKES! SEIICHI!!
WHAT'S WRONG WITH YOU?! HEY, YOU'RE THE KID FROM THE GOTOH LIQUOR STORE?
SEIICHI ...
HIRO
MINORU
WHAT'RE YOU THINKING?! YOU COULD'VE AT LEAST BROUGHT OVER SOME SAKE!
SAKE?
DON'T YOU KNOW ANY-THING ?!
THE BEST CURE FOR A COLD IS SAKE EGG-NOG.
TAKUYA, I'M GONNA USE YOUR KITCHEN.
UH... OKAY ...
IS IT SAFE?
HEY...
...GIMME A HAND, LIQUOR STORE KID.
WHY DO I HAVE TO...?
FIND A POT.
I'VE GOT EGGS.
THERE'S SOME SAKE LEFT. CAN'T LET IT GO TO WASTE.
GLUG GLUG
DON'T DRINK WHILE YOU'RE COOKING.
WHAT A RACK-ET!
KLANK
KLANK
ARE YOU SURE YOU CAN DO IT?
WHADDAYA MEAN?! I'LL HAVE YOU KNOW I MAKE A VERY HAND-SOME CHEF.
HAVE A TASTE.
OKAY.

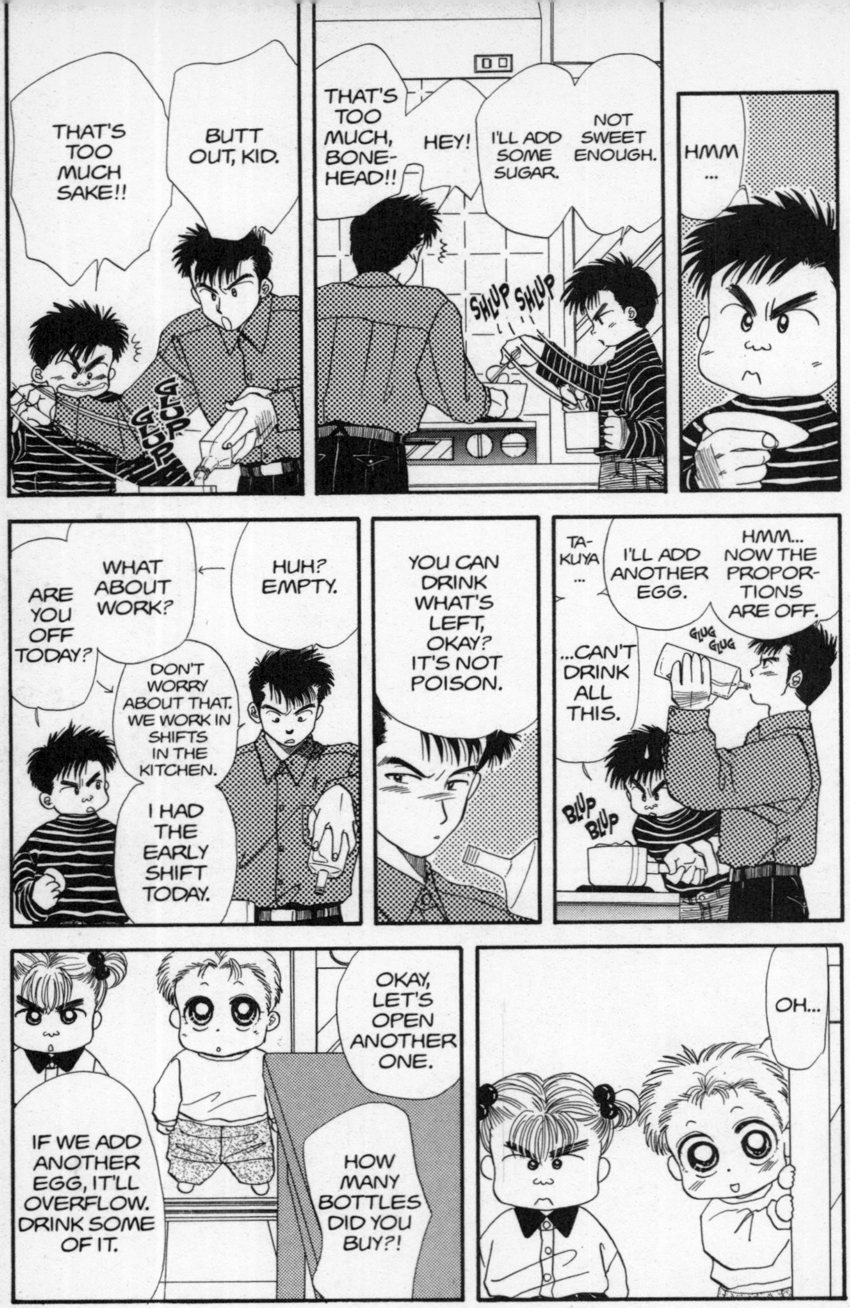
HMM...
NOT SWEET ENOUGH.
I'LL ADD SOME SUGAR.
HEY!
THAT'S TOO MUCH, BONE-HEAD!!
SHLUP SHLUP
BUTT OUT, KID.
THAT'S TOO MUCH SAKE!!
GLUP GLUP
HMM... NOW THE PROPOR-TIONS ARE OFF.
I'LL ADD ANOTHER EGG.
TA-KUYA...
GLUG GLUG
...CAN'T DRINK ALL THIS.
BLUP BLUP
YOU CAN DRINK WHAT'S LEFT, OKAY? IT'S NOT POISON.
HUH? EMPTY.
WHAT ABOUT WORK?
ARE YOU OFF TODAY?
DON'T WORRY ABOUT THAT. WE WORK IN SHIFTS IN THE KITCHEN.
I HAD THE EARLY SHIFT TODAY.
OH...
OKAY, LET'S OPEN ANOTHER ONE.
HOW MANY BOTTLES DID YOU BUY?!
IF WE ADD ANOTHER EGG, IT'LL OVERFLOW. DRINK SOME OF IT.

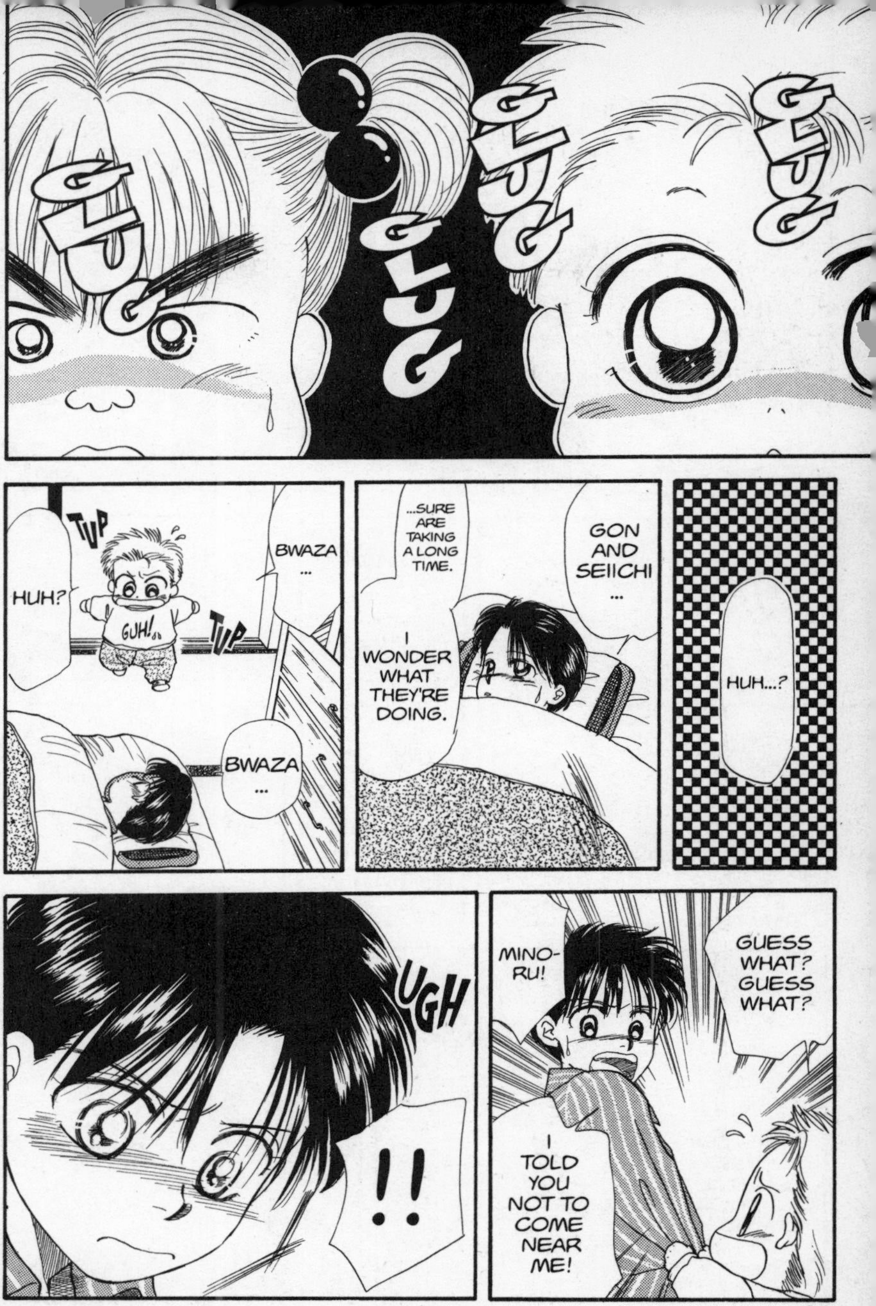
GLUG
GLUG
GLUG
GLUG
HUH...?
GON AND SEIICHI...
...SURE ARE TAKING A LONG TIME.
I WONDER WHAT THEY'RE DOING.
BWAZA...
TUP
HUH?
TUP
GUH!
BWAZA...
GUESS WHAT? GUESS WHAT?
MINO-RU!
I TOLD YOU NOT TO COME NEAR ME!
UGH
!!

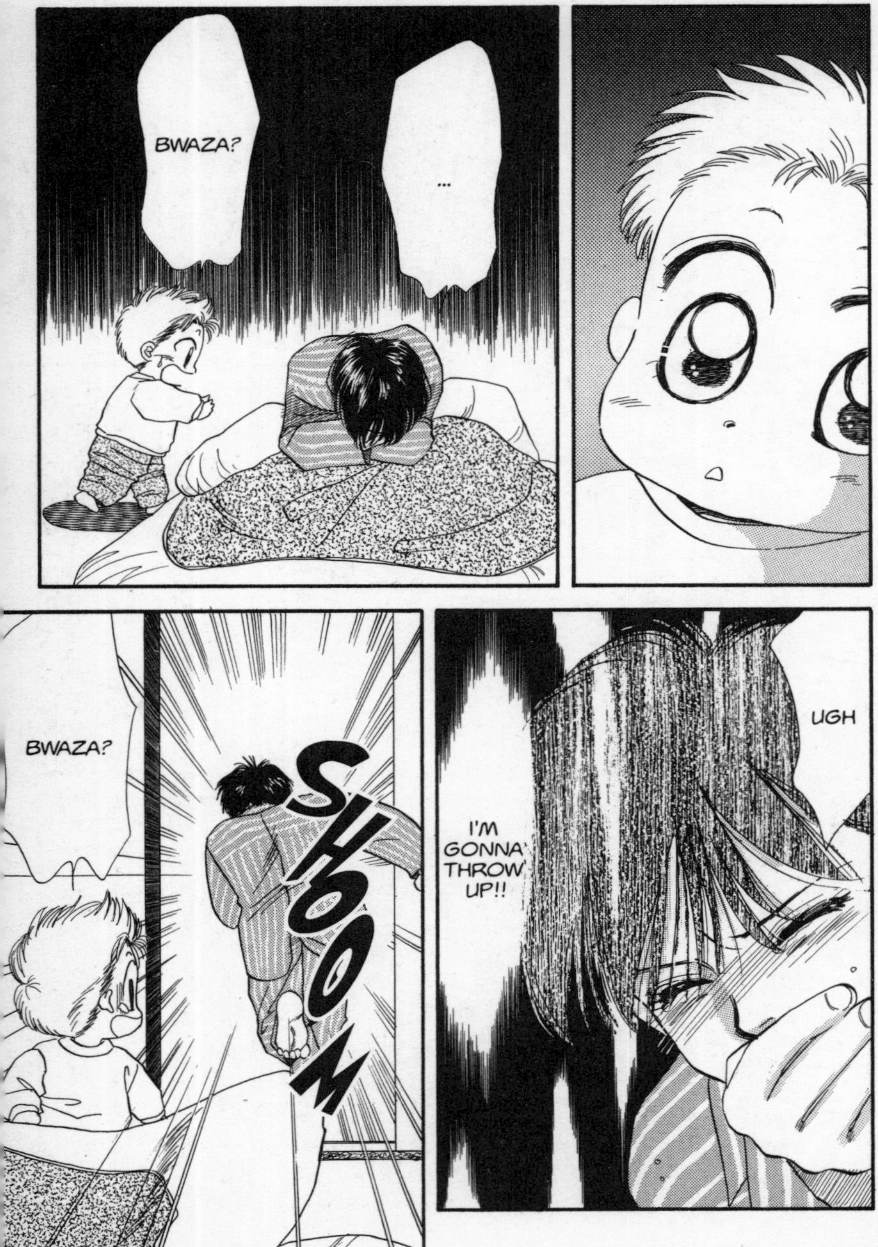
...
BWAZA?
UGH
I'M GONNA THROW UP!!
SHOOM
BWAZA?

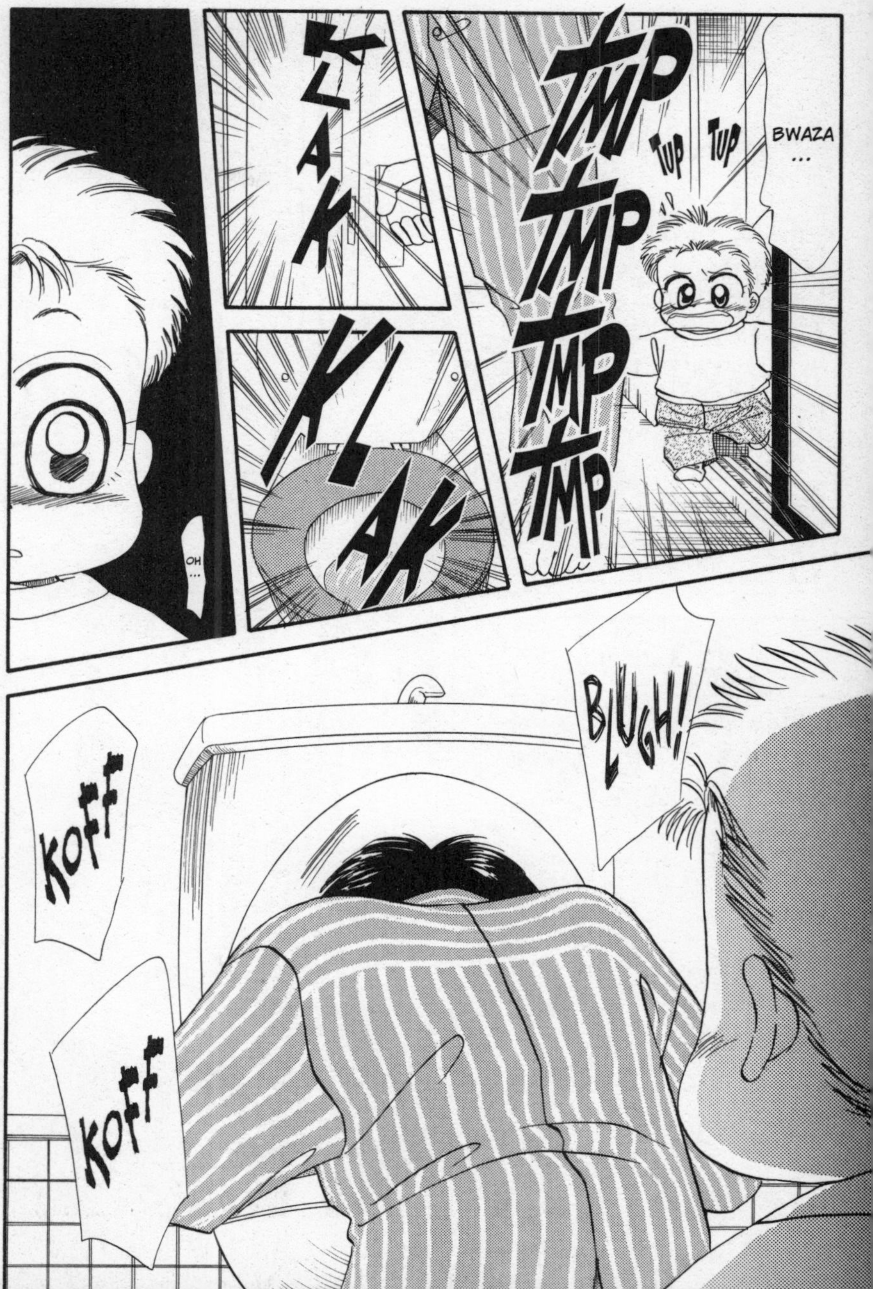
BWAZA ...
TUP TUP
TMP TMP TMP TMP
KLAK
KLAK
OH ...
BLUGH!
KOFF
KOFF

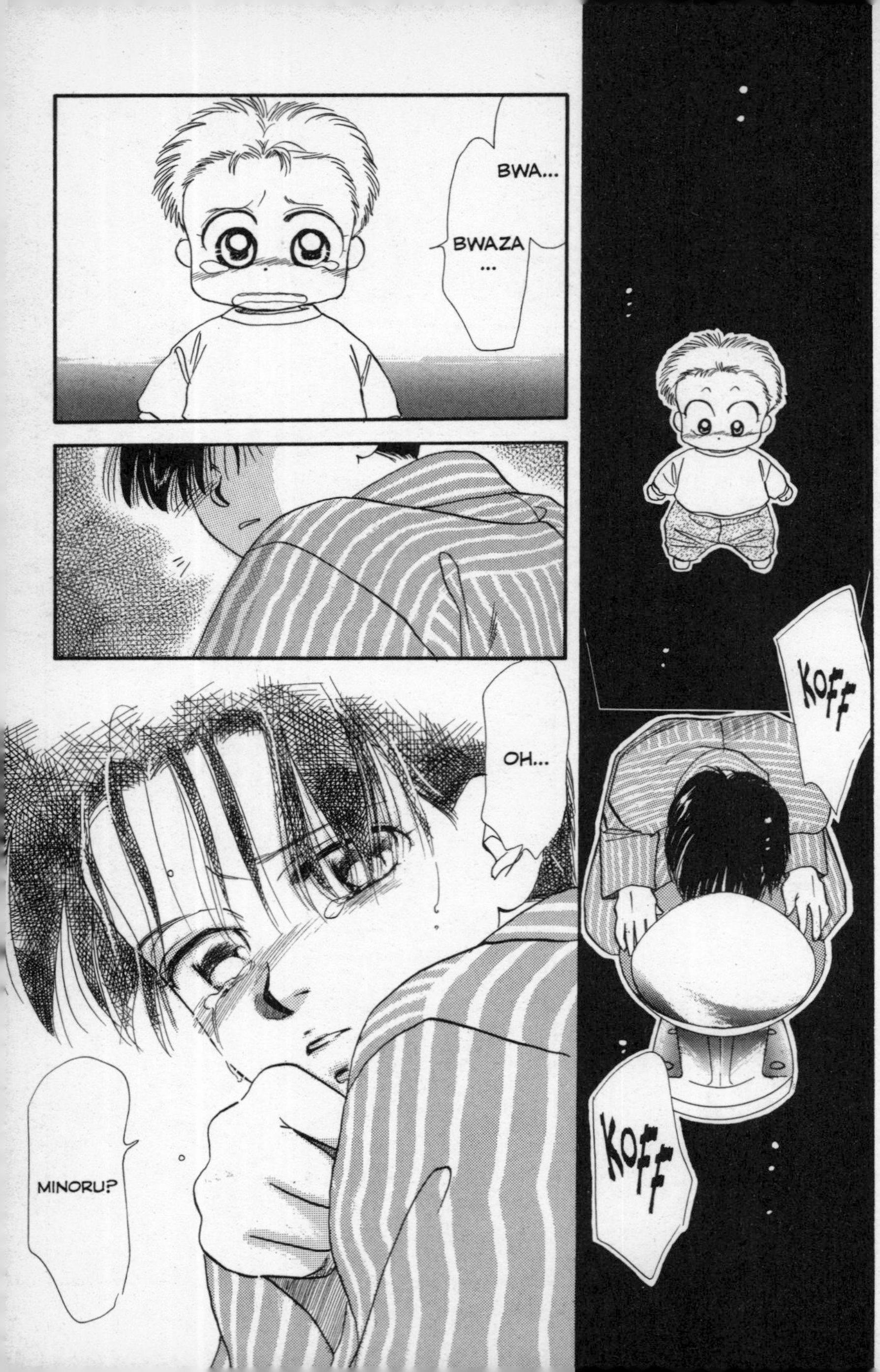
KOFF
KOFF
BWA...
BWAZA ...
OH...
MINORU?

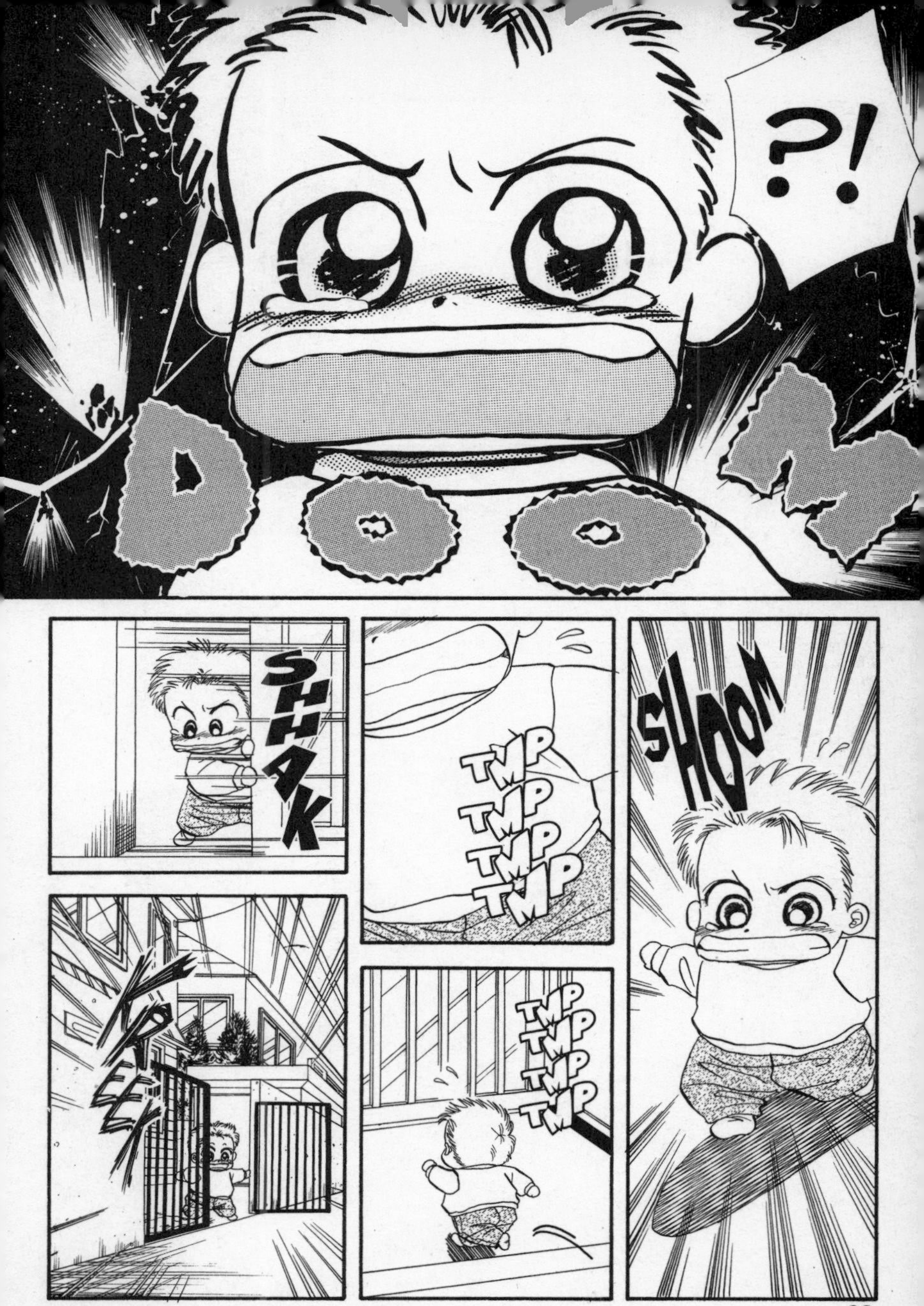
?!
DOOM
SHOOM
TMP TMP TMP TMP
SHAK
TMP TMP TMP TMP
KREEK

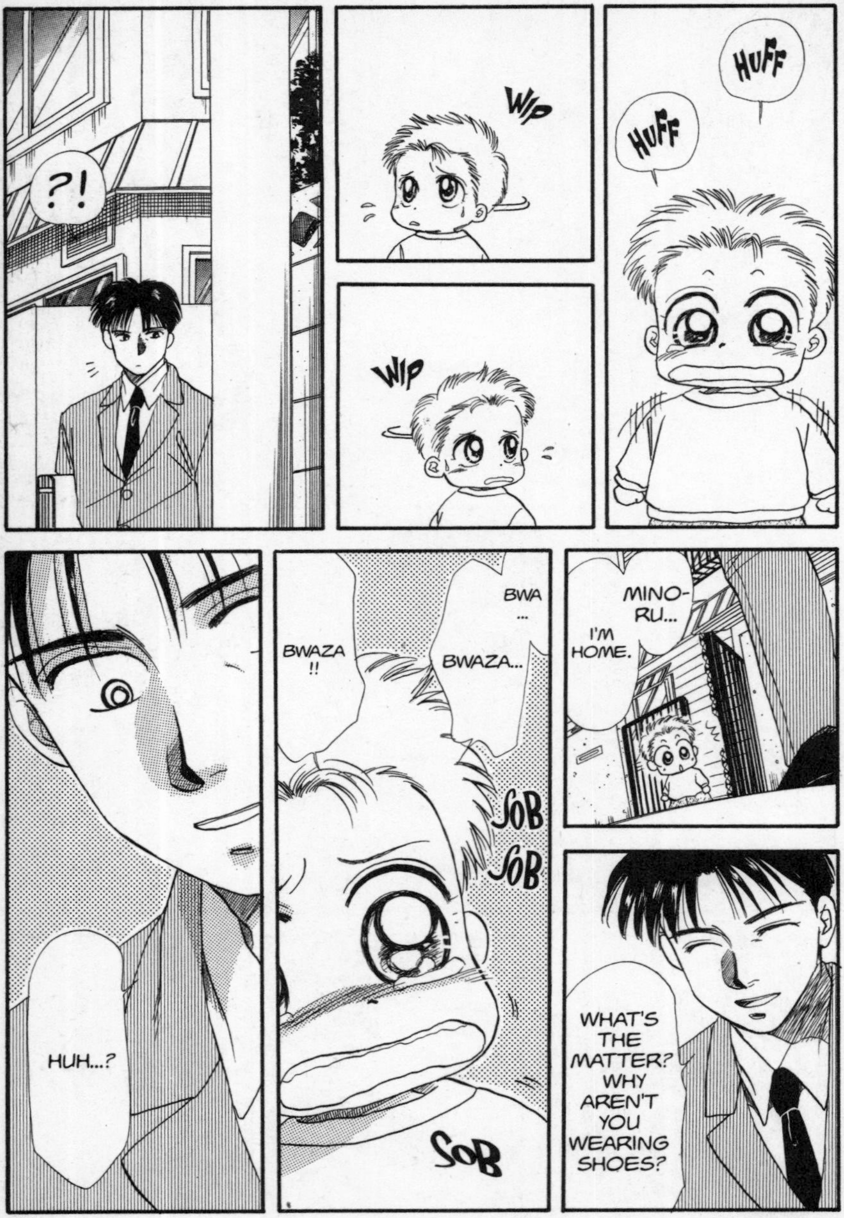
HUFF
HUFF
WIP
WIP
?!
MINO-RU...
I'M HOME.
WHAT'S THE MATTER? WHY AREN'T YOU WEARING SHOES?
BWA ...
BWAZA...
BWAZA !!
SOB
SOB
SOB
HUH...?

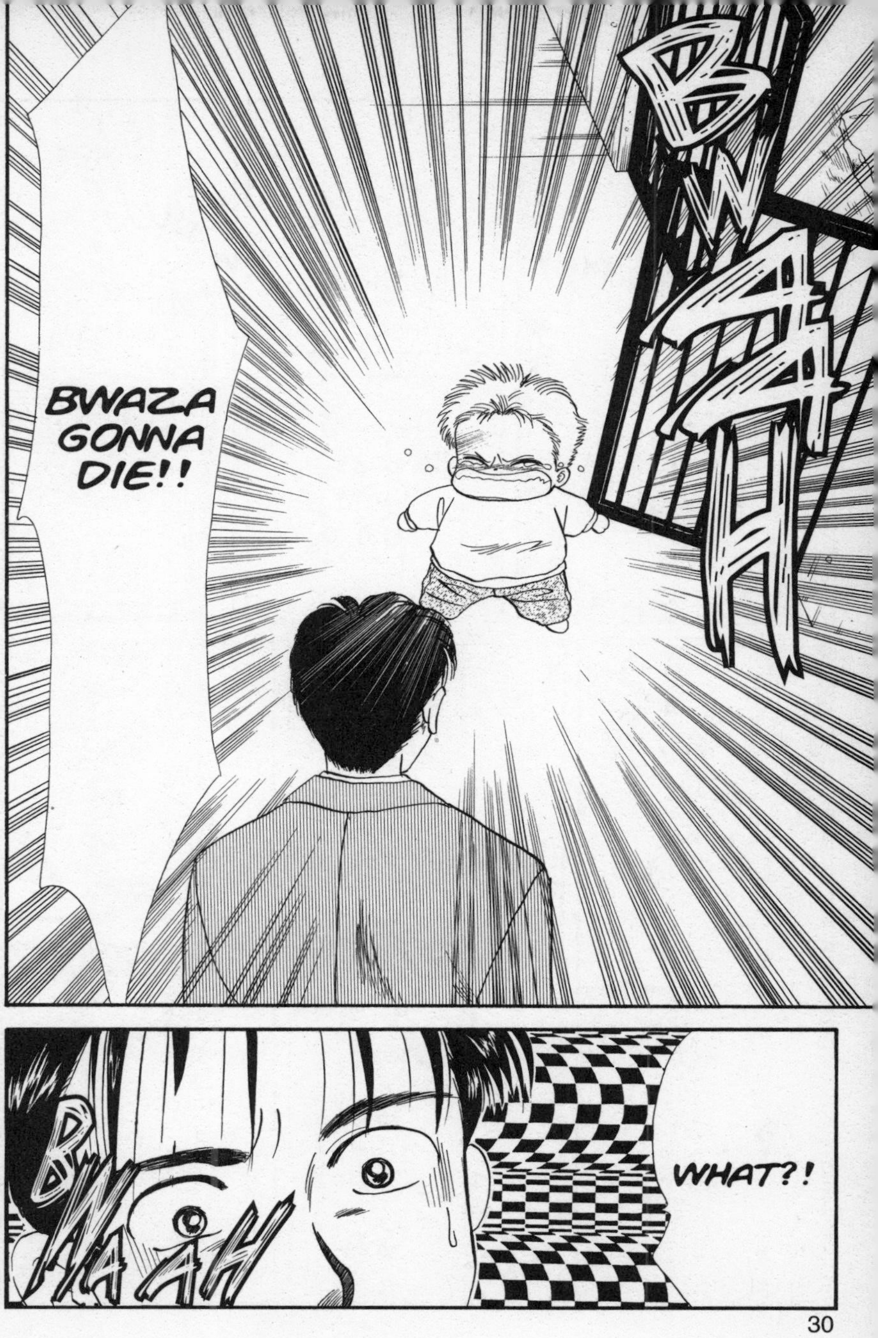
BWAAAH
BWAZA GONNA DIE!!
WHAT?!
BWAAH

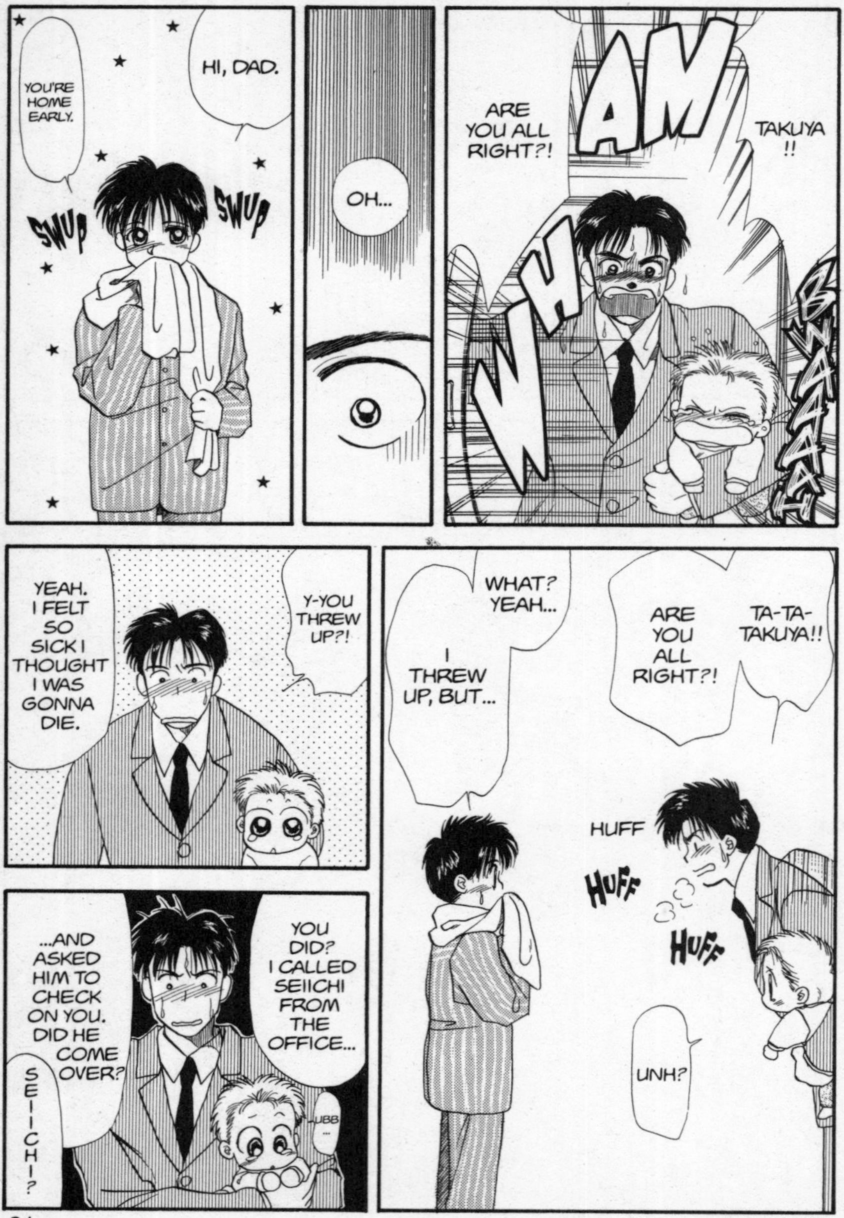
WHAM
TAKUYA !!
ARE YOU ALL RIGHT?!
BWAAAAH
OH...
HI, DAD.
YOU'RE HOME EARLY.
SWUP
SWUP
TA-TA-TAKUYA!!
ARE YOU ALL RIGHT?!
WHAT? YEAH...
I THREW UP, BUT...
HUFF
HUFF
HUFF
UNH?
Y-YOU THREW UP?!
YEAH. I FELT SO SICK I THOUGHT I WAS GONNA DIE.
YOU DID? I CALLED SEIICHI FROM THE OFFICE...
...AND ASKED HIM TO CHECK ON YOU. DID HE COME OVER?
UBB ...
SEIICHI?

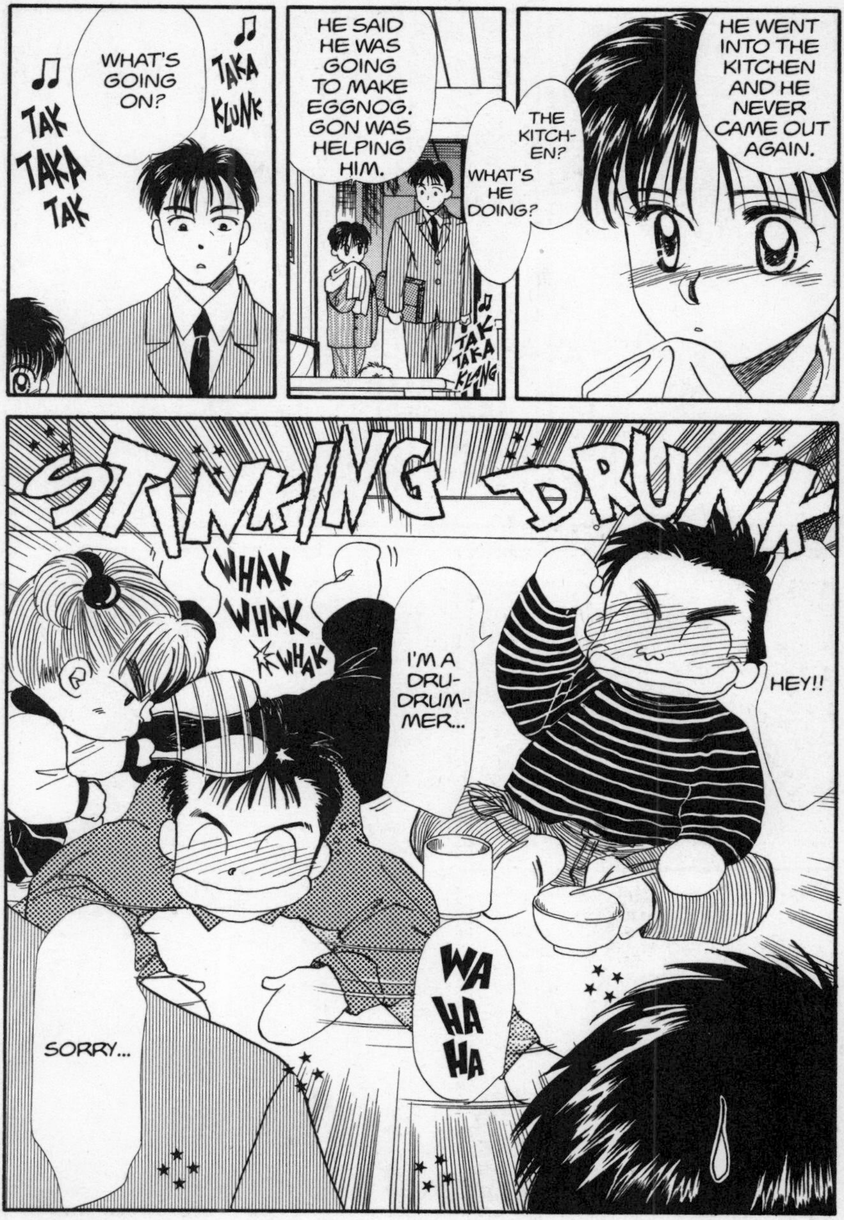
HE WENT INTO THE KITCHEN AND HE NEVER CAME OUT AGAIN.
THE KITCHEN? WHAT'S HE DOING?
HE SAID HE WAS GOING TO MAKE EGGNOG. GON WAS HELPING HIM.
TAK TAKA KLANG
TAKA KLUNK
WHAT'S GOING ON?
TAK TAKA TAK
STINKING DRUNK
HEY!!
I'M A DRU-DRUMMER...
WHAK WHAK WHAK
WA HA HA
SORRY...

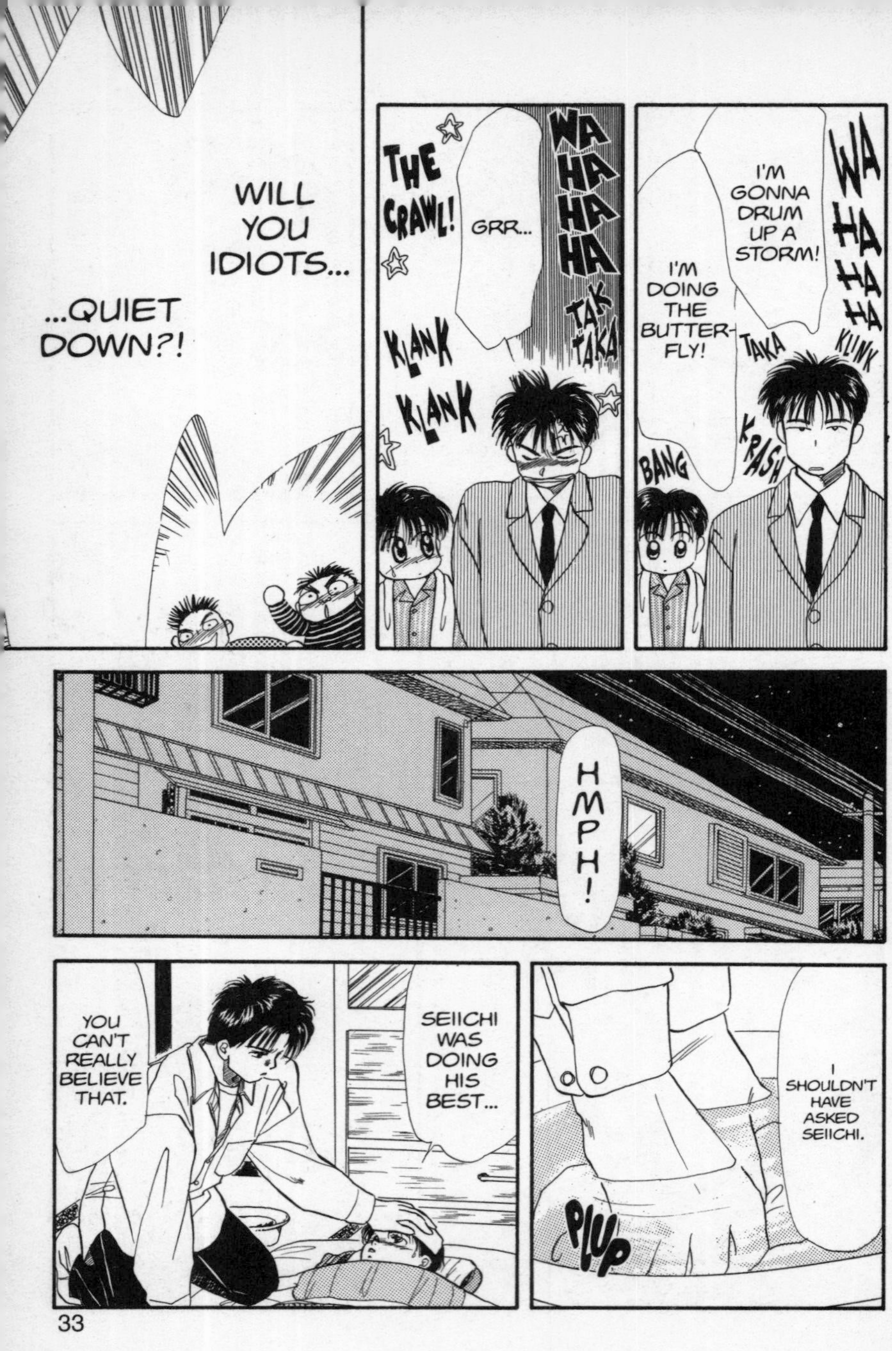
WA HA HA HA
I'M GONNA DRUM UP A STORM!
I'M DOING THE BUTTER-FLY!
KLINK
TAKA
KRASH
BANG
WA HA HA HA
TAK TAKA
GRR...
THE CRAWL!
KLANK
KLANK
WILL YOU IDIOTS...
...QUIET DOWN?!
HMPH!
I SHOULDN'T HAVE ASKED SEIICHI.
PLUP
SEIICHI WAS DOING HIS BEST...
YOU CAN'T REALLY BELIEVE THAT.

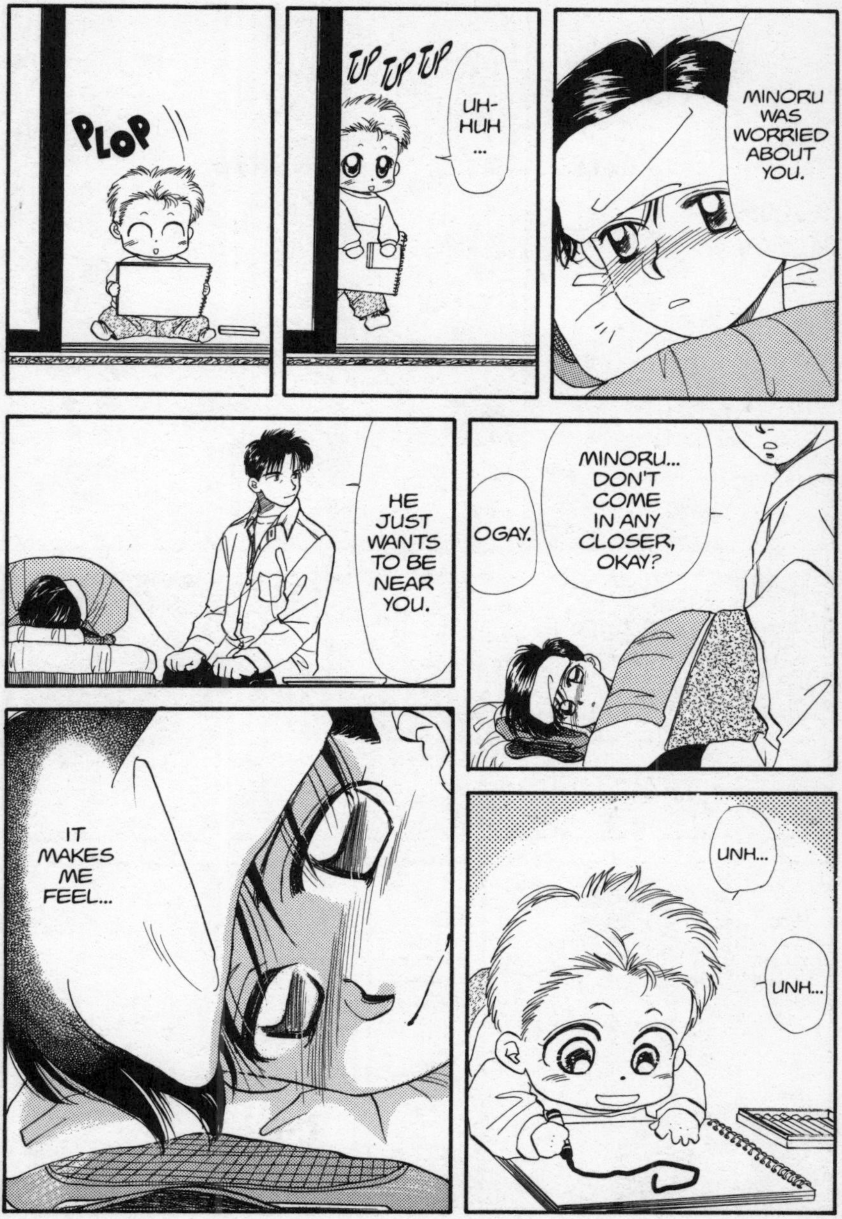
MINORU WAS WORRIED ABOUT YOU.
TUP TUP TUP
UH-HUH ...
PLOP
MINORU... DON'T COME IN ANY CLOSER, OKAY?
OGAY.
HE JUST WANTS TO BE NEAR YOU.
UNH...
UNH...
IT MAKES ME FEEL...

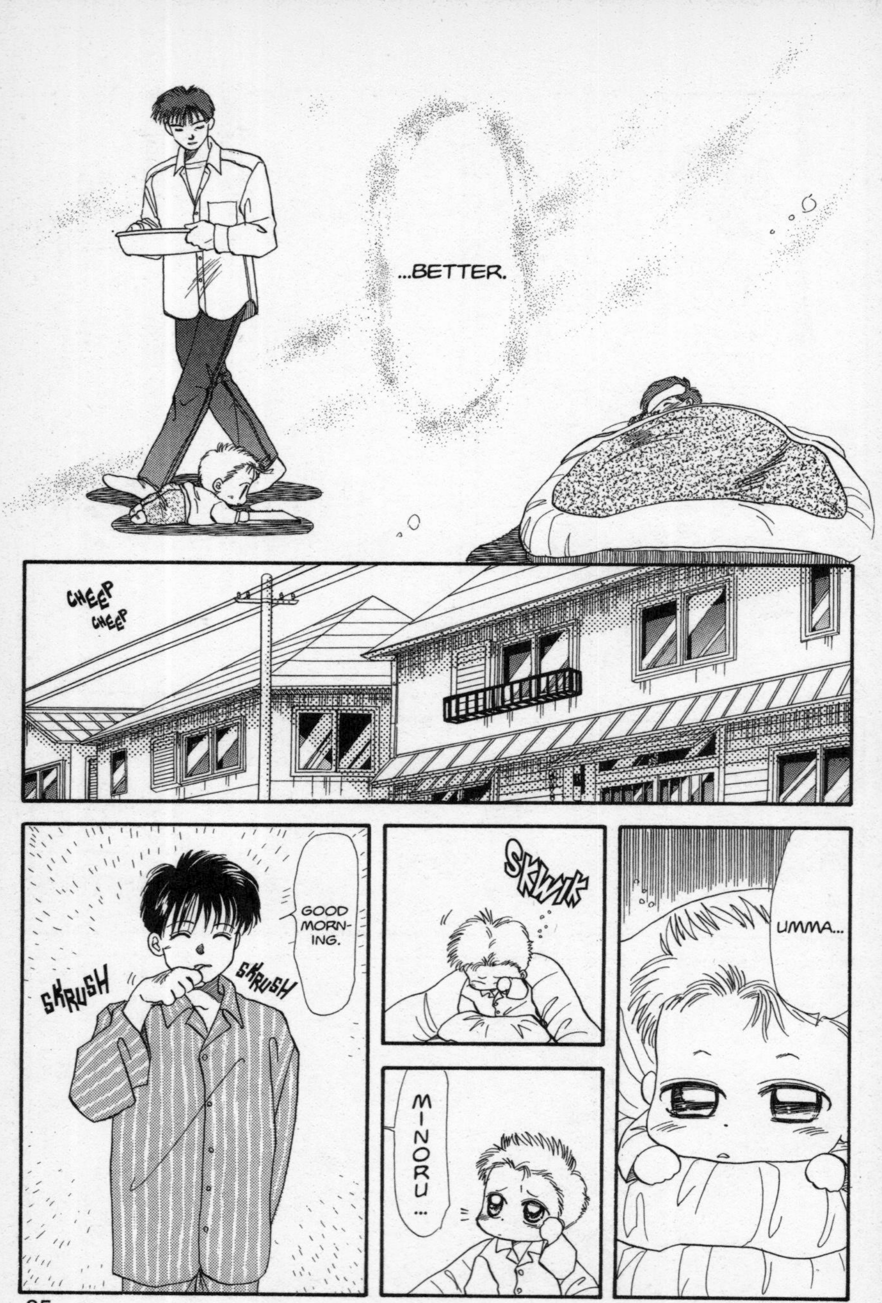
...BETTER.
CHEEP
CHEEP
UMMA...
SKWIK
MINORU...
GOOD MORNING.
SKRUSH
SKRUSH

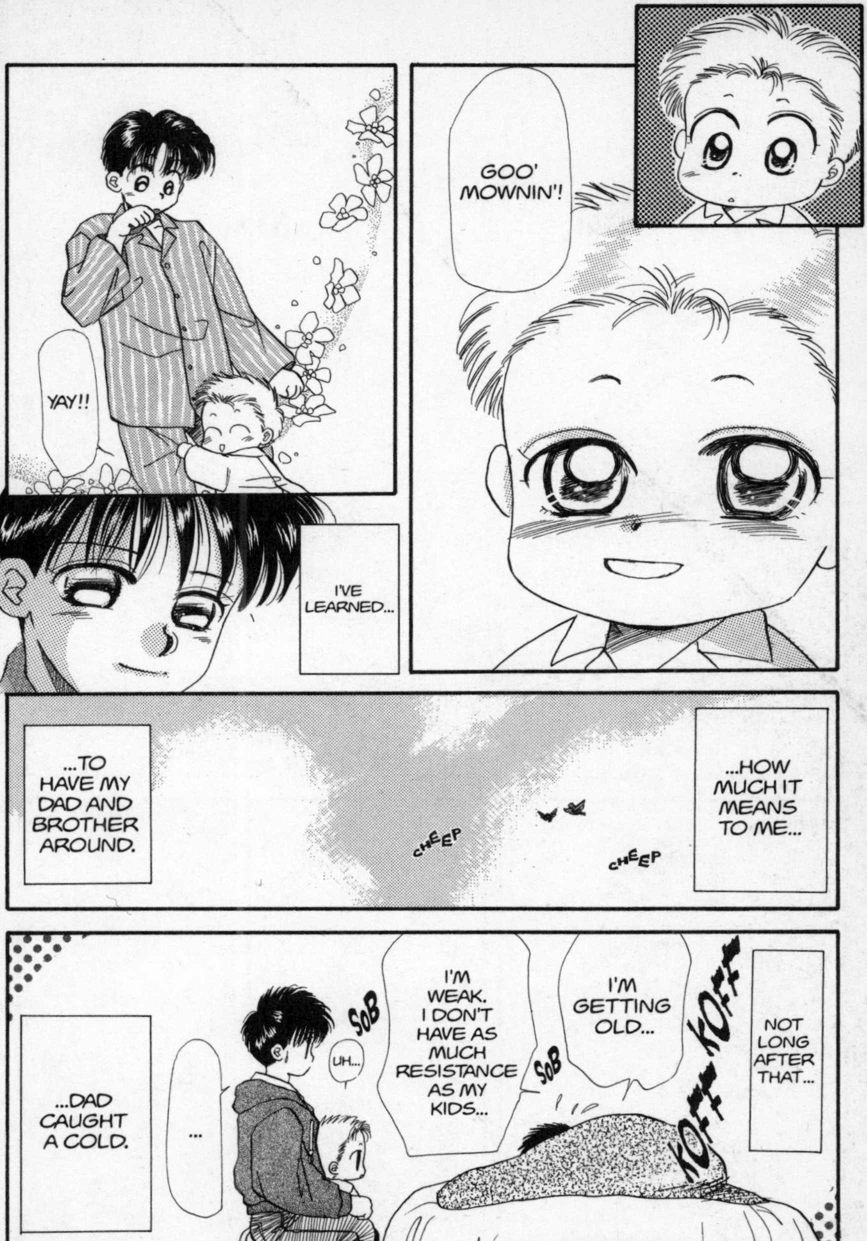
GOO' MOWNIN'!
YAY!!
I'VE LEARNED...
...HOW MUCH IT MEANS TO ME...
CHEEP
CHEEP
...TO HAVE MY DAD AND BROTHER AROUND.
NOT LONG AFTER THAT...
KOFF KOFF KOFF
I'M GETTING OLD...
SOB
I'M WEAK. I DON'T HAVE AS MUCH RESISTANCE AS MY KIDS...
SOB
UH...
...
...DAD CAUGHT A COLD.

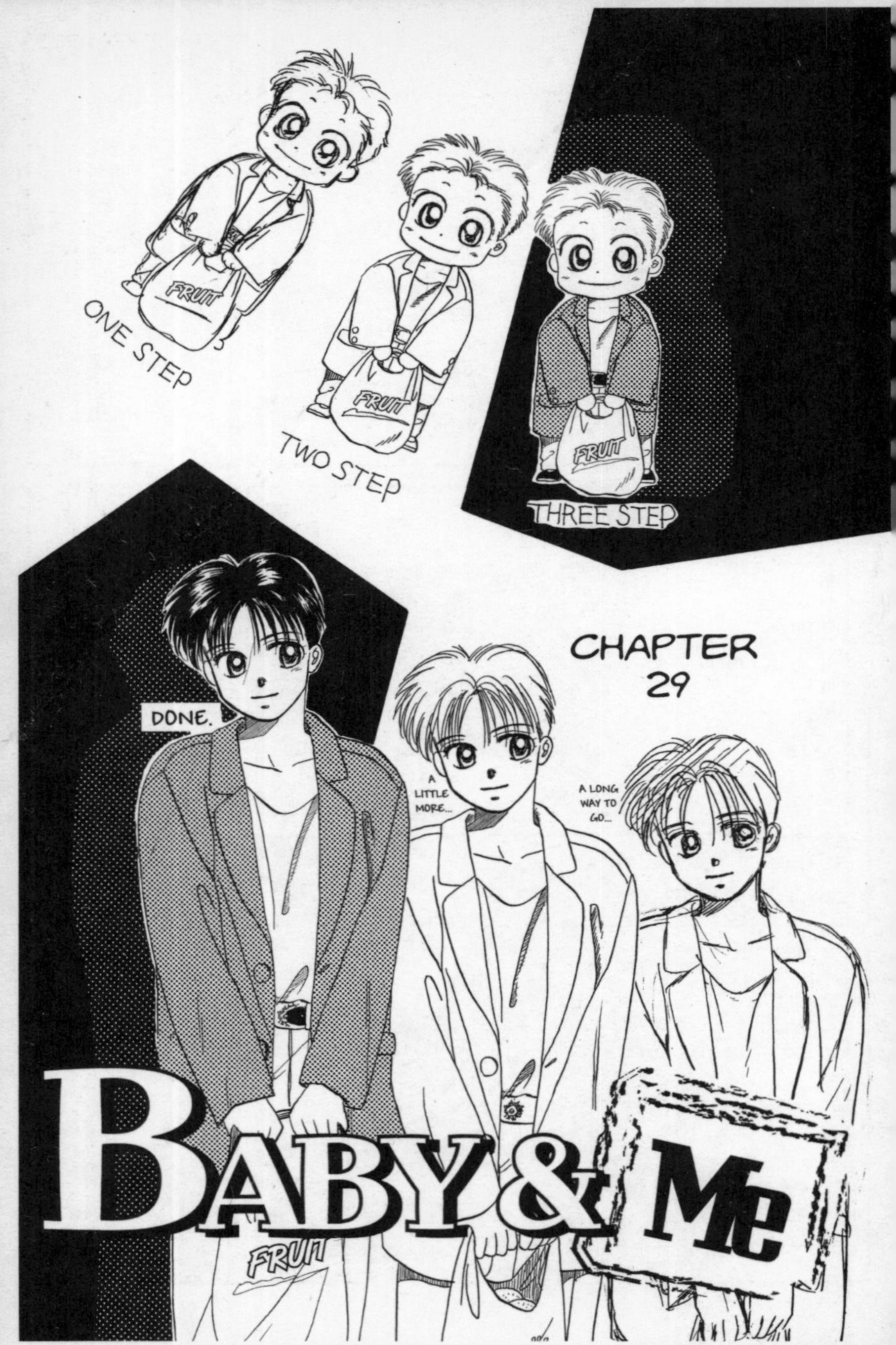
FRUIT
ONE STEP
FRUIT
TWO STEP
FRUIT
THREE STEP
CHAPTER 29
DONE.
A LITTLE MORE...
A LONG WAY TO GO...
BABY & Me
FRUIT

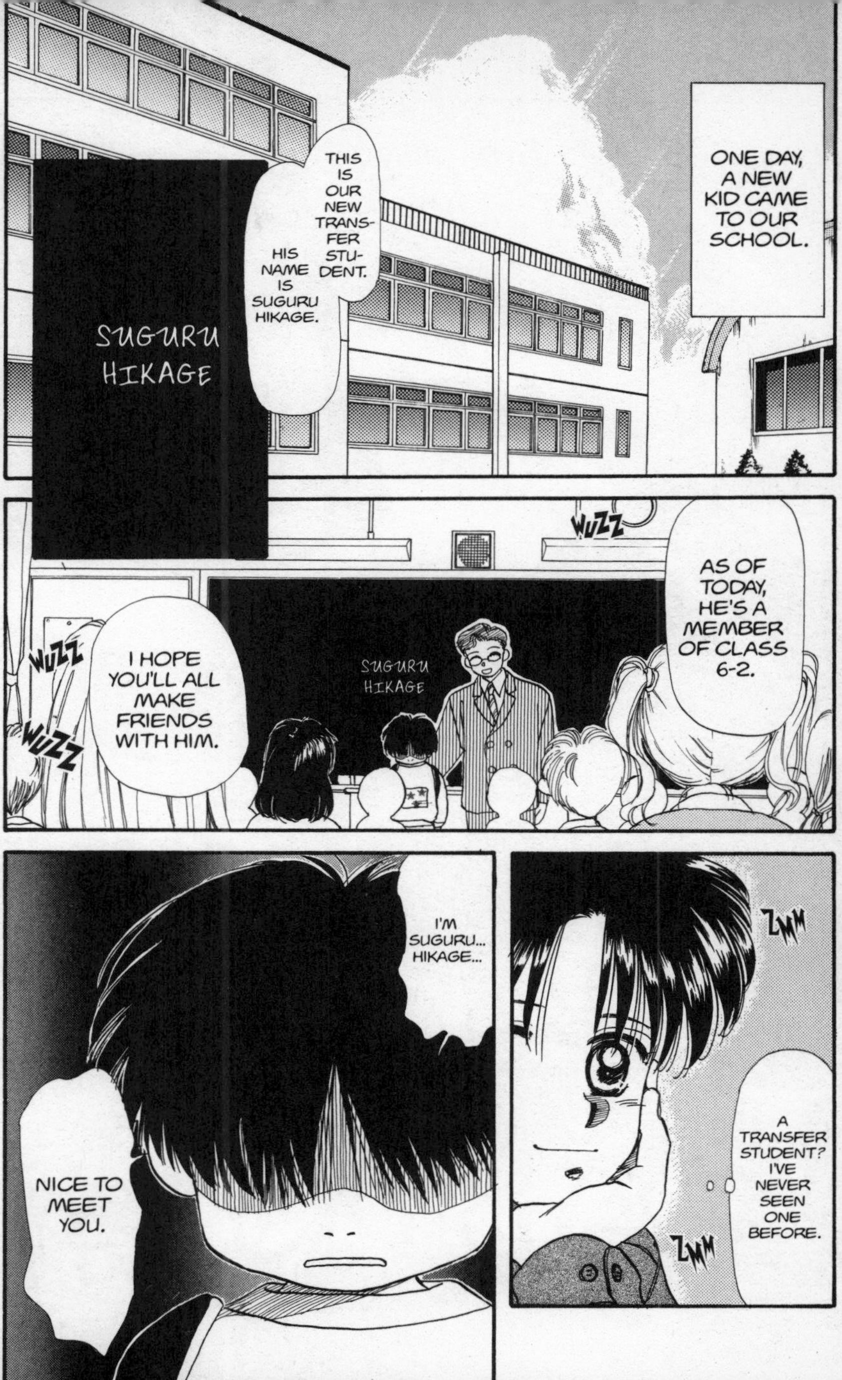
ONE DAY, A NEW KID CAME TO OUR SCHOOL.
THIS IS OUR NEW TRANSFER STUDENT.
HIS NAME IS SUGURU HIKAGE.
SUGURU HIKAGE
WUZZ
AS OF TODAY, HE'S A MEMBER OF CLASS 6-2.
SUGURU HIKAGE
I HOPE YOU'LL ALL MAKE FRIENDS WITH HIM.
WUZZ
WUZZ
ZMM
A TRANSFER STUDENT? I'VE NEVER SEEN ONE BEFORE.
ZMM
I'M SUGURU... HIKAGE...
NICE TO MEET YOU.

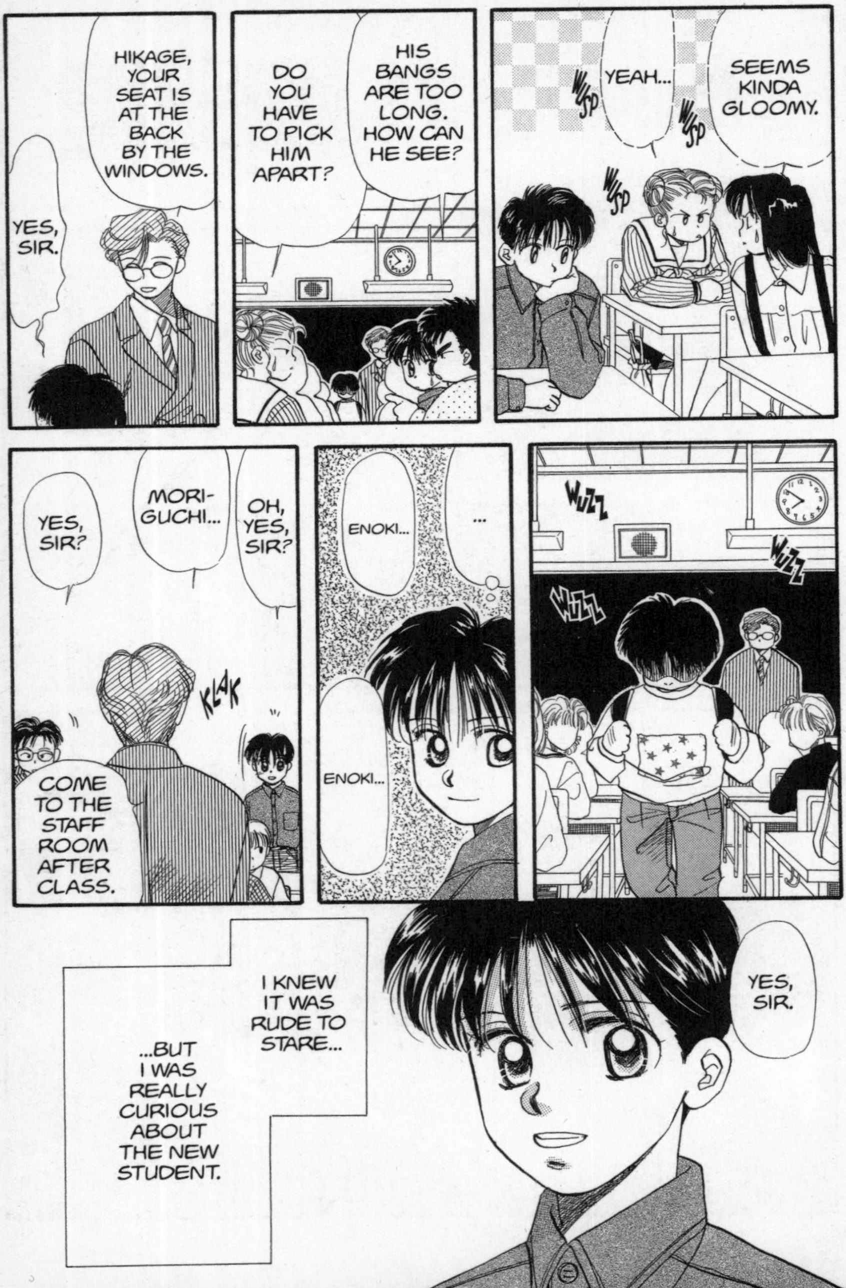
SEEMS KINDA GLOOMY.
YEAH...
WISP
WISP
WISP
HIS BANGS ARE TOO LONG. HOW CAN HE SEE?
DO YOU HAVE TO PICK HIM APART?
HIKAGE, YOUR SEAT IS AT THE BACK BY THE WINDOWS.
YES, SIR.
WUZZ
WUZZ
WUZZ
...
ENOKI...
ENOKI...
OH, YES, SIR?
MORI-GUCHI...
YES, SIR?
KLAK
COME TO THE STAFF ROOM AFTER CLASS.
YES, SIR.
I KNEW IT WAS RUDE TO STARE...
...BUT I WAS REALLY CURIOUS ABOUT THE NEW STUDENT.

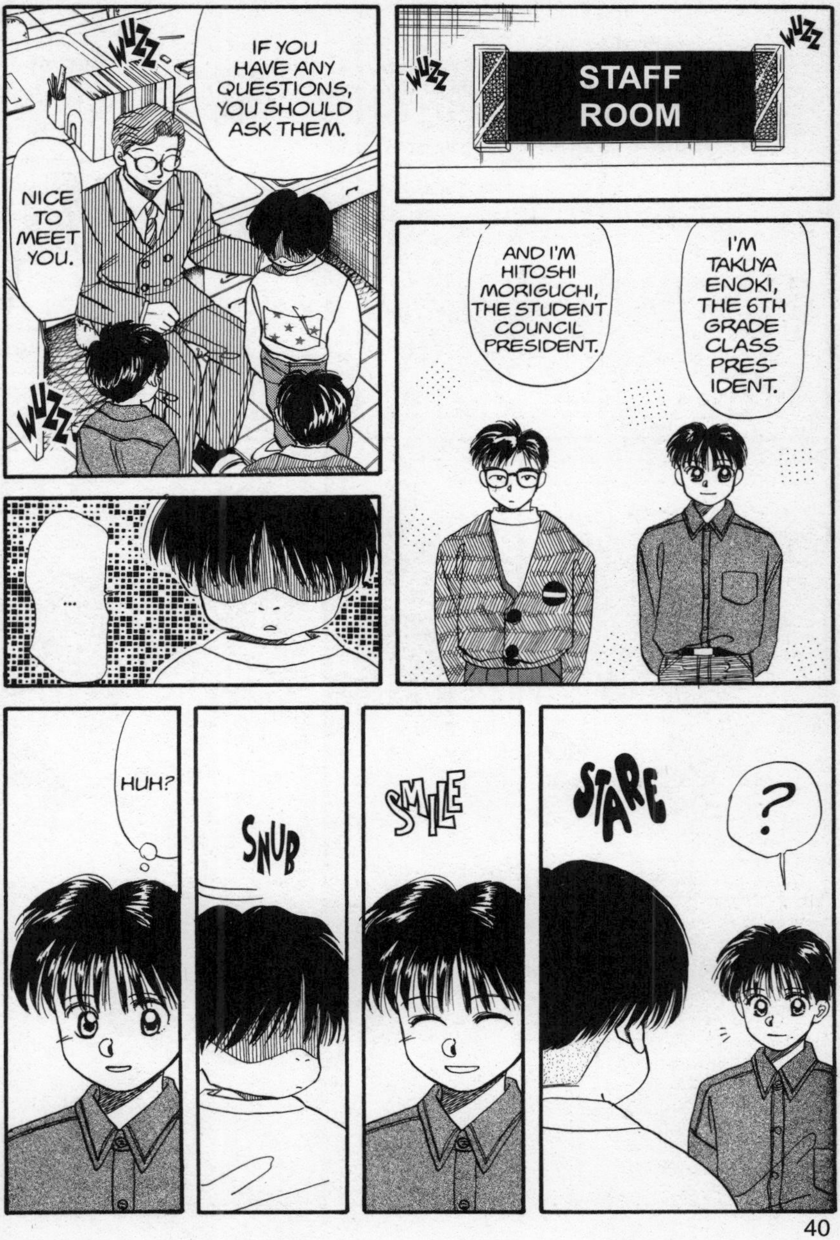
WUZZ
STAFF ROOM
WUZZ
I'M TAKUYA ENOKI, THE 6TH GRADE CLASS PRES-IDENT.
AND I'M HITOSHI MORIGUCHI, THE STUDENT COUNCIL PRESIDENT.
WUZZ
IF YOU HAVE ANY QUESTIONS, YOU SHOULD ASK THEM.
NICE TO MEET YOU.
WUZZ
...
?
STARE
SMILE
SNUB
HUH?

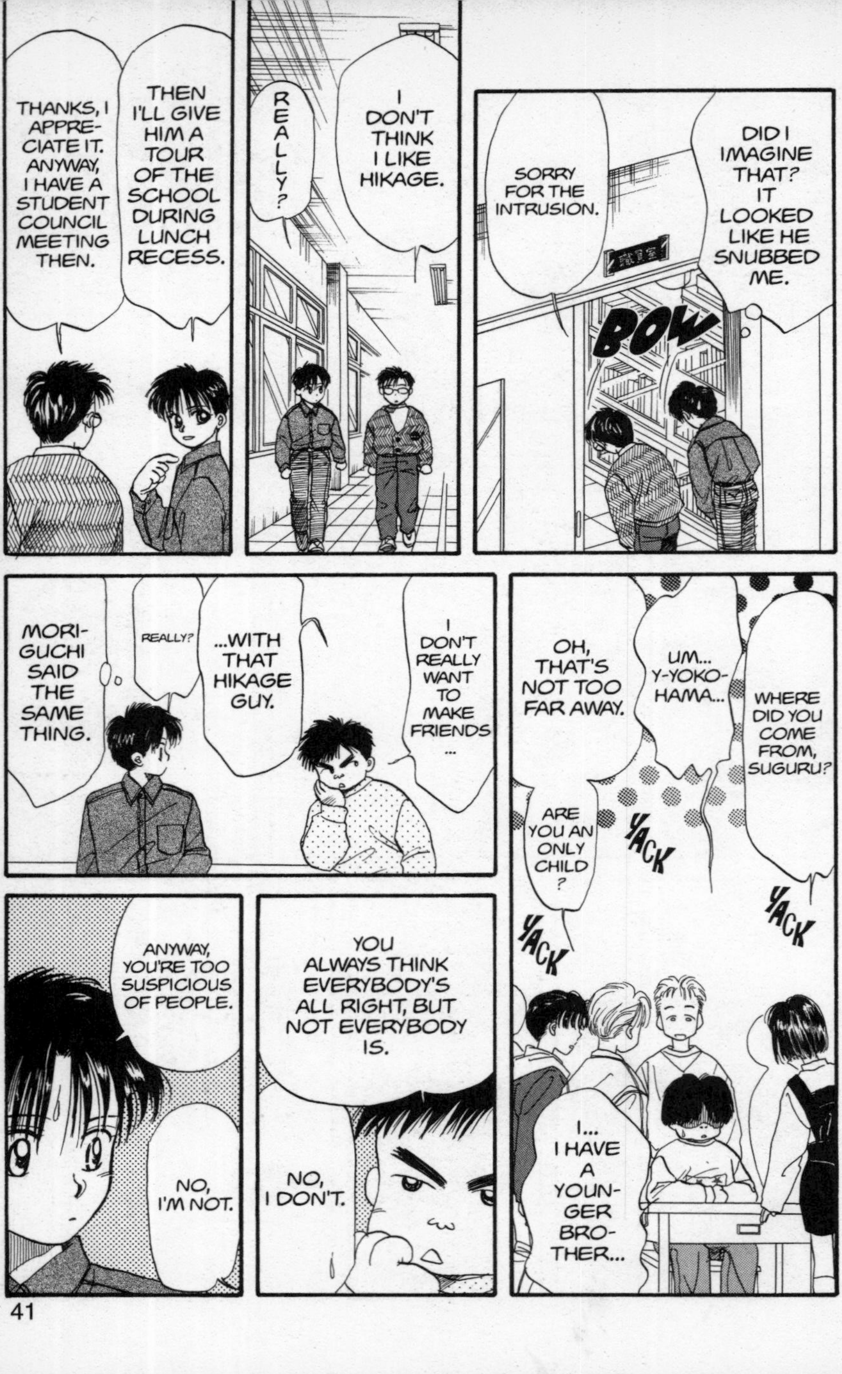
DID I IMAGINE THAT? IT LOOKED LIKE HE SNUBBED ME.
SORRY FOR THE INTRUSION.
BOW
I DON'T THINK I LIKE HIKAGE.
REALLY?
THEN I'LL GIVE HIM A TOUR OF THE SCHOOL DURING LUNCH RECESS.
THANKS, I APPRECIATE IT. ANYWAY, I HAVE A STUDENT COUNCIL MEETING THEN.
WHERE DID YOU COME FROM, SUGURU?
UM... Y-YOKOHAMA...
OH, THAT'S NOT TOO FAR AWAY.
YACK
ARE YOU AN ONLY CHILD?
YACK
YACK
I... I HAVE A YOUNGER BROTHER...
I DON'T REALLY WANT TO MAKE FRIENDS...
...WITH THAT HIKAGE GUY.
REALLY?
MORIGUCHI SAID THE SAME THING.
YOU ALWAYS THINK EVERYBODY'S ALL RIGHT, BUT NOT EVERYBODY IS.
NO, I DON'T.
ANYWAY, YOU'RE TOO SUSPICIOUS OF PEOPLE.
NO, I'M NOT.

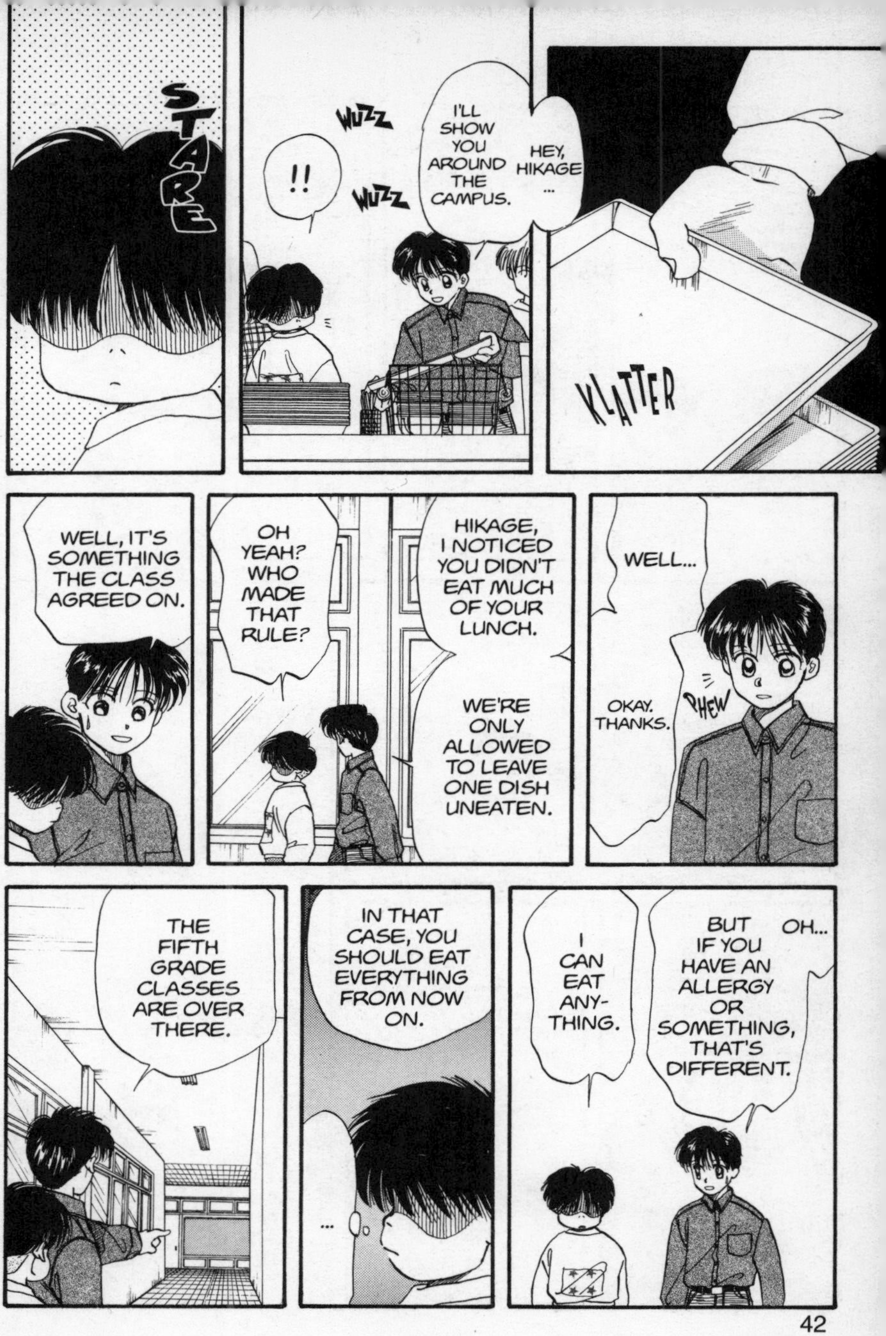
KLATTER
HEY, HIKAGE ...
I'LL SHOW YOU AROUND THE CAMPUS.
!!
WUZZ
WUZZ
STARE
WELL...
OKAY. THANKS.
PHEW
HIKAGE, I NOTICED YOU DIDN'T EAT MUCH OF YOUR LUNCH.
WE'RE ONLY ALLOWED TO LEAVE ONE DISH UNEATEN.
OH YEAH? WHO MADE THAT RULE?
WELL, IT'S SOMETHING THE CLASS AGREED ON.
OH...
BUT IF YOU HAVE AN ALLERGY OR SOMETHING, THAT'S DIFFERENT.
I CAN EAT ANY-THING.
IN THAT CASE, YOU SHOULD EAT EVERYTHING FROM NOW ON.
...
THE FIFTH GRADE CLASSES ARE OVER THERE.

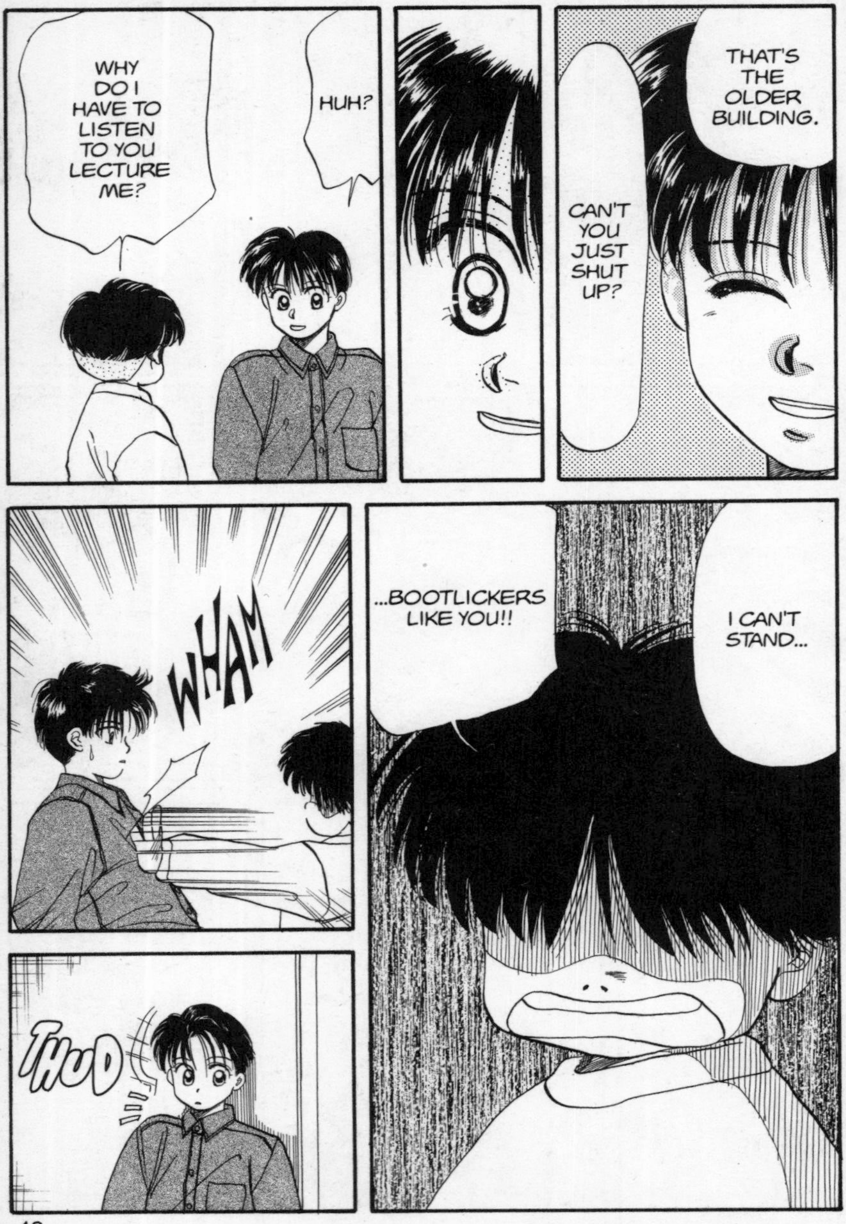
THAT'S THE OLDER BUILDING.
CAN'T YOU JUST SHUT UP?
HUH?
WHY DO I HAVE TO LISTEN TO YOU LECTURE ME?
I CAN'T STAND...
...BOOTLICKERS LIKE YOU!!
WHAM
THUD

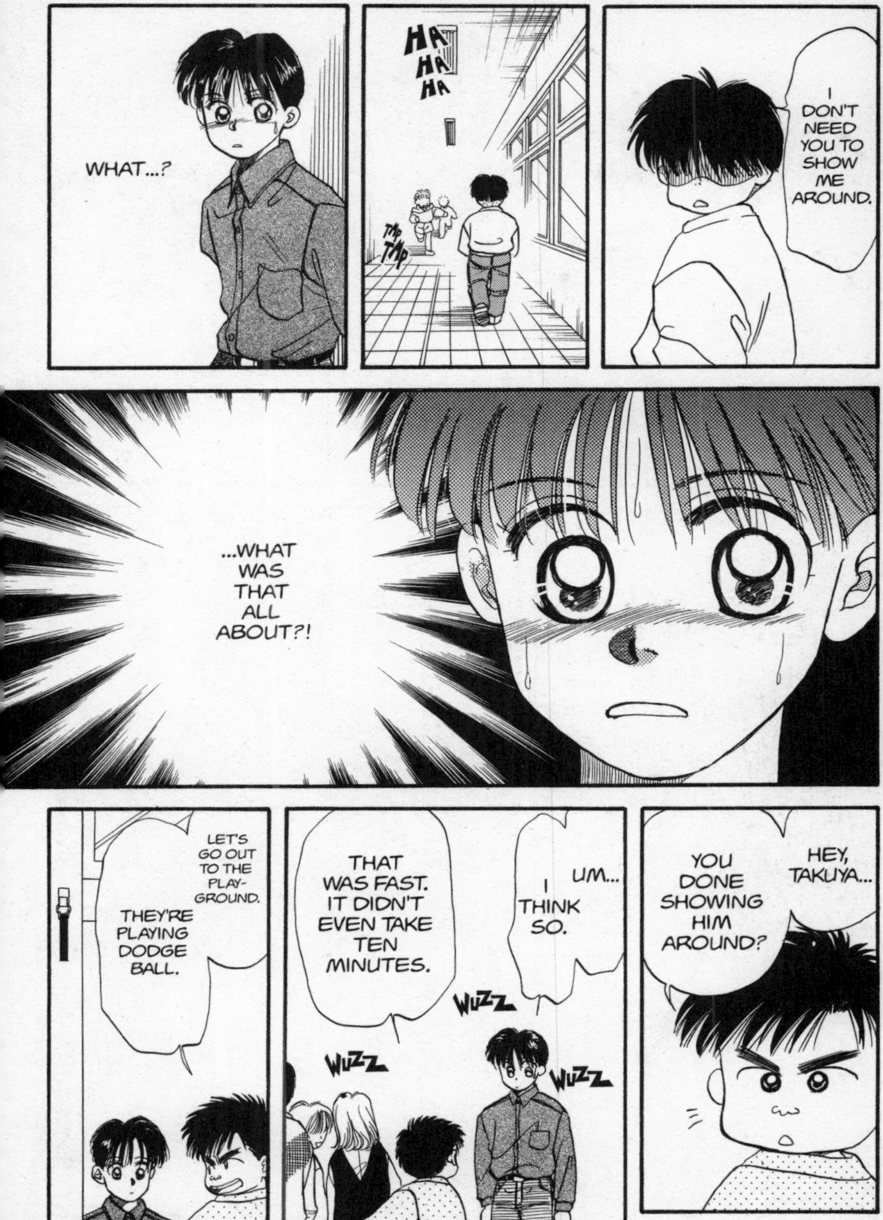
I DON'T NEED YOU TO SHOW ME AROUND.
HA HA HA
TMP TMP
WHAT...?
...WHAT WAS THAT ALL ABOUT?!
HEY, TAKUYA...
YOU DONE SHOWING HIM AROUND?
UM...
I THINK SO.
THAT WAS FAST. IT DIDN'T EVEN TAKE TEN MINUTES.
WUZZ
WUZZ
WUZZ
LET'S GO OUT TO THE PLAY-GROUND.
THEY'RE PLAYING DODGE BALL.

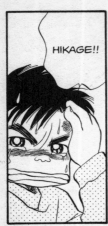

HIKAGE!!

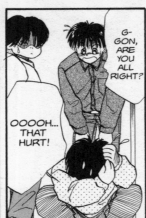

G-GON, ARE YOU ALL RIGHT?

OOOOH... THAT HURT!

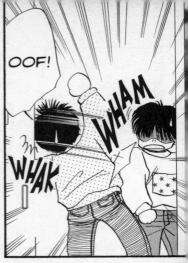

OOF!

WHAM

WHAK

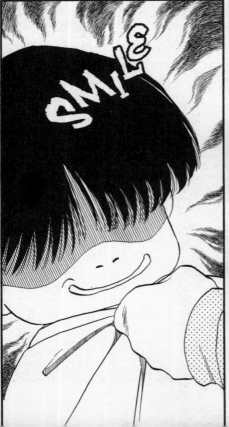

SMILE

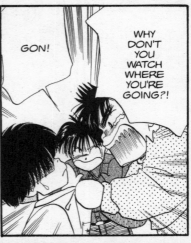

GON!

WHY DON'T YOU WATCH WHERE YOU'RE GOING?!

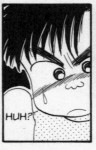

HUH?

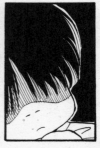

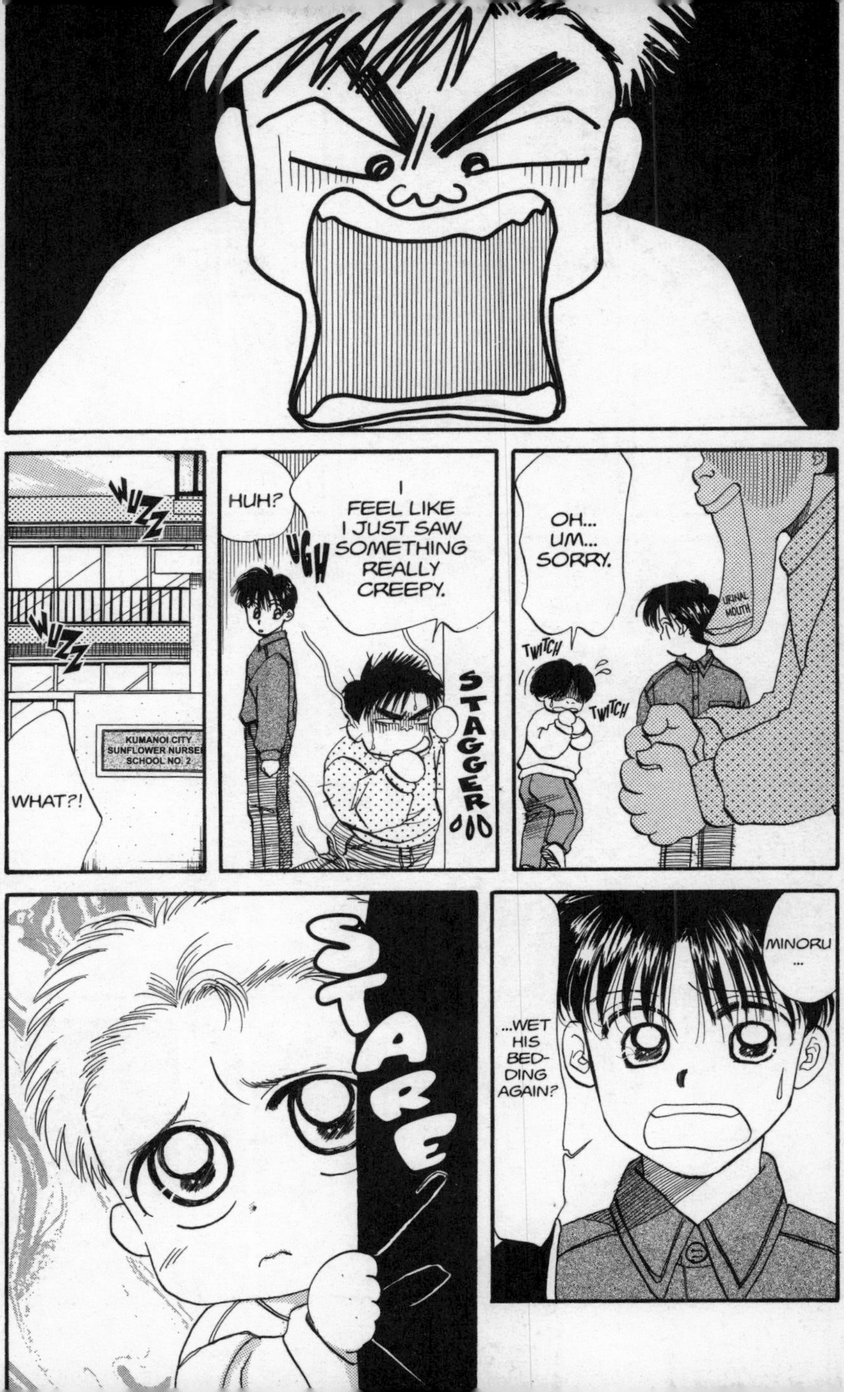

OH... UM... SORRY.
URINAL MOUTH
TWITCH
TWITCH
I FEEL LIKE I JUST SAW SOMETHING REALLY CREEPY.
HUH?
UGH
STAGGER
WUZZ
WUZZ
KUMANOI CITY SUNFLOWER NURSE SCHOOL NO. 2
WHAT?!
MINORU ...
...WET HIS BED-DING AGAIN?
STARE

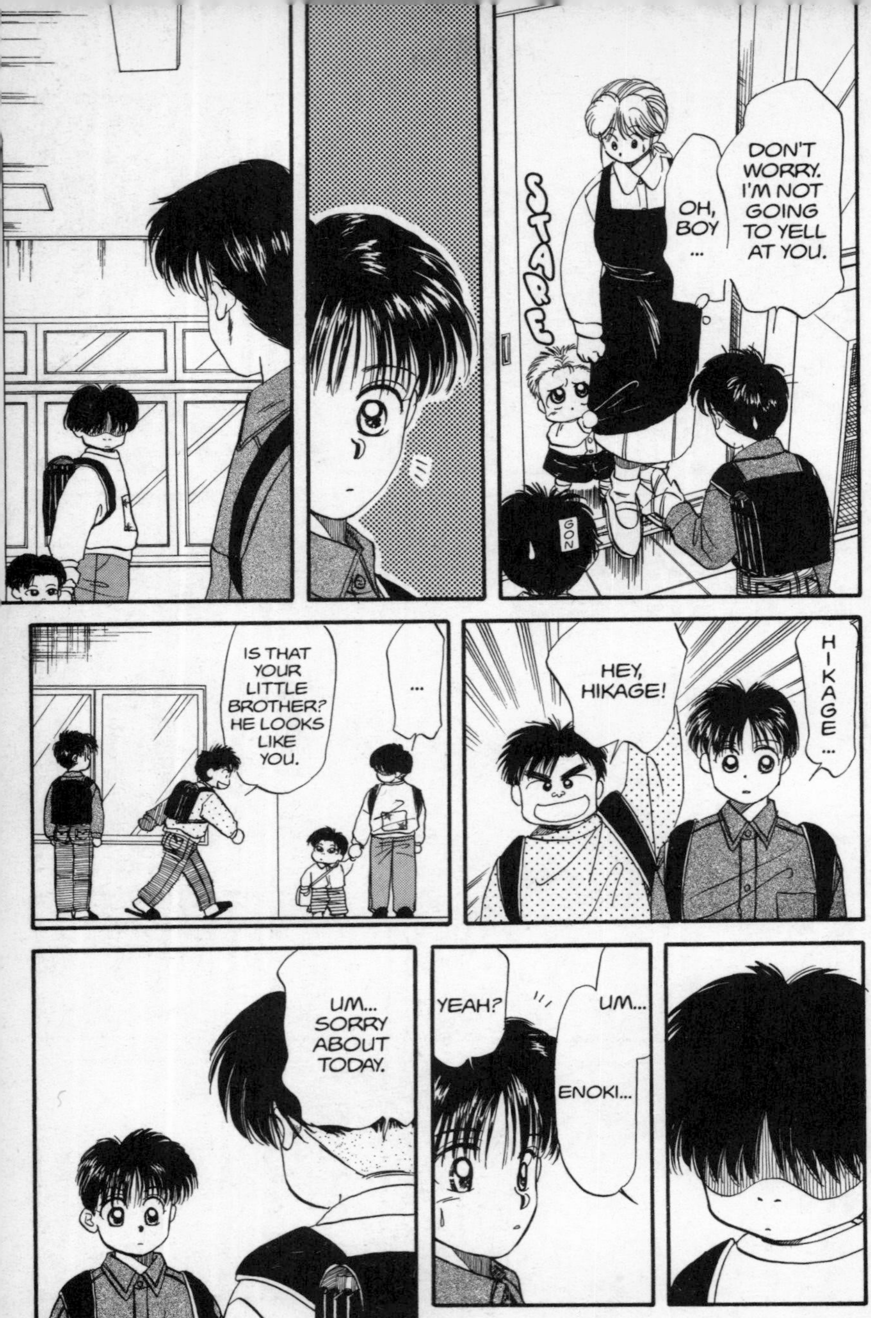
DON'T WORRY. I'M NOT GOING TO YELL AT YOU.
OH, BOY ...
STARE
GON
HIKAGE ...
HEY, HIKAGE!
...
IS THAT YOUR LITTLE BROTHER? HE LOOKS LIKE YOU.
UM...
ENOKI...
YEAH?
UM... SORRY ABOUT TODAY.

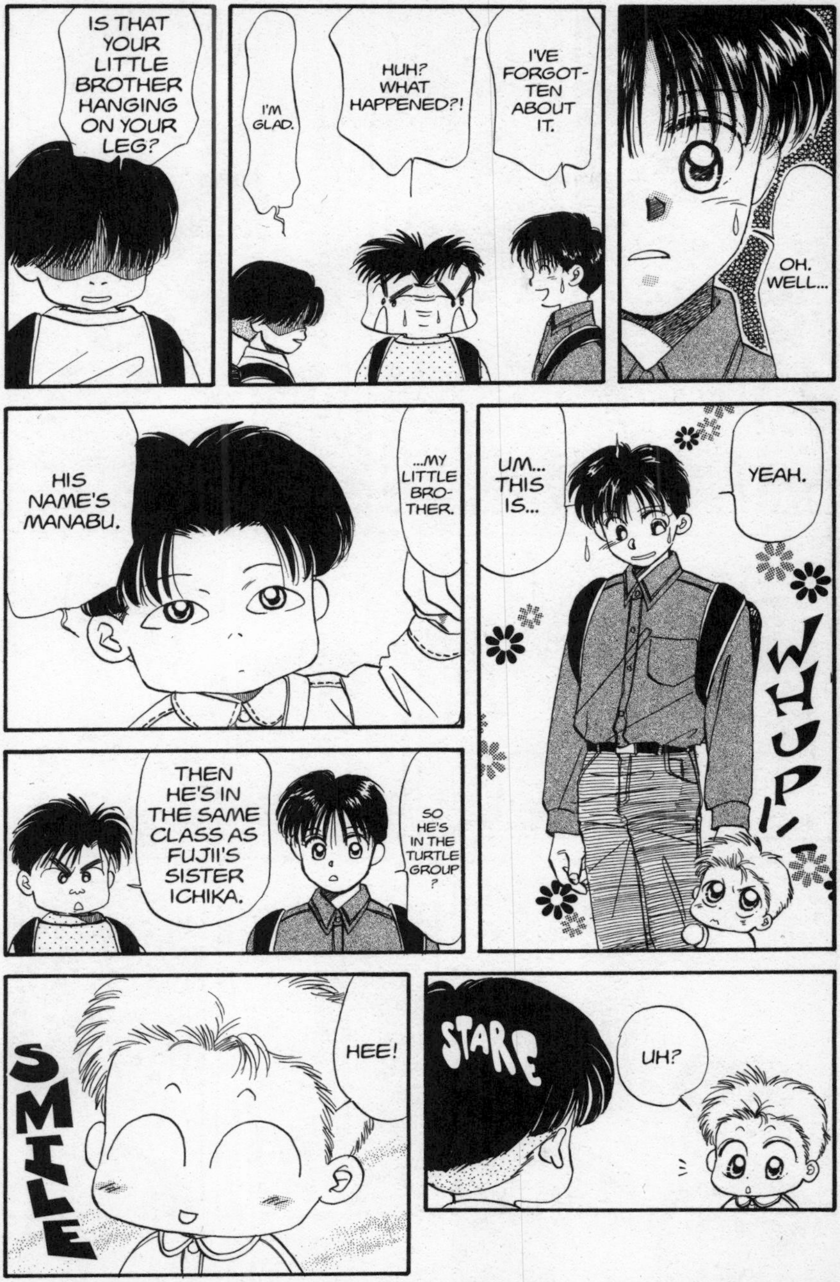

OH. WELL...
I'VE FORGOTTEN ABOUT IT.
HUH? WHAT HAPPENED?!
I'M GLAD.
IS THAT YOUR LITTLE BROTHER HANGING ON YOUR LEG?
YEAH.
UM... THIS IS...
WHUP!!
...MY LITTLE BROTHER.
HIS NAME'S MANABU.
SO HE'S IN THE TURTLE GROUP?
THEN HE'S IN THE SAME CLASS AS FUJII'S SISTER ICHIKA.
UH?
STARE
HEE!
SMILE

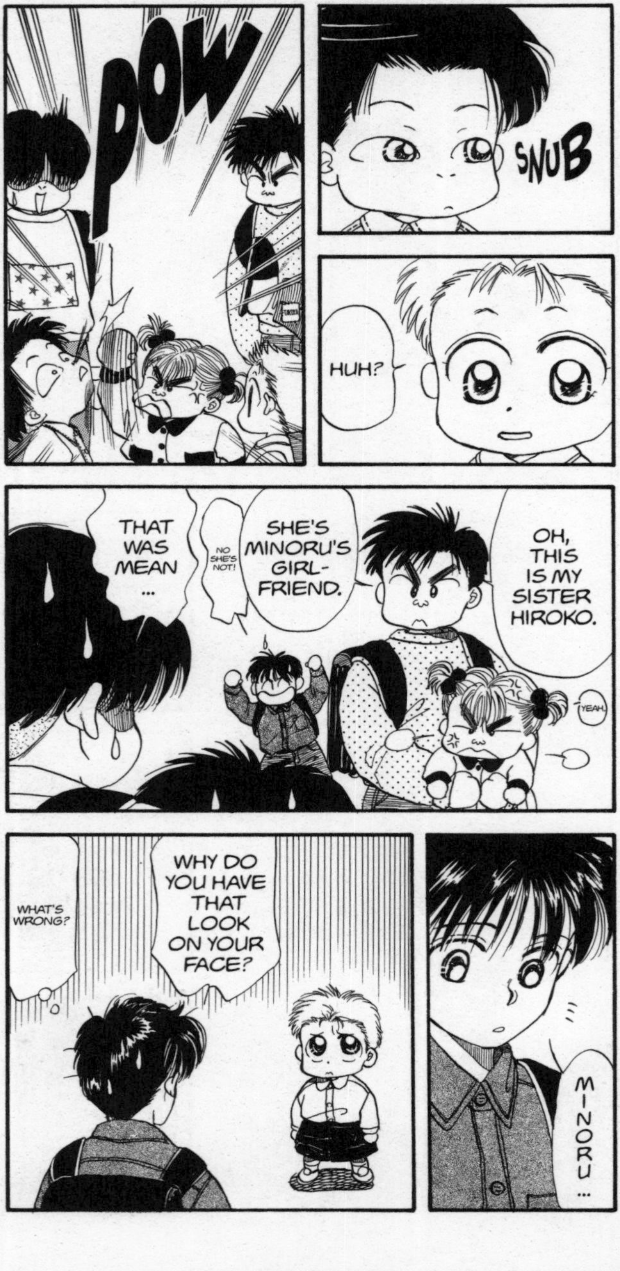
SNUB
HUH?
POW
OH, THIS IS MY SISTER HIROKO.
YEAH.
SHE'S MINORU'S GIRLFRIEND.
NO SHE'S NOT!
THAT WAS MEAN ...
MINORU ...
WHY DO YOU HAVE THAT LOOK ON YOUR FACE?
WHAT'S WRONG?

Author's Note, Part 2

Q: It's funny that on page 14 of volume 3, the Kimuras, who live right across the street, were on a different team than the Enoki's because the dividing line ran down their street, but according to the map on page 36 of volume 5, Gon--who was on the Blue team with Takuya--lives much farther away.

Ragawa: Well yes, that's true, but allow me to make up an excuse. The town of Nagara is divided because of its large population, but it's still considered to be one town. The Enokis and the Kimuras are from District 1, and Gon lives in District 2.

Q: In chapter 17 (page 6 of volume 4) all the kids took a share of the 5,000 yen for the festival, and there should have only been 500 yen left at the end, but the story has it that 1,500 yen was left. Wasn't that a mistake?

Ragawa: Well... Big sister Akemi took her share of the 5,000 yen, but there was actually 6,000 yen on the table to begin with. So it wasn't a mistake.

Q: In chapter 19 (volume 4), you say it's a pity that the man had to go to a home for the elderly, but please don't say that. I work at a home for the elderly, and it's a very nice place.

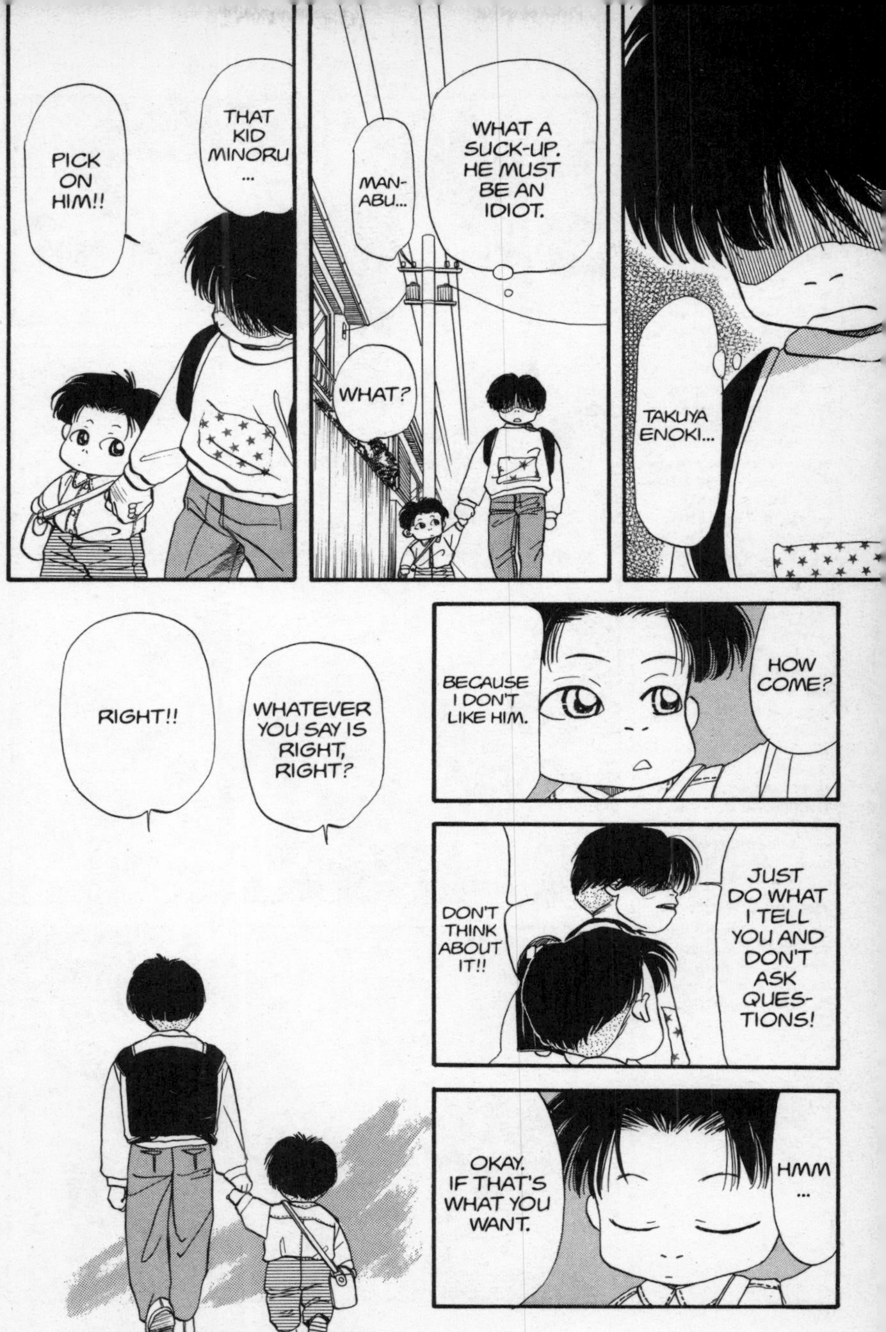
TAKUYA ENOKI...
WHAT A SUCK-UP. HE MUST BE AN IDIOT.
MAN-ABU...
WHAT?
THAT KID MINORU ...
PICK ON HIM!!
HOW COME?
BECAUSE I DON'T LIKE HIM.
JUST DO WHAT I TELL YOU AND DON'T ASK QUES-TIONS!
DON'T THINK ABOUT IT!!
HMM ...
OKAY. IF THAT'S WHAT YOU WANT.
WHATEVER YOU SAY IS RIGHT, RIGHT?
RIGHT!!

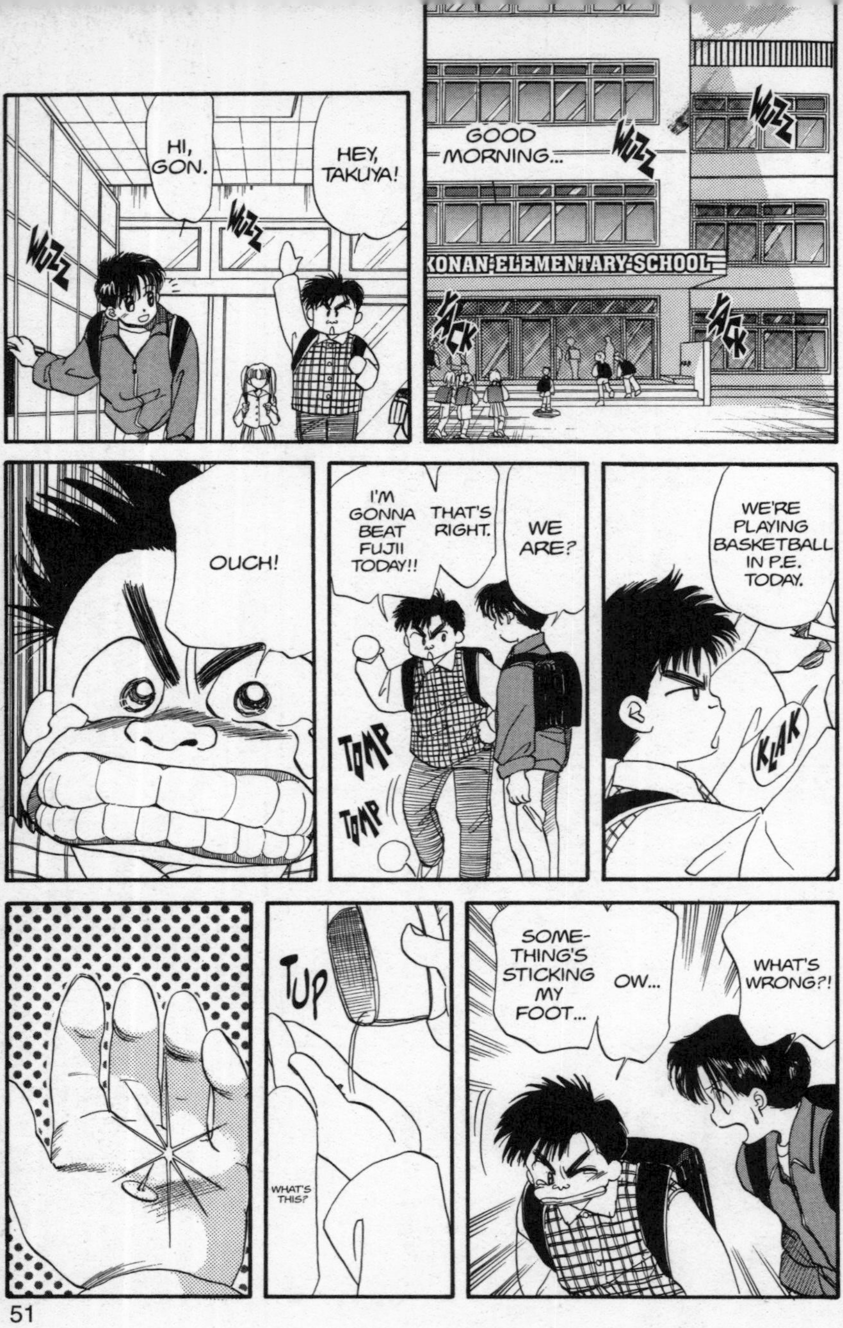
GOOD MORNING...
WUZZ
WUZZ
KONAN ELEMENTARY SCHOOL
YACK
YACK
HEY, TAKUYA!
HI, GON.
WUZZ
WUZZ
WE'RE PLAYING BASKETBALL IN P.E. TODAY.
KLAK
WE ARE?
THAT'S RIGHT.
I'M GONNA BEAT FUJII TODAY!!
TOMP
TOMP
OUCH!
WHAT'S WRONG?!
OW...
SOME-THING'S STICKING MY FOOT...
TUP
WHAT'S THIS?

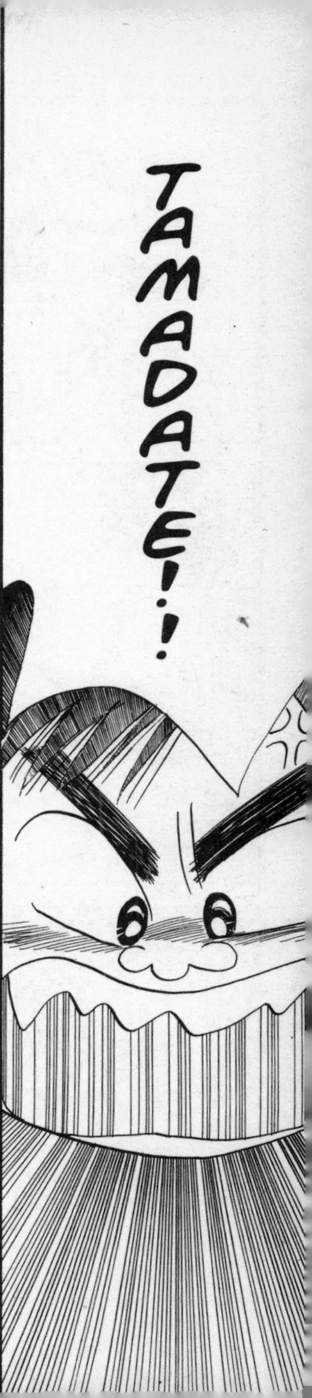
TAMADATE!!

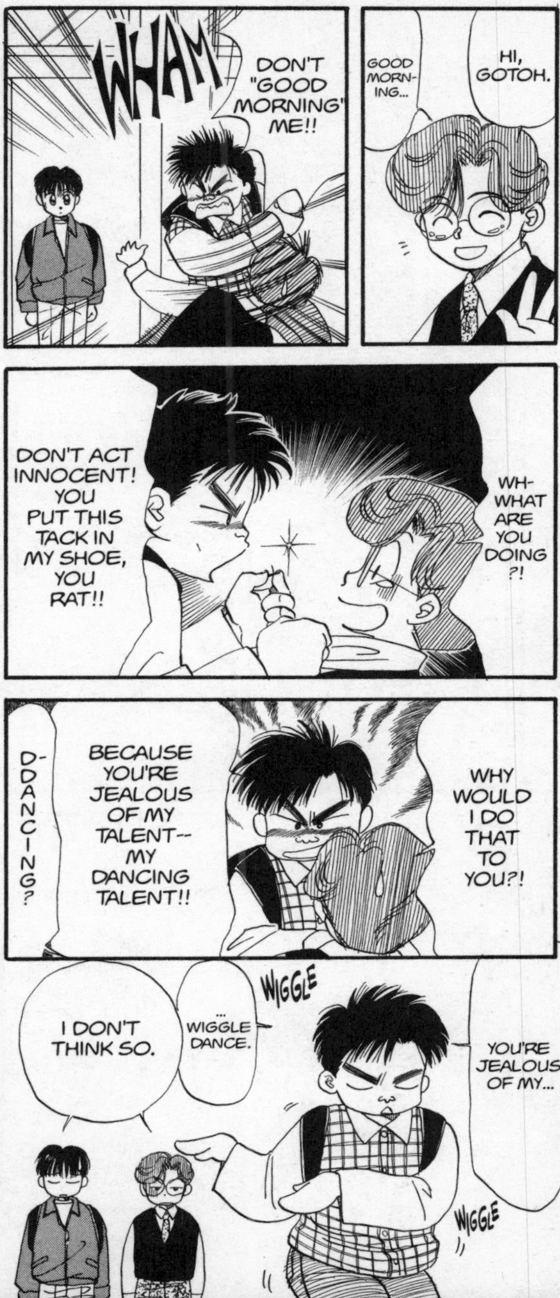
HI, GOTOH.
GOOD MORNING...
WHAM
DON'T "GOOD MORNING" ME!!
WH-WHAT ARE YOU DOING?!
DON'T ACT INNOCENT! YOU PUT THIS TACK IN MY SHOE, YOU RAT!!
WHY WOULD I DO THAT TO YOU?!
BECAUSE YOU'RE JEALOUS OF MY TALENT-- MY DANCING TALENT!!
D-DDANCING?
YOU'RE JEALOUS OF MY...
WIGGLE
... WIGGLE DANCE.
I DON'T THINK SO.
WIGGLE

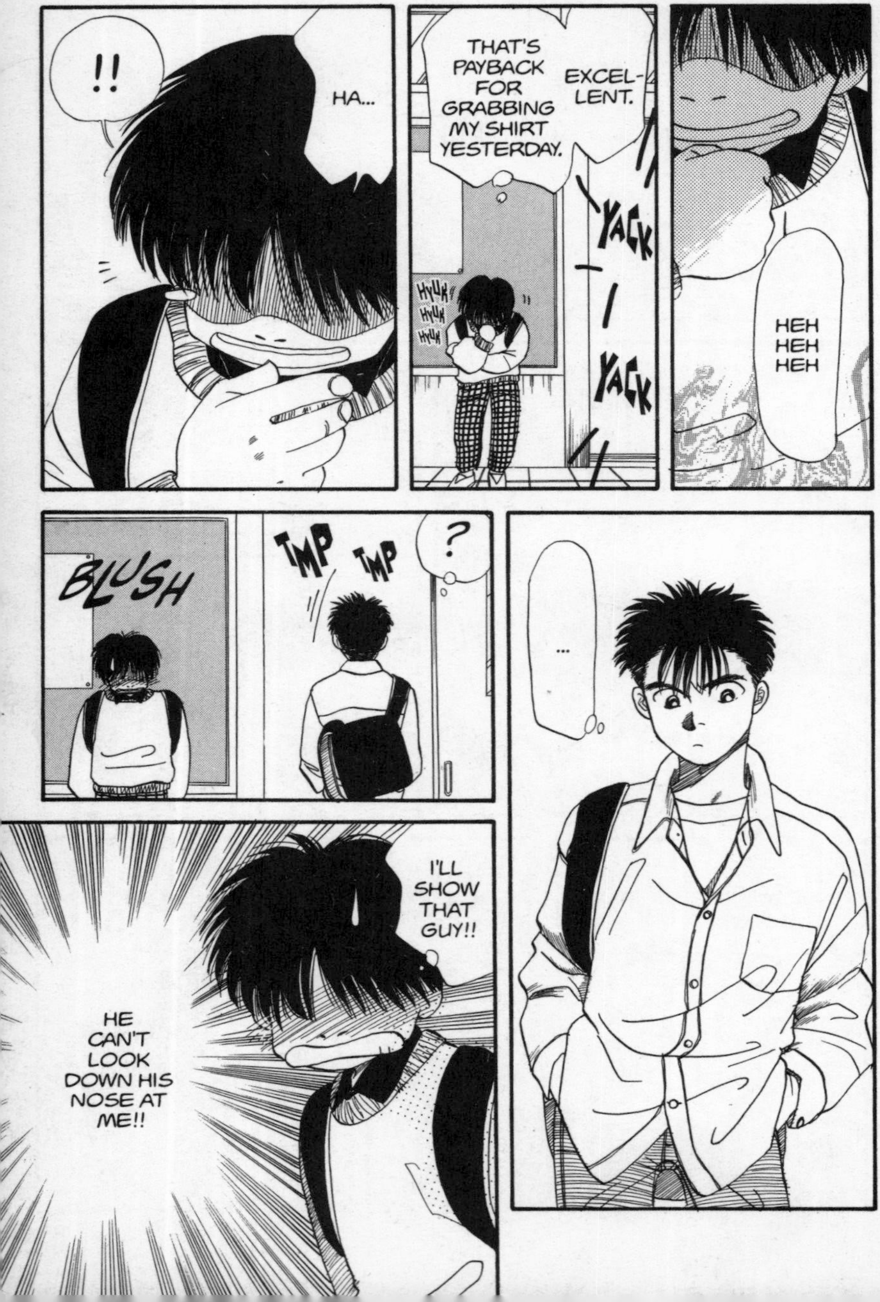
HEH HEH HEH
EXCEL-LENT.
THAT'S PAYBACK FOR GRABBING MY SHIRT YESTERDAY.
YACK
YACK
HYUK HYUK HYUK
HA...
!!
...
?
TMP TMP
BLUSH
I'LL SHOW THAT GUY!!
HE CAN'T LOOK DOWN HIS NOSE AT ME!!

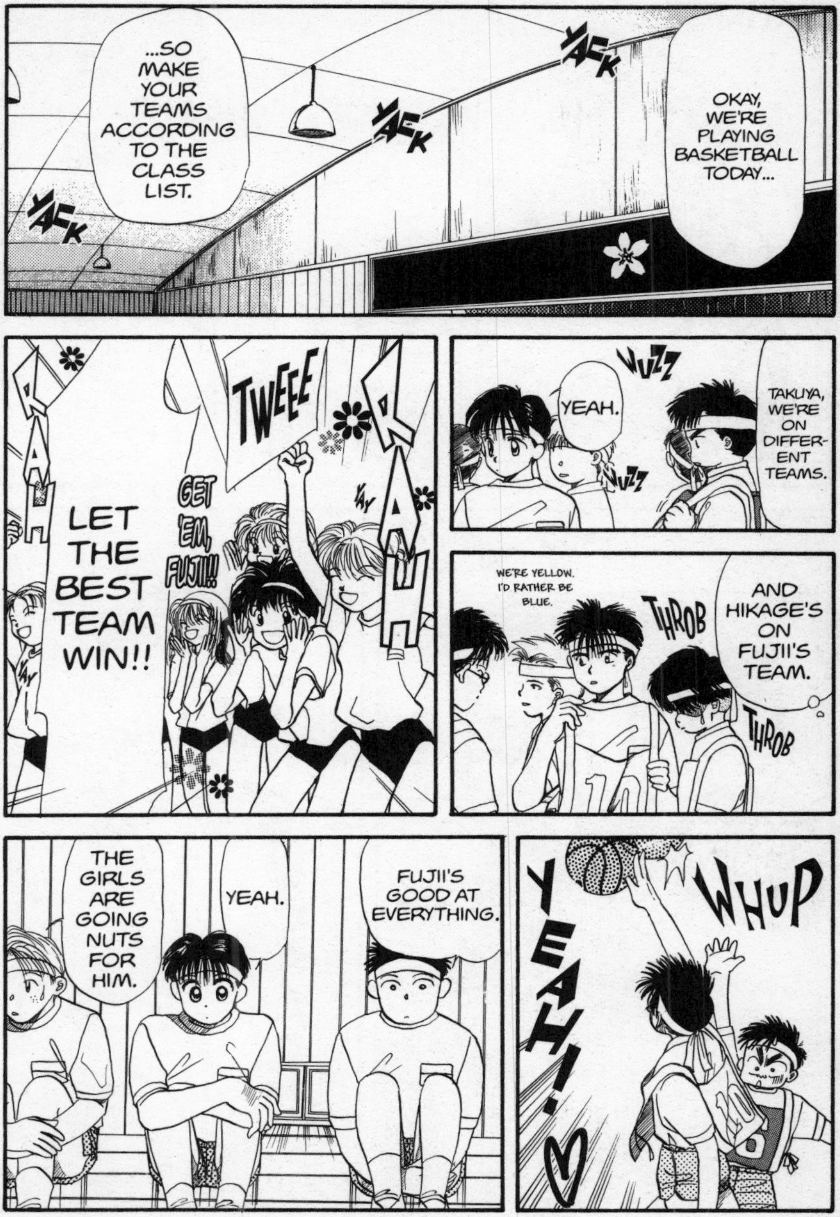
OKAY, WE'RE PLAYING BASKETBALL TODAY...
YACK
YACK
YACK
...SO MAKE YOUR TEAMS ACCORDING TO THE CLASS LIST.
TAKUYA, WE'RE ON DIFFERENT TEAMS.
WUZZ
YEAH.
WUZZ
AND HIKAGE'S ON FUJII'S TEAM.
THROB
THROB
WE'RE YELLOW. I'D RATHER BE BLUE.
RAAH
TWEEEE
YAY
GET 'EM, FUJII!!
RAAH
LET THE BEST TEAM WIN!!
YAY
WHUP
YEAH!!
FUJII'S GOOD AT EVERYTHING.
YEAH.
THE GIRLS ARE GOING NUTS FOR HIM.

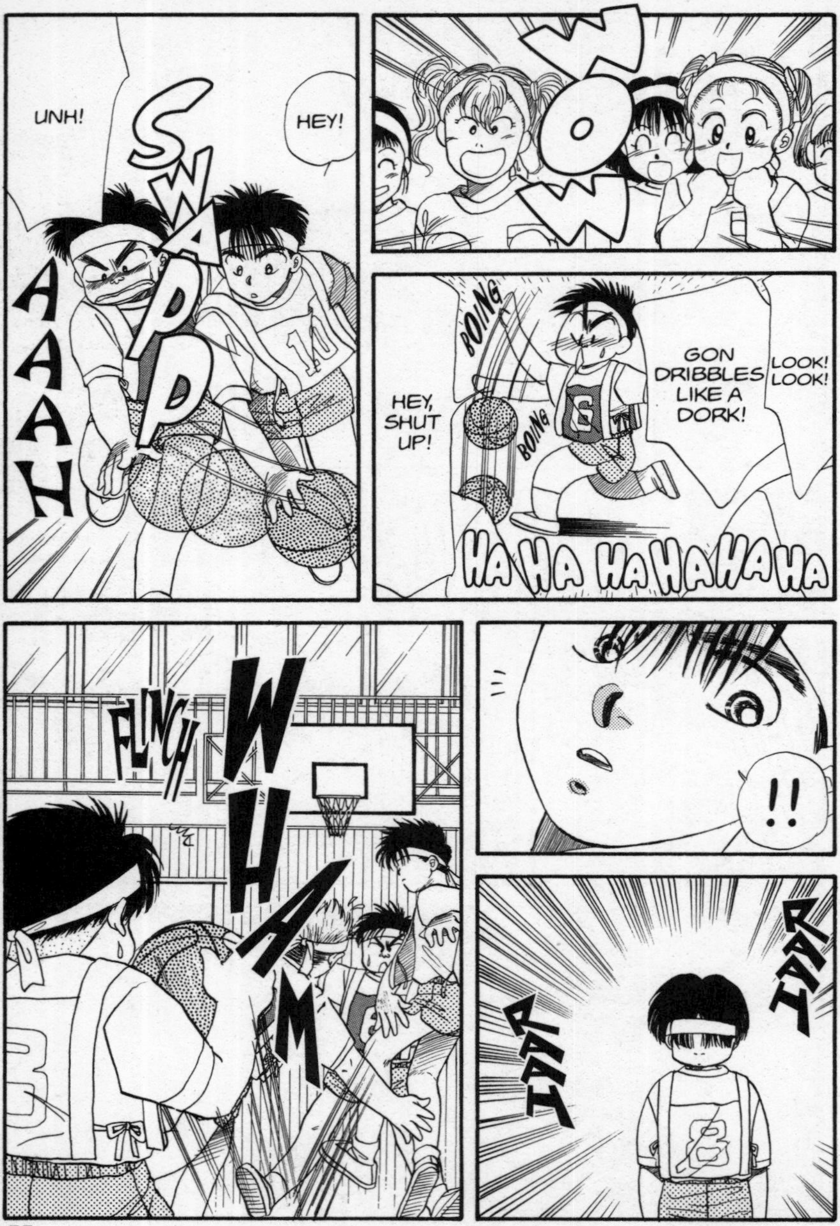
WOW
LOOK! LOOK!
GON DRIBBLES LIKE A DORK!
HEY, SHUT UP!
BOING
BOING
HA HA HA HA HA HA HA
HEY!
UNH!
SWAPP
AAAAH
!!
RAAH
RAAH
WHAM
FLINCH

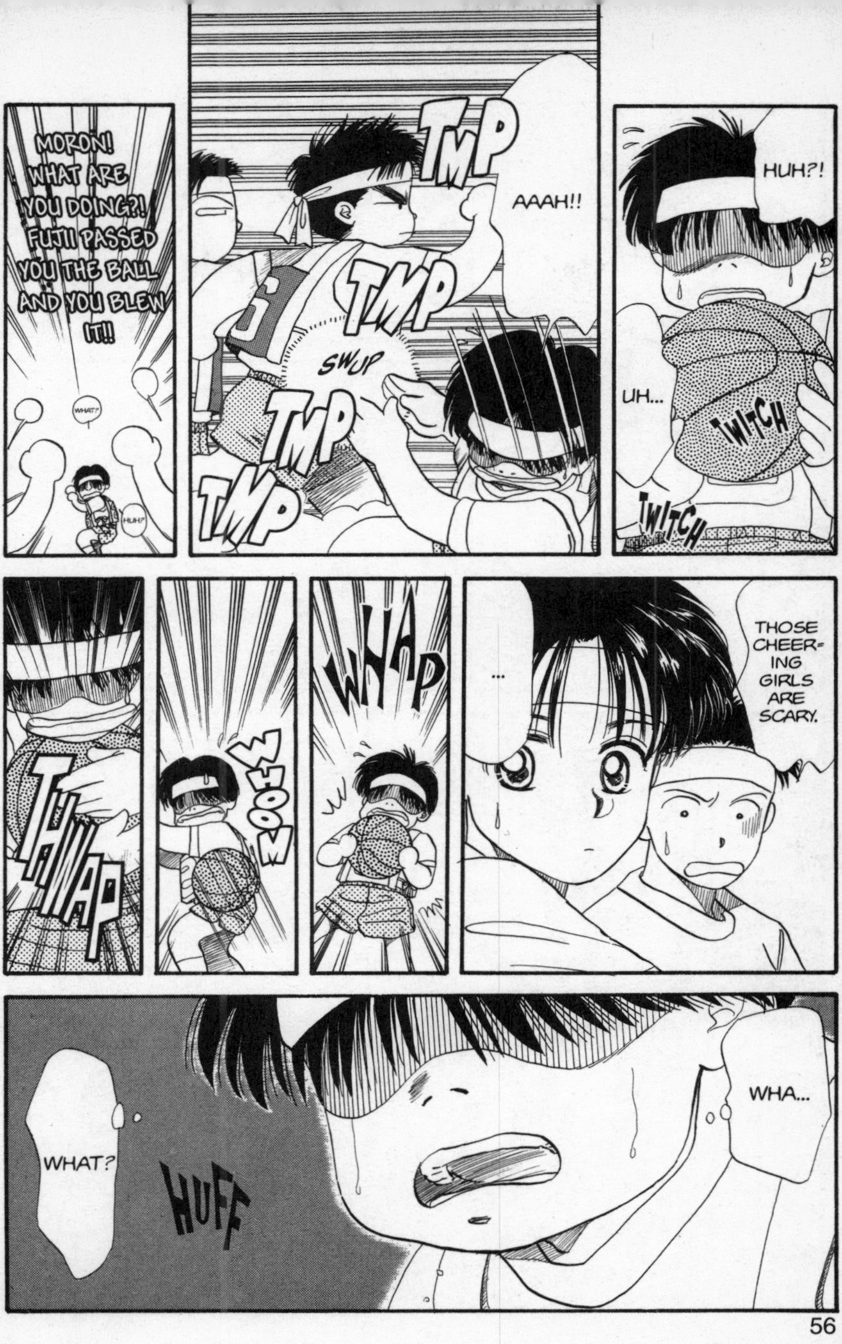
HUH?!
UH...
TWITCH
TWITCH
TMP
AAAH!!
TMP
SWUP
TMP
TMP
MORON! WHAT ARE YOU DOING?! FUJII PASSED YOU THE BALL AND YOU BLEW IT!!
WHAT?
HUH?
THOSE CHEER-ING GIRLS ARE SCARY.
...
WHAP
WHOOM
THWAP
WHA...
HUFF
WHAT?

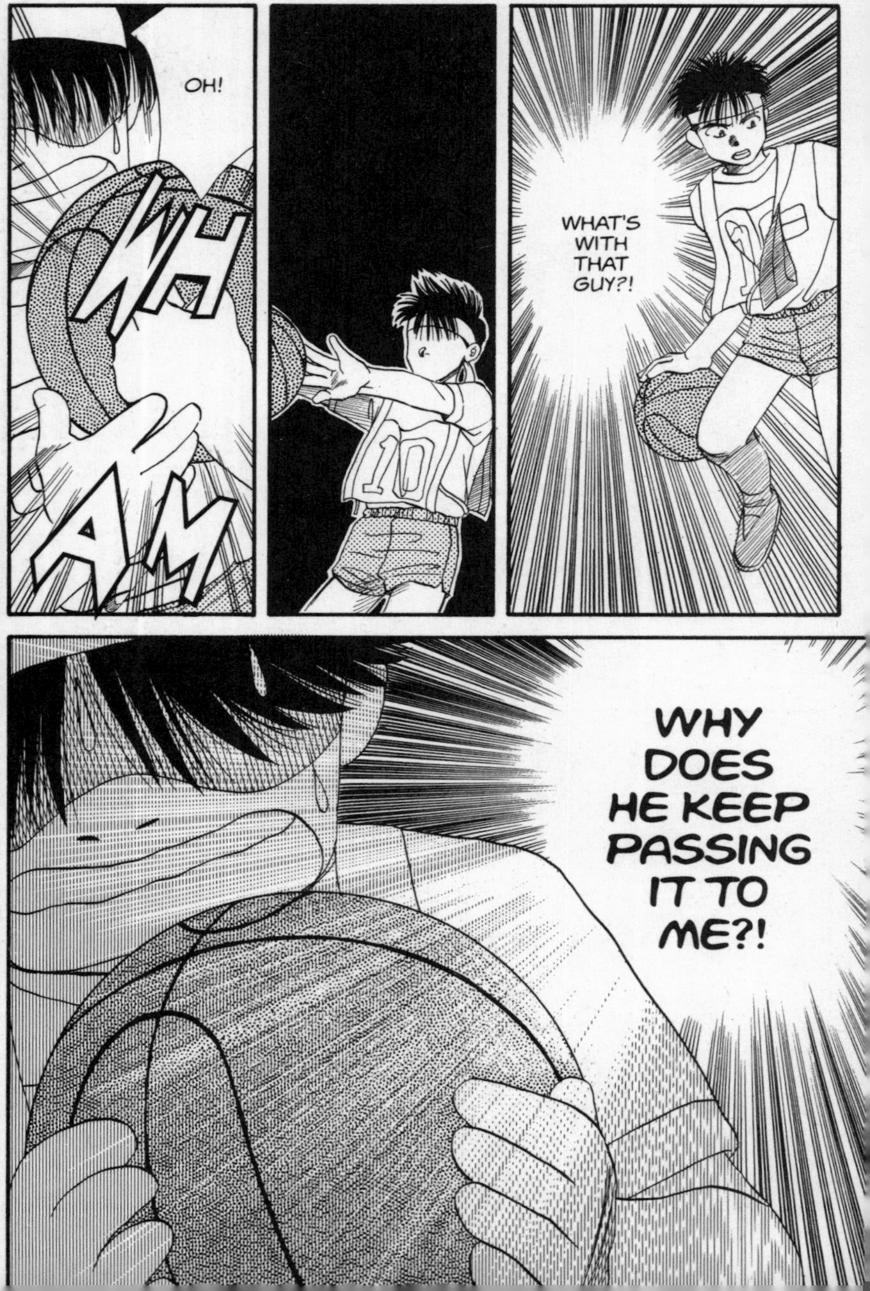
WHAT'S WITH THAT GUY?!
OH!
WHAM
WHY DOES HE KEEP PASSING IT TO ME?!

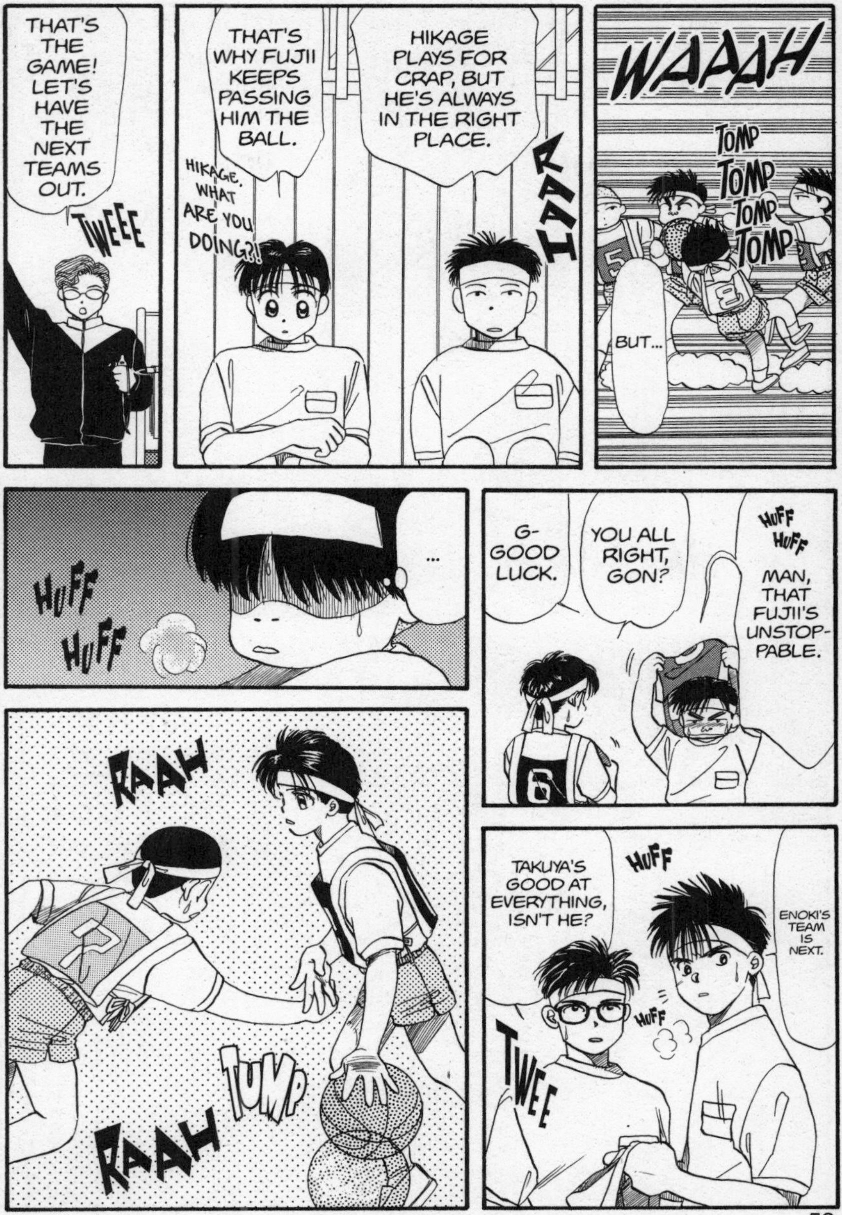
WAAAH
TOMP TOMP TOMP TOMP
BUT...
HIKAGE PLAYS FOR CRAP, BUT HE'S ALWAYS IN THE RIGHT PLACE.
THAT'S WHY FUJII KEEPS PASSING HIM THE BALL.
HIKAGE. WHAT ARE YOU DOING?!
RAAH
THAT'S THE GAME! LET'S HAVE THE NEXT TEAMS OUT.
TWEEE
HUFF HUFF
MAN, THAT FUJII'S UNSTOPPABLE.
YOU ALL RIGHT, GON?
G-GOOD LUCK.
...
HUFF HUFF
RAAH
TUMP
RAAH
ENOKI'S TEAM IS NEXT.
HUFF
TAKUYA'S GOOD AT EVERYTHING, ISN'T HE?
HUFF
TWEE

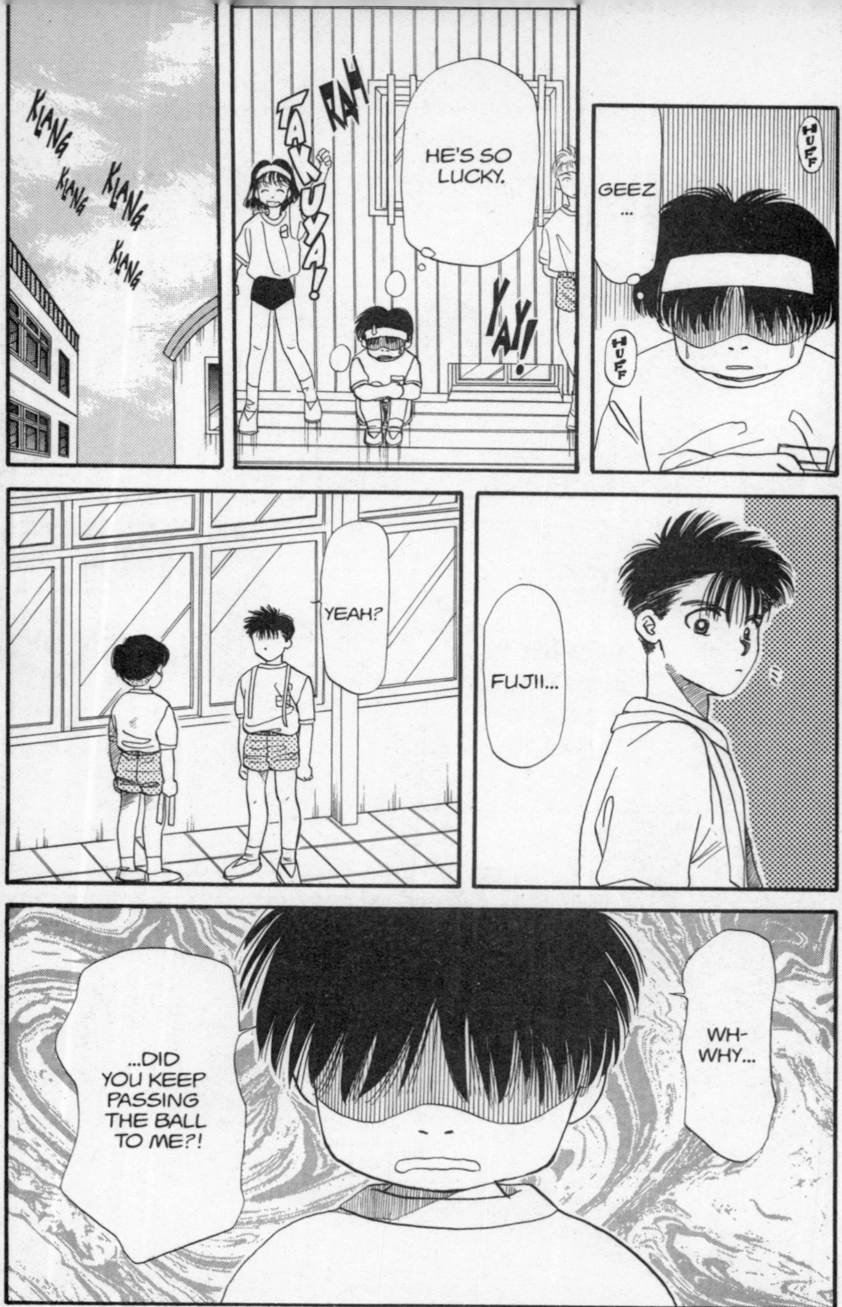
HUFF
GEEZ ...
HUFF
RAH
TAKUYA!
HE'S SO LUCKY.
YAY!
KLANG KLANG KLANG KLANG KLANG
FUJII...
YEAH?
WH- WHY...
...DID YOU KEEP PASSING THE BALL TO ME?!

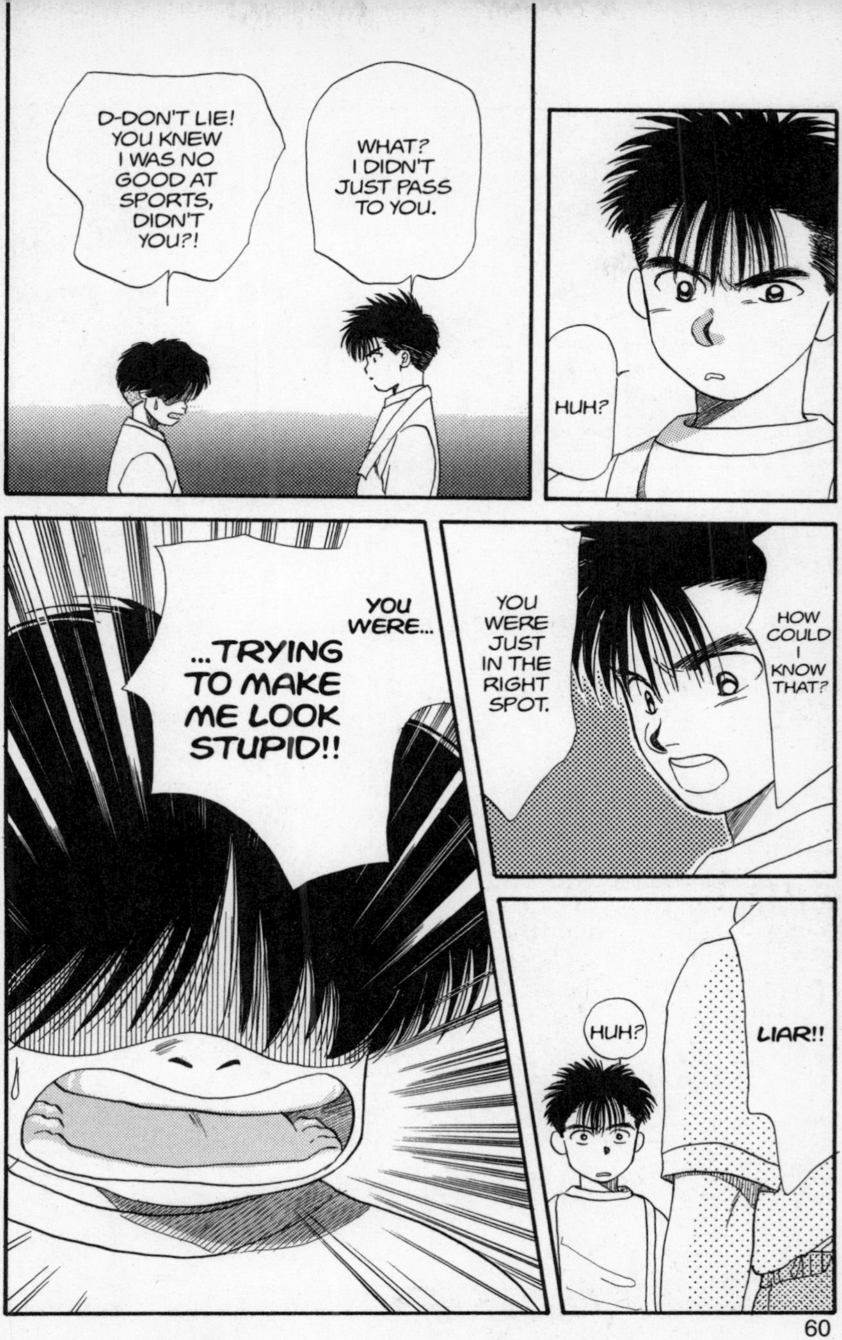
HUH?
WHAT? I DIDN'T JUST PASS TO YOU.
D-DON'T LIE! YOU KNEW I WAS NO GOOD AT SPORTS, DIDN'T YOU?!
HOW COULD I KNOW THAT?
YOU WERE JUST IN THE RIGHT SPOT.
LIAR!!
HUH?
YOU WERE...
...TRYING TO MAKE ME LOOK STUPID!!

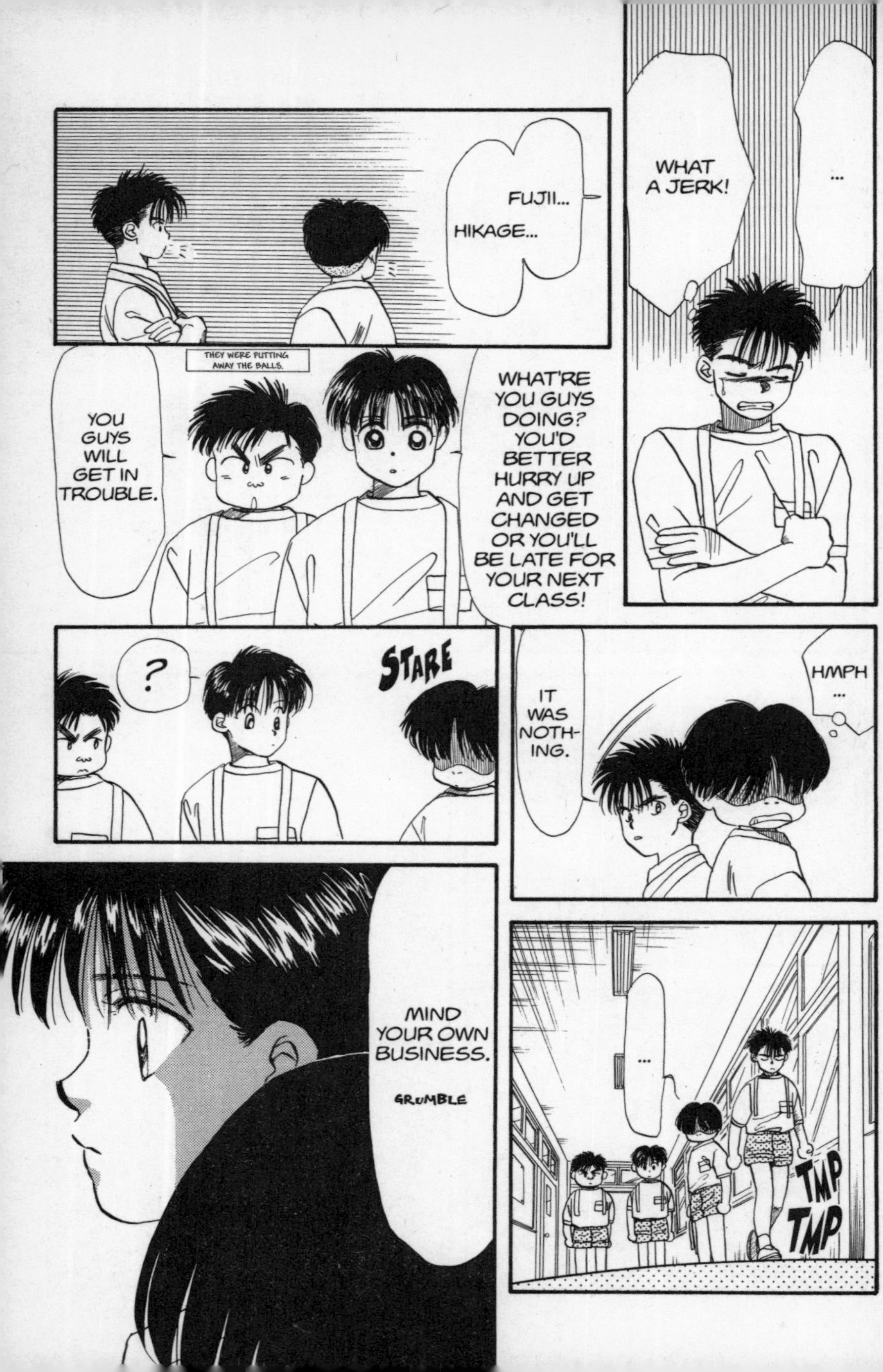
...
WHAT A JERK!
FUJII...
HIKAGE...
WHAT'RE YOU GUYS DOING? YOU'D BETTER HURRY UP AND GET CHANGED OR YOU'LL BE LATE FOR YOUR NEXT CLASS!
THEY WERE PUTTING AWAY THE BALLS.
YOU GUYS WILL GET IN TROUBLE.
HMPH ...
IT WAS NOTHING.
STARE
?
...
TMP TMP
MIND YOUR OWN BUSINESS.
GRUMBLE

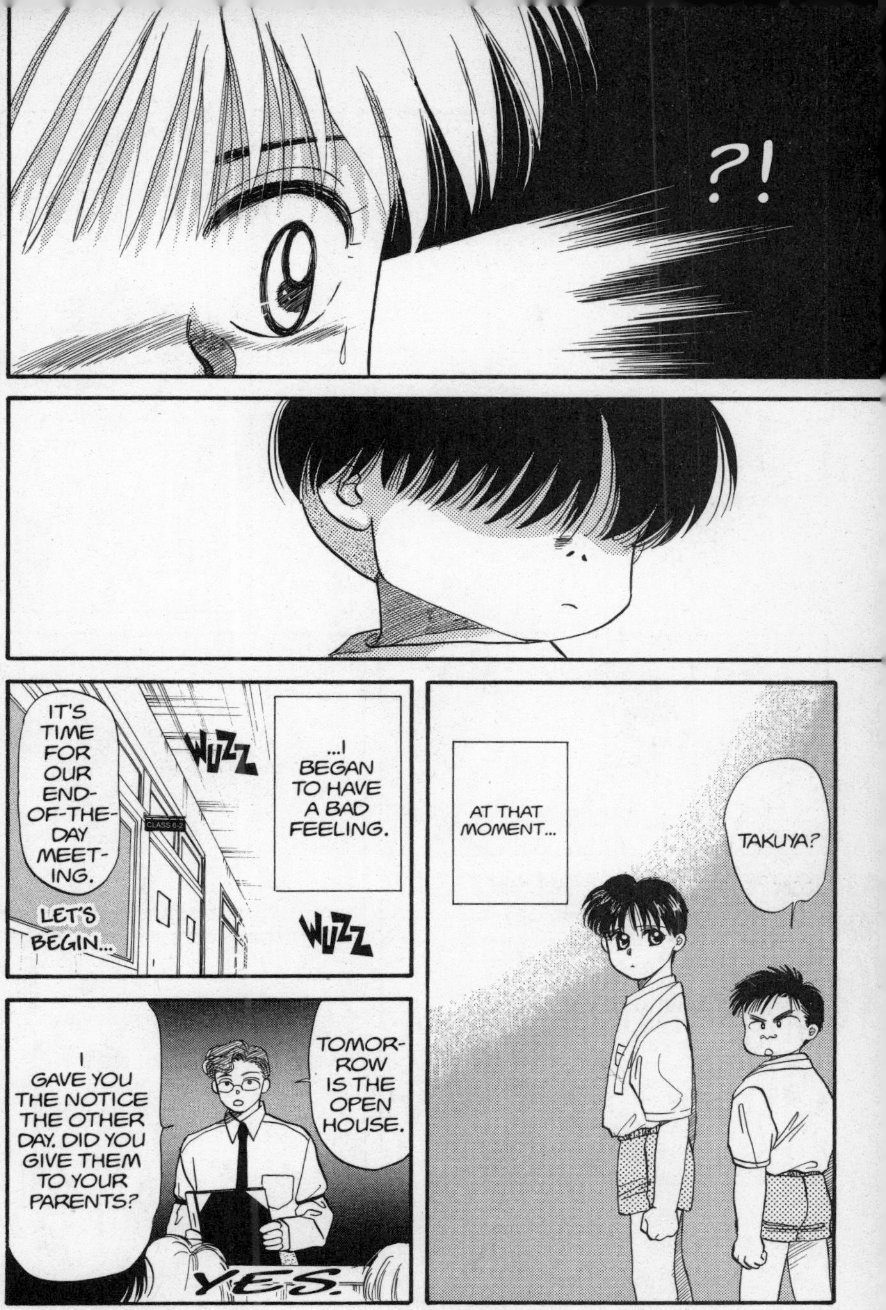
?!
AT THAT MOMENT...
TAKUYA?
...I BEGAN TO HAVE A BAD FEELING.
WUZZ
IT'S TIME FOR OUR END-OF-THE-DAY MEETING.
LET'S BEGIN...
WUZZ
CLASS 6-2
TOMORROW IS THE OPEN HOUSE.
I GAVE YOU THE NOTICE THE OTHER DAY. DID YOU GIVE THEM TO YOUR PARENTS?
YES.

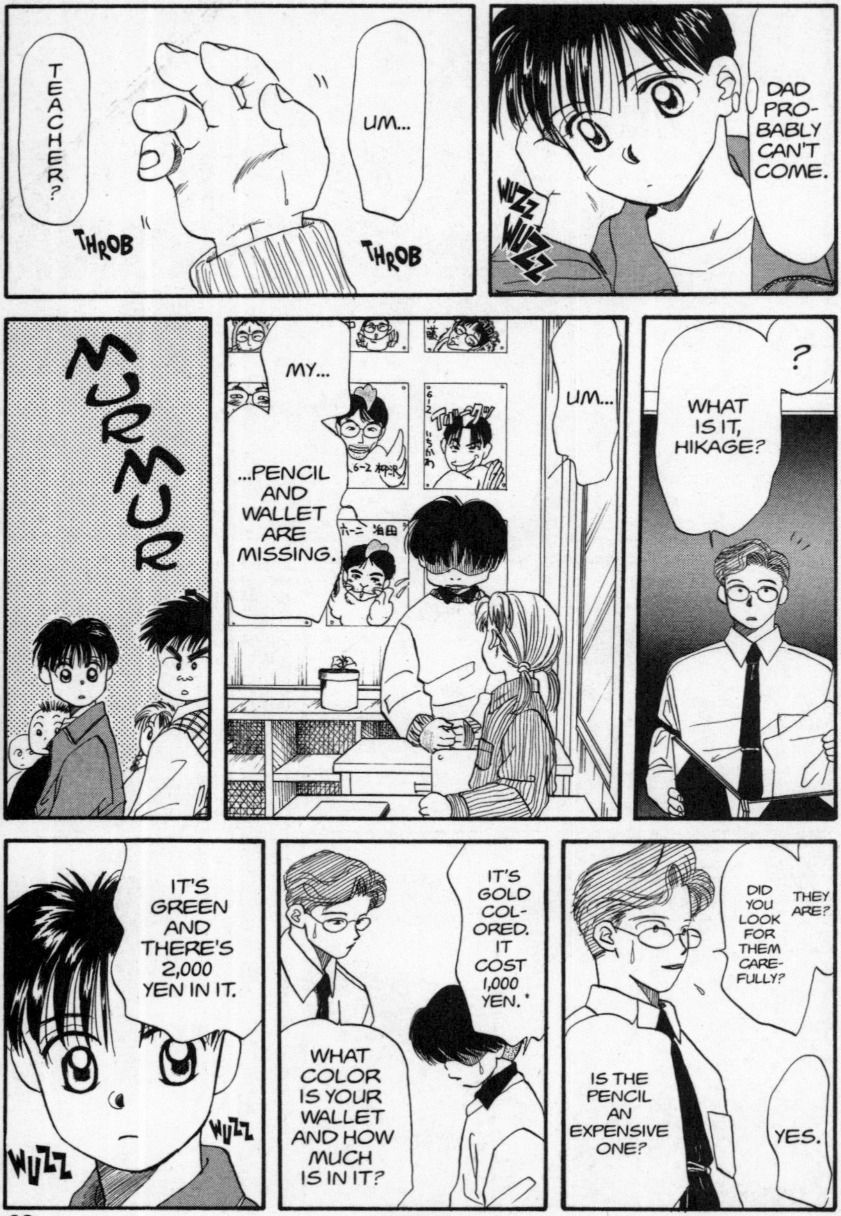
DAD PRO-BABLY CAN'T COME.
WUZZ WUZZ
UM...
TEACHER?
THROB
THROB
?
WHAT IS IT, HIKAGE?
UM...
MY...
...PENCIL AND WALLET ARE MISSING.
MURMUR
THEY ARE?
DID YOU LOOK FOR THEM CARE-FULLY?
YES.
IS THE PENCIL AN EXPENSIVE ONE?
IT'S GOLD COL-ORED. IT COST 1,000 YEN.*
WHAT COLOR IS YOUR WALLET AND HOW MUCH IS IN IT?
IT'S GREEN AND THERE'S 2,000 YEN IN IT.
WUZZ
WUZZ

*ABOUT $10

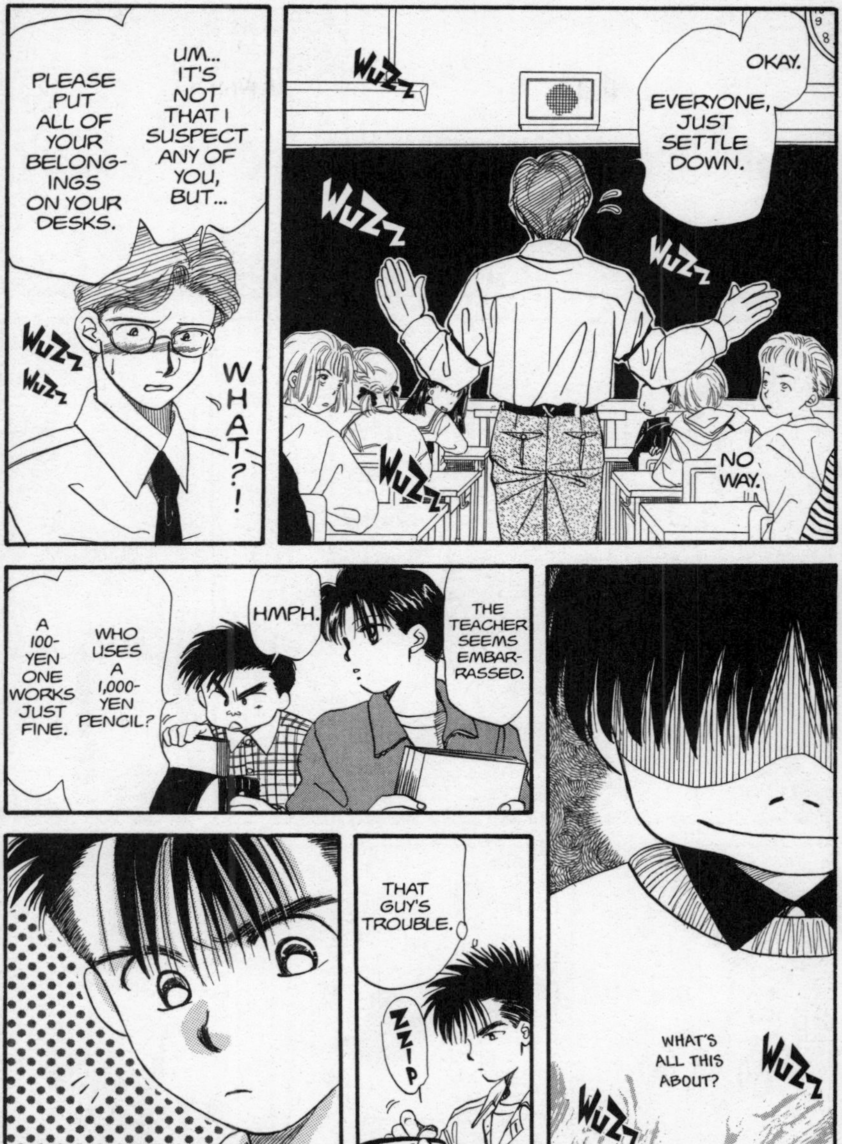
OKAY.
EVERYONE, JUST SETTLE DOWN.
WUZZZ
WUZZ
WUZZ
WUZZ
NO WAY.
UM... IT'S NOT THAT I SUSPECT ANY OF YOU, BUT...
PLEASE PUT ALL OF YOUR BELONG-INGS ON YOUR DESKS.
WUZZZ
WUZZ
WHAT?!
WHAT'S ALL THIS ABOUT?
WUZZ
WUZZ
THE TEACHER SEEMS EMBAR-RASSED.
HMPH.
WHO USES A 1,000-YEN PENCIL?
A 100-YEN ONE WORKS JUST FINE.
THAT GUY'S TROUBLE.
ZZIP

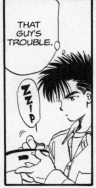

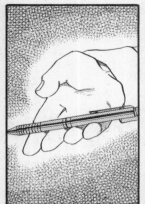

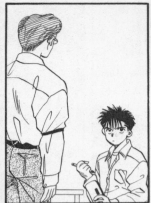

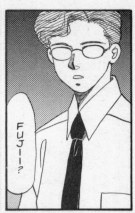

FUJII?

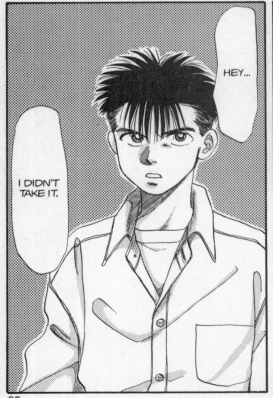

HEY...

I DIDN'T TAKE IT.

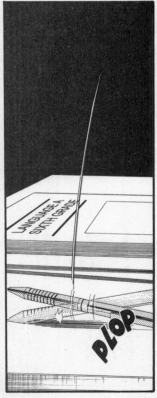

LANGUAGE A SIXTH GRADE

PLOP

NO WAY! FUJII HAD THE PENCIL?!
IT'S GOTTA BE A MIS-TAKE!
WHAT? THAT CAN'T BE!
BA-BUMP
BA-BUMP
SWUFF
BA-BUMP
BA-BUMP
BA-BUMP
WHAT?!

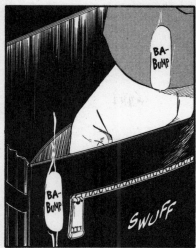

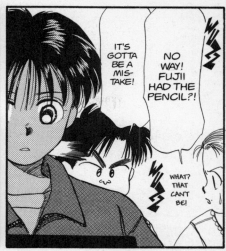

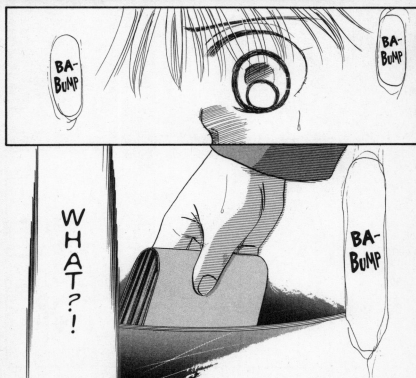

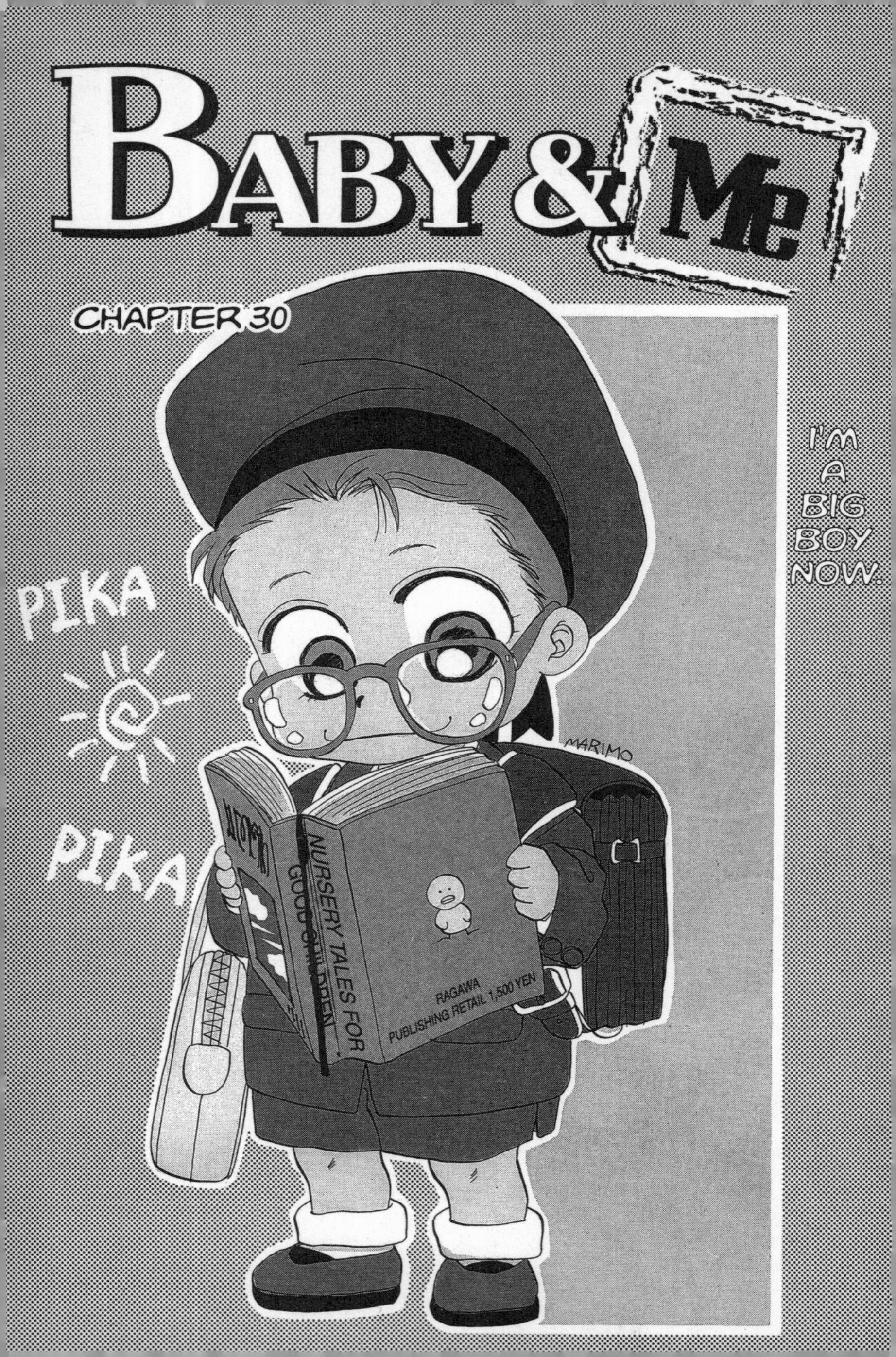

BABY & ME
CHAPTER 30
I'M A BIG BOY NOW.
PIKA PIKA
MARIMO
NURSERY TALES FOR GOOD CHILDREN
RAGAWA PUBLISHING RETAIL 1,500 YEN

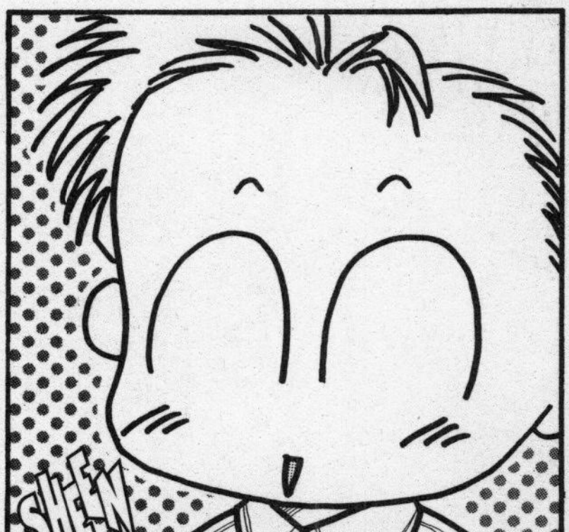
SHEEN

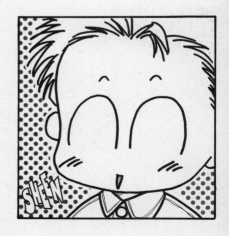

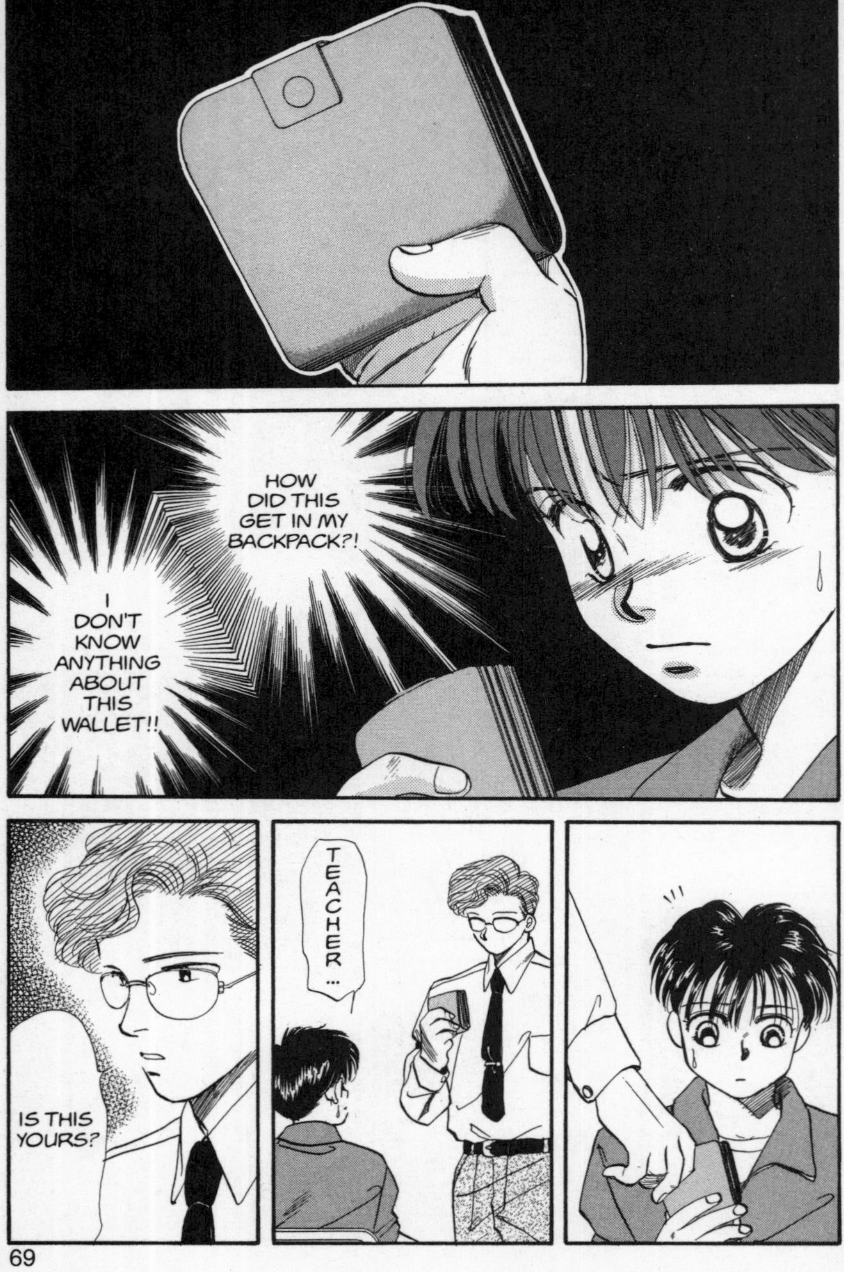
HOW DID THIS GET IN MY BACKPACK?!
I DON'T KNOW ANYTHING ABOUT THIS WALLET!!
TEACHER...
IS THIS YOURS?

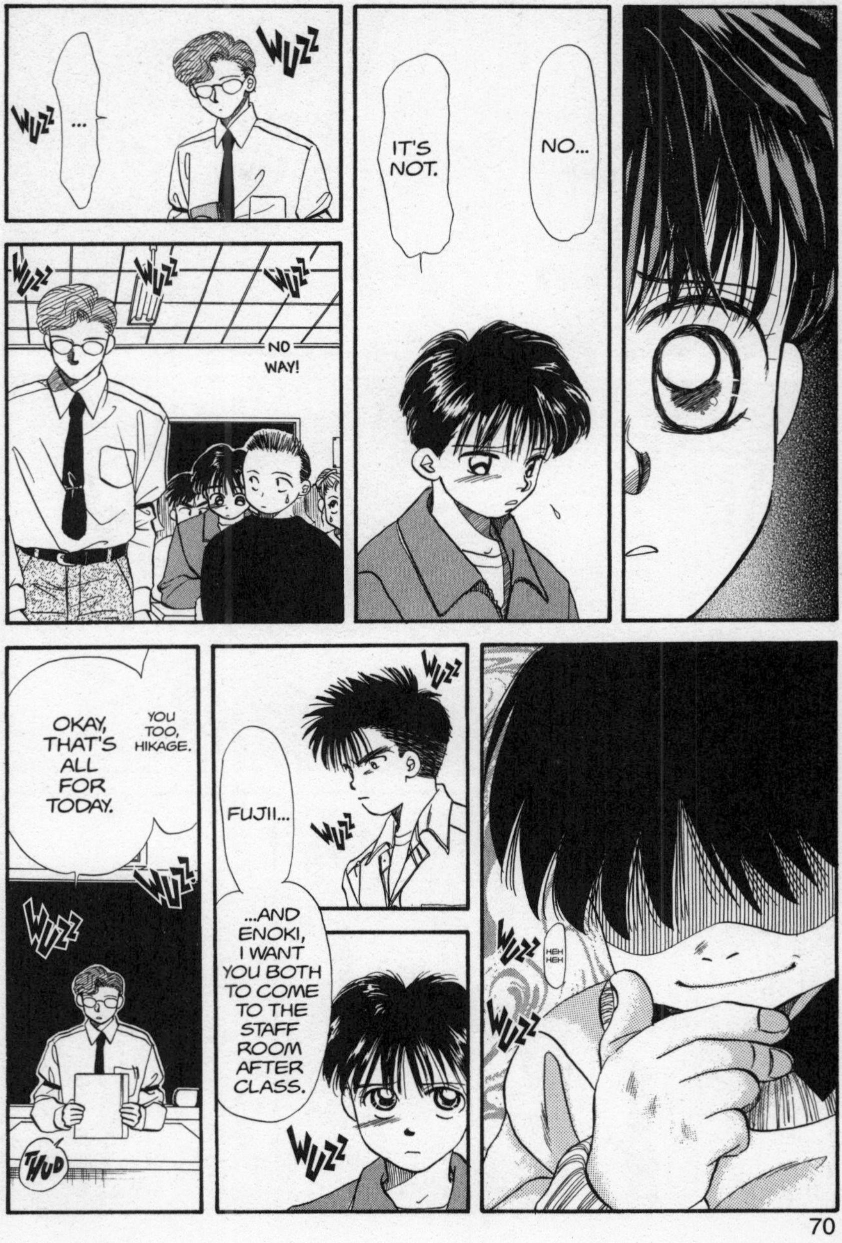
NO...
IT'S NOT.
WUZZ
...
WUZZ
WUZZ
WUZZ
WUZZ
NO WAY!
HEH HEH
WUZZ
WUZZ
WUZZ
FUJII...
WUZZ
...AND ENOKI, I WANT YOU BOTH TO COME TO THE STAFF ROOM AFTER CLASS.
WUZZ
OKAY, THAT'S ALL FOR TODAY.
YOU TOO, HIKAGE.
WUZZ
WUZZ
THUD

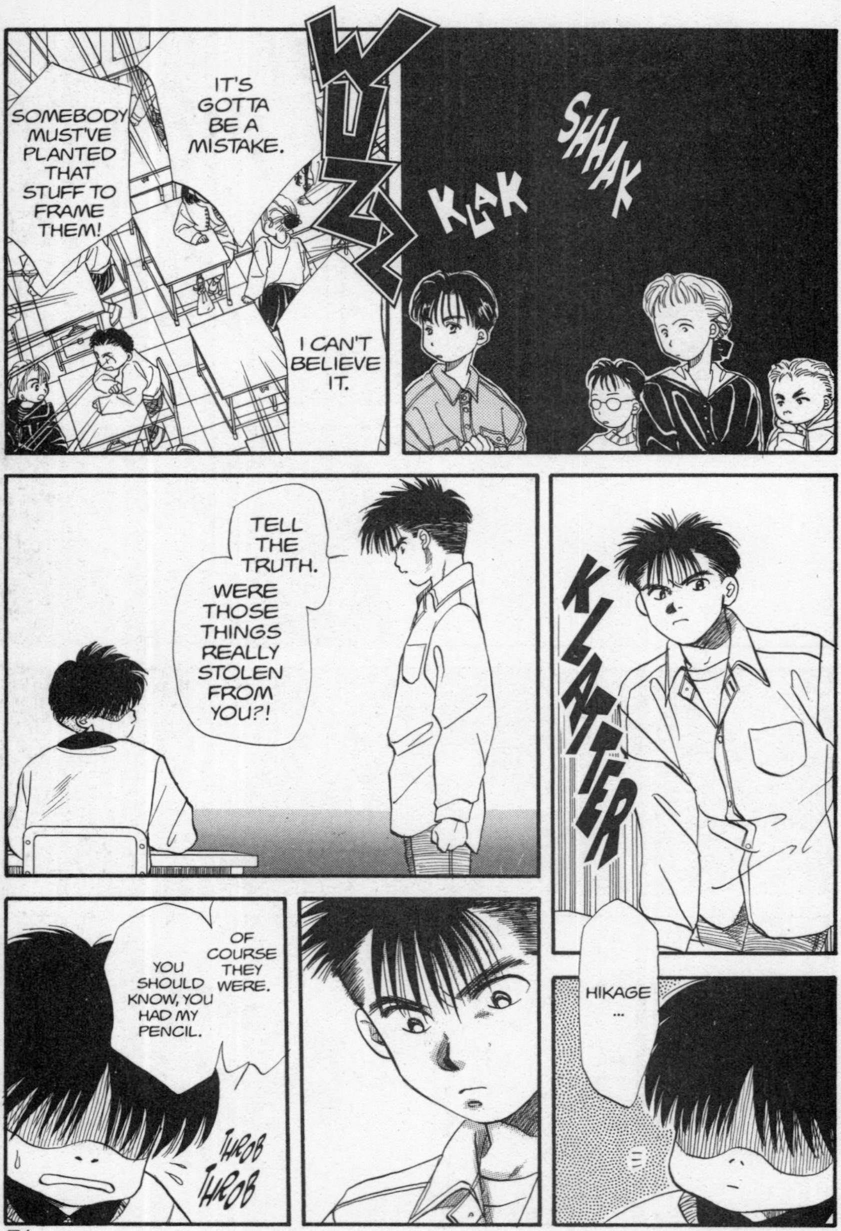
SHHAK
KLAK
IT'S GOTTA BE A MISTAKE.
SOMEBODY MUST'VE PLANTED THAT STUFF TO FRAME THEM!
I CAN'T BELIEVE IT.
KLATTER
TELL THE TRUTH.
WERE THOSE THINGS REALLY STOLEN FROM YOU?!
HIKAGE ...
OF COURSE THEY WERE.
YOU SHOULD KNOW, YOU HAD MY PENCIL.
THROB THROB

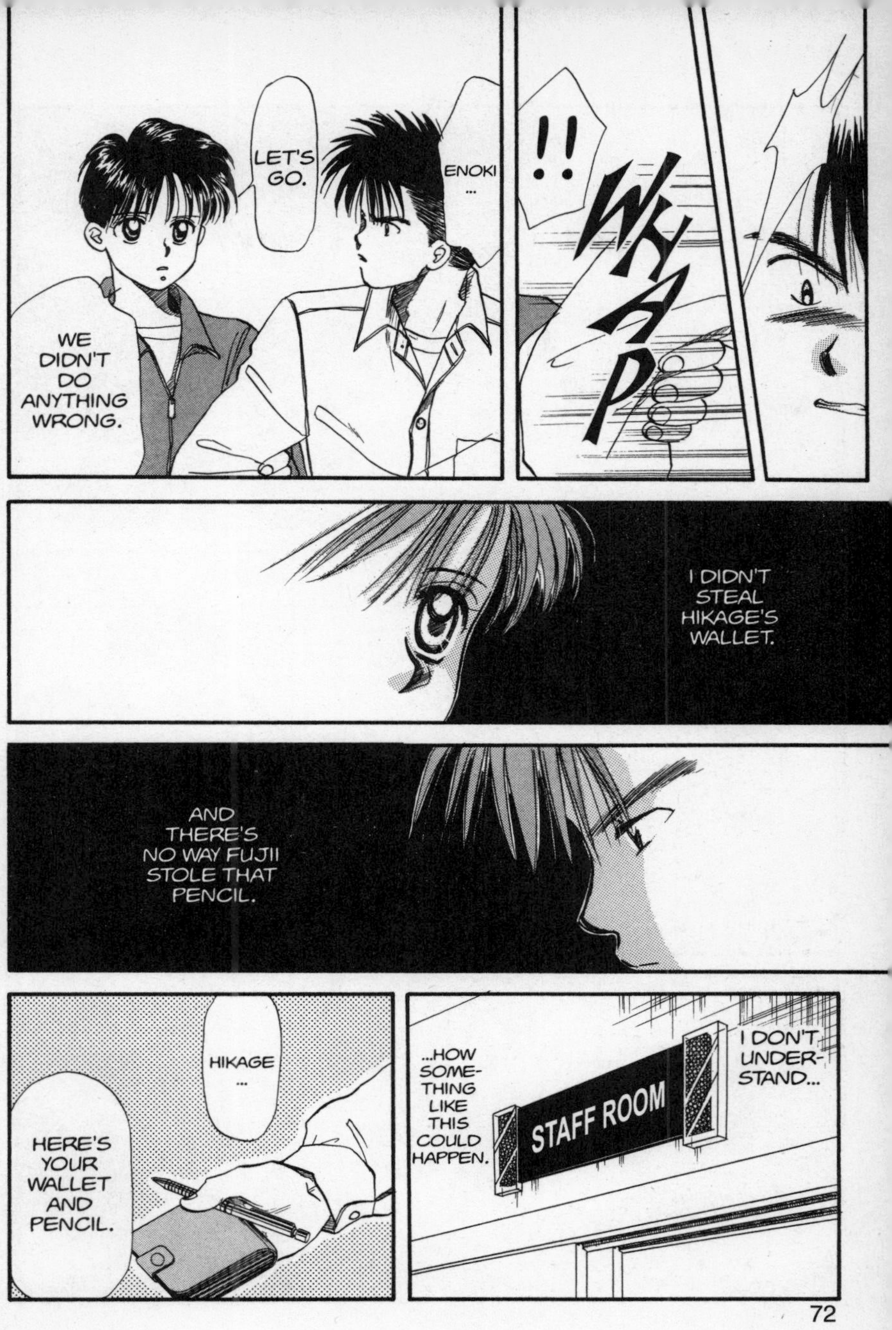
!!
WHAP
ENOKI ...
LET'S GO.
WE DIDN'T DO ANYTHING WRONG.
I DIDN'T STEAL HIKAGE'S WALLET.
AND THERE'S NO WAY FUJII STOLE THAT PENCIL.
I DON'T UNDER-STAND...
...HOW SOME-THING LIKE THIS COULD HAPPEN.
STAFF ROOM
HIKAGE ...
HERE'S YOUR WALLET AND PENCIL.

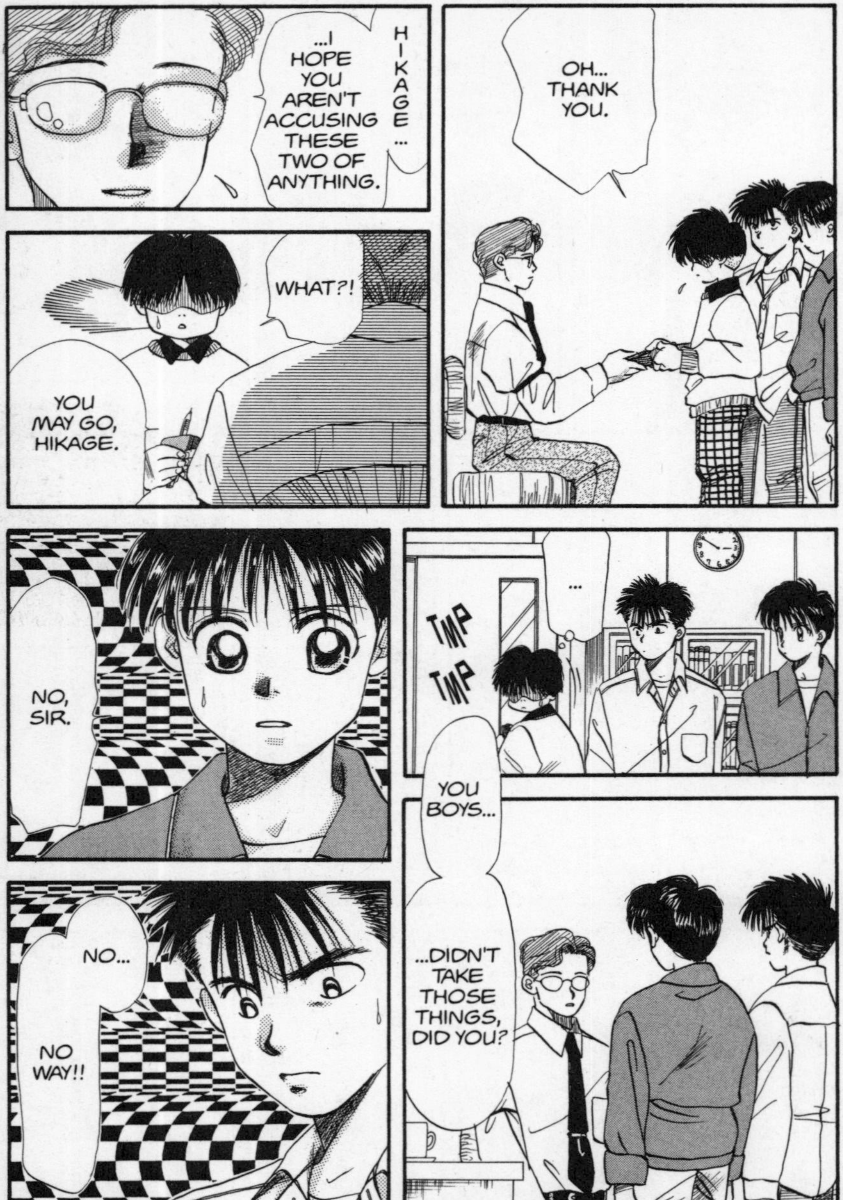
OH... THANK YOU.
HIKAGE...
...I HOPE YOU AREN'T ACCUSING THESE TWO OF ANYTHING.
WHAT?!
YOU MAY GO, HIKAGE.
...
TMP
TMP
YOU BOYS...
...DIDN'T TAKE THOSE THINGS, DID YOU?
NO, SIR.
NO...
NO WAY!!

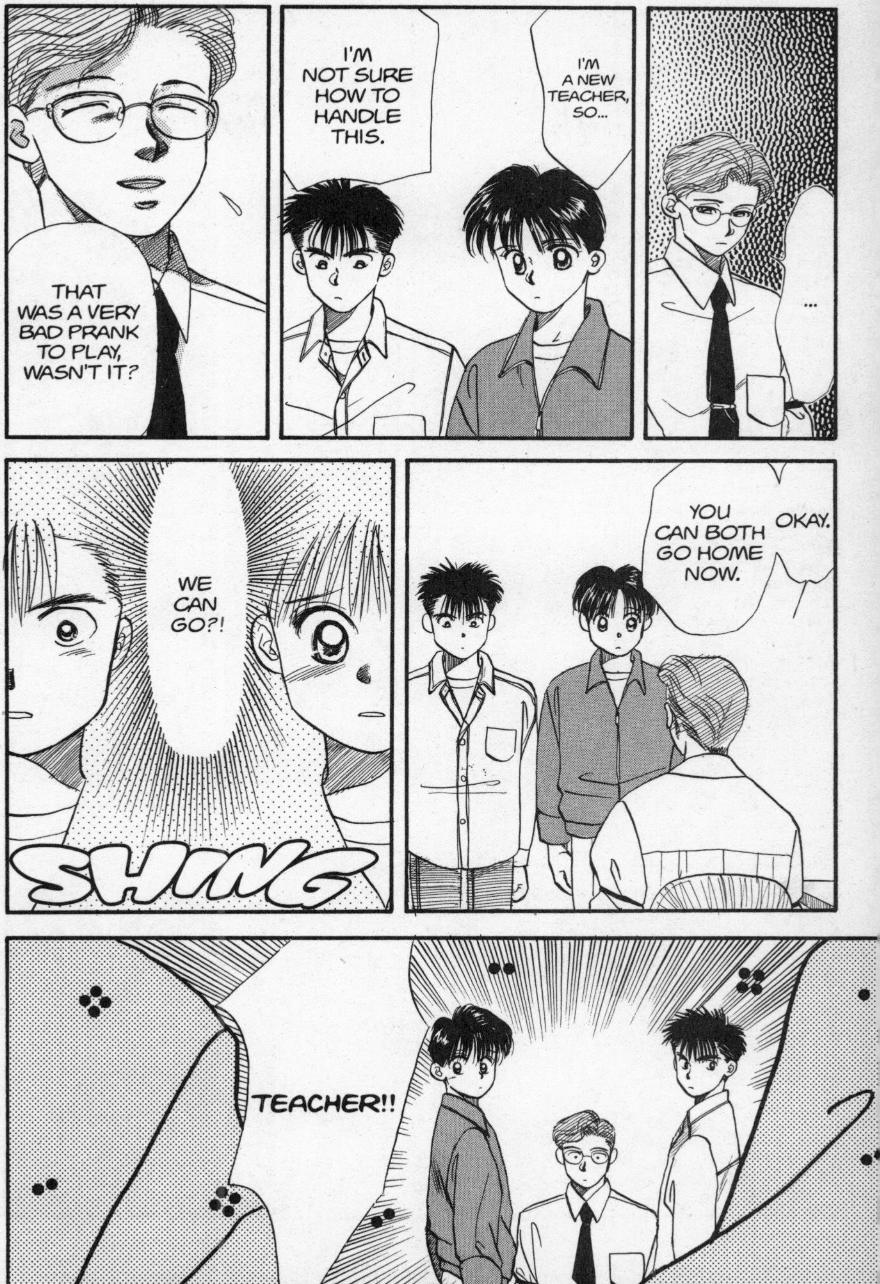
...
I'M A NEW TEACHER, SO...
I'M NOT SURE HOW TO HANDLE THIS.
THAT WAS A VERY BAD PRANK TO PLAY, WASN'T IT?
OKAY.
YOU CAN BOTH GO HOME NOW.
WE CAN GO?!
SHING
TEACHER!!

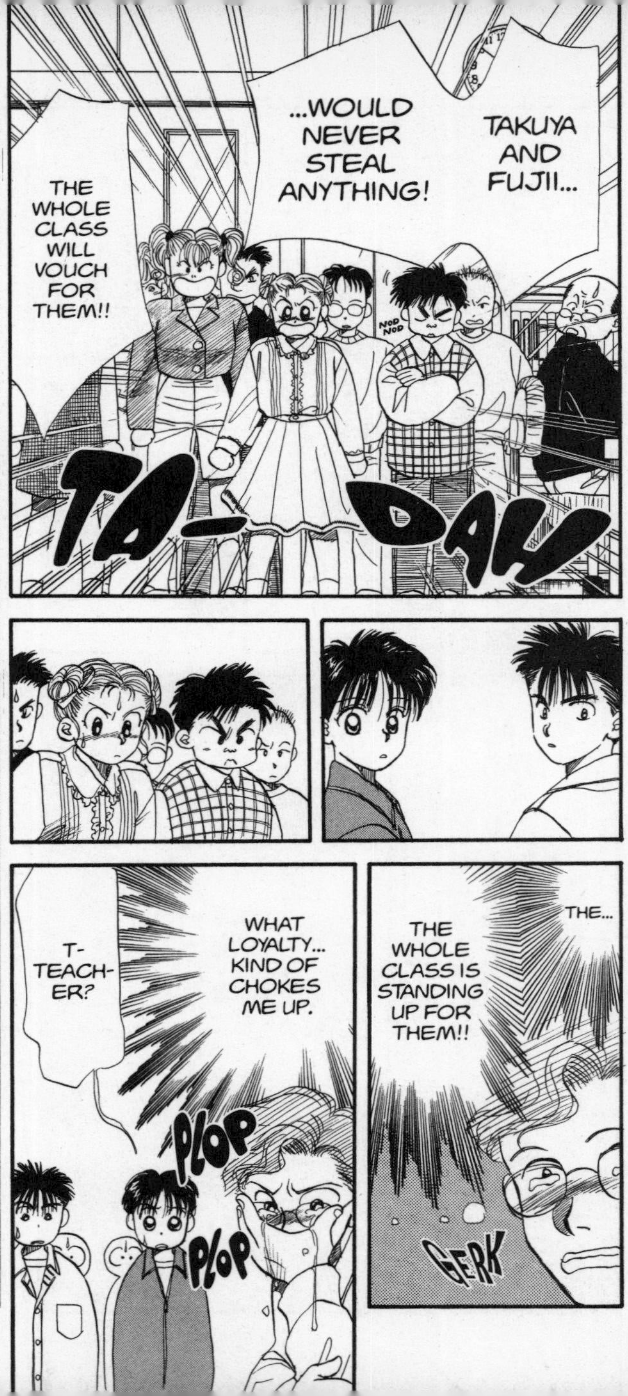
TAKUYA AND FUJII...
...WOULD NEVER STEAL ANYTHING!
THE WHOLE CLASS WILL VOUCH FOR THEM!!
NOD NOD
TA-DAH
THE...
THE WHOLE CLASS IS STANDING UP FOR THEM!!
GERK
WHAT LOYALTY... KIND OF CHOKES ME UP.
T-TEACHER?
PLOP
PLOP

Author's Note, Part 3 Continued from Part 2.

Ragawa: I'm sorry. I didn't mean to put down old folks' homes, I was just trying to suggest that the old man craved the love of his family. I guess I didn't make that clear enough. My apologies.

Q: I'm a nursery school teacher. In chapters 29-30 (included in this volume), the teacher scolds Minoru. No nursery school teacher would scold a child without finding out the reason behind his actions, or lay the blame on one child without getting the facts. I'm very disappointed.
Ragawa: Oh!! Please forgive me. That's probably true in the real world, but this is a manga, and there's the flow of the story to consider, and... Oh, but that's just an excuse! I know that nursery school teachers are very kind.

And finally...
Q: Will Takuya and the others ever grow older?
Ragawa: They will not. I'll make that clear. Since the title is *Baby and Me*, I intend to keep them just the way they are. There's really not much choice--if they got older, it wouldn't be Baby and Me anymore.
End of my excuses.

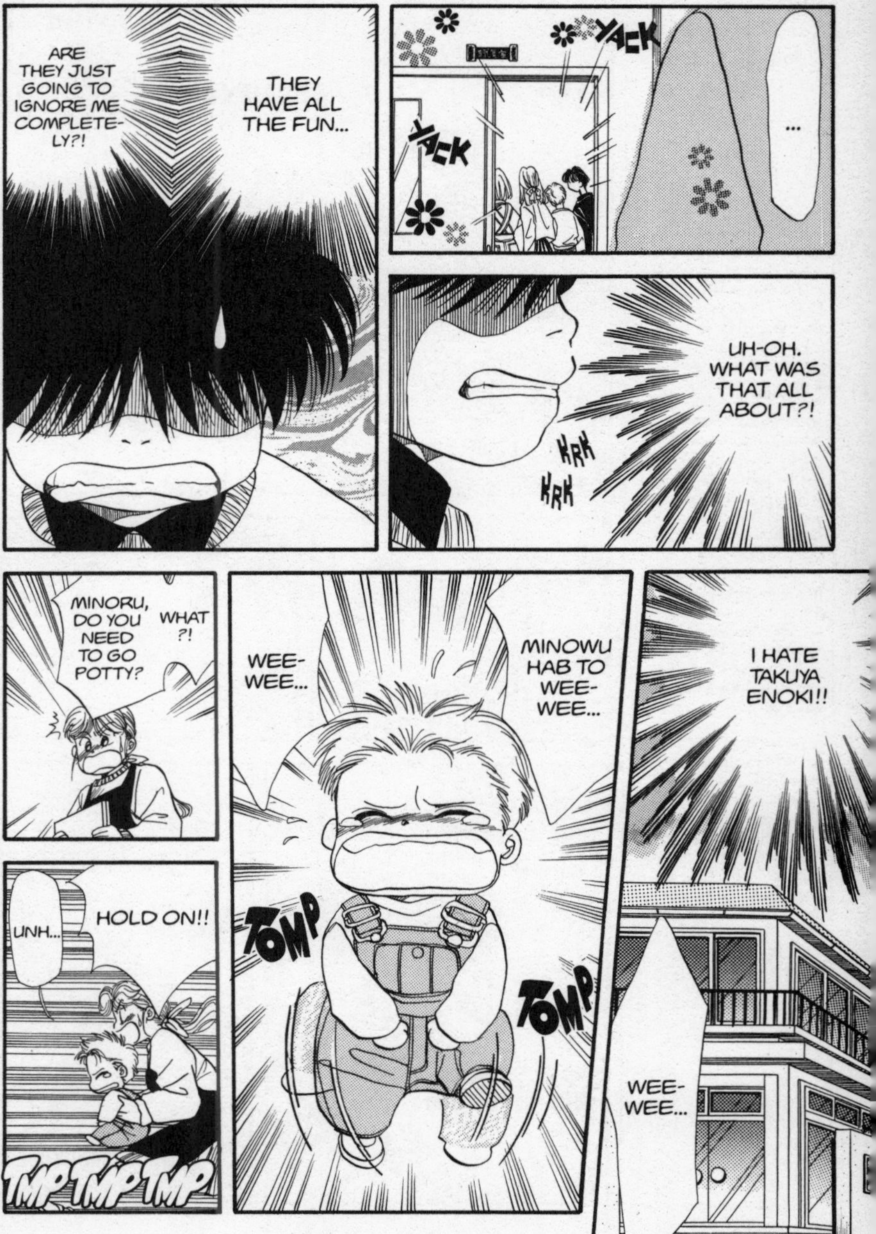
YACK
...
YACK
UH-OH. WHAT WAS THAT ALL ABOUT?!
KRK
KRK
THEY HAVE ALL THE FUN...
ARE THEY JUST GOING TO IGNORE ME COMPLETELY?!
I HATE TAKUYA ENOKI!!
WEE-WEE...
MINOWU HAB TO WEE-WEE...
WEE-WEE...
TOMP
TOMP
WHAT?!
MINORU, DO YOU NEED TO GO POTTY?
HOLD ON!!
UNH...
TMP TMP TMP

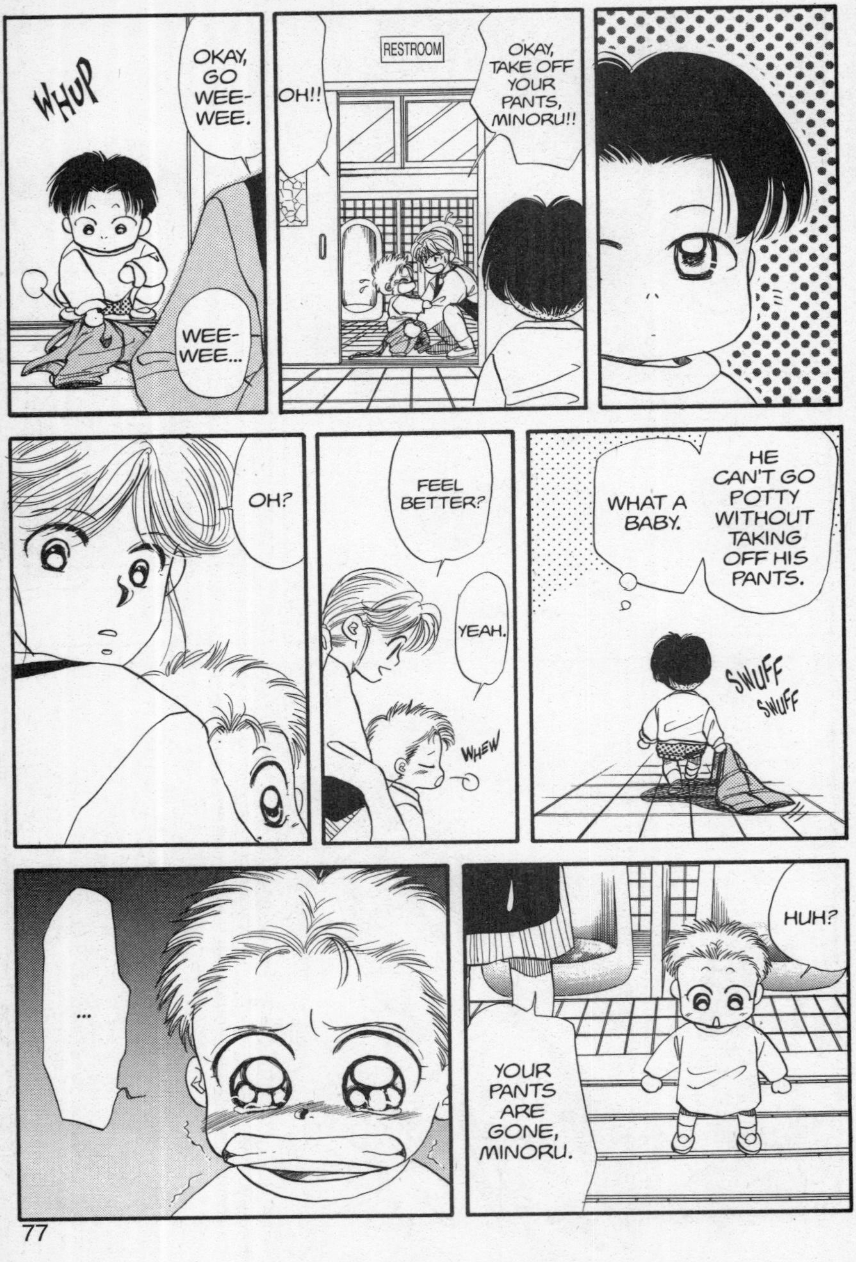
OKAY, TAKE OFF YOUR PANTS, MINORU!!
RESTROOM
OH!!
OKAY, GO WEE-WEE.
WHUP
WEE-WEE...
HE CAN'T GO POTTY WITHOUT TAKING OFF HIS PANTS.
WHAT A BABY.
SWUFF
SWUFF
FEEL BETTER?
YEAH.
WHEW
OH?
HUH?
YOUR PANTS ARE GONE, MINORU.
...

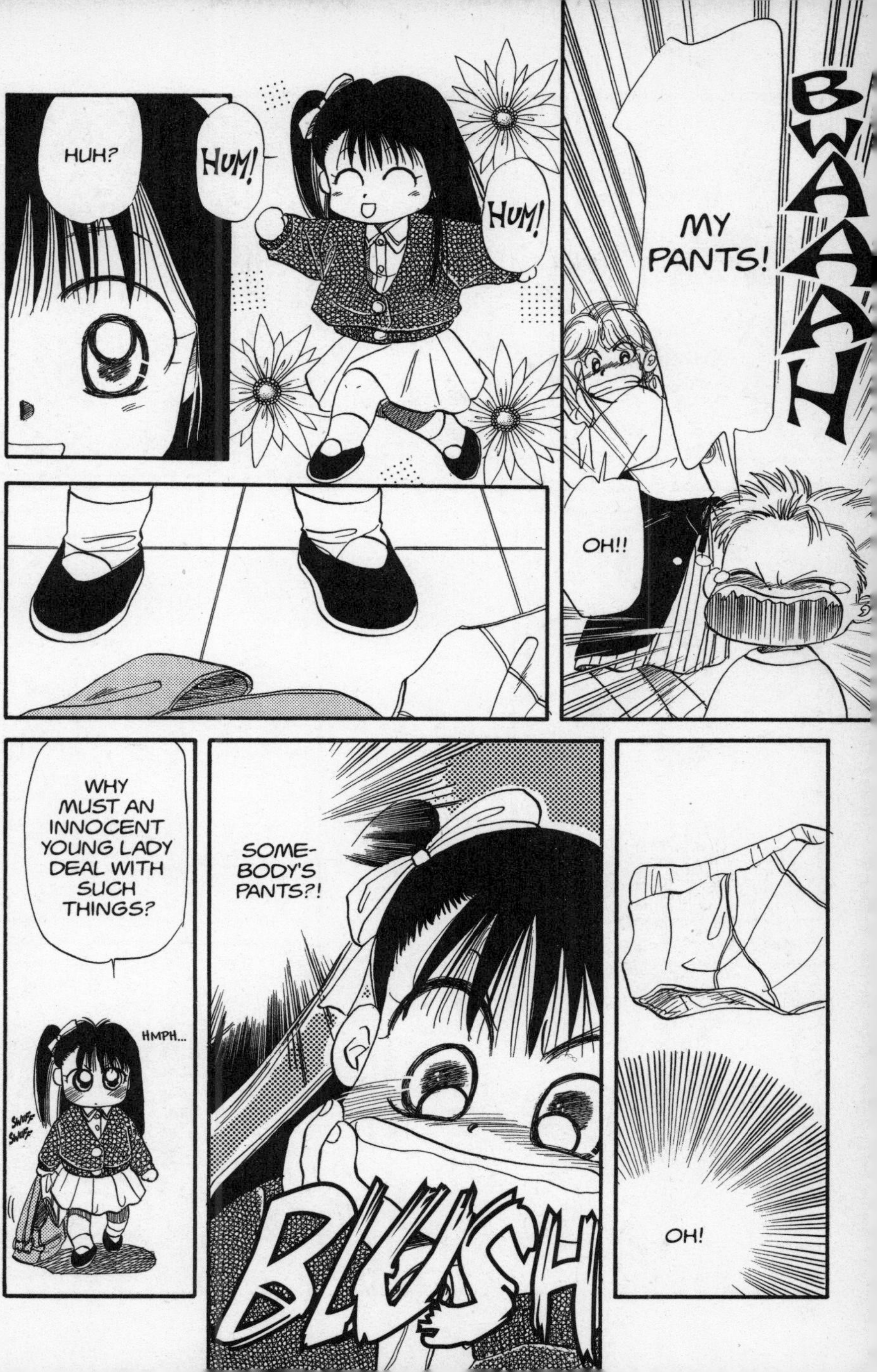
BWAAAH
MY PANTS!
OH!!
HUM!
HUM!
HUH?
OH!
SOME-BODY'S PANTS?!
BLUSH
WHY MUST AN INNOCENT YOUNG LADY DEAL WITH SUCH THINGS?
HMPH...
SNIFF SNIFF

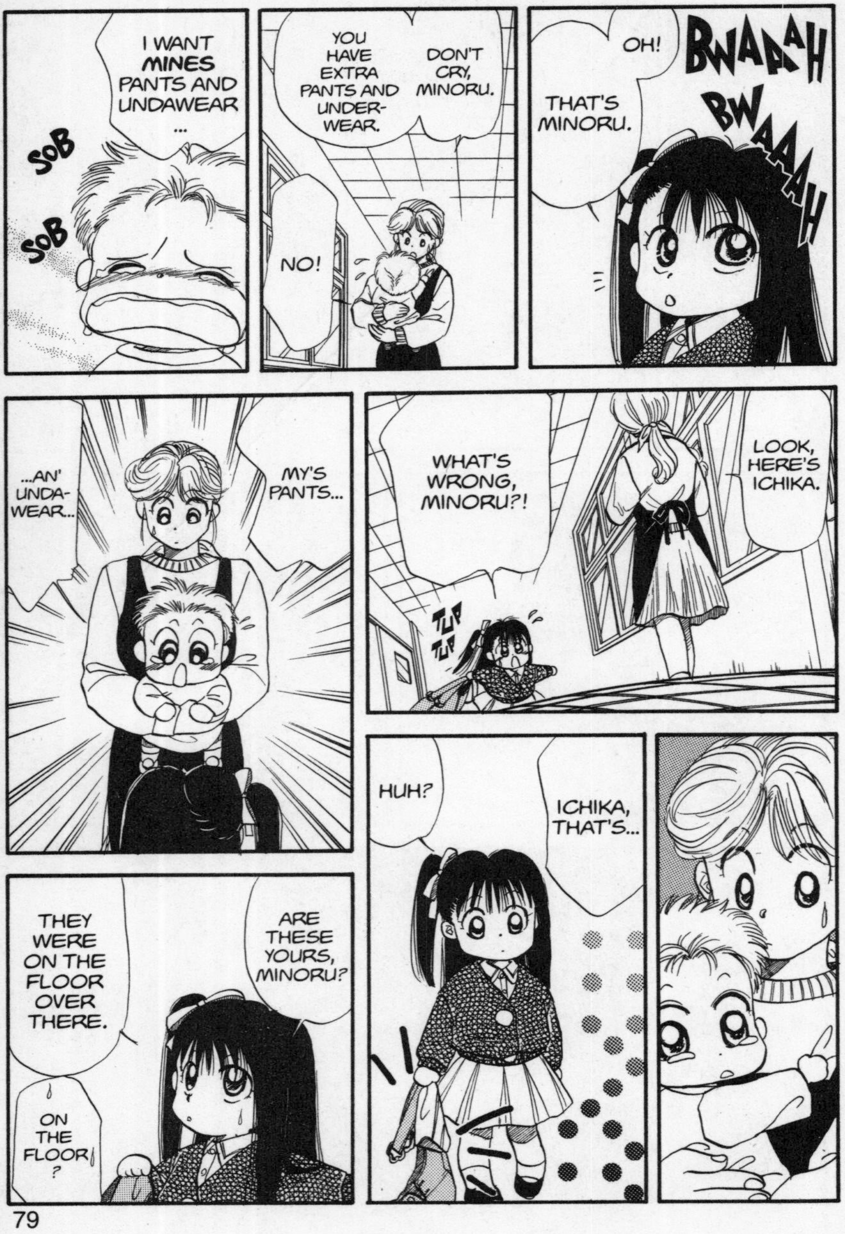
OH!
THAT'S MINORU.
BWAAAH
BWAAAAH
DON'T CRY, MINORU.
YOU HAVE EXTRA PANTS AND UNDER-WEAR.
NO!
I WANT **MINES** PANTS AND UNDAWEAR ...
SOB
SOB
LOOK, HERE'S ICHIKA.
WHAT'S WRONG, MINORU?!
TUP TUP
MY'S PANTS...
...AN' UNDA-WEAR...
ICHIKA, THAT'S...
HUH?
ARE THESE YOURS, MINORU?
THEY WERE ON THE FLOOR OVER THERE.
ON THE FLOOR?

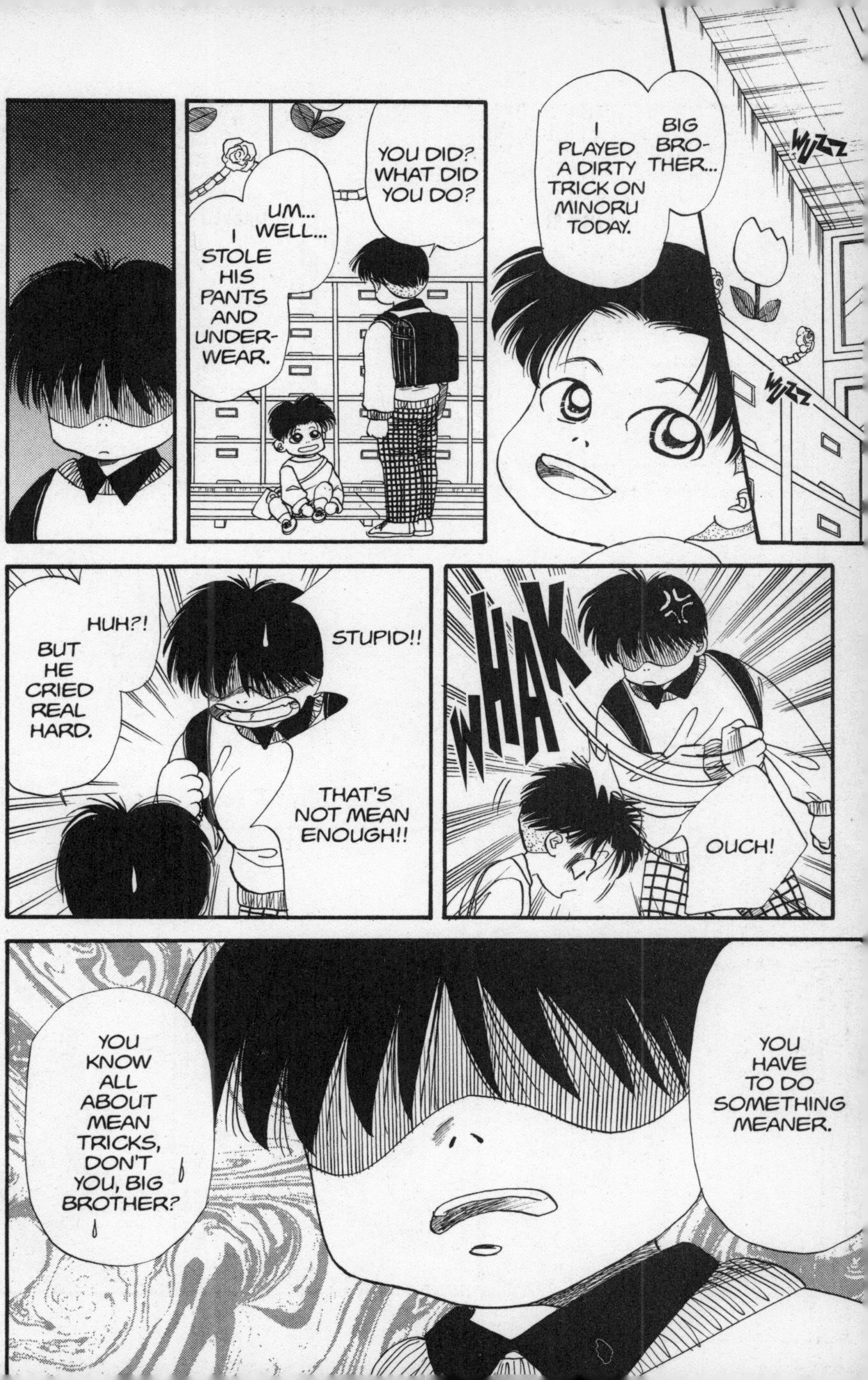
WUZZZ
WUZZZ
BIG BROTHER...
I PLAYED A DIRTY TRICK ON MINORU TODAY.
YOU DID? WHAT DID YOU DO?
UM... WELL...
I STOLE HIS PANTS AND UNDERWEAR.
WHAK
OUCH!
STUPID!!
THAT'S NOT MEAN ENOUGH!!
HUH?!
BUT HE CRIED REAL HARD.
YOU HAVE TO DO SOMETHING MEANER.
YOU KNOW ALL ABOUT MEAN TRICKS, DON'T YOU, BIG BROTHER?

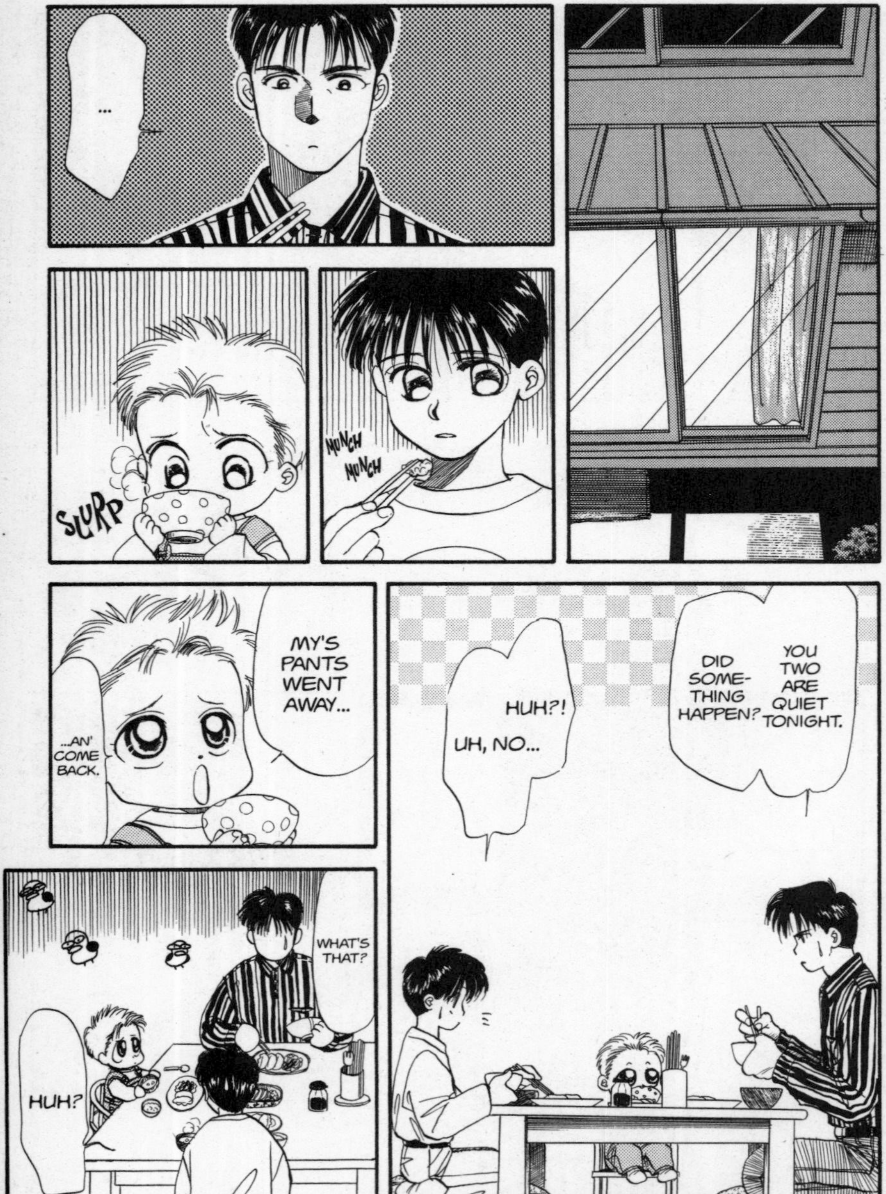
...
MUNCH MUNCH
SLURP
YOU TWO ARE QUIET TONIGHT.
DID SOME-THING HAPPEN?
HUH?!
UH, NO...
MY'S PANTS WENT AWAY...
...AN' COME BACK.
WHAT'S THAT?
HUH?

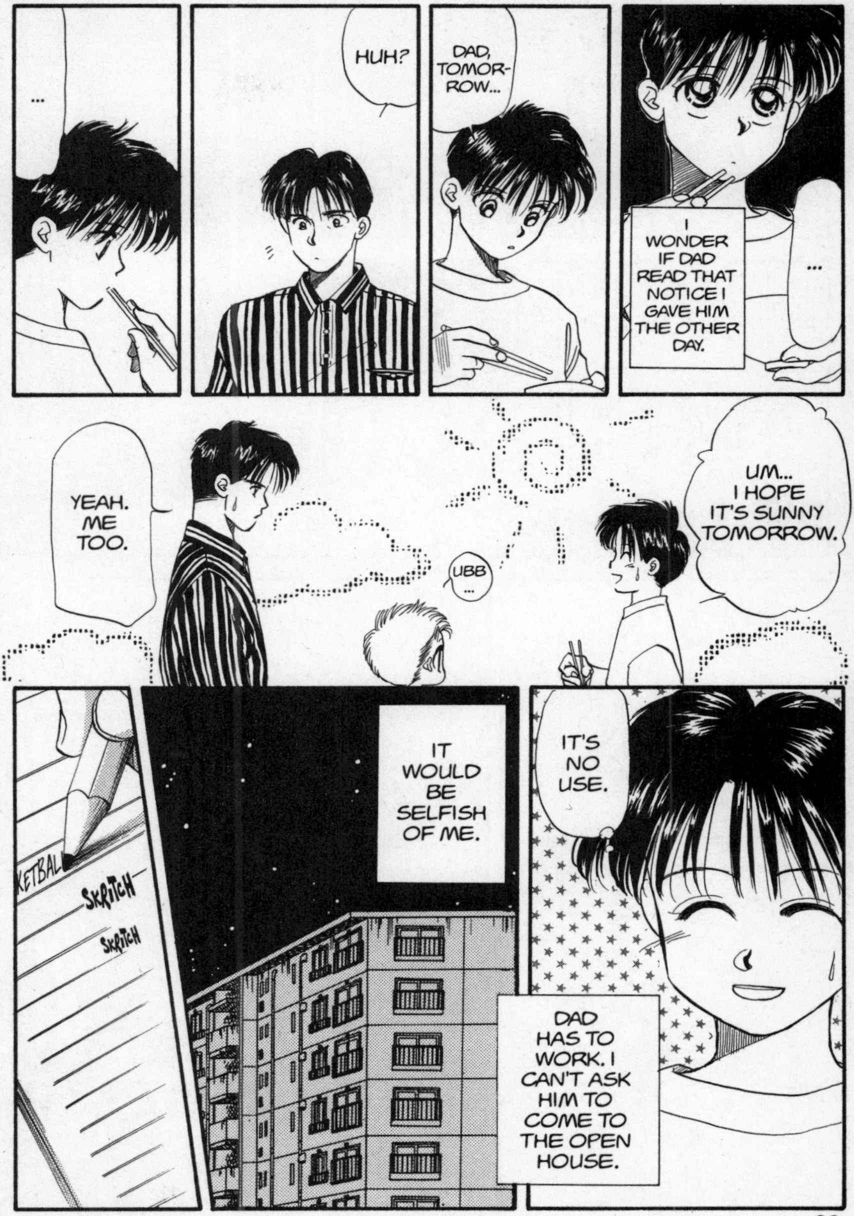
I WONDER IF DAD READ THAT NOTICE I GAVE HIM THE OTHER DAY.
...
DAD, TOMORROW...
HUH?
...
UM... I HOPE IT'S SUNNY TOMORROW.
UBB ...
YEAH. ME TOO.
IT'S NO USE.
DAD HAS TO WORK. I CAN'T ASK HIM TO COME TO THE OPEN HOUSE.
IT WOULD BE SELFISH OF ME.
KETBAL
SKRITCH
SKRITCH

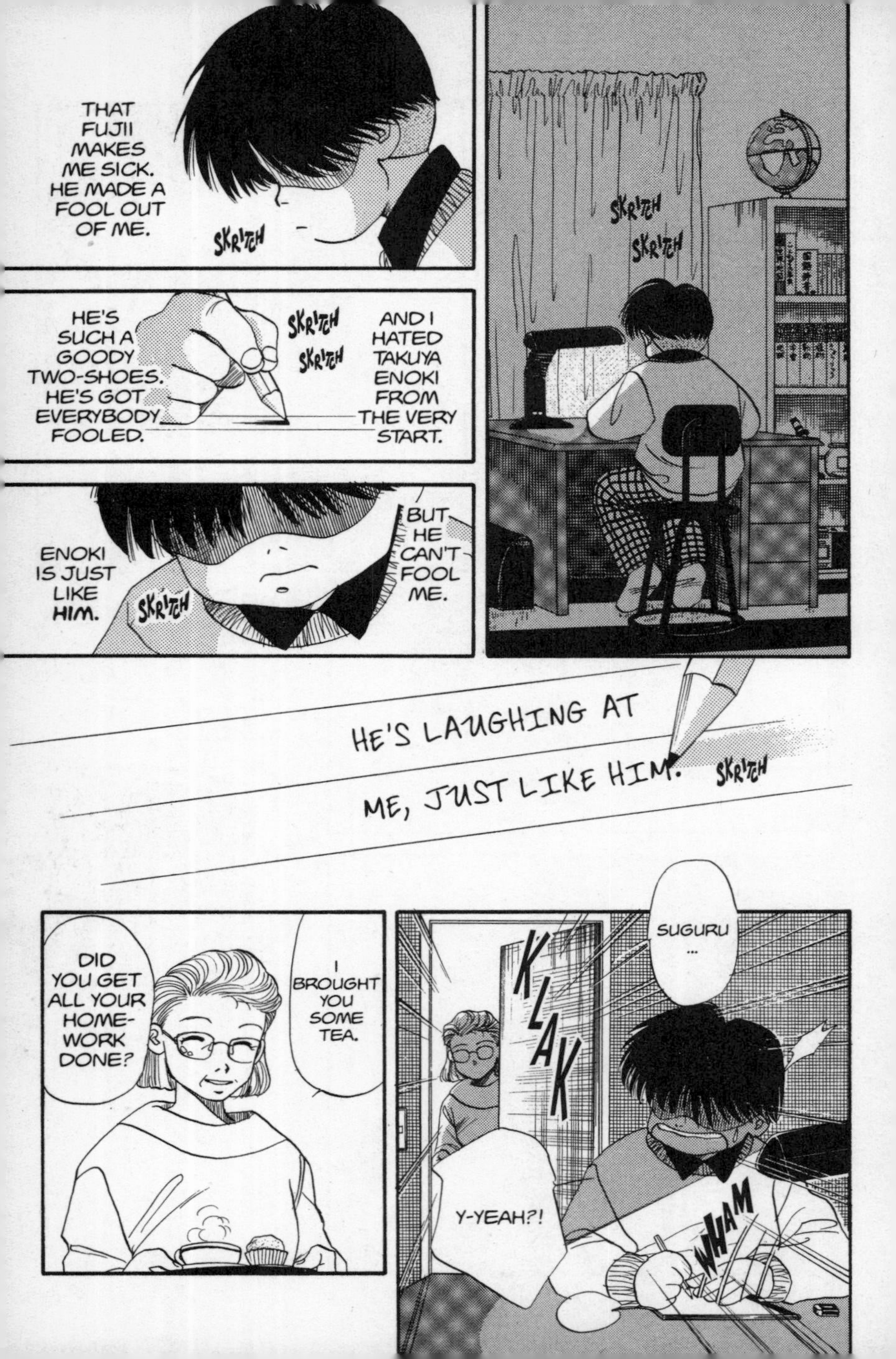
SKRITCH
SKRITCH
SKRITCH
THAT FUJII MAKES ME SICK. HE MADE A FOOL OUT OF ME.
SKRITCH
SKRITCH
AND I HATED TAKUYA ENOKI FROM THE VERY START.
HE'S SUCH A GOODY TWO-SHOES. HE'S GOT EVERYBODY FOOLED.
BUT HE CAN'T FOOL ME.
ENOKI IS JUST LIKE HIM.
SKRITCH
HE'S LAUGHING AT ME, JUST LIKE HIM.
SKRITCH
SUGURU ...
KLAK
Y-YEAH?!
WHAM
I BROUGHT YOU SOME TEA.
DID YOU GET ALL YOUR HOME-WORK DONE?

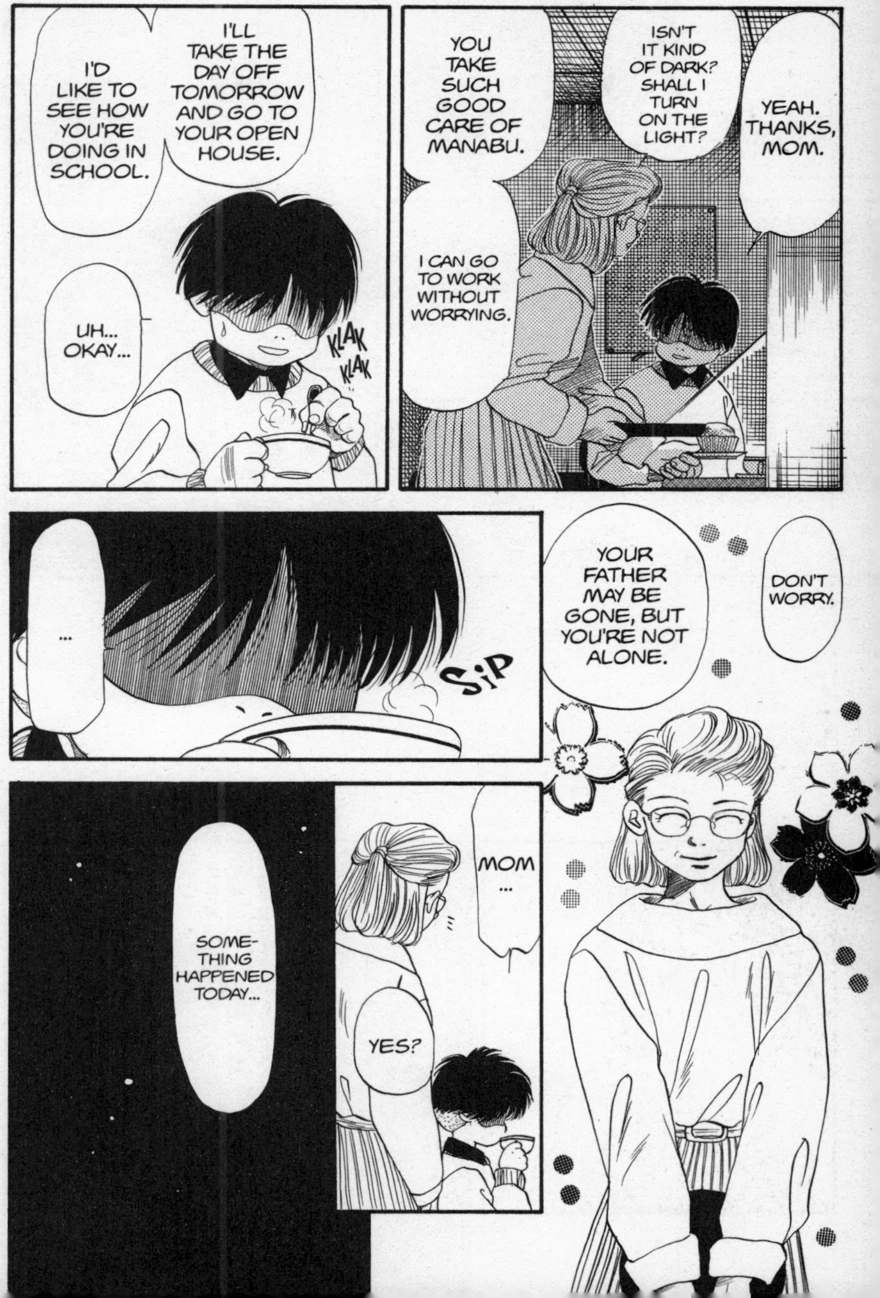
YEAH. THANKS, MOM.
ISN'T IT KIND OF DARK? SHALL I TURN ON THE LIGHT?
YOU TAKE SUCH GOOD CARE OF MANABU.
I CAN GO TO WORK WITHOUT WORRYING.
I'LL TAKE THE DAY OFF TOMORROW AND GO TO YOUR OPEN HOUSE.
I'D LIKE TO SEE HOW YOU'RE DOING IN SCHOOL.
KLAK KLAK
UH... OKAY...
DON'T WORRY.
YOUR FATHER MAY BE GONE, BUT YOU'RE NOT ALONE.
SIP
...
MOM ...
YES?
SOME-THING HAPPENED TODAY...

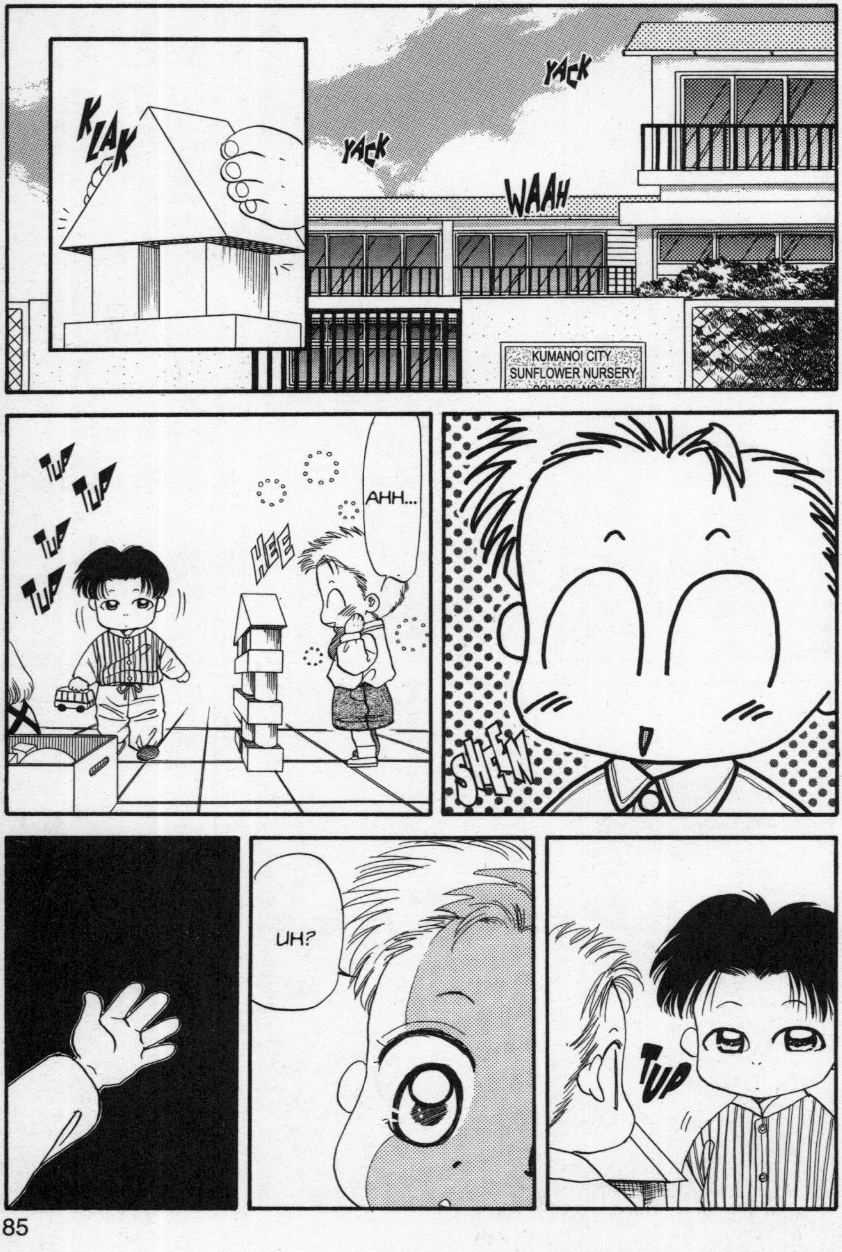
YACK
YACK
WAAH
KUMANOI CITY
SUNFLOWER NURSERY
KLAK
SHEEN
AHH...
HEE
TUP
TUP
TUP
TUP
TUP
UH?

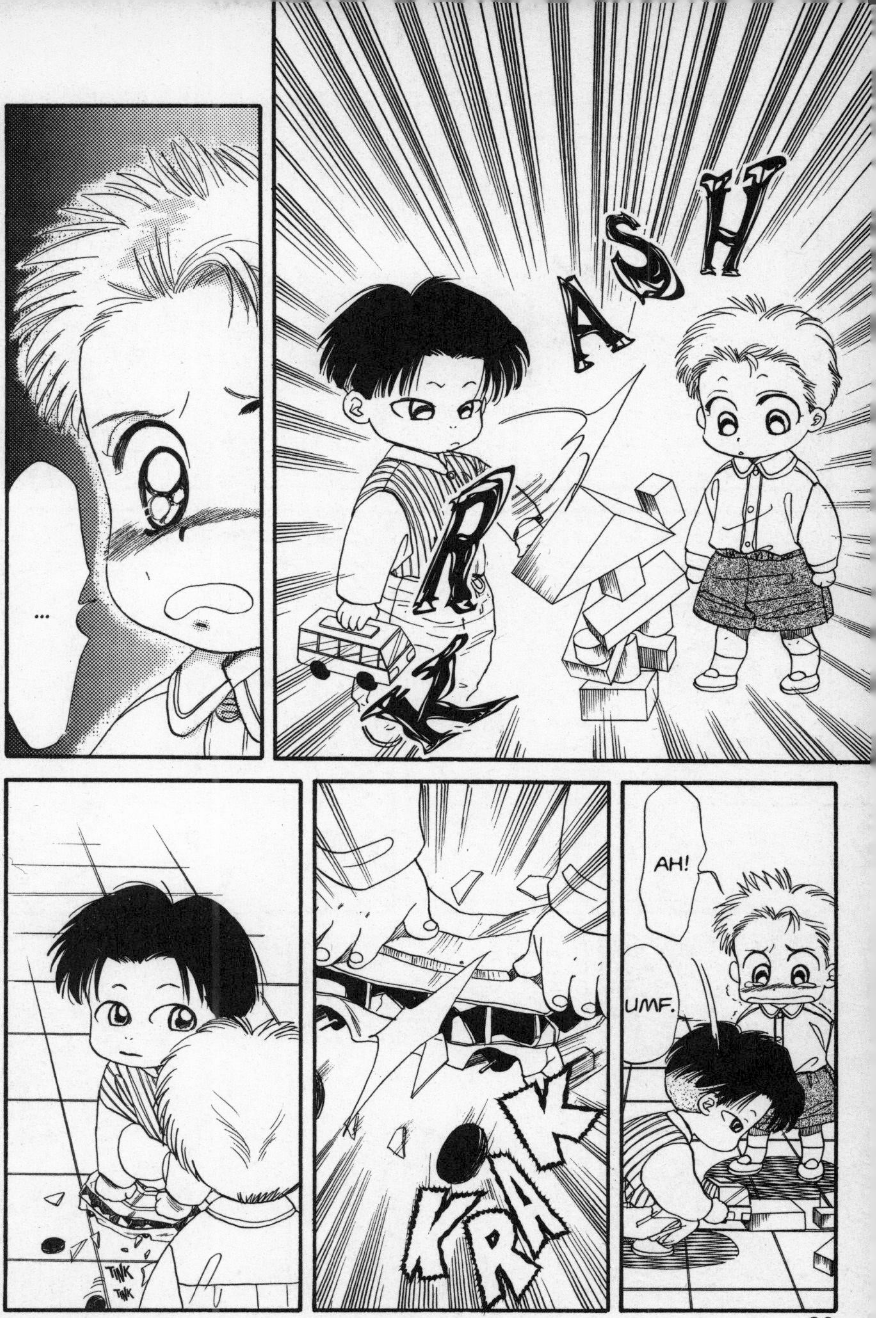
KRASH
...
AH!
UMF.
KRAK
TINK
TINK

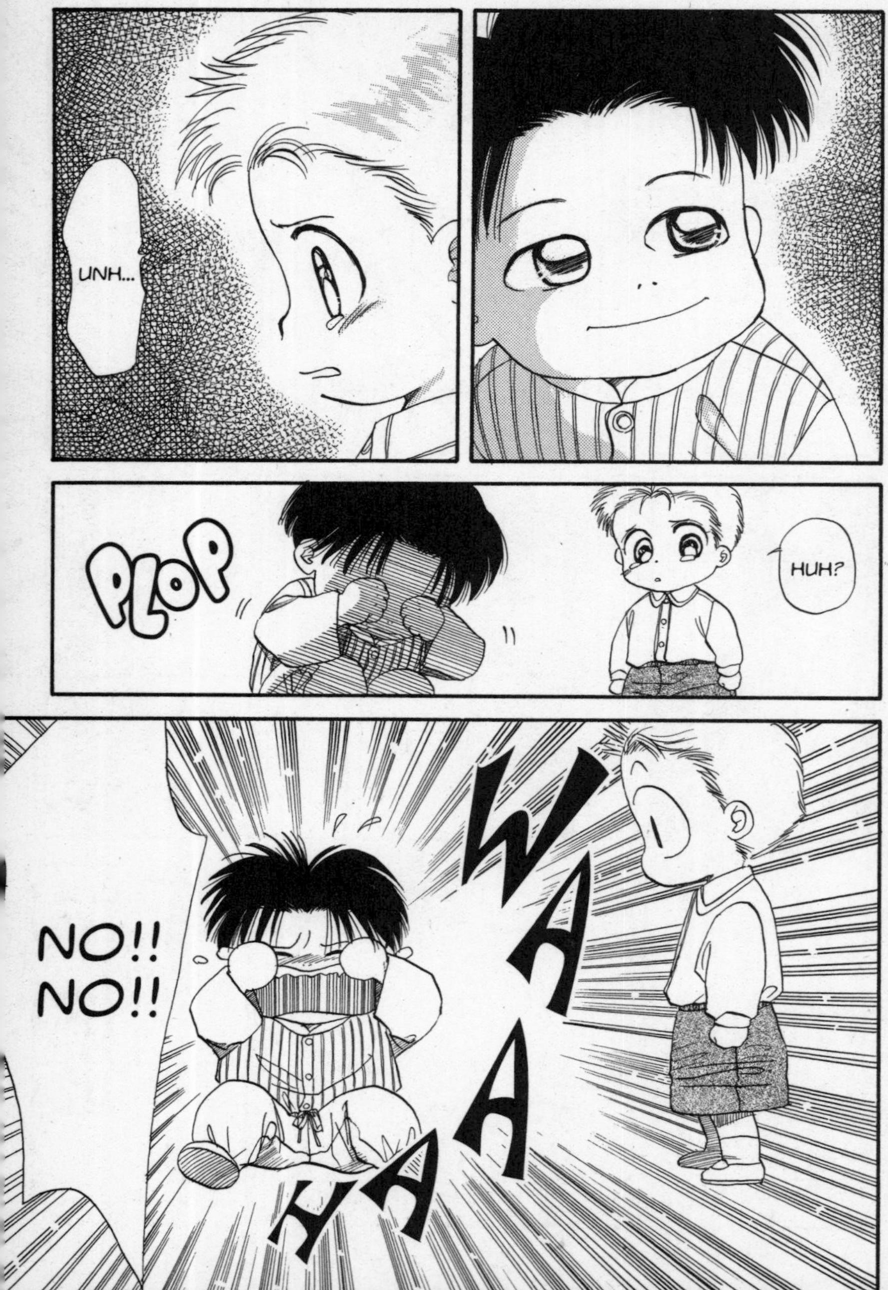
UNH...
HUH?
PLOP
WAAAH
NO!! NO!!

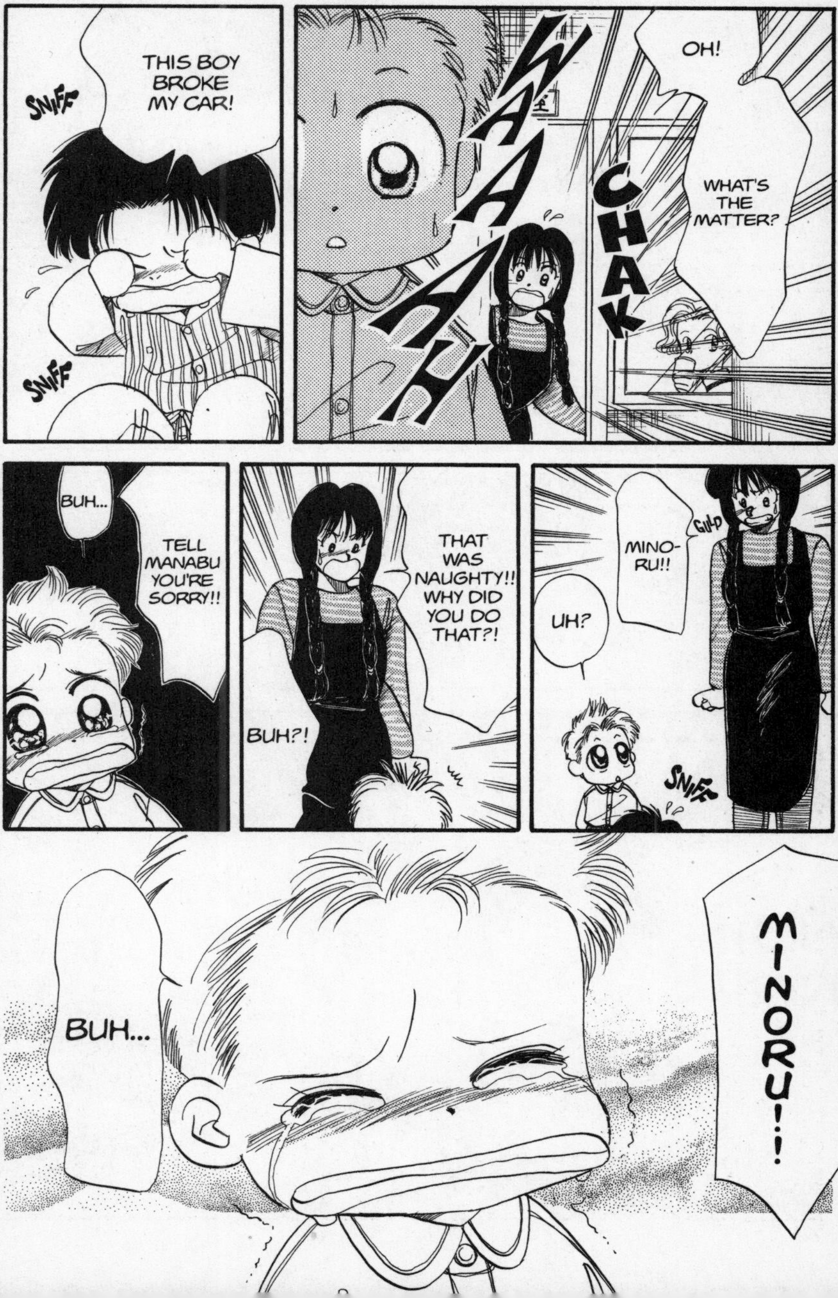
OH!
CHAK
WHAT'S THE MATTER?
WAAAAH
THIS BOY BROKE MY CAR!
SNIFF
SNIFF
GULP
MINO-RU!!
UH?
SNIFF
THAT WAS NAUGHTY!! WHY DID YOU DO THAT?!
BUH?!
BUH...
TELL MANABU YOU'RE SORRY!!
MINORU!!
BUH...

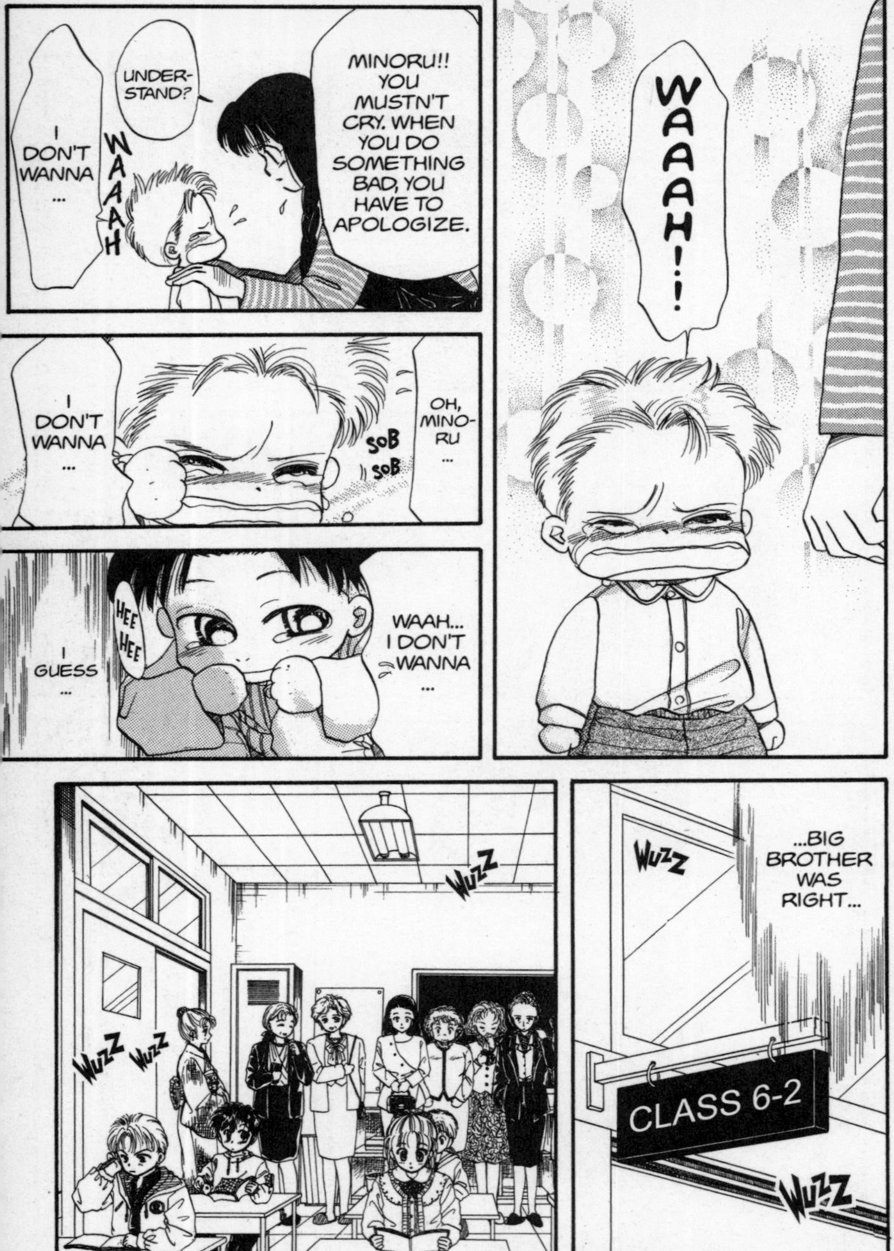
WAAAH!!
MINORU!! YOU MUSTN'T CRY. WHEN YOU DO SOMETHING BAD, YOU HAVE TO APOLOGIZE.
UNDER-STAND?
WAAAH
I DON'T WANNA ...
OH, MINO-RU ...
SOB SOB
I DON'T WANNA ...
WAAH... I DON'T WANNA ...
HEE HEE
I GUESS ...
...BIG BROTHER WAS RIGHT...
WUZZ
CLASS 6-2
WUZZ
WUZZ
WUZZ
WUZZ

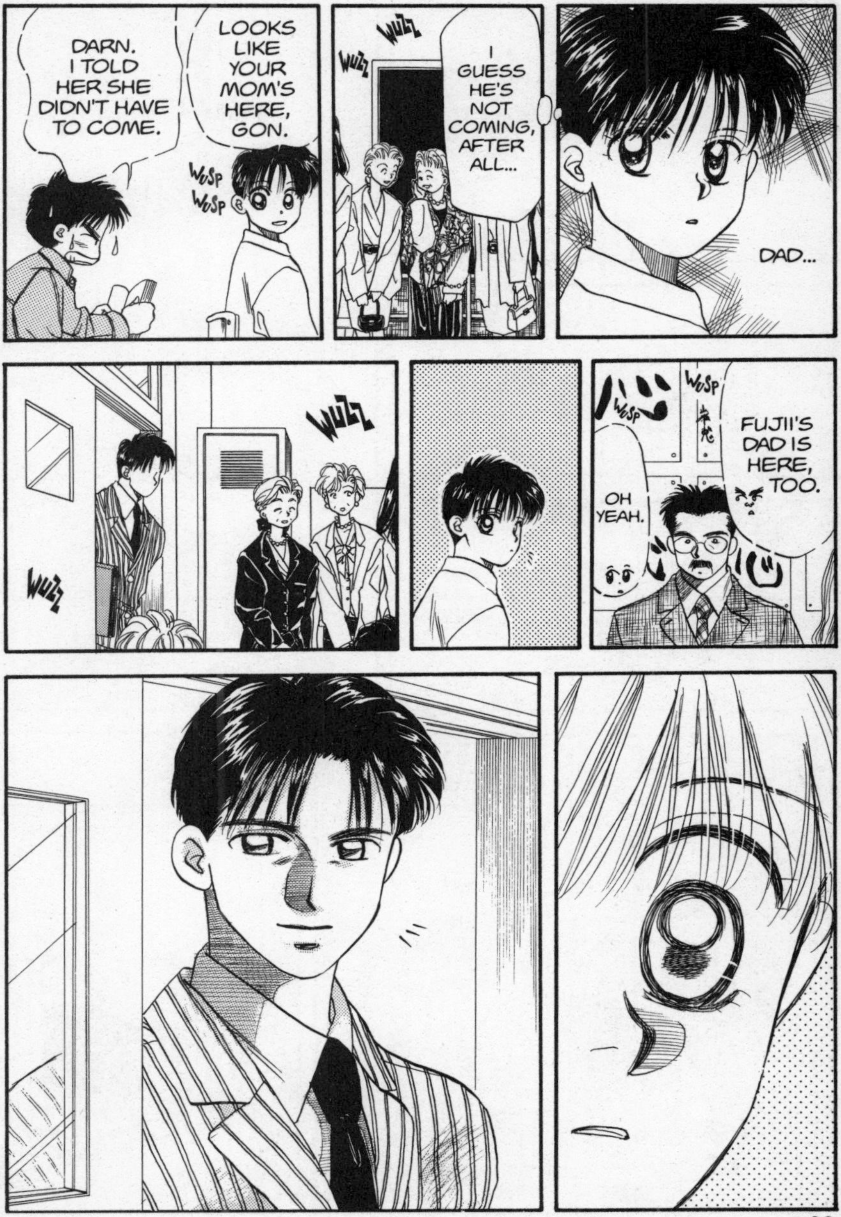
DAD...
WUZZ
WUZZ
I GUESS HE'S NOT COMING, AFTER ALL...
LOOKS LIKE YOUR MOM'S HERE, GON.
WUSP
WUSP
DARN. I TOLD HER SHE DIDN'T HAVE TO COME.
WUSP
WUSP
FUJII'S DAD IS HERE, TOO.
OH YEAH.
WUZZ
WUZZ

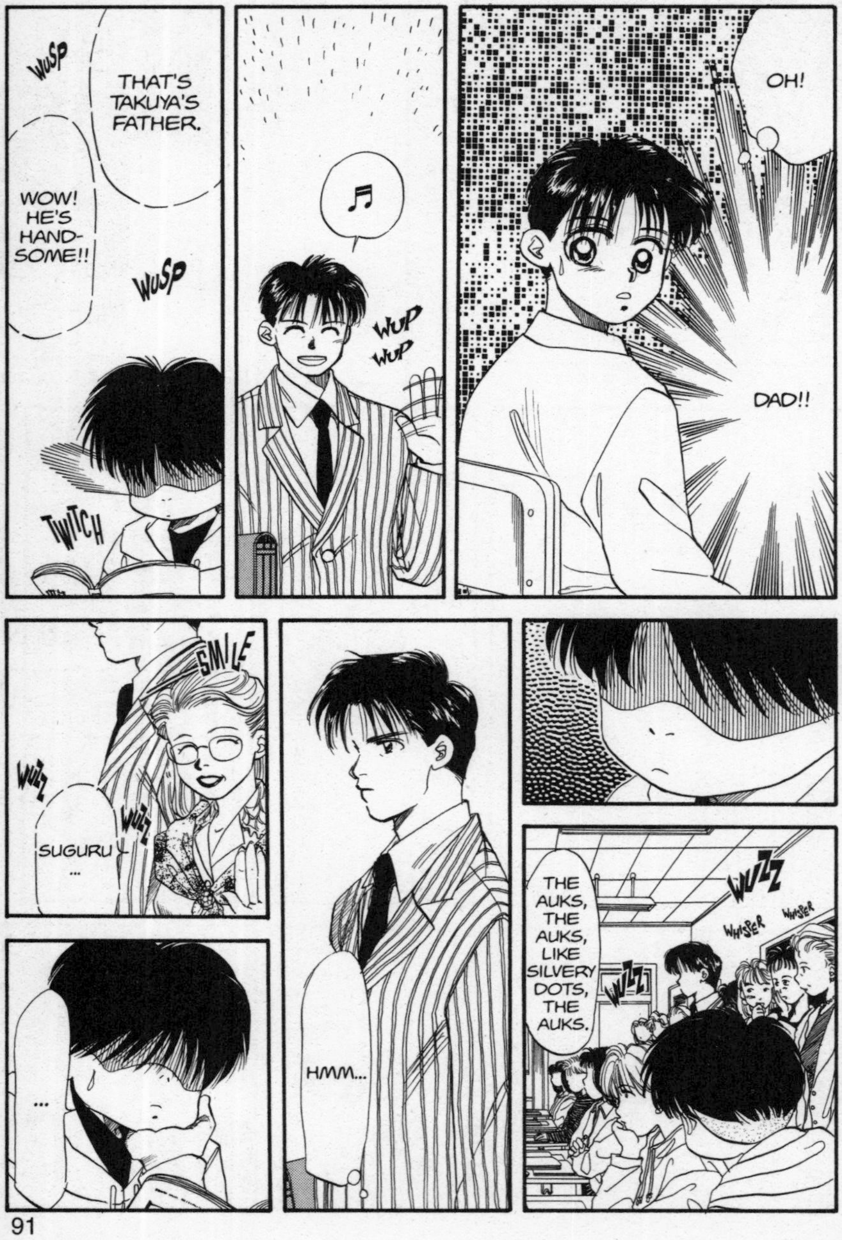
OH!
DAD!!
♬
WUP WUP
WUSP
THAT'S TAKUYA'S FATHER.
WOW! HE'S HANDSOME!!
WUSP
TWITCH
WUZZ
THE AUKS, THE AUKS, LIKE SILVERY DOTS, THE AUKS.
WHISPER
WHISPER
WUZZ
HMM...
SMILE
WUZZ
SUGURU ...
WUZZ
...

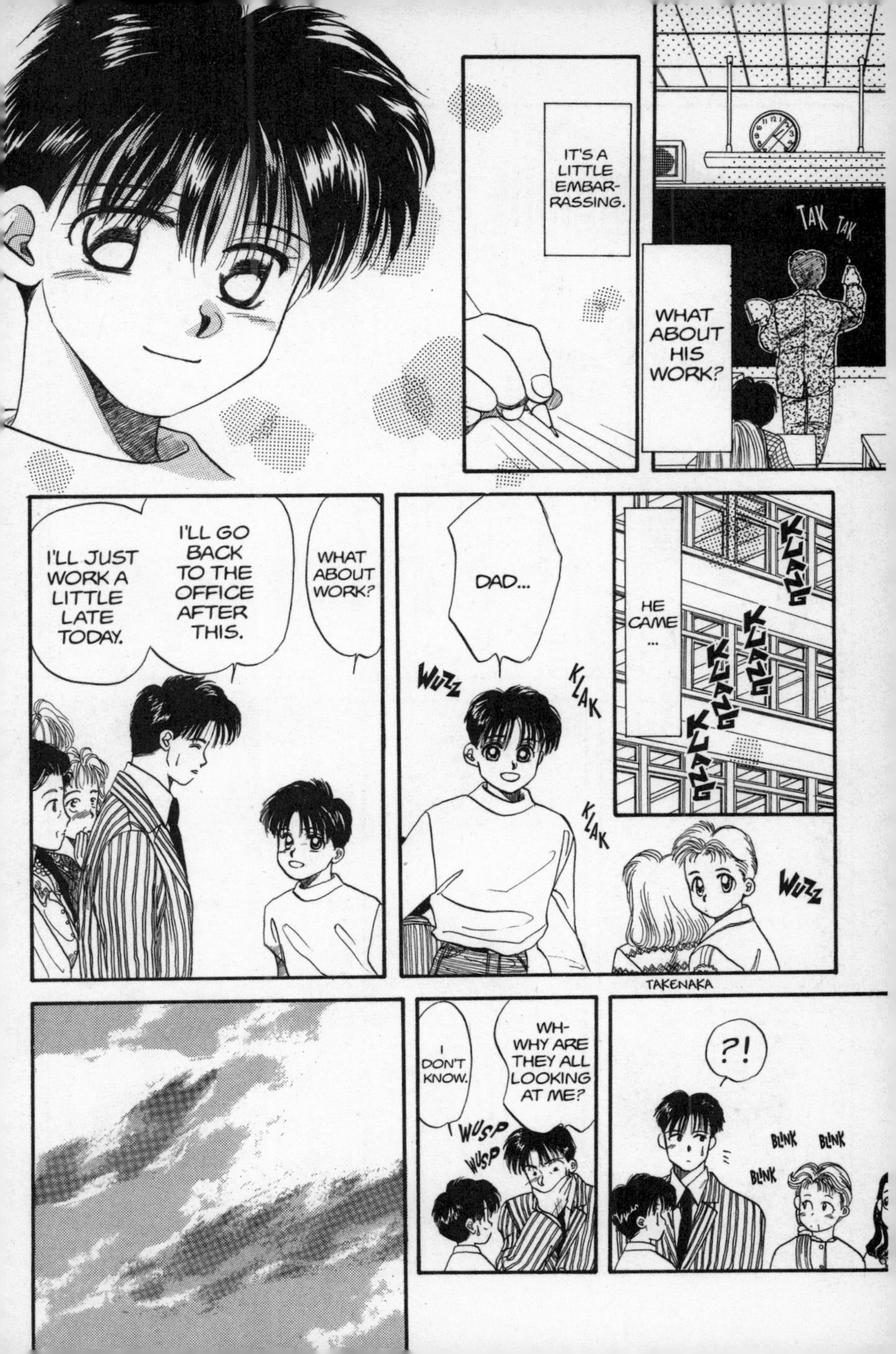
TAK TAK
WHAT ABOUT HIS WORK?
IT'S A LITTLE EMBARRASSING.
HE CAME...
KUANG KUANG KUANG KUANG
DAD...
WUZZ
KLAK
KLAK
WUZZ
TAKENAKA
WHAT ABOUT WORK?
I'LL GO BACK TO THE OFFICE AFTER THIS.
I'LL JUST WORK A LITTLE LATE TODAY.
?!
BLINK BLINK
BLINK
WH- WHY ARE THEY ALL LOOKING AT ME?
I DON'T KNOW.
WUSP WUSP

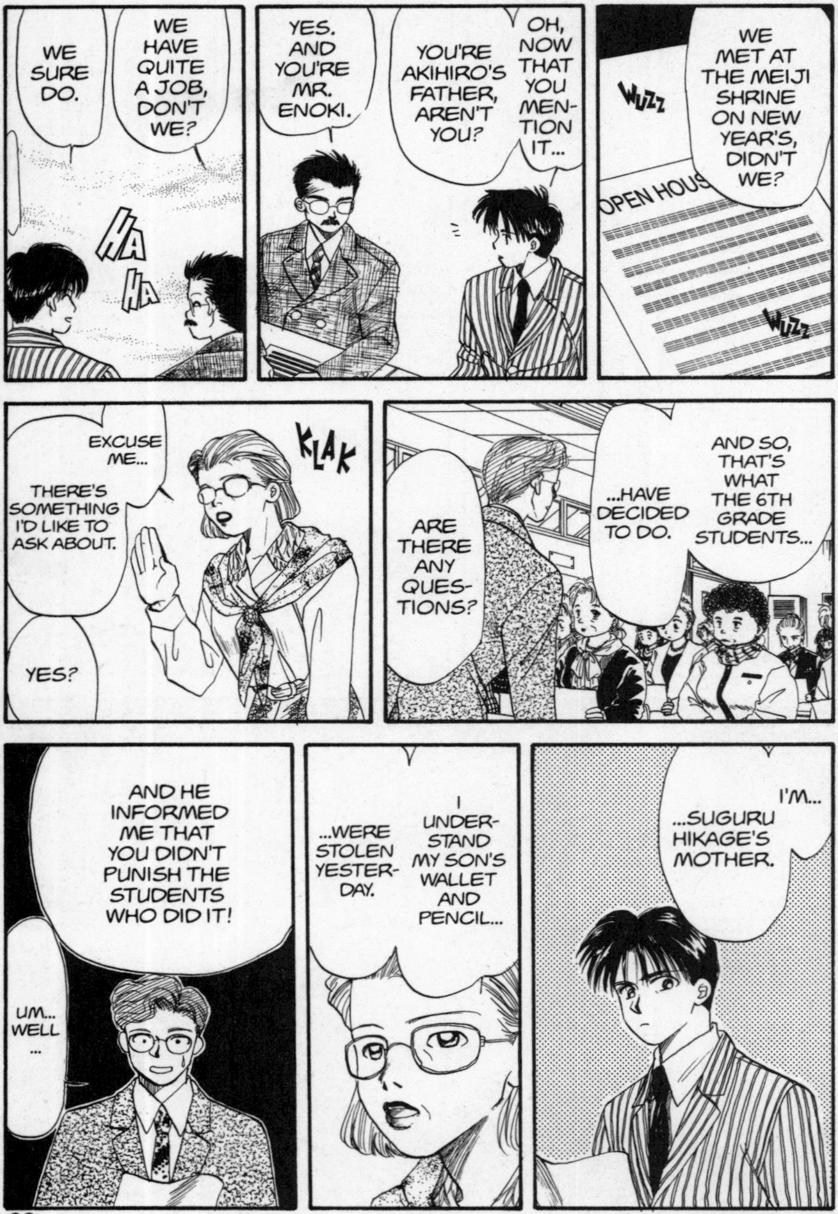
WE MET AT THE MEIJI SHRINE ON NEW YEAR'S, DIDN'T WE?
WUZZ
OPEN HOUS
WUZZ
OH, NOW THAT YOU MEN-TION IT...
YOU'RE AKIHIRO'S FATHER, AREN'T YOU?
YES. AND YOU'RE MR. ENOKI.
WE HAVE QUITE A JOB, DON'T WE?
WE SURE DO.
HA
HA
AND SO, THAT'S WHAT THE 6TH GRADE STUDENTS...
...HAVE DECIDED TO DO.
ARE THERE ANY QUES-TIONS?
KLAK
EXCUSE ME...
THERE'S SOMETHING I'D LIKE TO ASK ABOUT.
YES?
I'M...
...SUGURU HIKAGE'S MOTHER.
I UNDER-STAND MY SON'S WALLET AND PENCIL...
...WERE STOLEN YESTER-DAY.
AND HE INFORMED ME THAT YOU DIDN'T PUNISH THE STUDENTS WHO DID IT!
UM... WELL ...

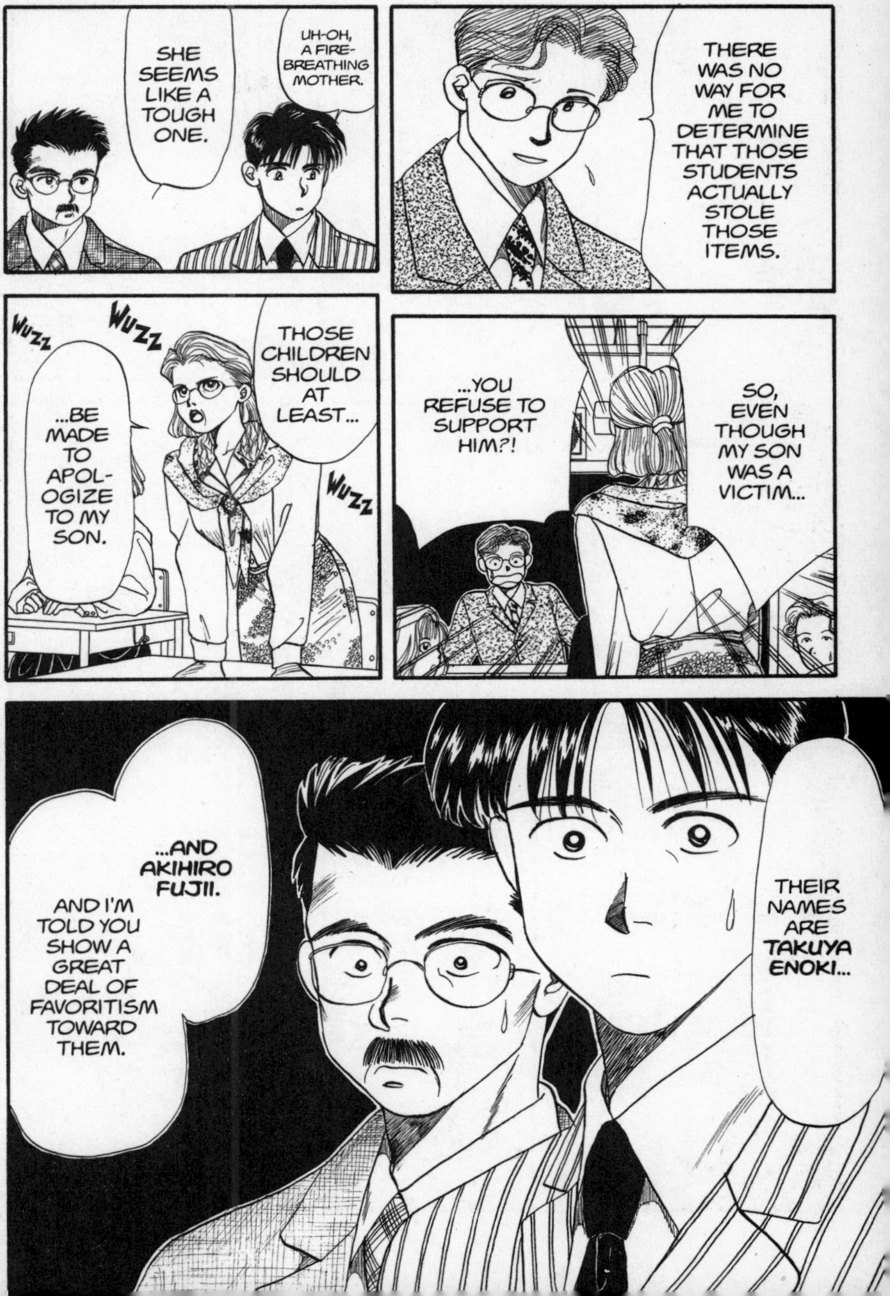
THERE WAS NO WAY FOR ME TO DETERMINE THAT THOSE STUDENTS ACTUALLY STOLE THOSE ITEMS.
UH-OH, A FIRE-BREATHING MOTHER.
SHE SEEMS LIKE A TOUGH ONE.
SO, EVEN THOUGH MY SON WAS A VICTIM...
...YOU REFUSE TO SUPPORT HIM?!
WUZZ
THOSE CHILDREN SHOULD AT LEAST...
WUZZ
...BE MADE TO APOLOGIZE TO MY SON.
WUZZ
THEIR NAMES ARE TAKUYA ENOKI...
...AND AKIHIRO FUJII.
AND I'M TOLD YOU SHOW A GREAT DEAL OF FAVORITISM TOWARD THEM.

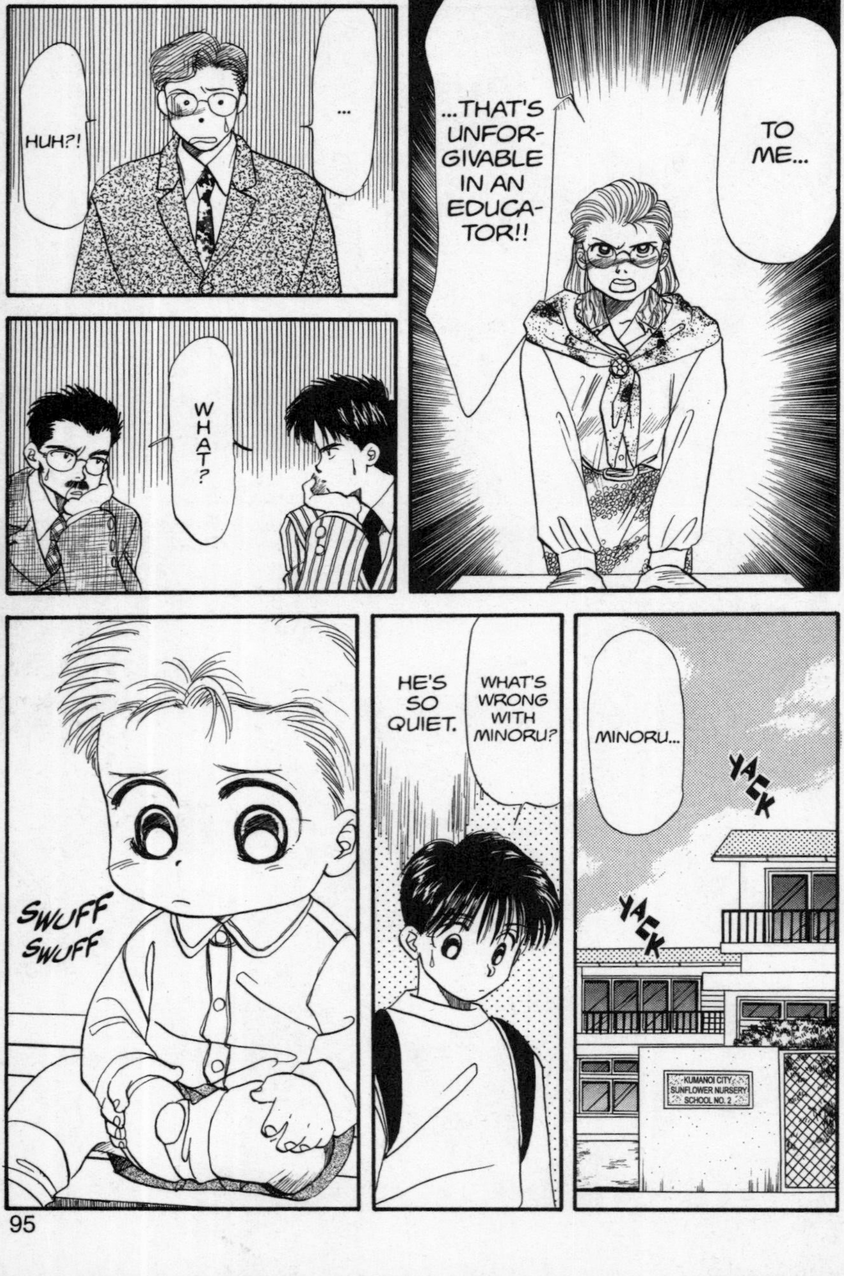
TO ME...
...THAT'S UNFORGIVABLE IN AN EDUCATOR!!
...
HUH?!
WHAT?
MINORU...
YACK
YACK
KUMANOI CITY SUNFLOWER NURSERY SCHOOL NO. 2
WHAT'S WRONG WITH MINORU?
HE'S SO QUIET.
SWUFF SWUFF

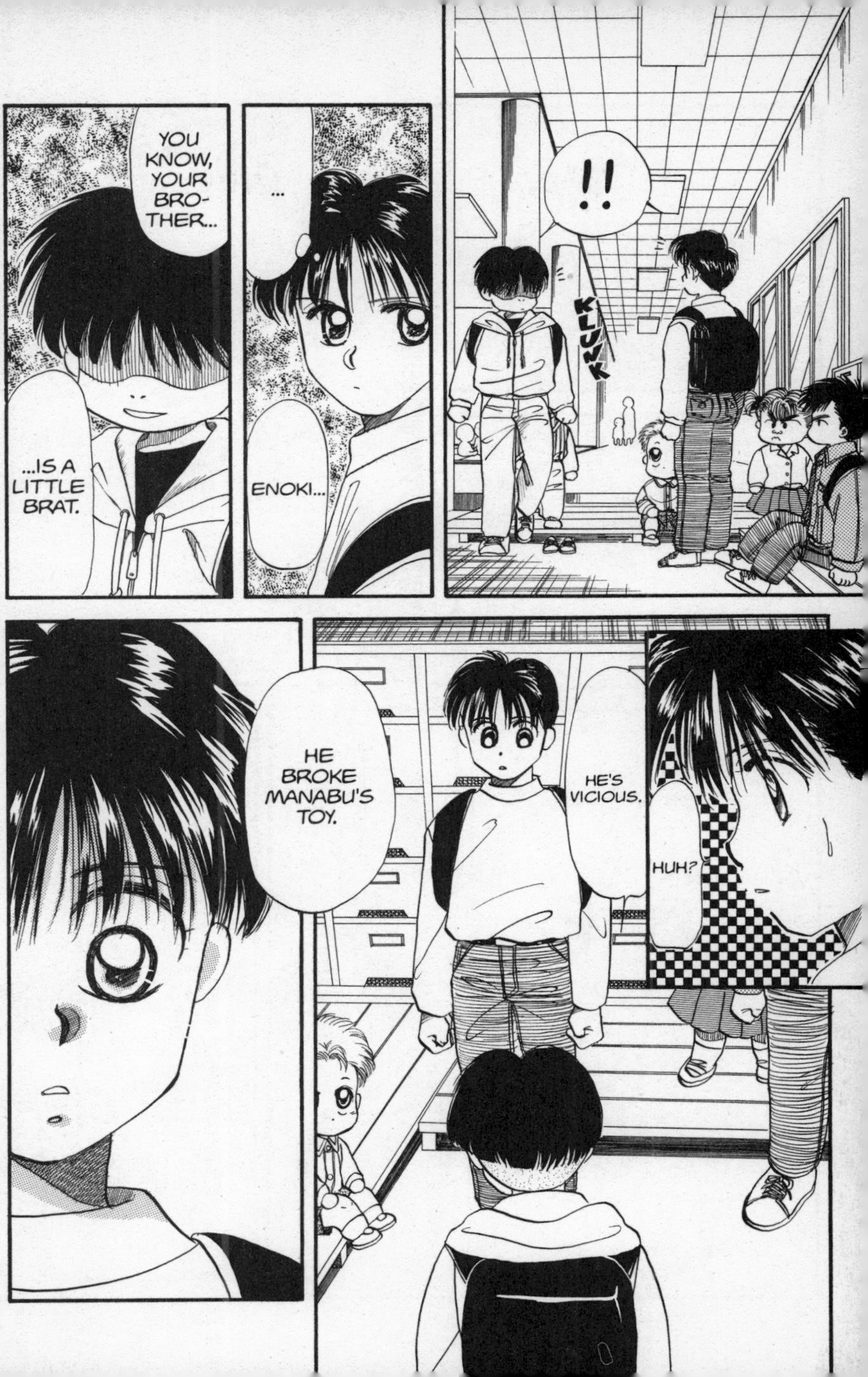
!!
KLUNK
...
ENOKI...
YOU KNOW, YOUR BRO-THER...
...IS A LITTLE BRAT.
HUH?
HE'S VICIOUS.
HE BROKE MANABU'S TOY.

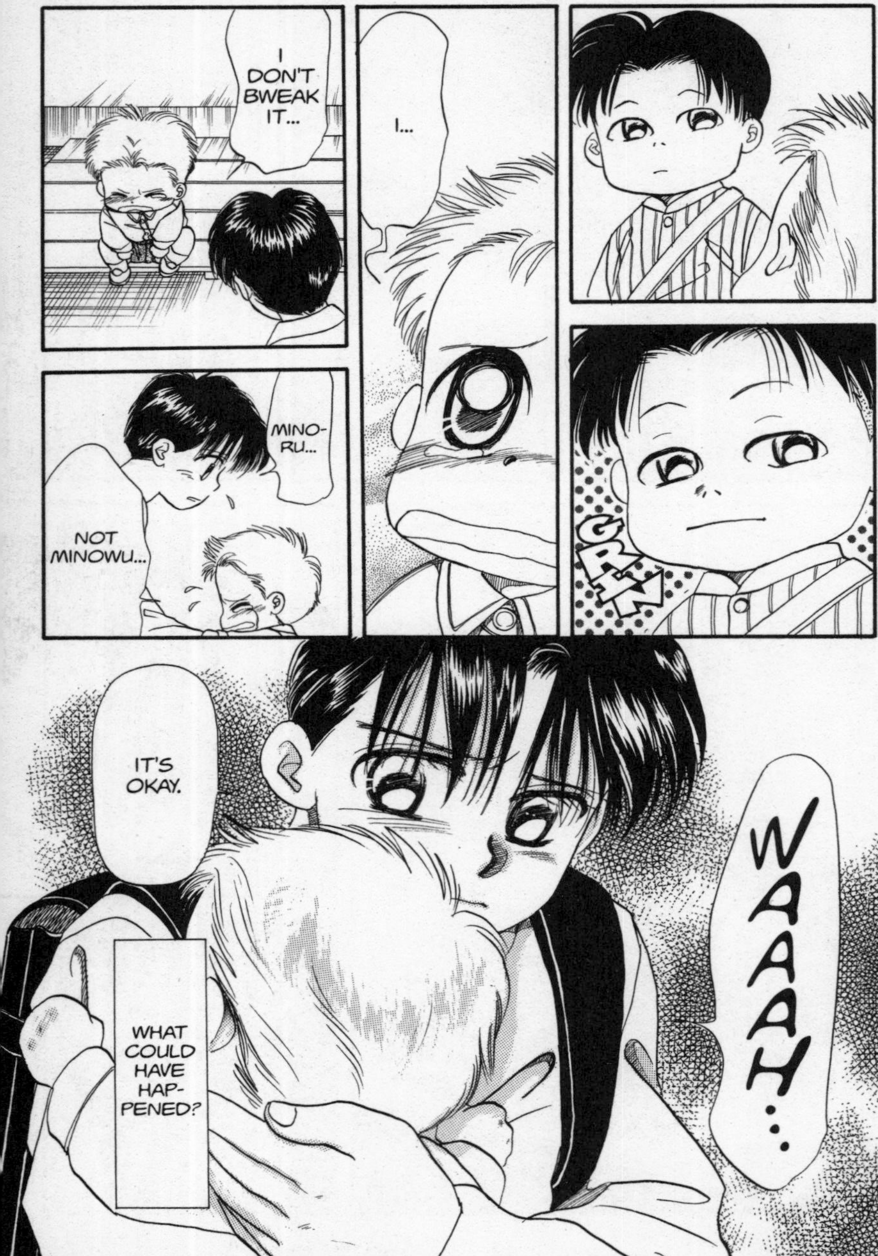
GRIN
I...
I DON'T BWEAK IT...
MINO-RU...
NOT MINOWU...
WAAAH...
IT'S OKAY.
WHAT COULD HAVE HAPPENED?

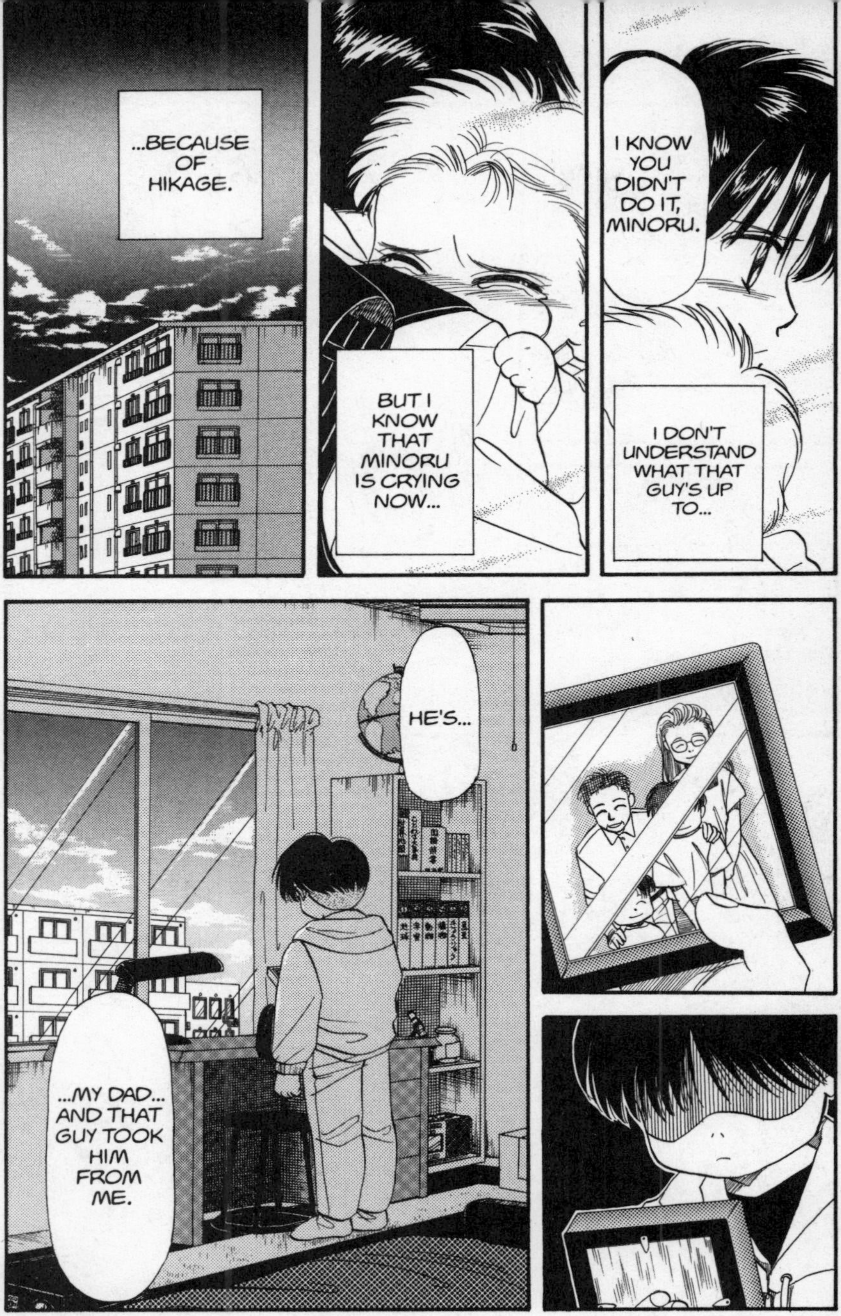
I KNOW YOU DIDN'T DO IT, MINORU.
I DON'T UNDERSTAND WHAT THAT GUY'S UP TO...
BUT I KNOW THAT MINORU IS CRYING NOW...
...BECAUSE OF HIKAGE.
HE'S...
...MY DAD... AND THAT GUY TOOK HIM FROM ME.

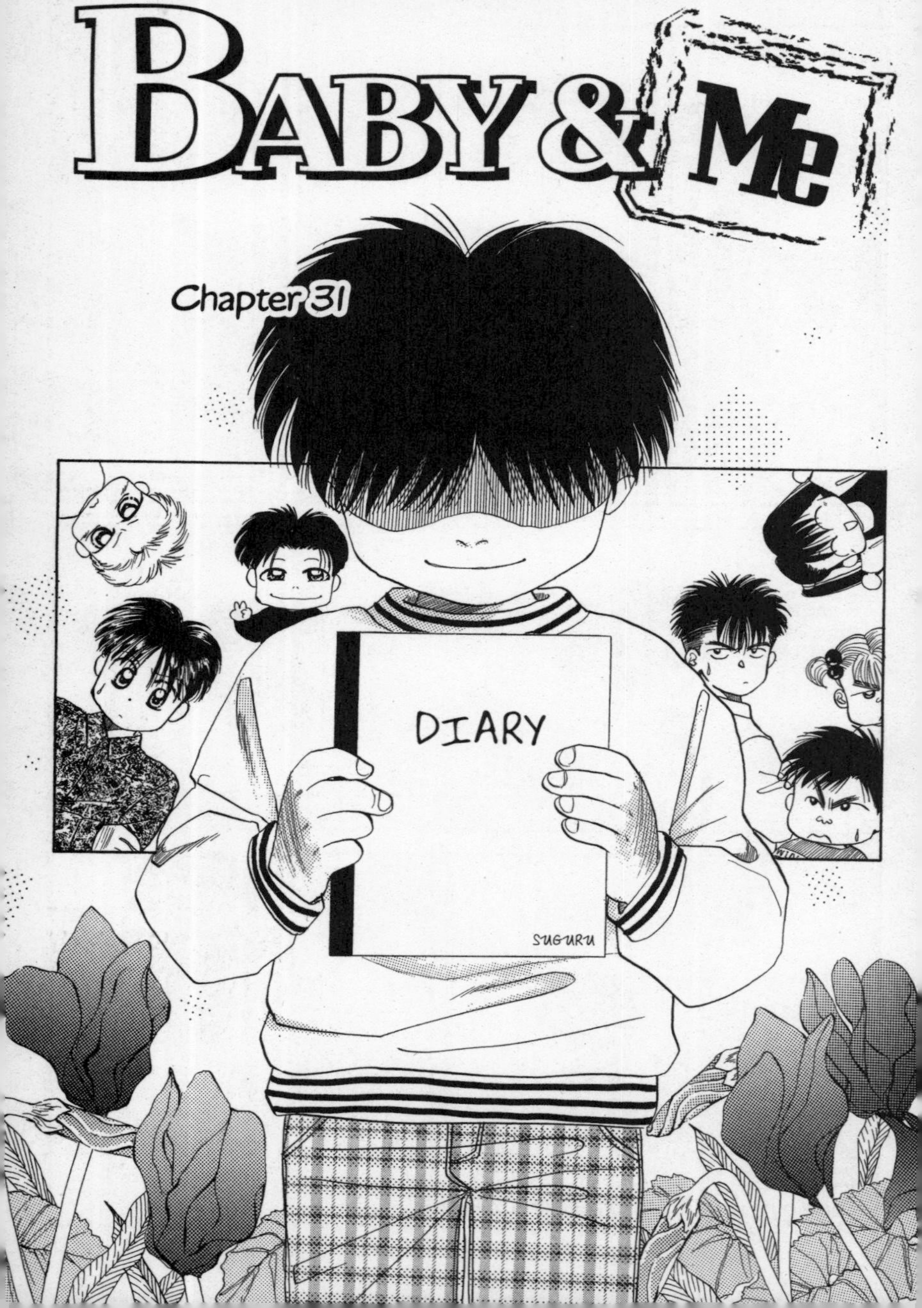
BABY & Me
Chapter 31
DIARY
SUGURU

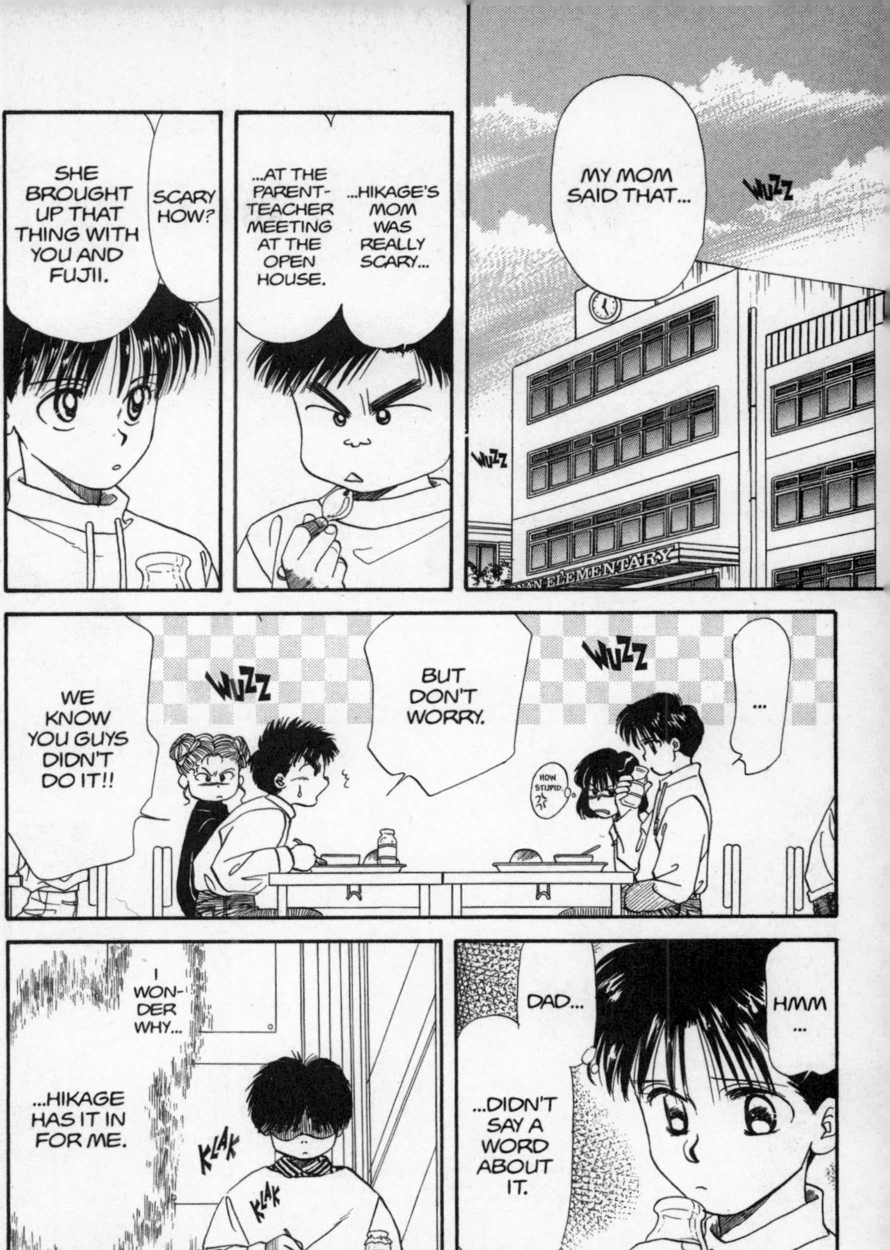
MY MOM SAID THAT...
WUZZ
WUZZ
ELEMENTARY
...HIKAGE'S MOM WAS REALLY SCARY...
...AT THE PARENT-TEACHER MEETING AT THE OPEN HOUSE.
SCARY HOW?
SHE BROUGHT UP THAT THING WITH YOU AND FUJII.
...
WUZZ
HOW STUPID.
BUT DON'T WORRY.
WUZZ
WE KNOW YOU GUYS DIDN'T DO IT!!
HMM ...
DAD...
...DIDN'T SAY A WORD ABOUT IT.
I WONDER WHY...
...HIKAGE HAS IT IN FOR ME.
KLAK
KLAK

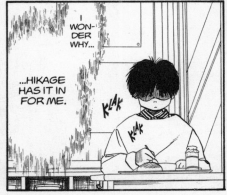

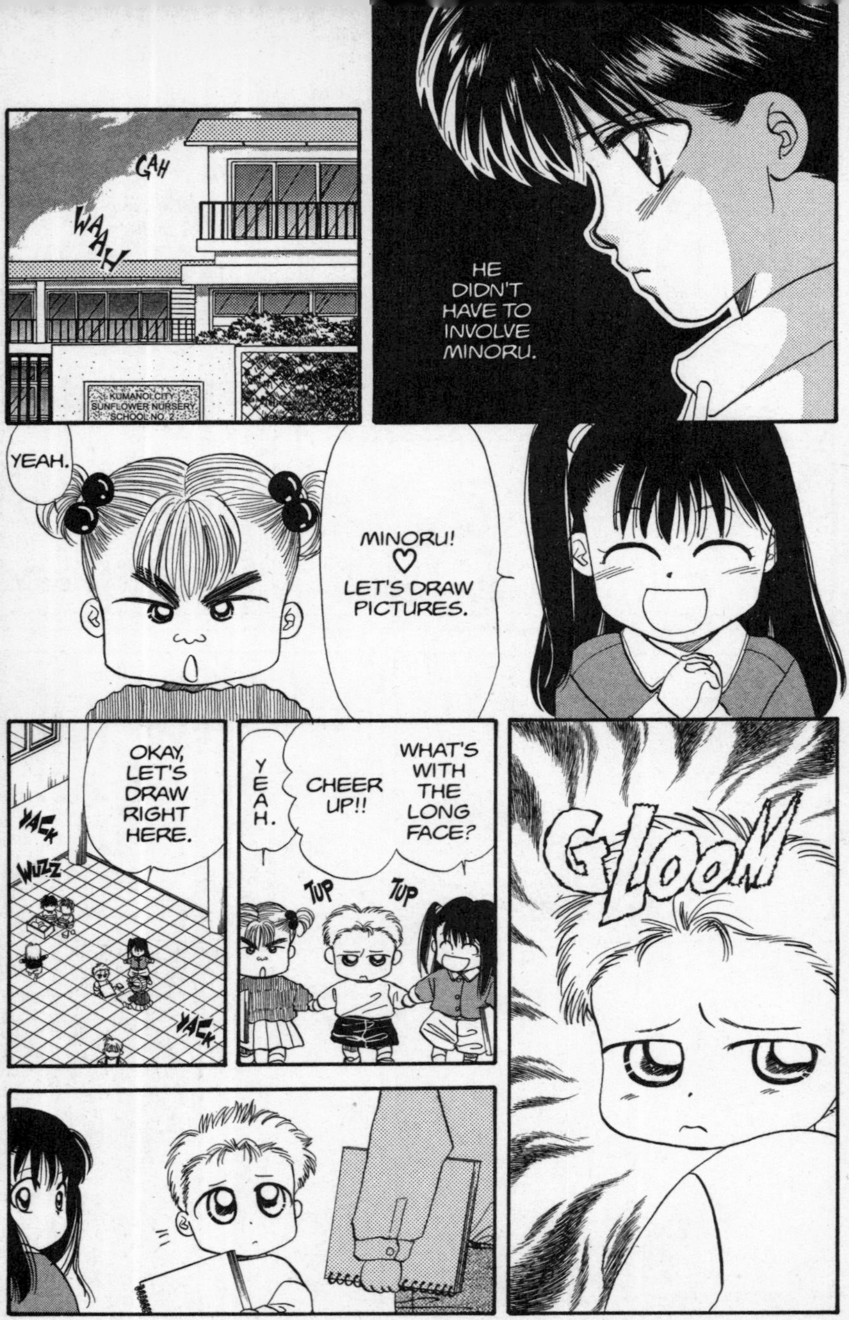
HE DIDN'T HAVE TO INVOLVE MINORU.
GAH
WAAAH
KUMANOI CITY SUNFLOWER NURSERY SCHOOL NO. 2
MINORU! ♡ LET'S DRAW PICTURES.
YEAH.
GLOOM
WHAT'S WITH THE LONG FACE?
CHEER UP!!
YEAH.
TUP
TUP
OKAY, LET'S DRAW RIGHT HERE.
YACK
WUZZ
YACK

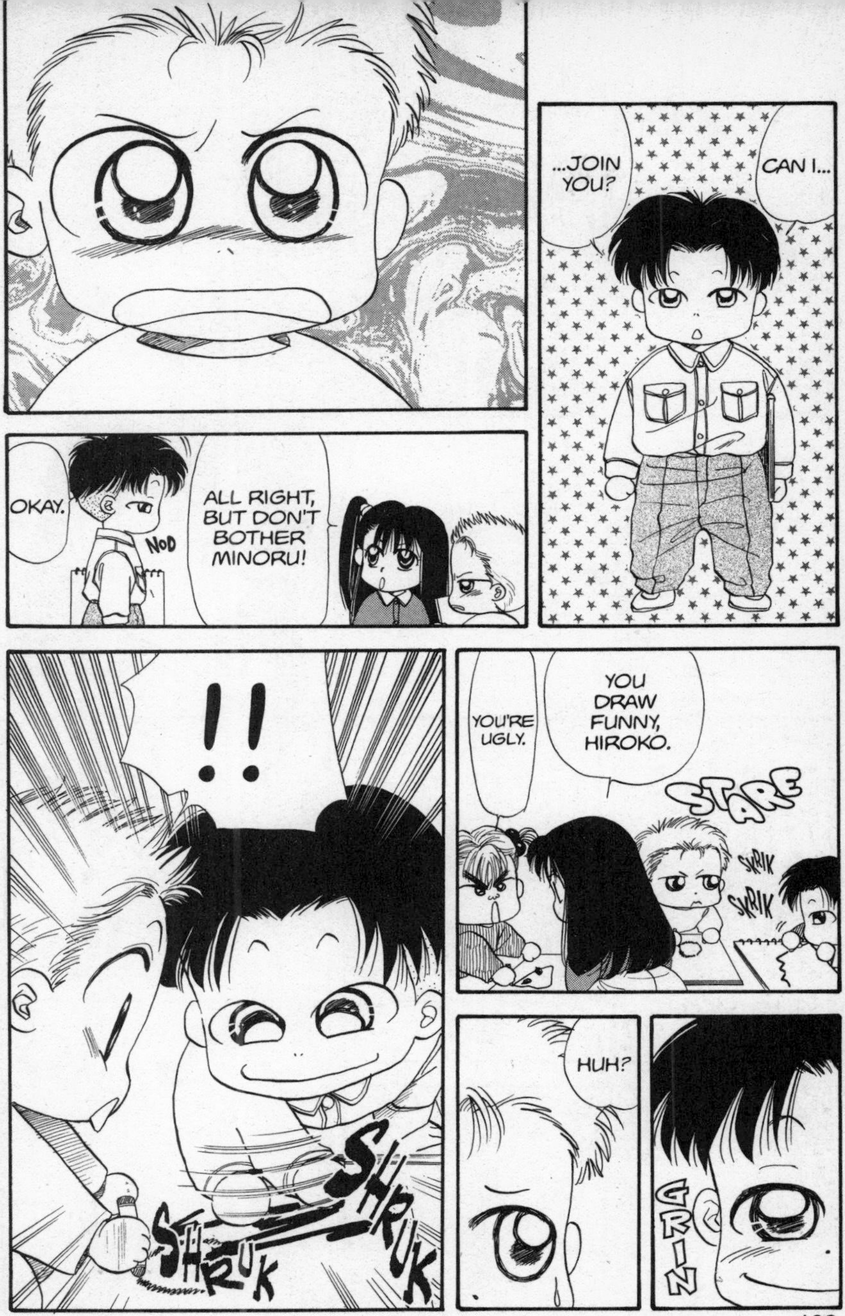
CAN I...
...JOIN YOU?
ALL RIGHT, BUT DON'T BOTHER MINORU!
NOD
OKAY.
YOU DRAW FUNNY, HIROKO.
YOU'RE UGLY.
STARE
SKRIK
SKRIK
GRIN
HUH?
!!
SHRUK
SHRUK

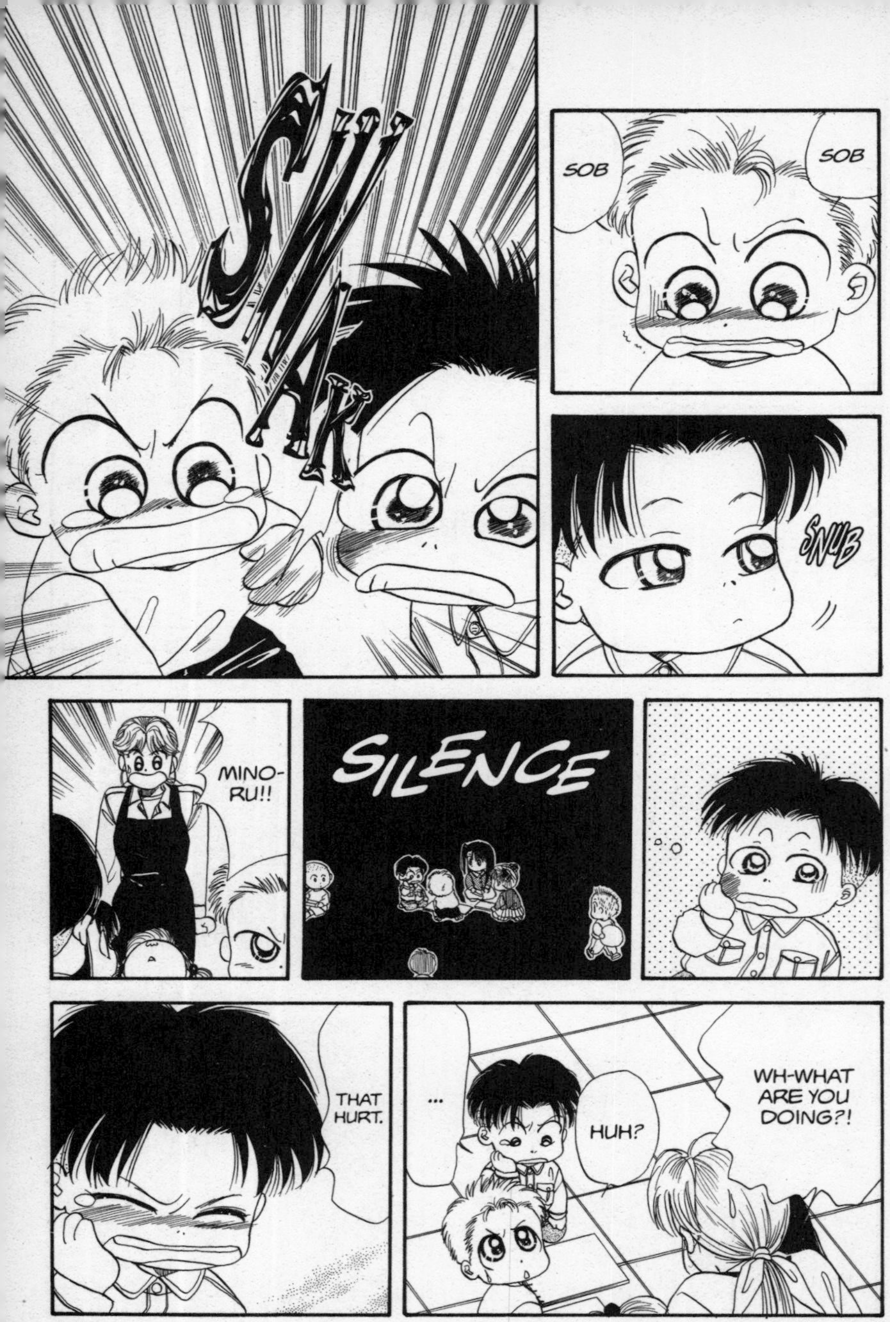
SOB
SOB
SNUB
SHAK
SILENCE
MINO-
RU!!
WH-WHAT ARE YOU DOING?!
HUH?
...
THAT HURT.

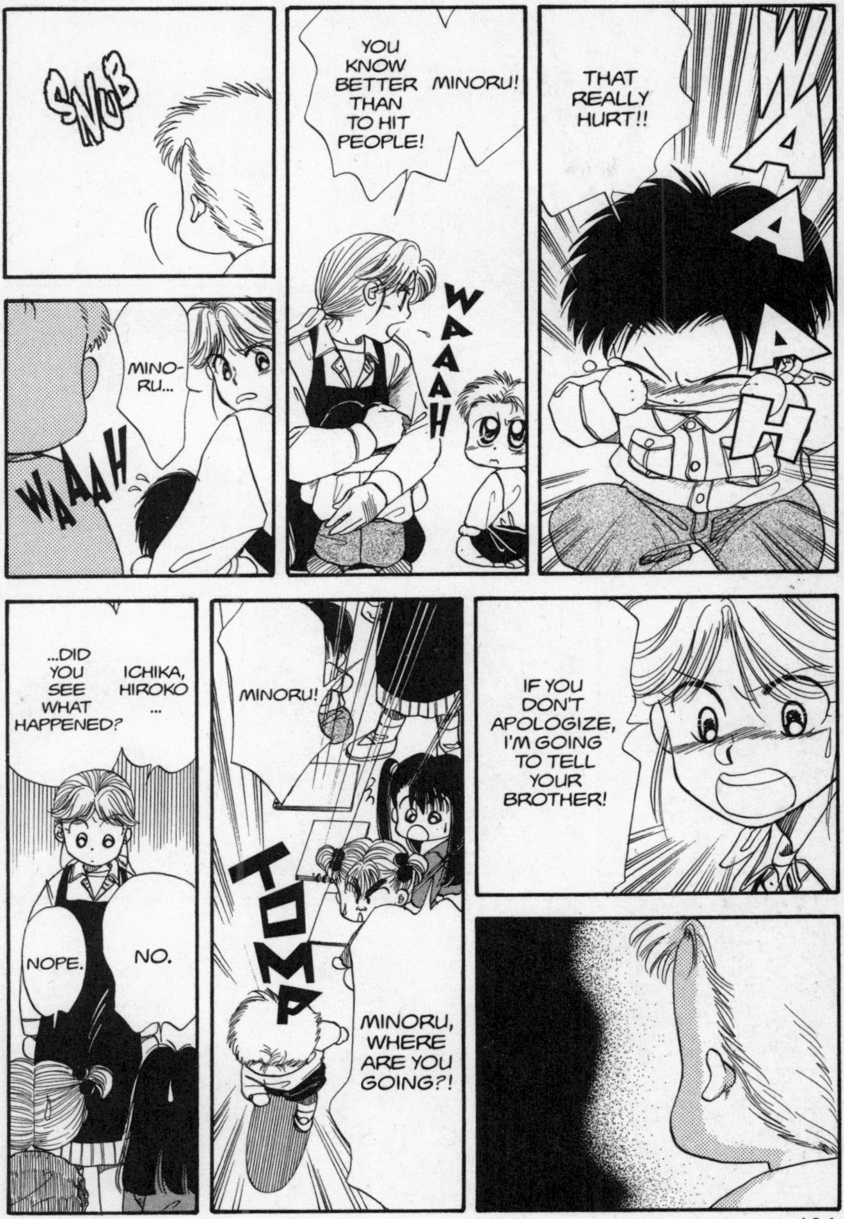
WAAAH
THAT REALLY HURT!!
MINORU!
YOU KNOW BETTER THAN TO HIT PEOPLE!
WAAAH
SNOB
MINO-RU...
WAAAH
IF YOU DON'T APOLOGIZE, I'M GOING TO TELL YOUR BROTHER!
MINORU!
TOMP
MINORU, WHERE ARE YOU GOING?!
ICHIKA, HIROKO...
...DID YOU SEE WHAT HAPPENED?
NO.
NOPE.

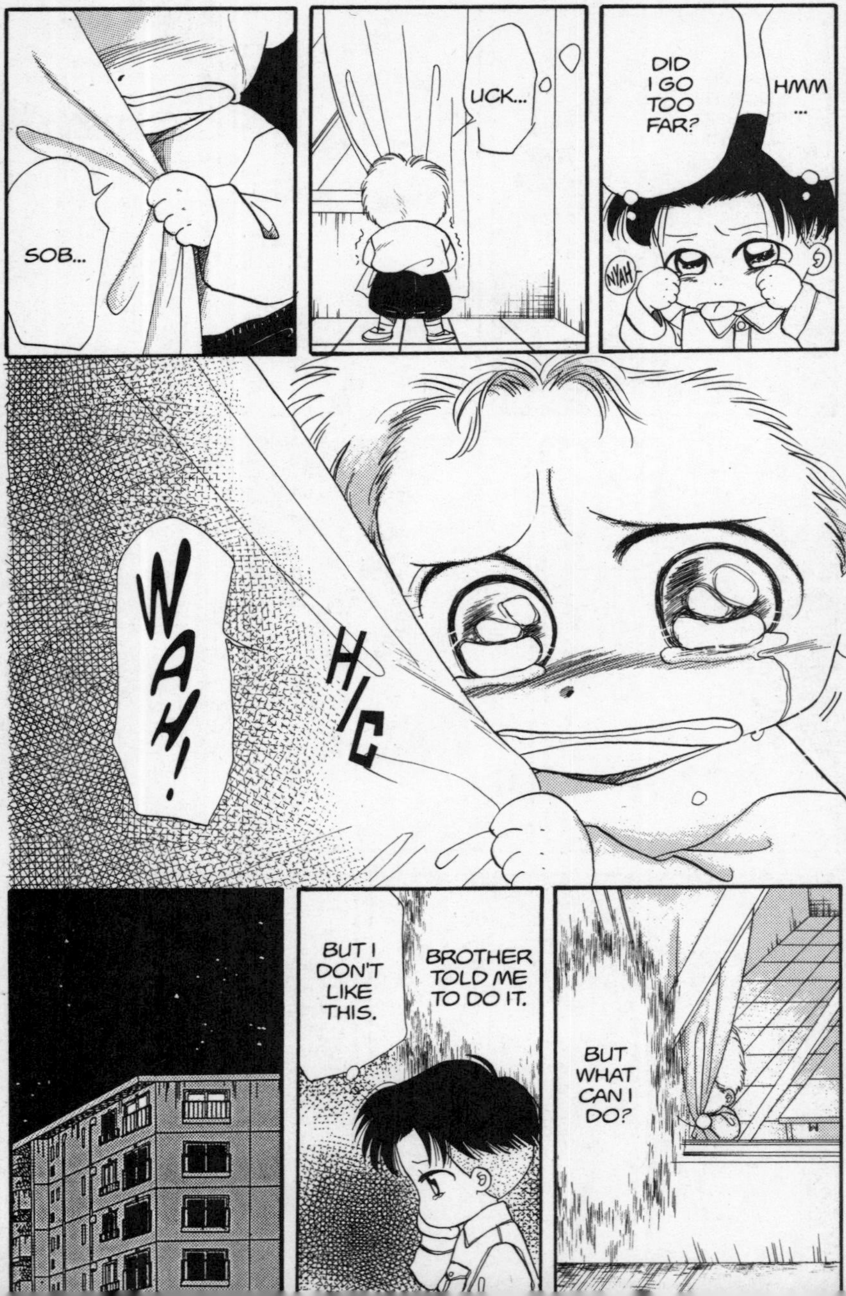
HMM ...
DID I GO TOO FAR?
NYAH
UCK...
SOB...
HIC
WAH!
BUT WHAT CAN I DO?
BROTHER TOLD ME TO DO IT.
BUT I DON'T LIKE THIS.

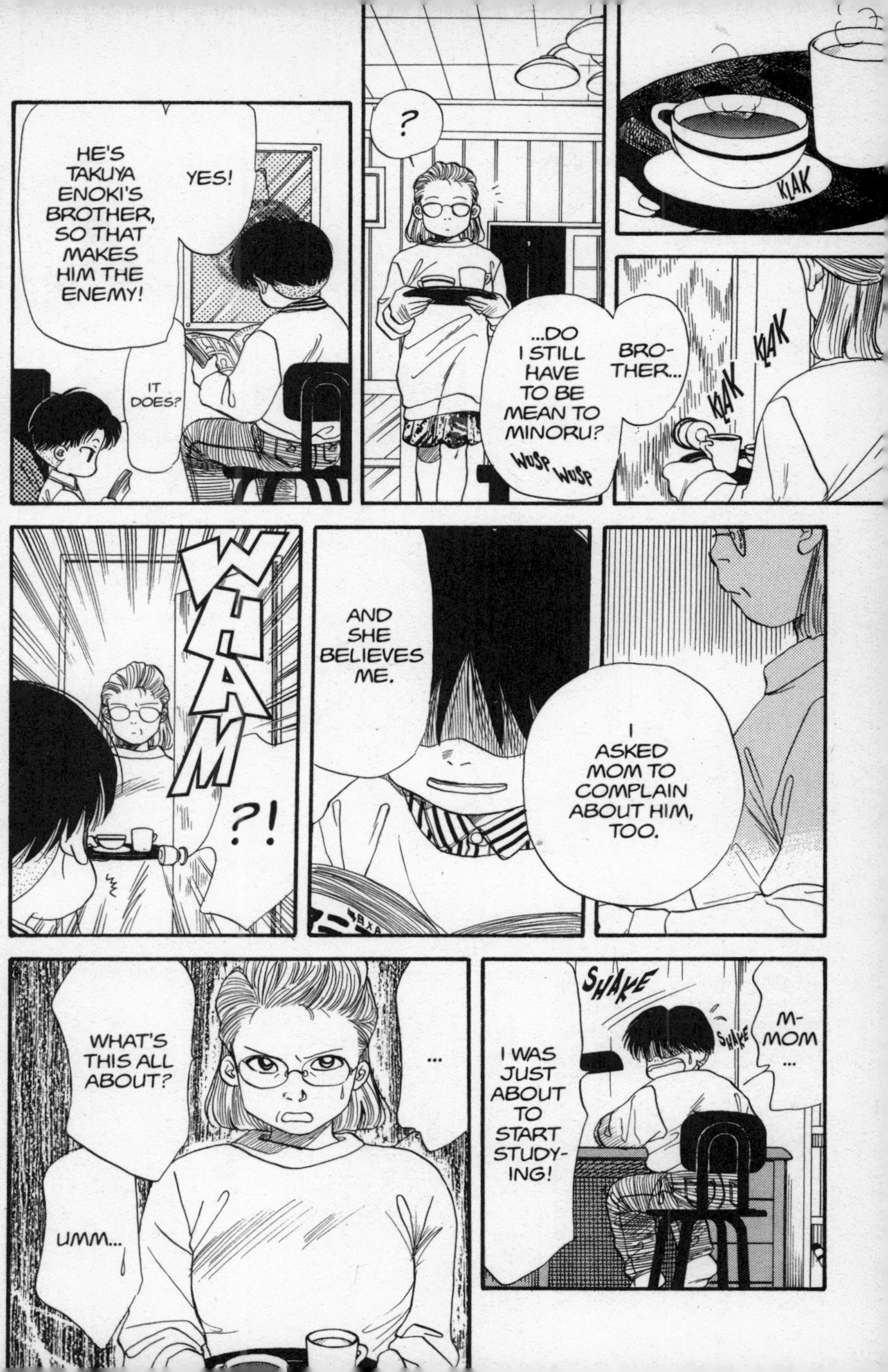
KLAK
BRO-THER...
...DO I STILL HAVE TO BE MEAN TO MINORU?
KLAK KLAK
?
WUSP WUSP
YES!
HE'S TAKUYA ENOKI'S BROTHER, SO THAT MAKES HIM THE ENEMY!
IT DOES?
I ASKED MOM TO COMPLAIN ABOUT HIM, TOO.
AND SHE BELIEVES ME.
WHAM
?!
M-MOM...
SHAKE
SHAKE
I WAS JUST ABOUT TO START STUDY-ING!
...
WHAT'S THIS ALL ABOUT?
UMM...

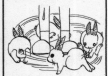

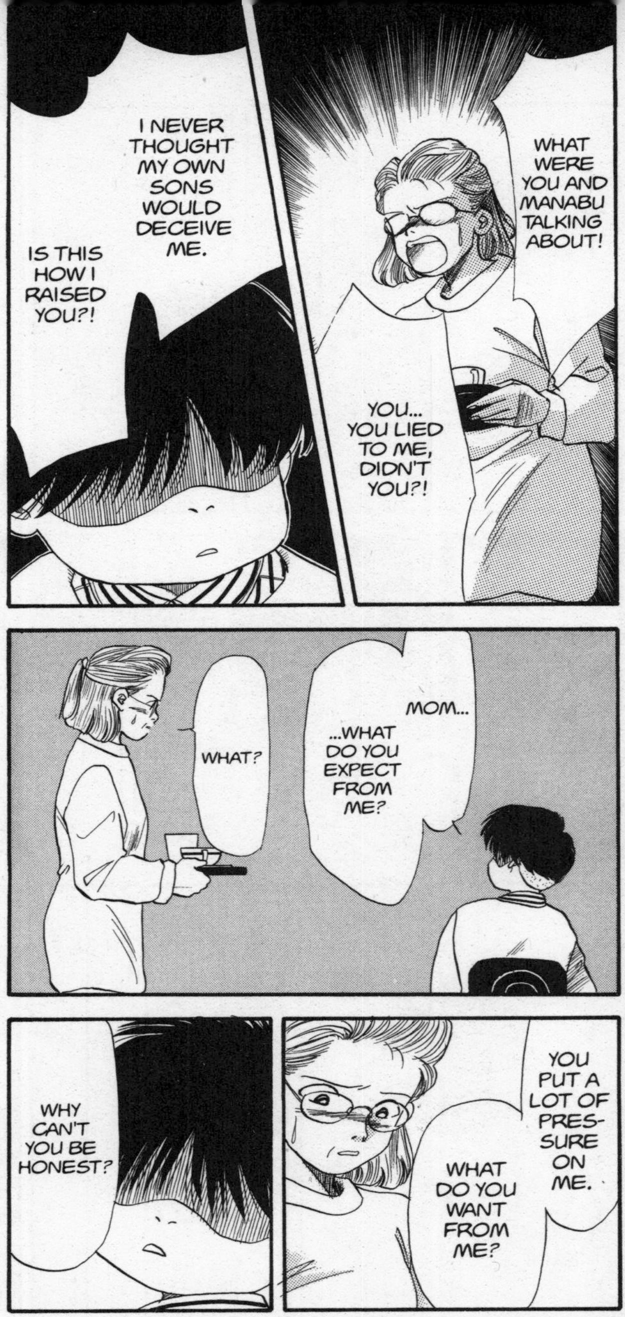
WHAT WERE YOU AND MANABU TALKING ABOUT!
YOU... YOU LIED TO ME, DIDN'T YOU?!
I NEVER THOUGHT MY OWN SONS WOULD DECEIVE ME.
IS THIS HOW I RAISED YOU?!
MOM...
...WHAT DO YOU EXPECT FROM ME?
WHAT?
YOU PUT A LOT OF PRESSURE ON ME.
WHAT DO YOU WANT FROM ME?
WHY CAN'T YOU BE HONEST?

Author's Note Part 4

Yoshizo today.

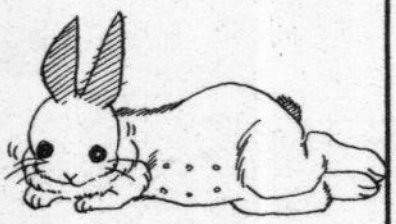

Yoshizo is a rabbit, but she lies down like this. I can see her nipples. That's weird, Yoshizo.

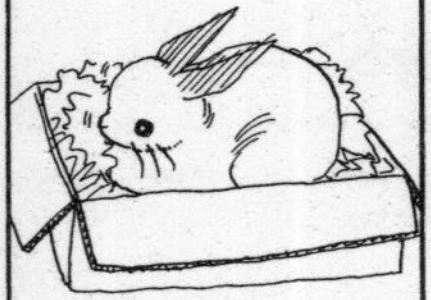

Yoshizo always sits in her litter box. If I can't find her, I just look in her litter box, and there she is.

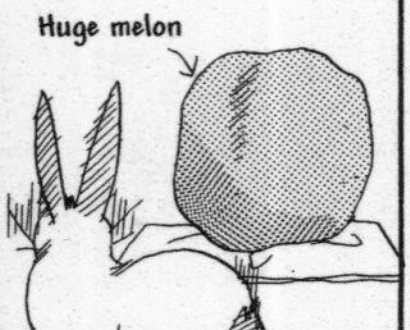
Huge melon

I didn't have any place to put it, so I put this melon on her bed. Yoshizo eyed it with suspicion. I wonder what she was afraid of.

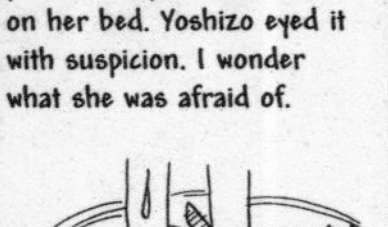

If I leave her alone for a while, she starts running round and round my feet. You're such a pest, Yoshizo.

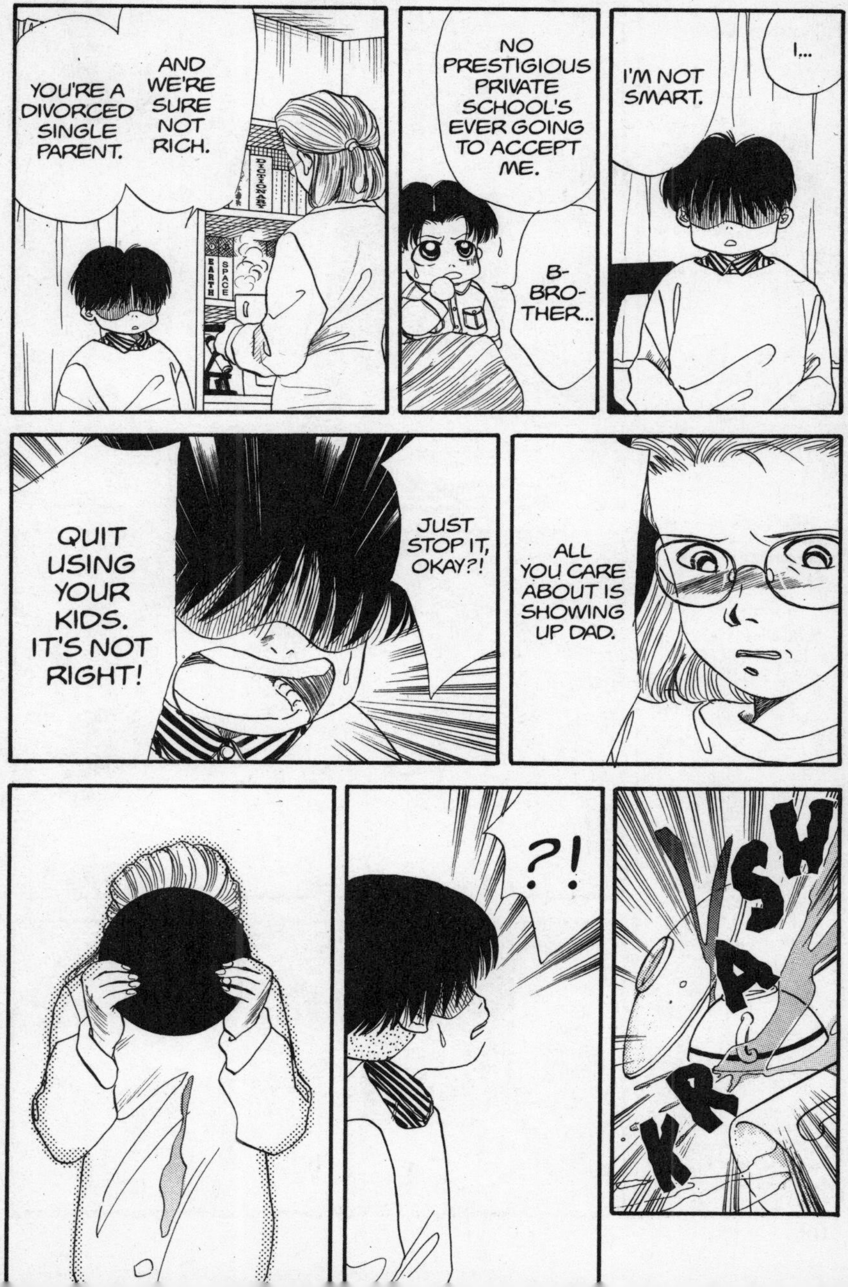
I...
I'M NOT SMART.
NO PRESTIGIOUS PRIVATE SCHOOL'S EVER GOING TO ACCEPT ME.
B-BRO-THER...
YOU'RE A DIVORCED SINGLE PARENT.
AND WE'RE SURE NOT RICH.
ALL YOU CARE ABOUT IS SHOWING UP DAD.
JUST STOP IT, OKAY?!
QUIT USING YOUR KIDS. IT'S NOT RIGHT!
KRASH
?!

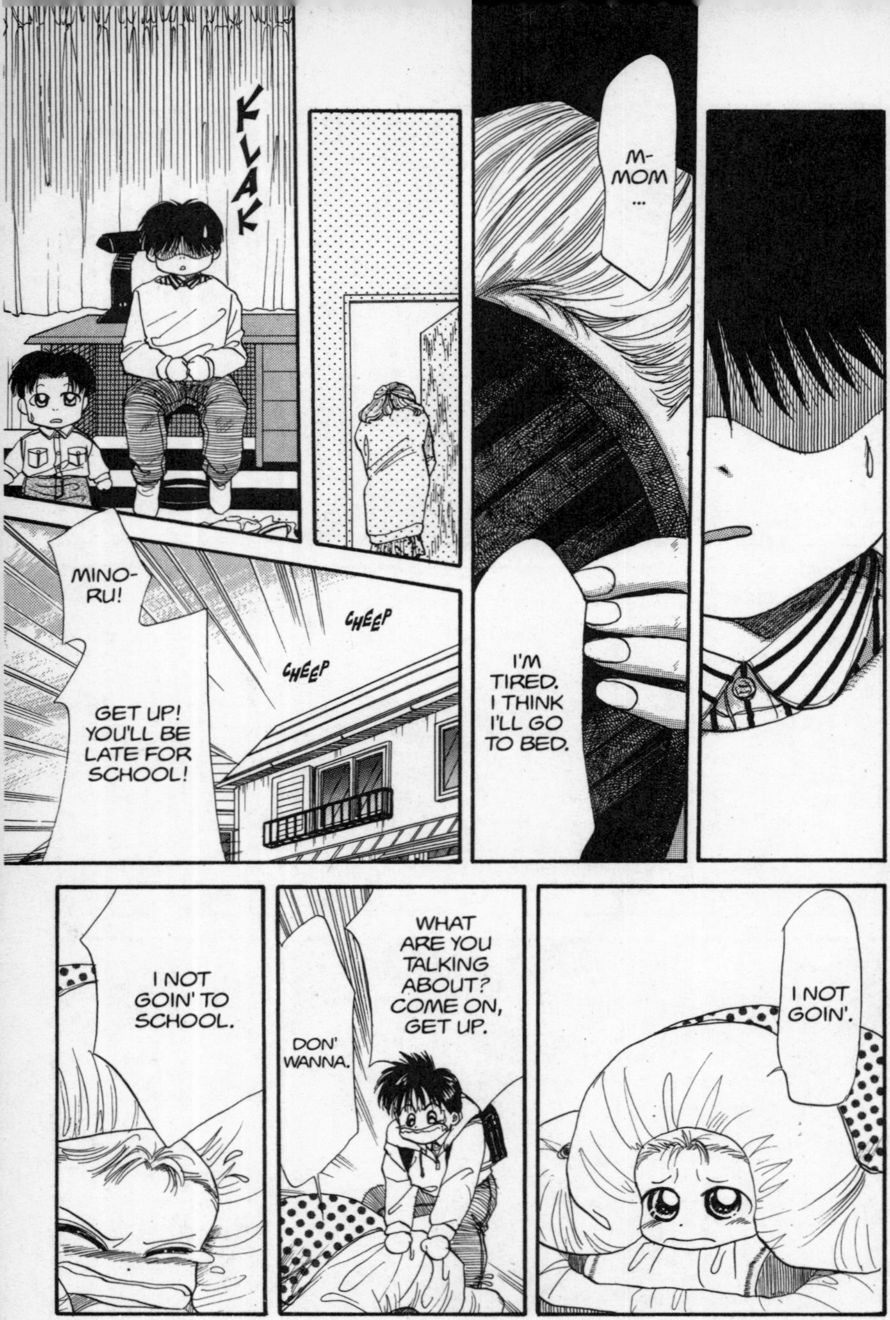
M-
MOM
...
I'M TIRED. I THINK I'LL GO TO BED.
KLAK
MINO-RU!
GET UP! YOU'LL BE LATE FOR SCHOOL!
CHEEP
CHEEP
I NOT GOIN'.
WHAT ARE YOU TALKING ABOUT? COME ON, GET UP.
DON' WANNA.
I NOT GOIN' TO SCHOOL.

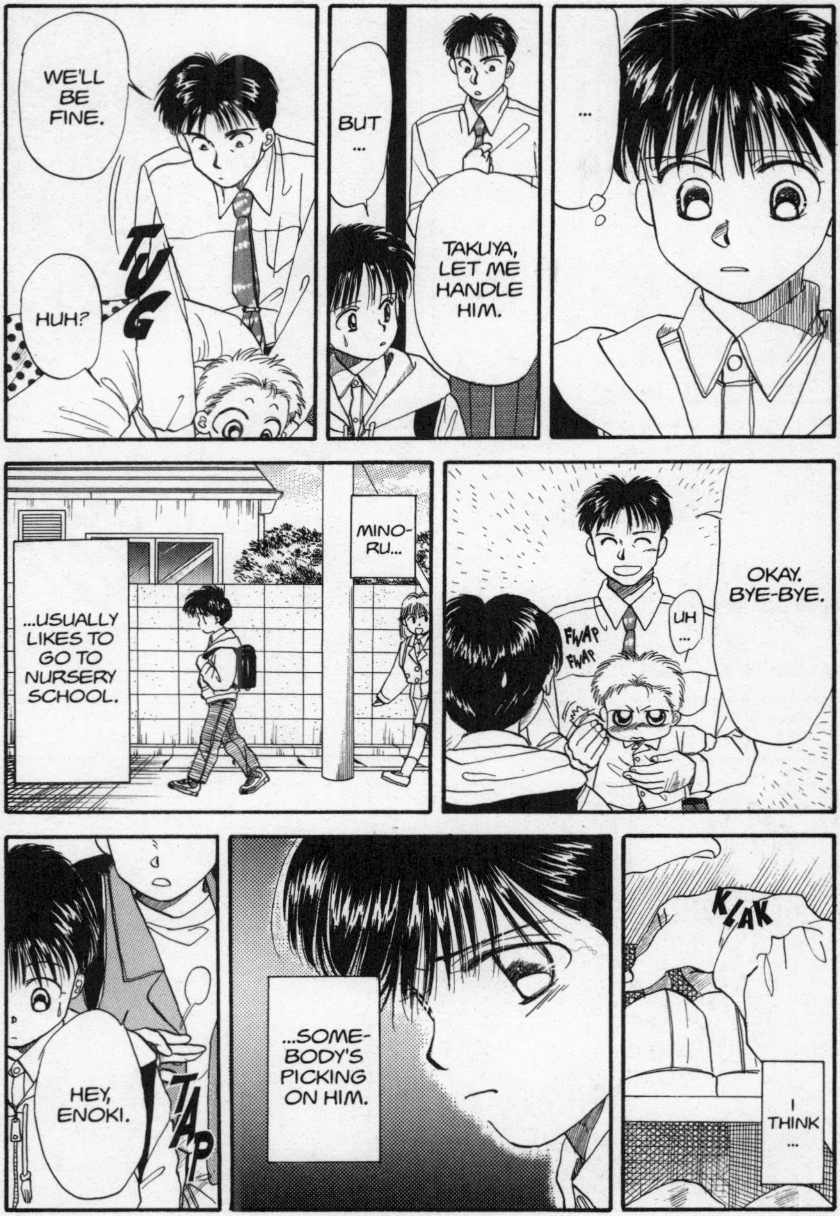
...
BUT ...
TAKUYA, LET ME HANDLE HIM.
WE'LL BE FINE.
TUG
HUH?
OKAY. BYE-BYE.
UH ...
FWAP FWAP
MINO-RU...
...USUALLY LIKES TO GO TO NURSERY SCHOOL.
KLAK
I THINK ...
...SOMEBODY'S PICKING ON HIM.
HEY, ENOKI.
TAP

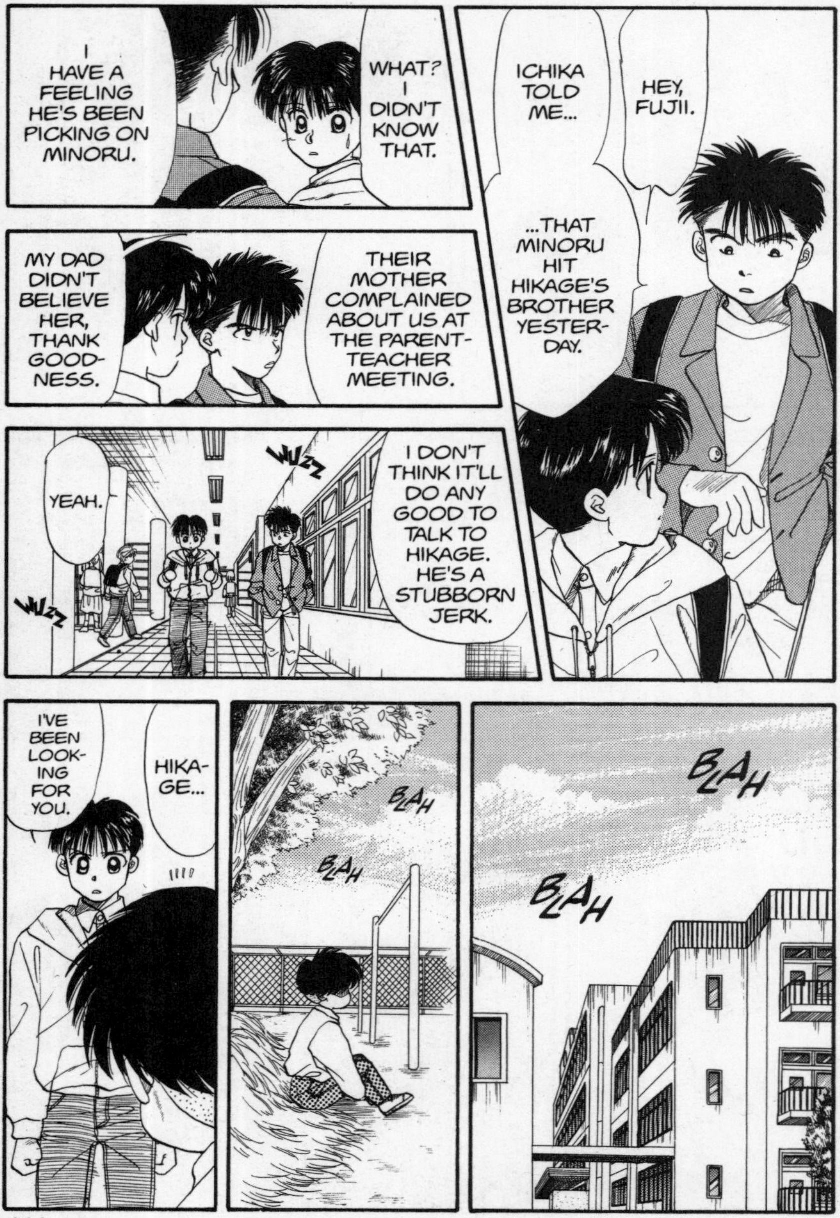
HEY, FUJII.
ICHIKA TOLD ME...
...THAT MINORU HIT HIKAGE'S BROTHER YESTER-DAY.
WHAT? I DIDN'T KNOW THAT.
I HAVE A FEELING HE'S BEEN PICKING ON MINORU.
THEIR MOTHER COMPLAINED ABOUT US AT THE PARENT-TEACHER MEETING.
MY DAD DIDN'T BELIEVE HER, THANK GOOD-NESS.
I DON'T THINK IT'LL DO ANY GOOD TO TALK TO HIKAGE. HE'S A STUBBORN JERK.
WUZZ
YEAH.
WUZZ
BLAH
BLAH
BLAH
BLAH
HIKA-GE...
I'VE BEEN LOOK-ING FOR YOU.

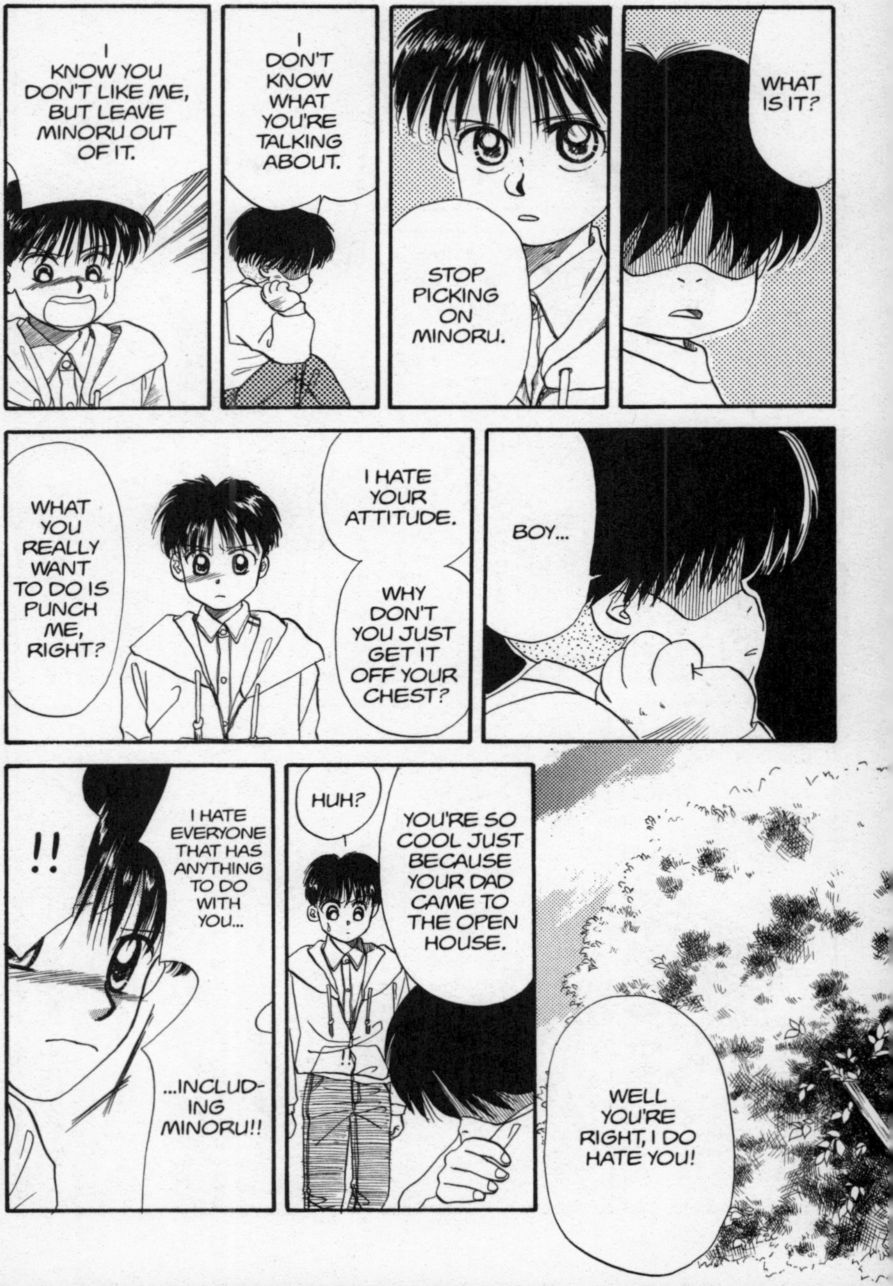
WHAT IS IT?
STOP PICKING ON MINORU.
I DON'T KNOW WHAT YOU'RE TALKING ABOUT.
I KNOW YOU DON'T LIKE ME, BUT LEAVE MINORU OUT OF IT.
BOY...
I HATE YOUR ATTITUDE.
WHY DON'T YOU JUST GET IT OFF YOUR CHEST?
WHAT YOU REALLY WANT TO DO IS PUNCH ME, RIGHT?
WELL YOU'RE RIGHT, I DO HATE YOU!
YOU'RE SO COOL JUST BECAUSE YOUR DAD CAME TO THE OPEN HOUSE.
HUH?
!!
I HATE EVERYONE THAT HAS ANYTHING TO DO WITH YOU...
!!
...INCLUD-ING MINORU!!

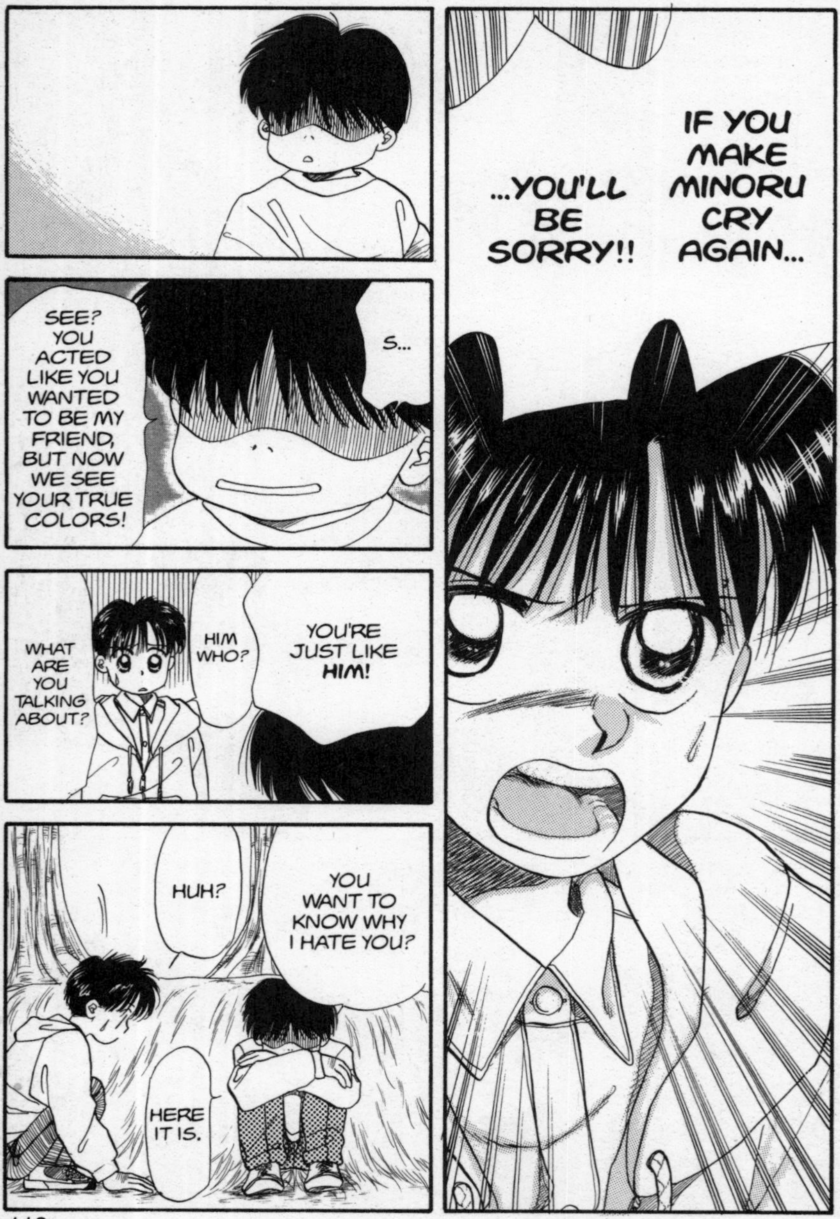
IF YOU MAKE MINORU CRY AGAIN...
...YOU'LL BE SORRY!!
S...
SEE? YOU ACTED LIKE YOU WANTED TO BE MY FRIEND, BUT NOW WE SEE YOUR TRUE COLORS!
YOU'RE JUST LIKE **HIM!**
HIM WHO?
WHAT ARE YOU TALKING ABOUT?
YOU WANT TO KNOW WHY I HATE YOU?
HUH?
HERE IT IS.

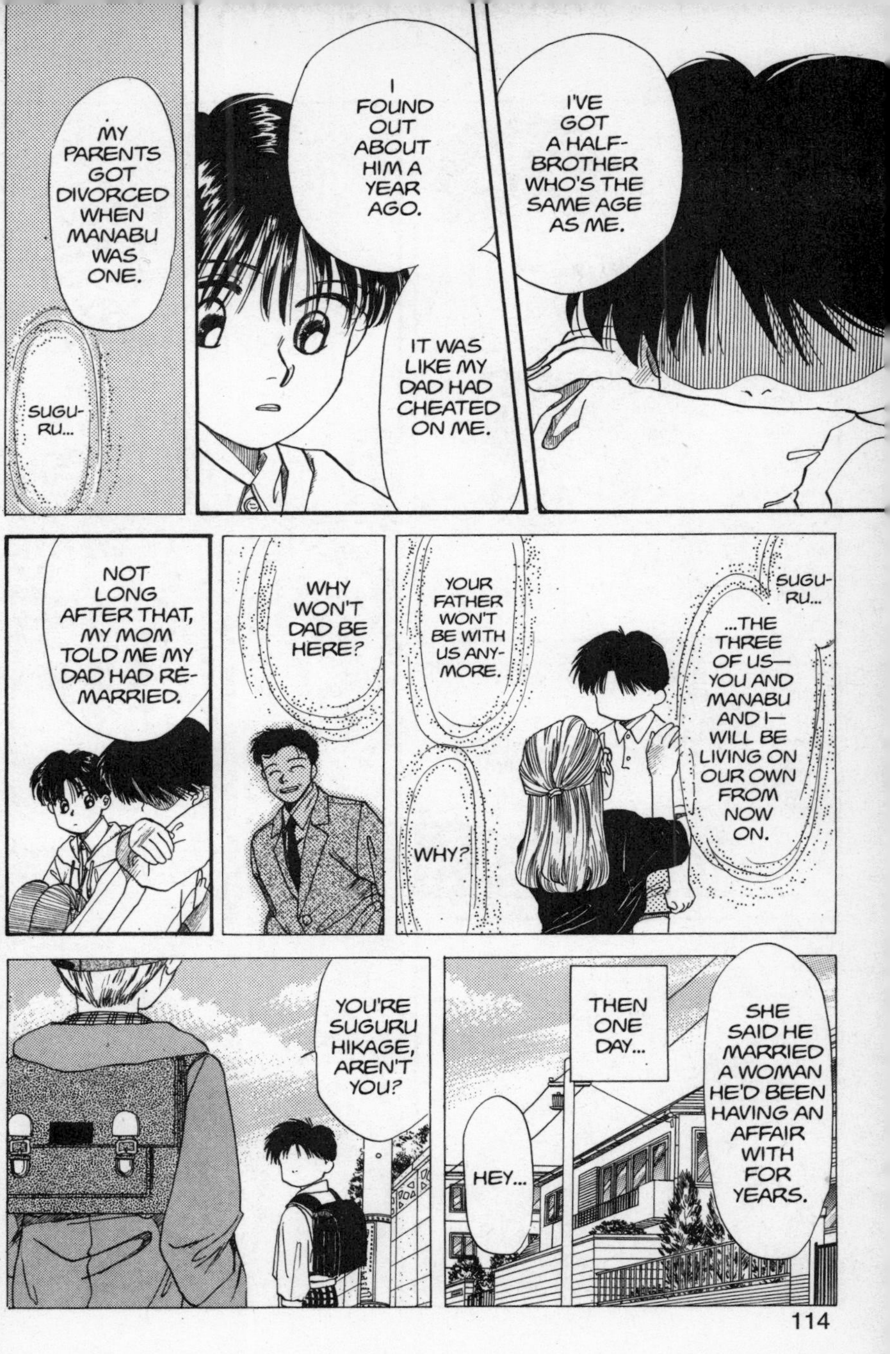
I'VE GOT A HALF-BROTHER WHO'S THE SAME AGE AS ME.
I FOUND OUT ABOUT HIM A YEAR AGO.
IT WAS LIKE MY DAD HAD CHEATED ON ME.
MY PARENTS GOT DIVORCED WHEN MANABU WAS ONE.
SUGU-RU...
SUGU-RU...
...THE THREE OF US— YOU AND MANABU AND I— WILL BE LIVING ON OUR OWN FROM NOW ON.
YOUR FATHER WON'T BE WITH US ANY-MORE.
WHY?
WHY WON'T DAD BE HERE?
NOT LONG AFTER THAT, MY MOM TOLD ME MY DAD HAD RE-MARRIED.
SHE SAID HE MARRIED A WOMAN HE'D BEEN HAVING AN AFFAIR WITH FOR YEARS.
THEN ONE DAY...
HEY...
YOU'RE SUGURU HIKAGE, AREN'T YOU?

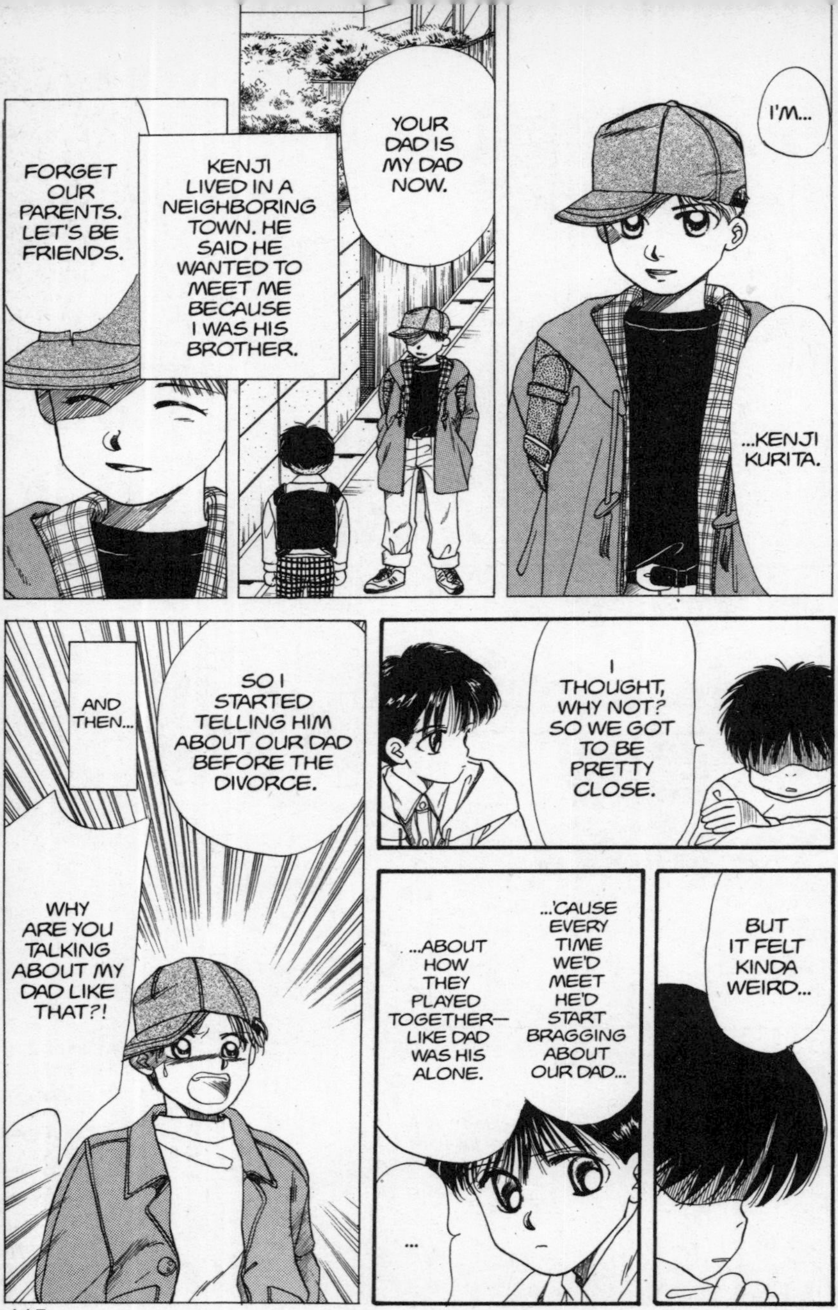
I'M...
...KENJI KURITA.
YOUR DAD IS MY DAD NOW.
KENJI LIVED IN A NEIGHBORING TOWN. HE SAID HE WANTED TO MEET ME BECAUSE I WAS HIS BROTHER.
FORGET OUR PARENTS. LET'S BE FRIENDS.
I THOUGHT, WHY NOT? SO WE GOT TO BE PRETTY CLOSE.
BUT IT FELT KINDA WEIRD...
...'CAUSE EVERY TIME WE'D MEET HE'D START BRAGGING ABOUT OUR DAD...
...ABOUT HOW THEY PLAYED TOGETHER—LIKE DAD WAS HIS ALONE.
...
SO I STARTED TELLING HIM ABOUT OUR DAD BEFORE THE DIVORCE.
AND THEN...
WHY ARE YOU TALKING ABOUT MY DAD LIKE THAT?!

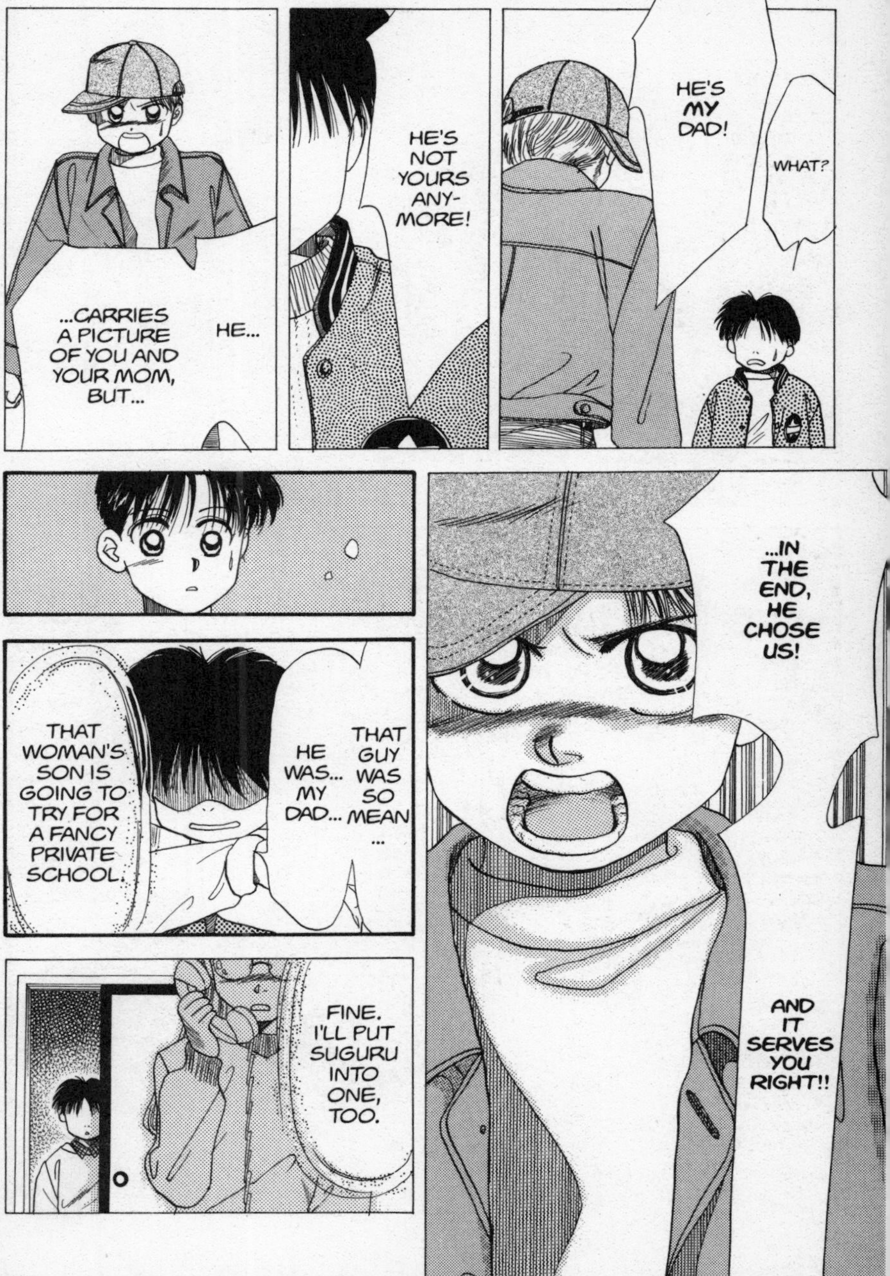
HE'S MY DAD!
WHAT?
HE'S NOT YOURS ANY-MORE!
HE...
...CARRIES A PICTURE OF YOU AND YOUR MOM, BUT...
...IN THE END, HE CHOSE US!
AND IT SERVES YOU RIGHT!!
THAT GUY WAS SO MEAN...
HE WAS... MY DAD...
THAT WOMAN'S SON IS GOING TO TRY FOR A FANCY PRIVATE SCHOOL.
FINE. I'LL PUT SUGURU INTO ONE, TOO.

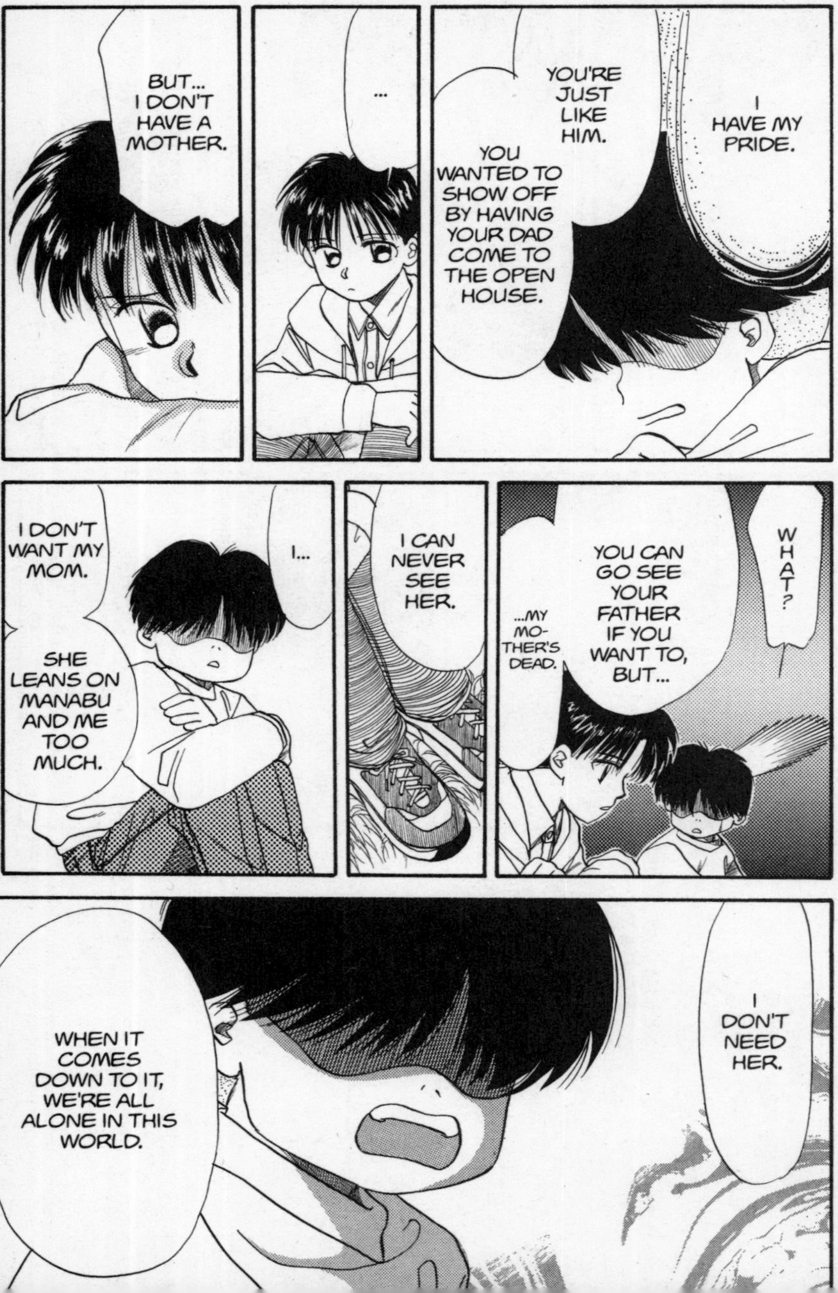
I HAVE MY PRIDE.
YOU'RE JUST LIKE HIM.
YOU WANTED TO SHOW OFF BY HAVING YOUR DAD COME TO THE OPEN HOUSE.
...
BUT... I DON'T HAVE A MOTHER.
WHAT?
YOU CAN GO SEE YOUR FATHER IF YOU WANT TO, BUT...
...MY MOTHER'S DEAD.
I CAN NEVER SEE HER.
I...
I DON'T WANT MY MOM.
SHE LEANS ON MANABU AND ME TOO MUCH.
I DON'T NEED HER.
WHEN IT COMES DOWN TO IT, WE'RE ALL ALONE IN THIS WORLD.

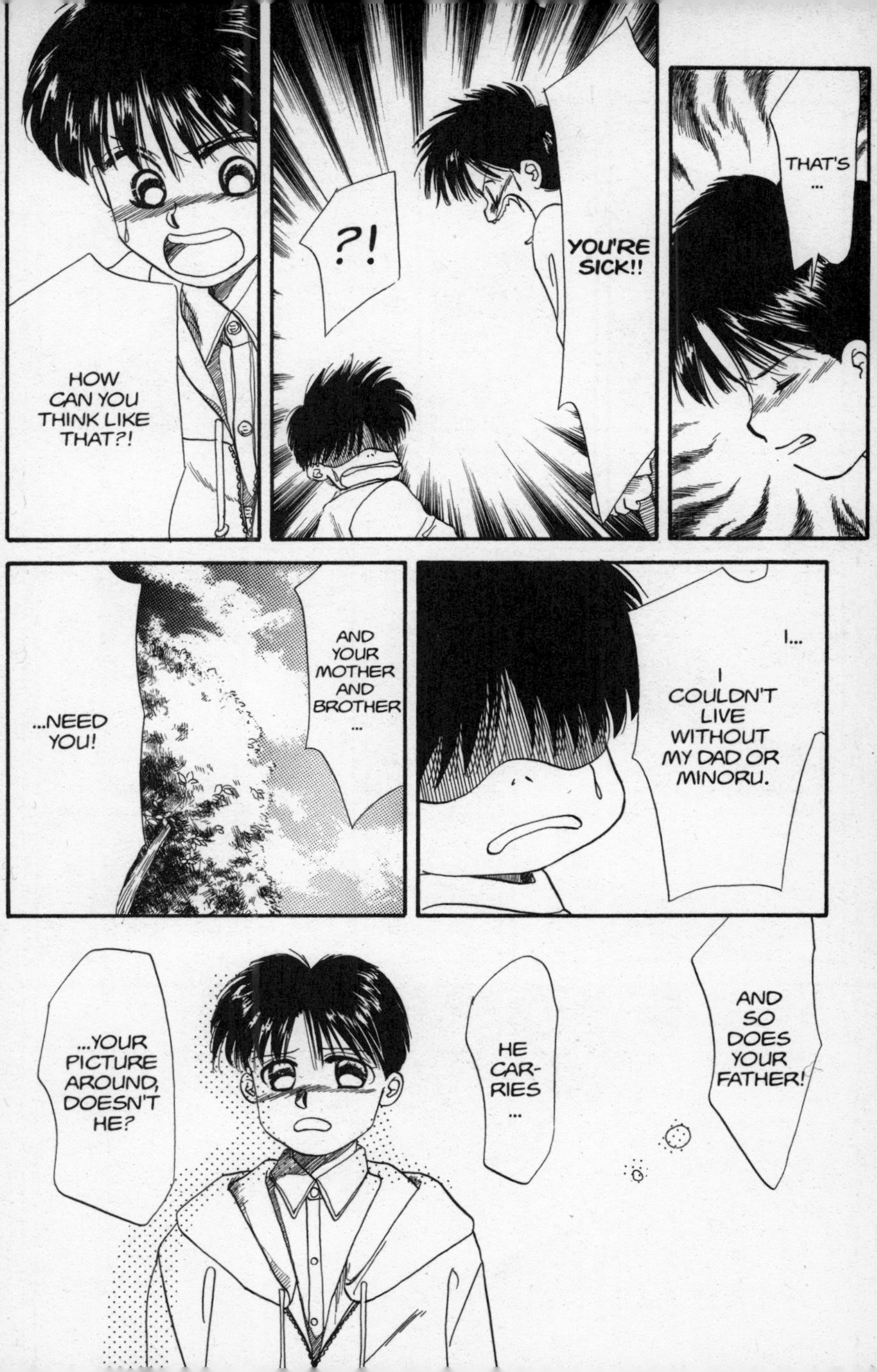
THAT'S ...
YOU'RE SICK!!
?!
HOW CAN YOU THINK LIKE THAT?!
I...
I COULDN'T LIVE WITHOUT MY DAD OR MINORU.
AND YOUR MOTHER AND BROTHER ...
...NEED YOU!
AND SO DOES YOUR FATHER!
HE CAR-RIES ...
...YOUR PICTURE AROUND, DOESN'T HE?

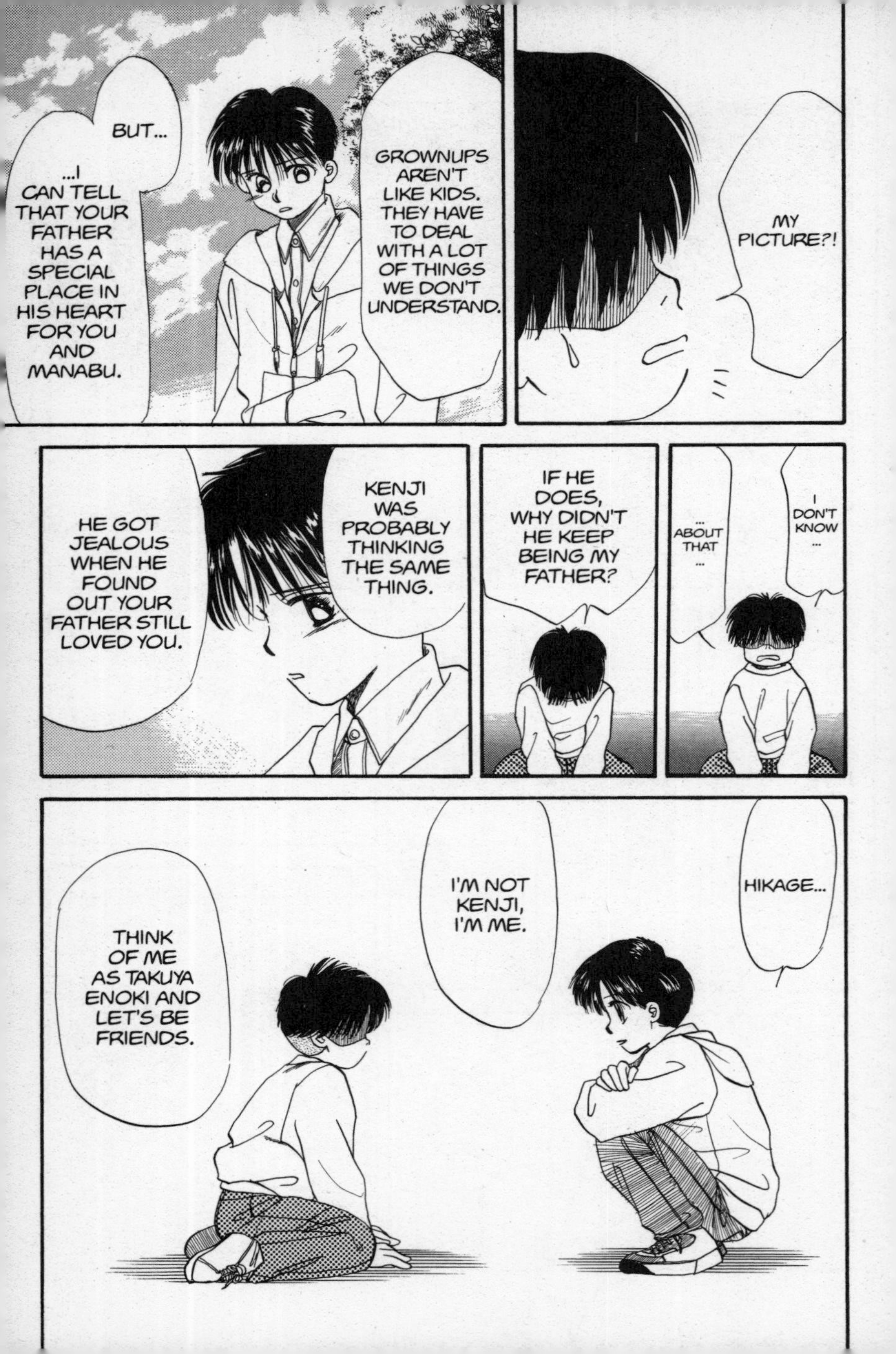
MY PICTURE?!
GROWNUPS AREN'T LIKE KIDS. THEY HAVE TO DEAL WITH A LOT OF THINGS WE DON'T UNDERSTAND.
BUT...
...I CAN TELL THAT YOUR FATHER HAS A SPECIAL PLACE IN HIS HEART FOR YOU AND MANABU.
I DON'T KNOW ...
... ABOUT THAT ...
IF HE DOES, WHY DIDN'T HE KEEP BEING MY FATHER?
KENJI WAS PROBABLY THINKING THE SAME THING.
HE GOT JEALOUS WHEN HE FOUND OUT YOUR FATHER STILL LOVED YOU.
HIKAGE...
I'M NOT KENJI, I'M ME.
THINK OF ME AS TAKUYA ENOKI AND LET'S BE FRIENDS.

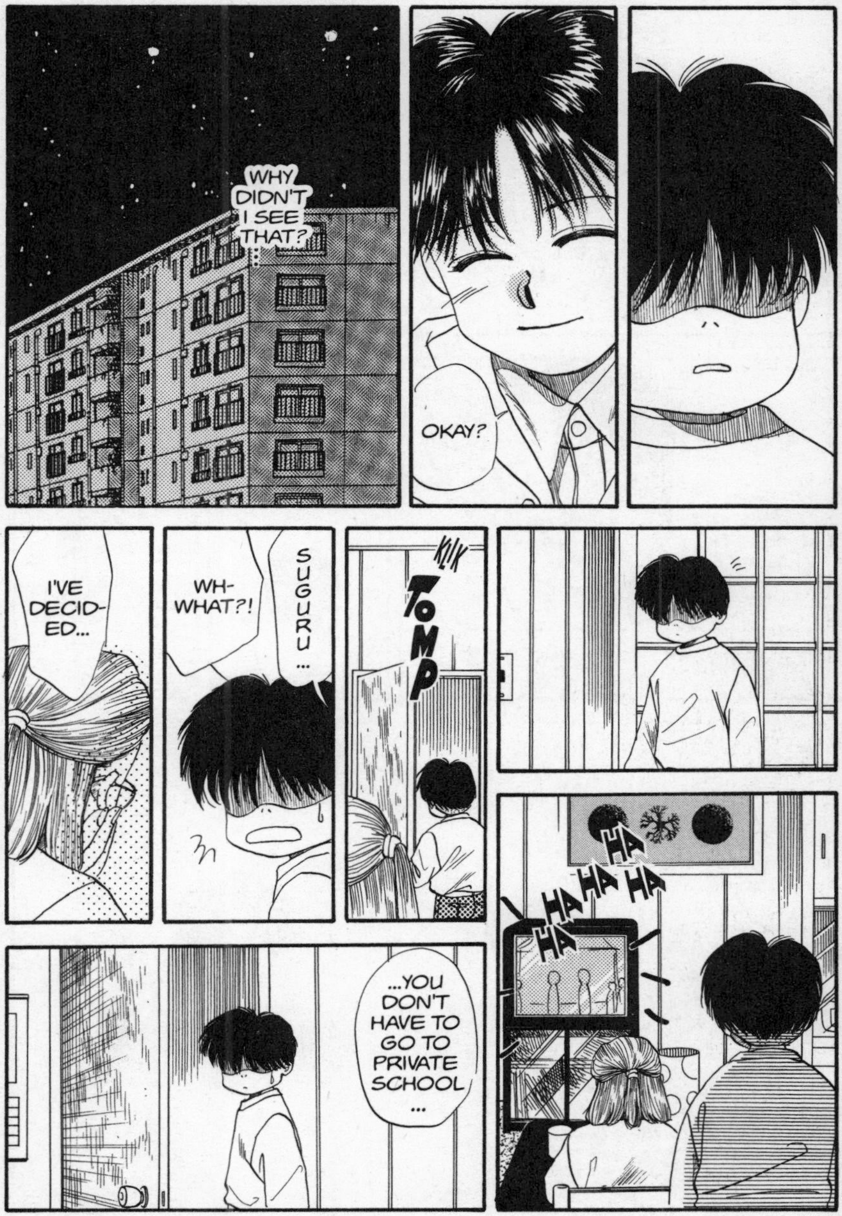
OKAY?
WHY DIDN'T I SEE THAT? ...
KLIK
TOMP
SUGURU ...
WH-WHAT?!
I'VE DECIDED...
HA HA HA HA HA HA
...YOU DON'T HAVE TO GO TO PRIVATE SCHOOL ...

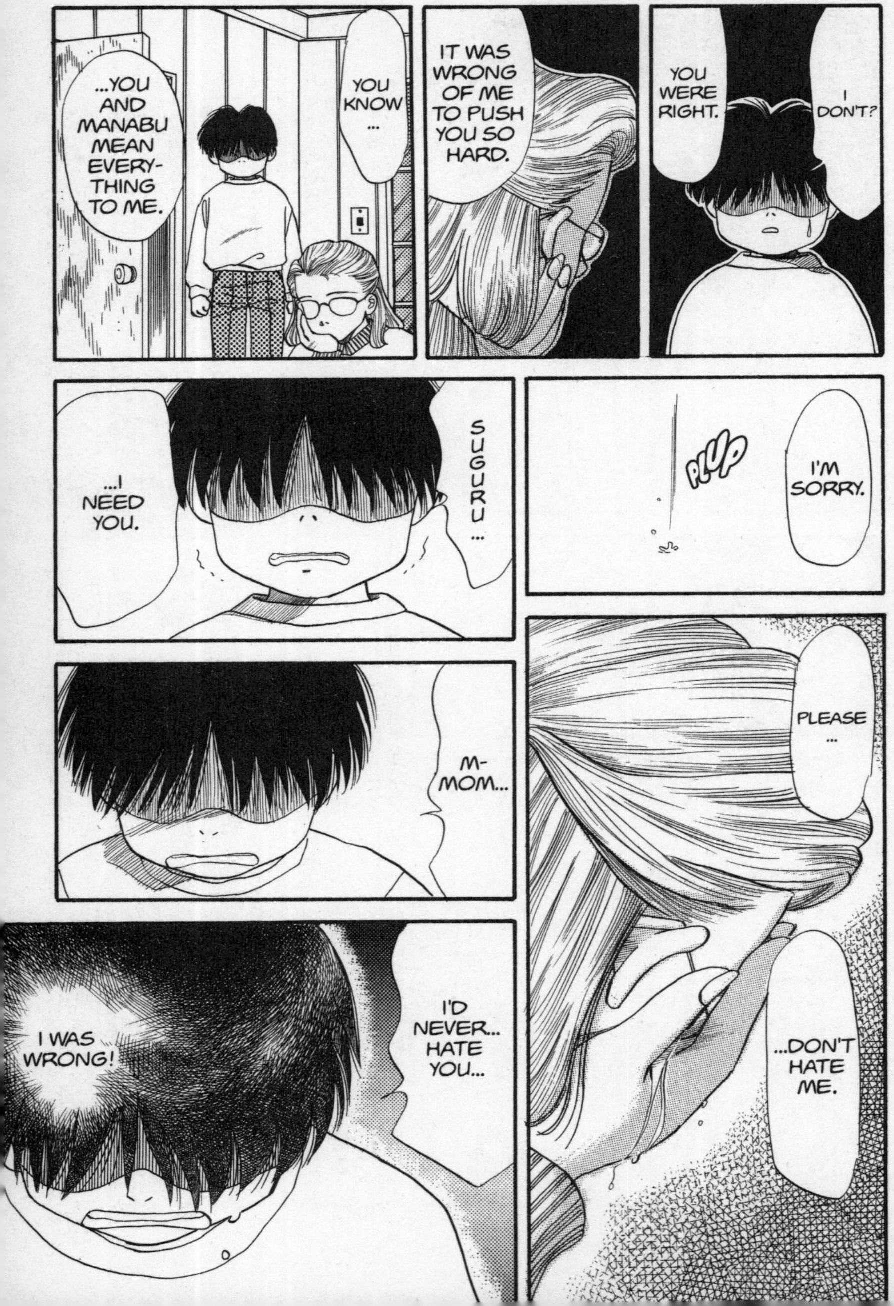
I DON'T?
YOU WERE RIGHT.
IT WAS WRONG OF ME TO PUSH YOU SO HARD.
YOU KNOW ...
...YOU AND MANABU MEAN EVERY-THING TO ME.
PLUP
I'M SORRY.
SUGURU ...
...I NEED YOU.
PLEASE ...
...DON'T HATE ME.
M-MOM...
I'D NEVER... HATE YOU...
I WAS WRONG!

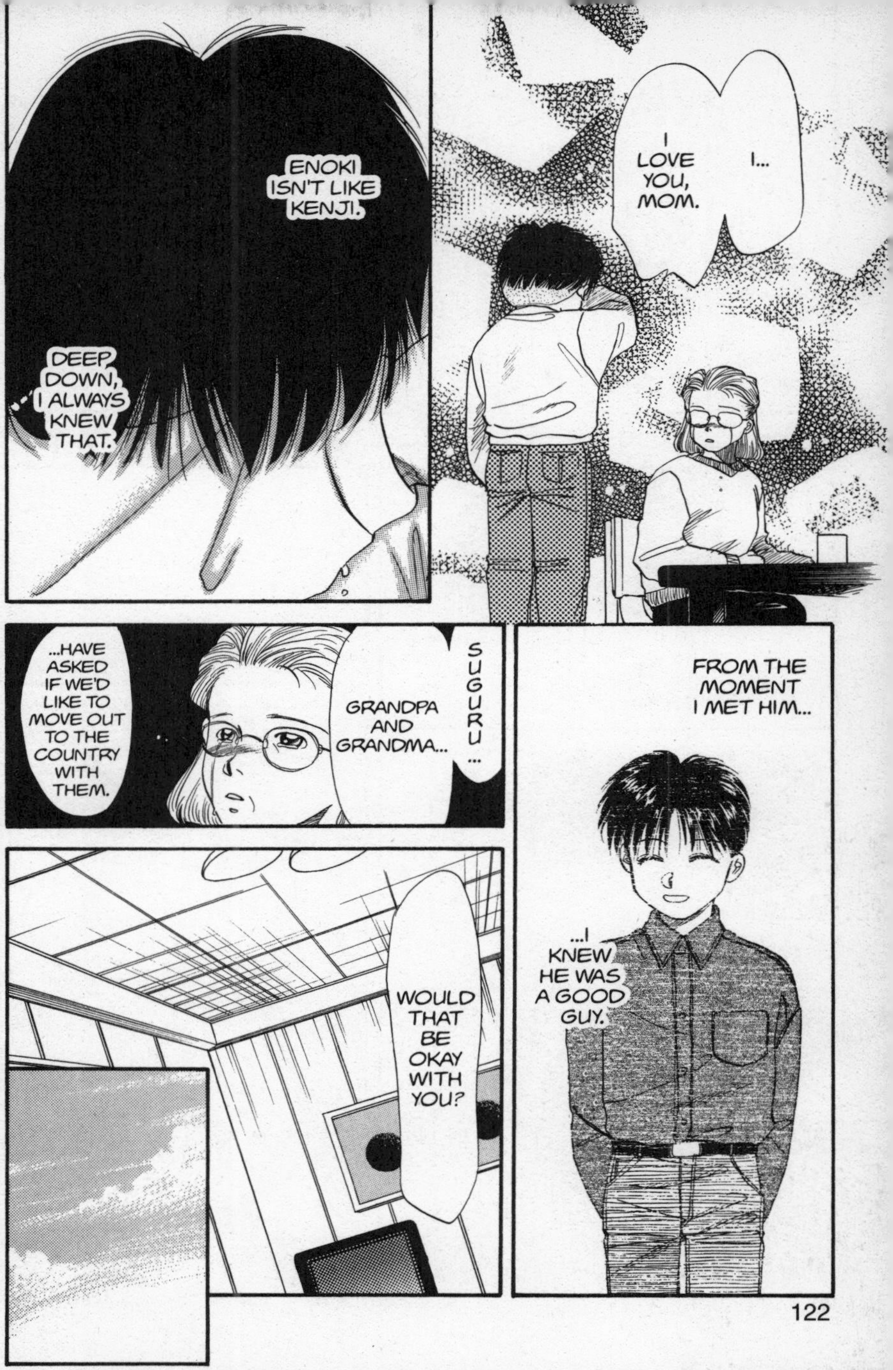
I...
I LOVE YOU, MOM.
ENOKI ISN'T LIKE KENJI.
DEEP DOWN, I ALWAYS KNEW THAT.
FROM THE MOMENT I MET HIM...
...I KNEW HE WAS A GOOD GUY.
SUGURU...
GRANDPA AND GRANDMA...
...HAVE ASKED IF WE'D LIKE TO MOVE OUT TO THE COUNTRY WITH THEM.
WOULD THAT BE OKAY WITH YOU?

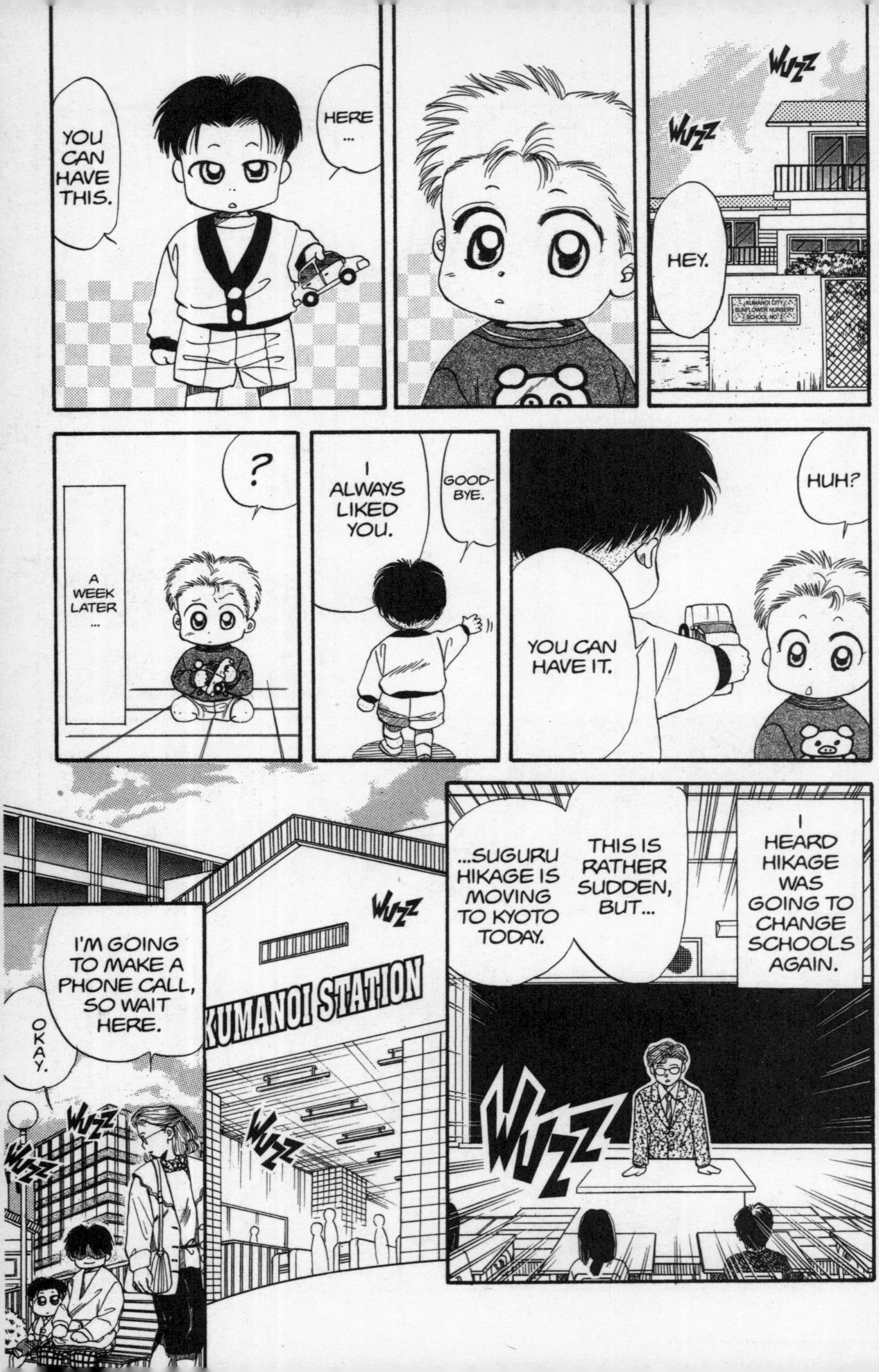
WUZZ
WUZZ
KUMANOI CITY SUNFLOWER NURSERY SCHOOL NO. 2
HEY.
HERE ...
YOU CAN HAVE THIS.
HUH?
YOU CAN HAVE IT.
GOOD-BYE.
I ALWAYS LIKED YOU.
?
A WEEK LATER ...
I HEARD HIKAGE WAS GOING TO CHANGE SCHOOLS AGAIN.
THIS IS RATHER SUDDEN, BUT...
...SUGURU HIKAGE IS MOVING TO KYOTO TODAY.
WUZZ
WUZZ
KUMANOI STATION
I'M GOING TO MAKE A PHONE CALL, SO WAIT HERE.
OKAY.
WUZZ
WUZZ
WUZZ

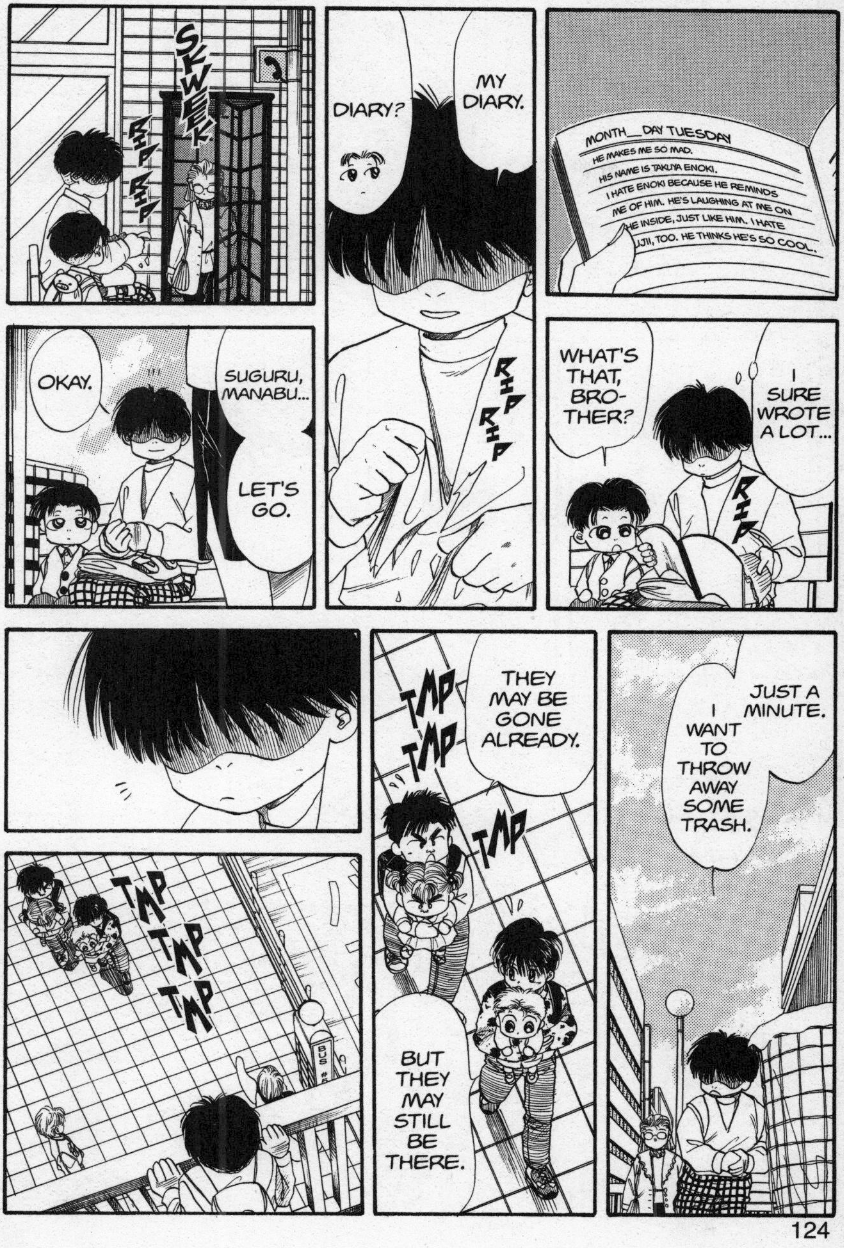

MONTH_ DAY TUESDAY
HE MAKES ME SO MAD.
HIS NAME IS TAKUYA ENOKI.
I HATE ENOKI BECAUSE HE REMINDS
ME OF HIM. HE'S LAUGHING AT ME ON
THE INSIDE, JUST LIKE HIM. I HATE
UJII, TOO. HE THINKS HE'S SO COOL.
I SURE WROTE A LOT...
WHAT'S THAT, BROTHER?
RIP
MY DIARY.
DIARY?
RIP RIP
SKWEEK
RIP RIP
SUGURU, MANABU...
LET'S GO.
OKAY.
JUST A MINUTE.
I WANT TO THROW AWAY SOME TRASH.
THEY MAY BE GONE ALREADY.
TMP TMP
TMP
BUT THEY MAY STILL BE THERE.
TMP TMP TMP TMP

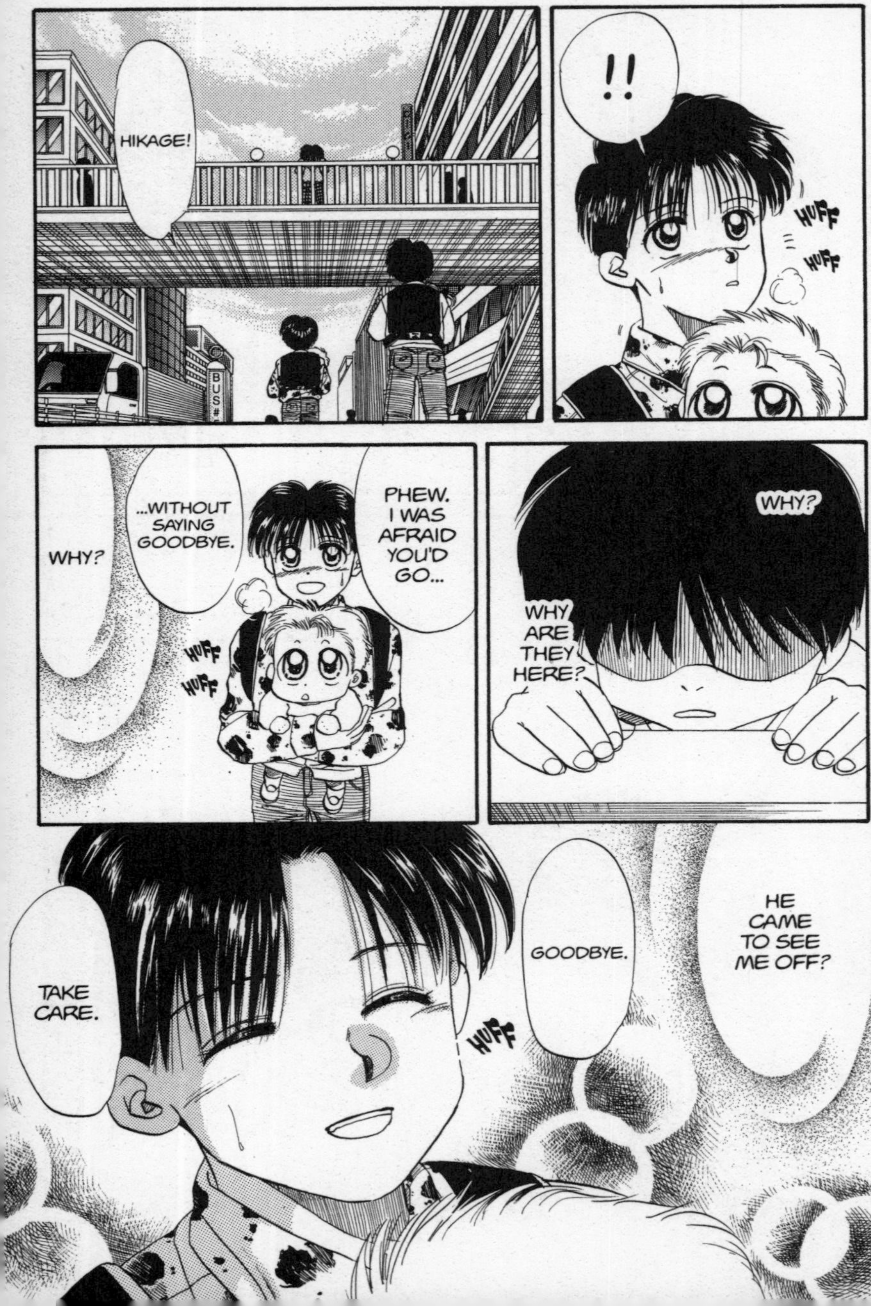
!!
HUFF
HUFF
HIKAGE!
WHY?
WHY ARE THEY HERE?
PHEW. I WAS AFRAID YOU'D GO...
...WITHOUT SAYING GOODBYE.
WHY?
HUFF
HUFF
HE CAME TO SEE ME OFF?
GOODBYE.
HUFF
TAKE CARE.

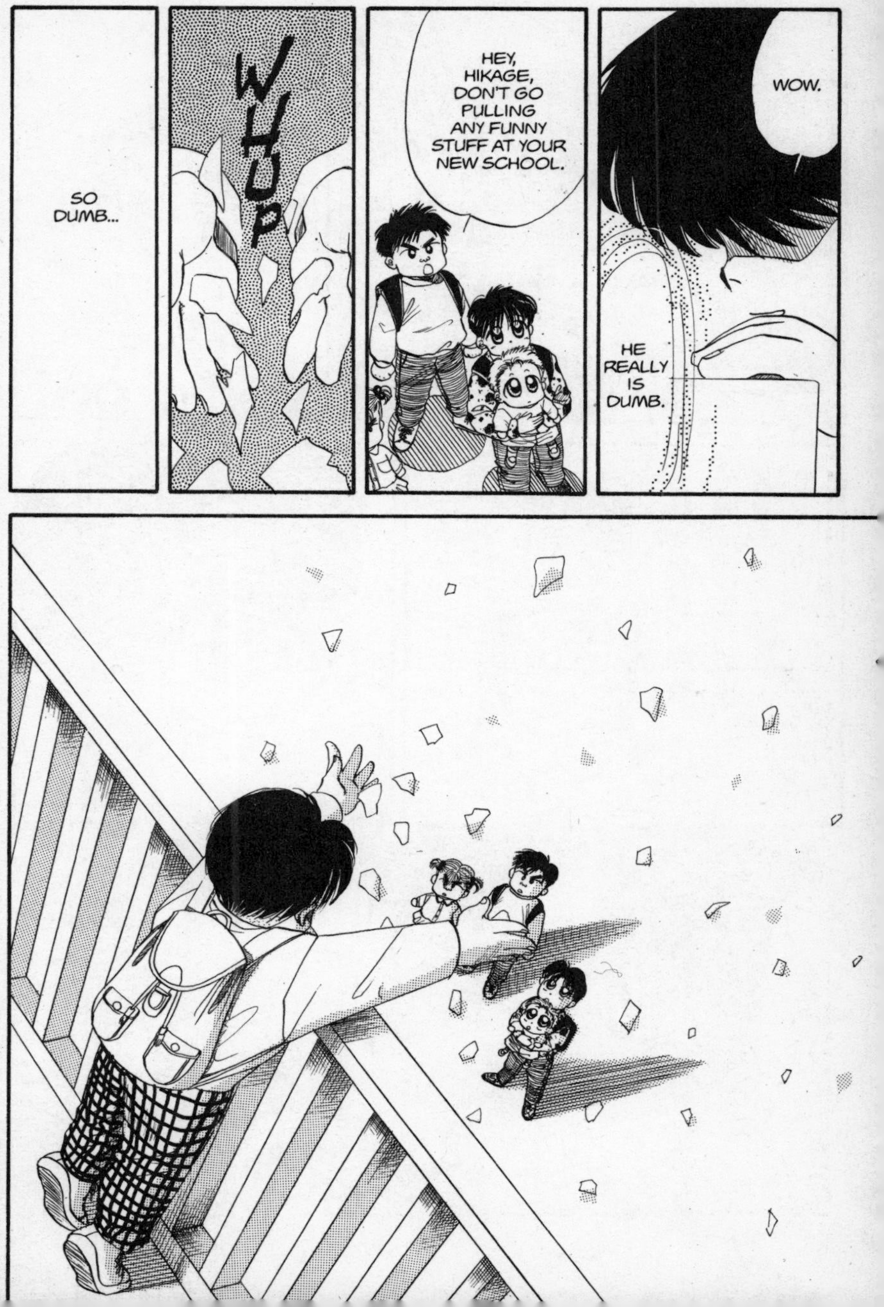
WOW.
HE REALLY IS DUMB.
HEY, HIKAGE, DON'T GO PULLING ANY FUNNY STUFF AT YOUR NEW SCHOOL.
WHUP
SO DUMB...

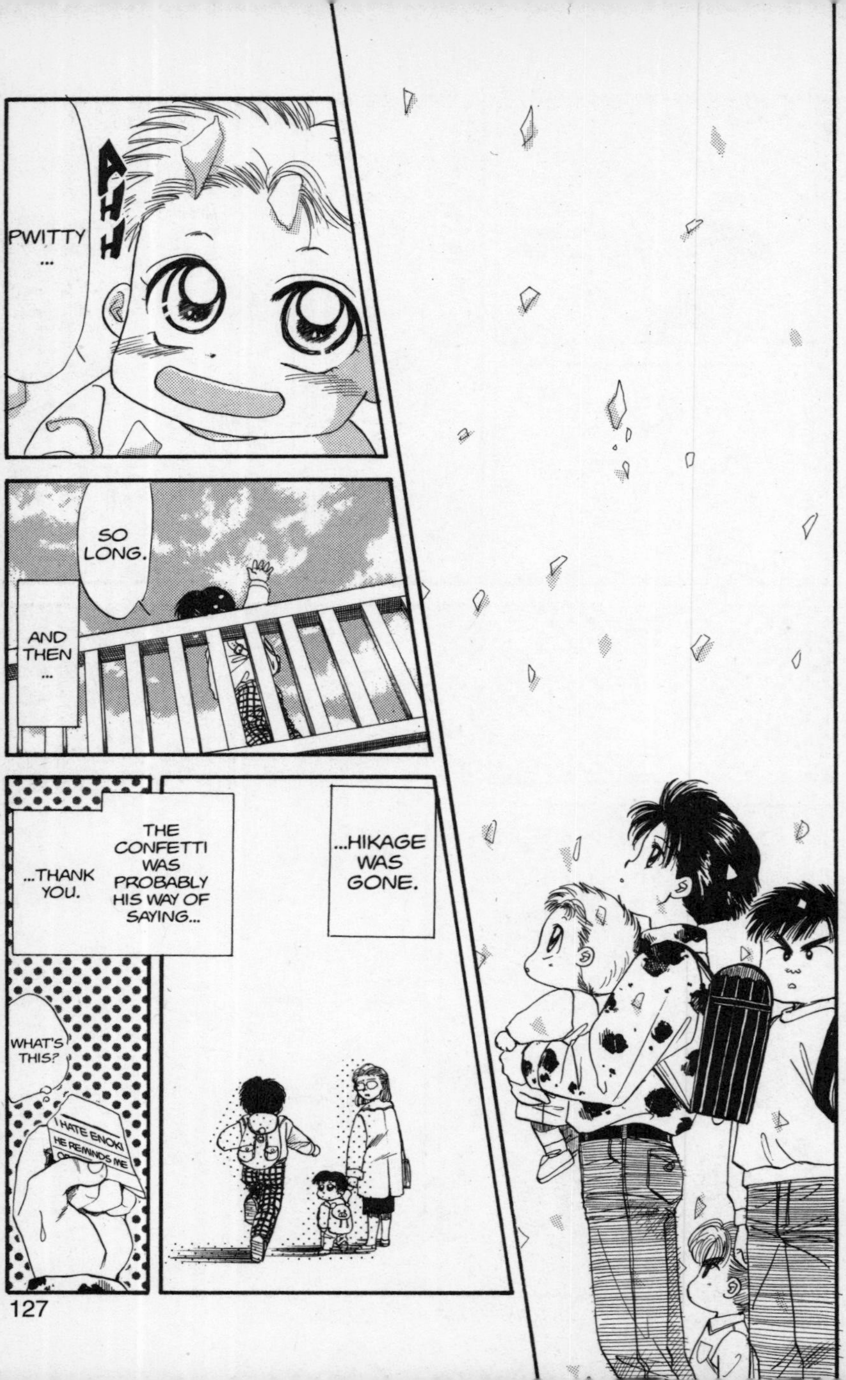
AHH
PWITTY ...
SO LONG.
AND THEN ...
...HIKAGE WAS GONE.
THE CONFETTI WAS PROBABLY HIS WAY OF SAYING...
...THANK YOU.
WHAT'S THIS?
I HATE ENOKI HE REMINDS ME

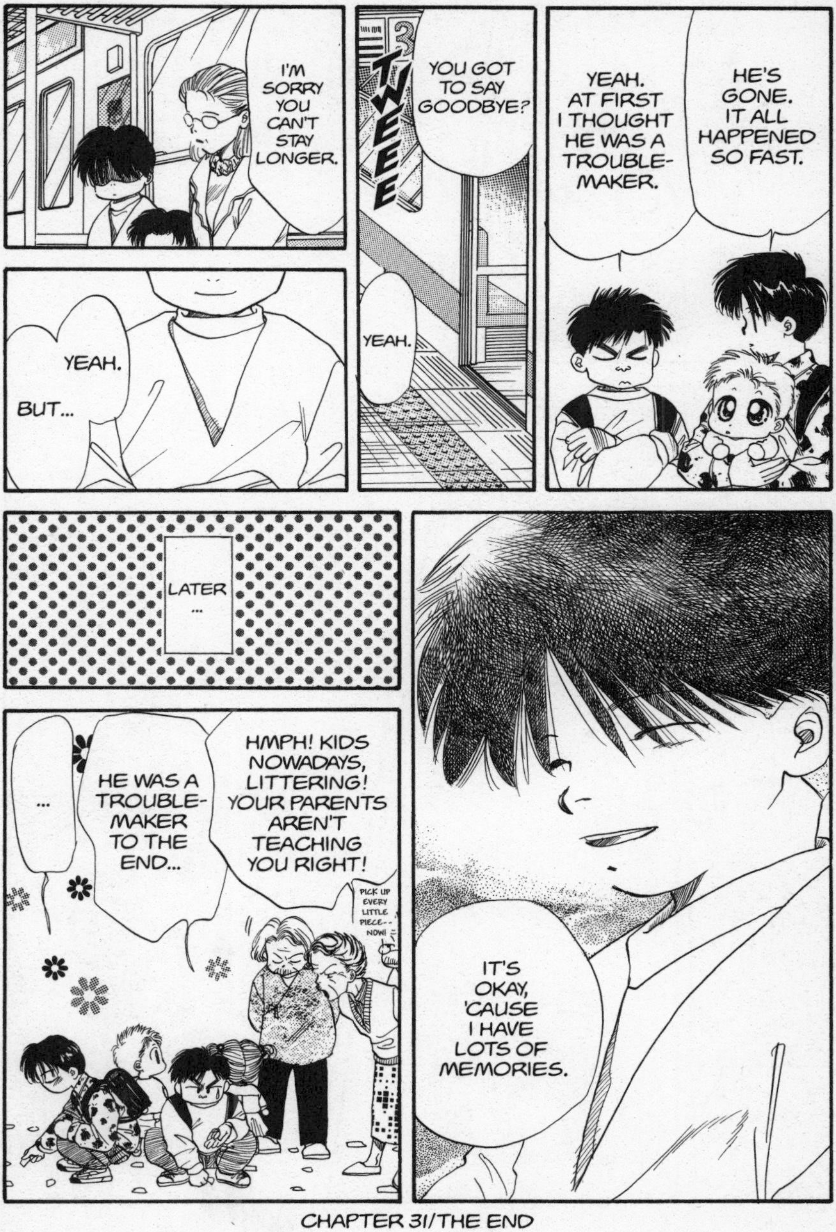
HE'S GONE. IT ALL HAPPENED SO FAST.
YEAH. AT FIRST I THOUGHT HE WAS A TROUBLE-MAKER.
3
TWEEE
YOU GOT TO SAY GOODBYE?
YEAH.
I'M SORRY YOU CAN'T STAY LONGER.
YEAH.
BUT...
IT'S OKAY, 'CAUSE I HAVE LOTS OF MEMORIES.
LATER ...
HMPH! KIDS NOWADAYS, LITTERING! YOUR PARENTS AREN'T TEACHING YOU RIGHT!
PICK UP EVERY LITTLE PIECE--NOW!
HE WAS A TROUBLE-MAKER TO THE END...
...

CHAPTER 31/THE END

Baby & Me

Chapter 32

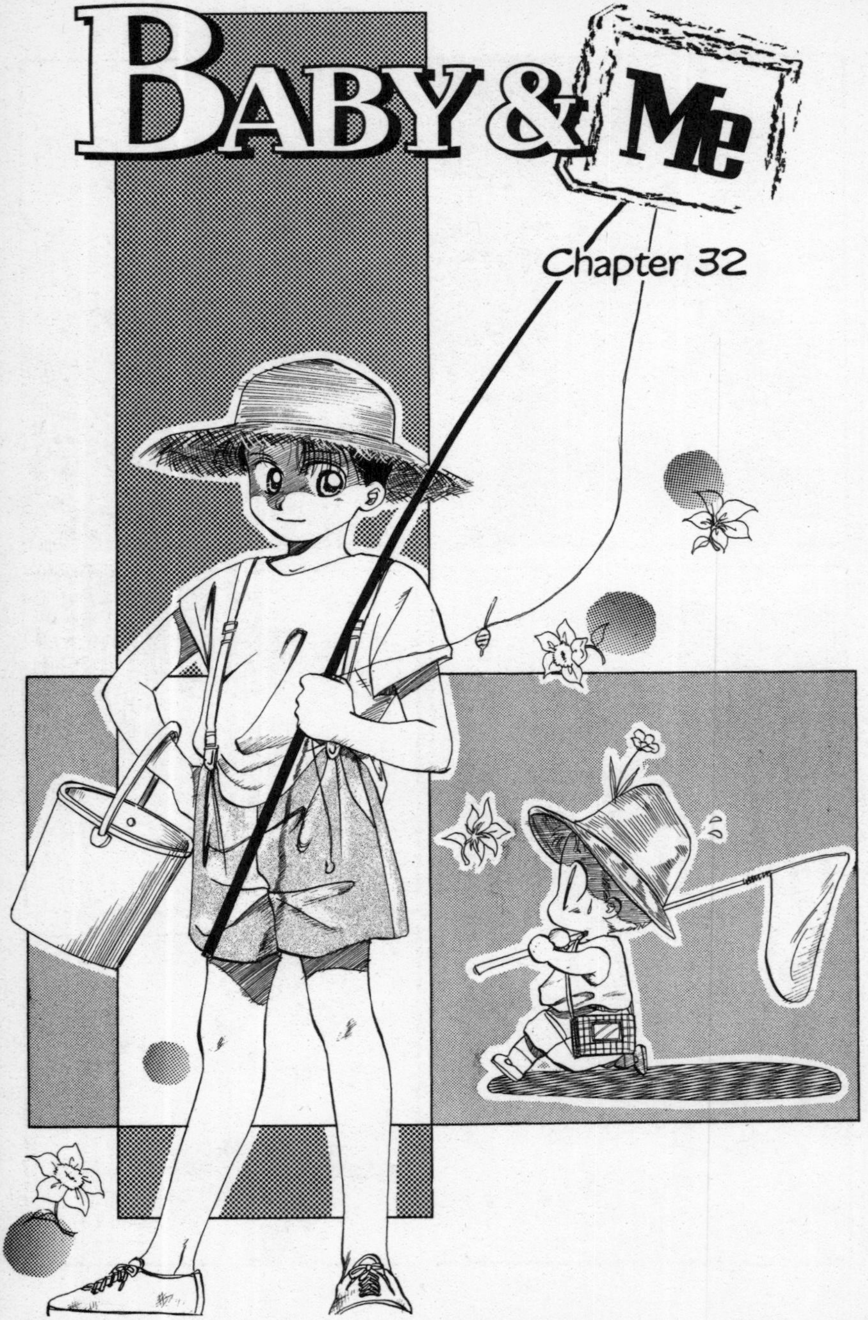

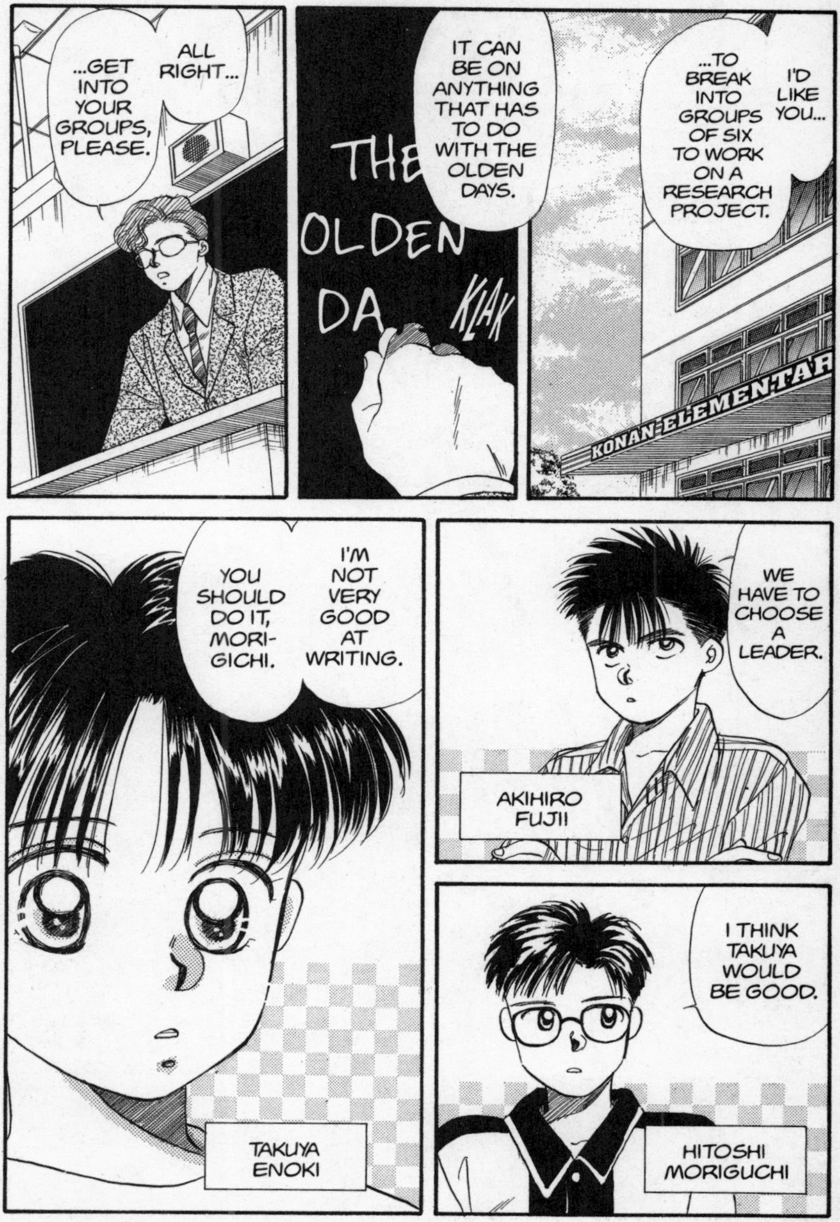
I'D LIKE YOU...
...TO BREAK INTO GROUPS OF SIX TO WORK ON A RESEARCH PROJECT.
KONAN ELEMENTAR
IT CAN BE ON ANYTHING THAT HAS TO DO WITH THE OLDEN DAYS.
THE OLDEN DA
KLAK
ALL RIGHT...
...GET INTO YOUR GROUPS, PLEASE.
WE HAVE TO CHOOSE A LEADER.
AKIHIRO FUJII
I THINK TAKUYA WOULD BE GOOD.
HITOSHI MORIGUCHI
I'M NOT VERY GOOD AT WRITING.
YOU SHOULD DO IT, MORI-GICHI.
TAKUYA ENOKI

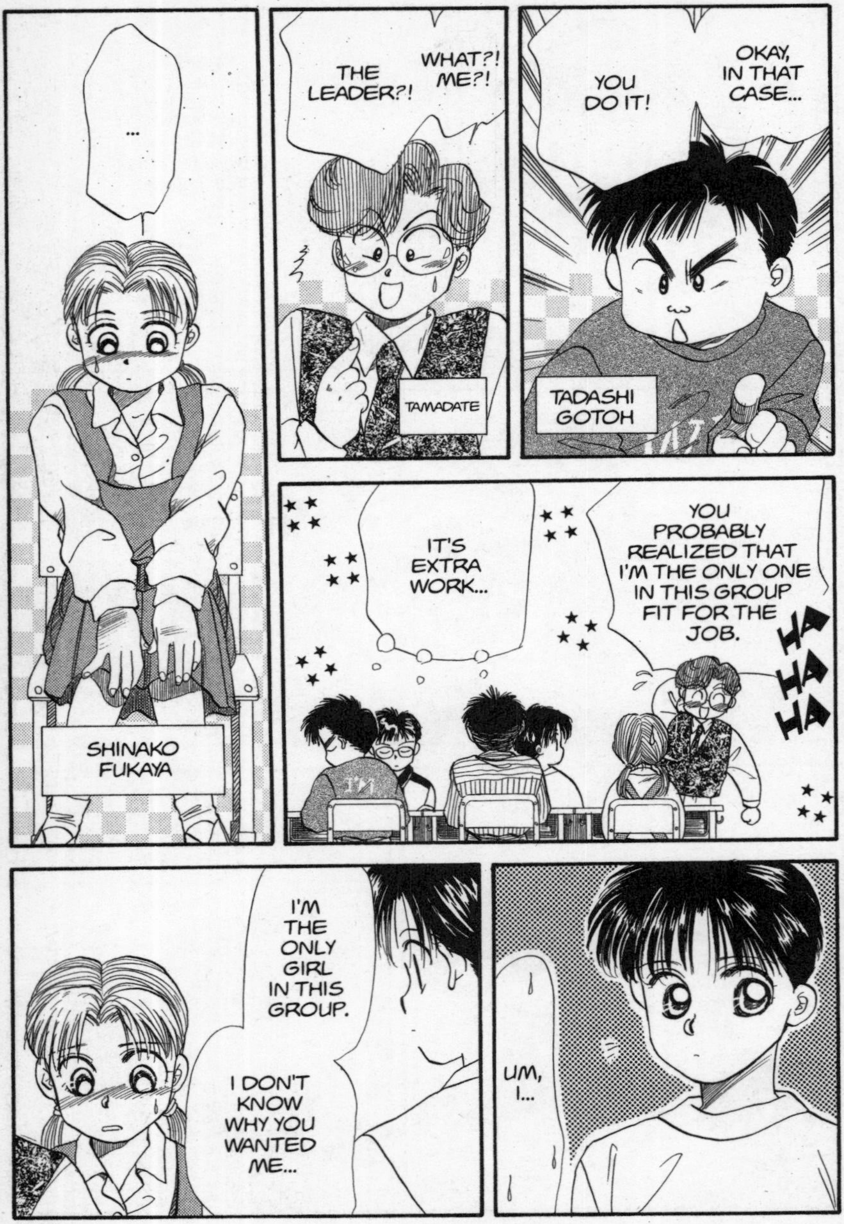
OKAY, IN THAT CASE...
YOU DO IT!
TADASHI GOTOH
WHAT?! ME?!
THE LEADER?!
TAMADATE
YOU PROBABLY REALIZED THAT I'M THE ONLY ONE IN THIS GROUP FIT FOR THE JOB.
HA HA HA
IT'S EXTRA WORK...
...
SHINAKO FUKAYA
UM, I...
I'M THE ONLY GIRL IN THIS GROUP.
I DON'T KNOW WHY YOU WANTED ME...

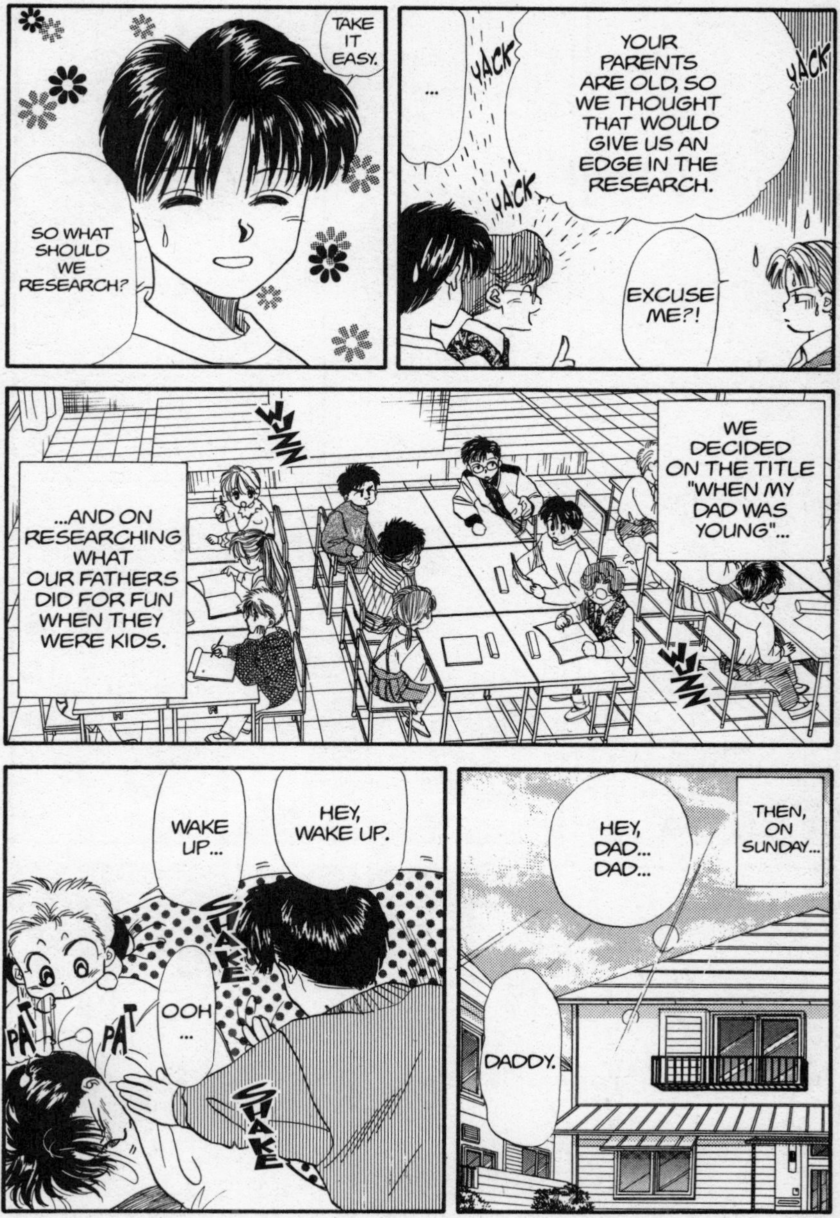
YACK
YOUR PARENTS ARE OLD, SO WE THOUGHT THAT WOULD GIVE US AN EDGE IN THE RESEARCH.
YACK
...
YACK
EXCUSE ME?!
TAKE IT EASY.
SO WHAT SHOULD WE RESEARCH?
WE DECIDED ON THE TITLE "WHEN MY DAD WAS YOUNG"...
WUNN
...AND ON RESEARCHING WHAT OUR FATHERS DID FOR FUN WHEN THEY WERE KIDS.
WUNN
THEN, ON SUNDAY...
HEY, DAD... DAD...
DADDY.
HEY, WAKE UP.
WAKE UP...
SHAKE
OOH ...
PAT
PAT
SHAKE

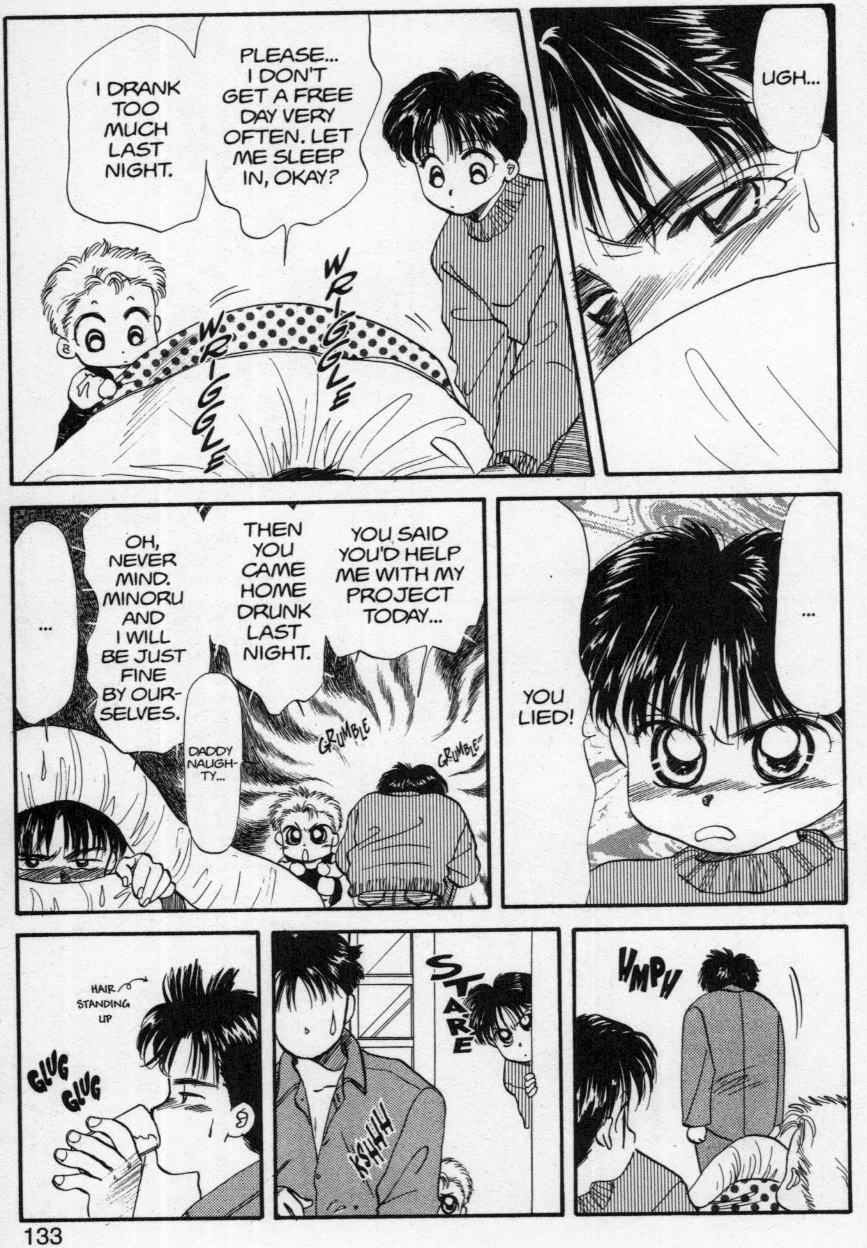
UGH...
PLEASE... I DON'T GET A FREE DAY VERY OFTEN. LET ME SLEEP IN, OKAY?
I DRANK TOO MUCH LAST NIGHT.
WRIGGLE
WRIGGLE
...
YOU LIED!
YOU SAID YOU'D HELP ME WITH MY PROJECT TODAY...
THEN YOU CAME HOME DRUNK LAST NIGHT.
OH, NEVER MIND. MINORU AND I WILL BE JUST FINE BY OURSELVES.
...
GRUMBLE
GRUMBLE
DADDY NAUGHTY...
HMPH
STARE
KSHHH
HAIR STANDING UP
GLUG GLUG

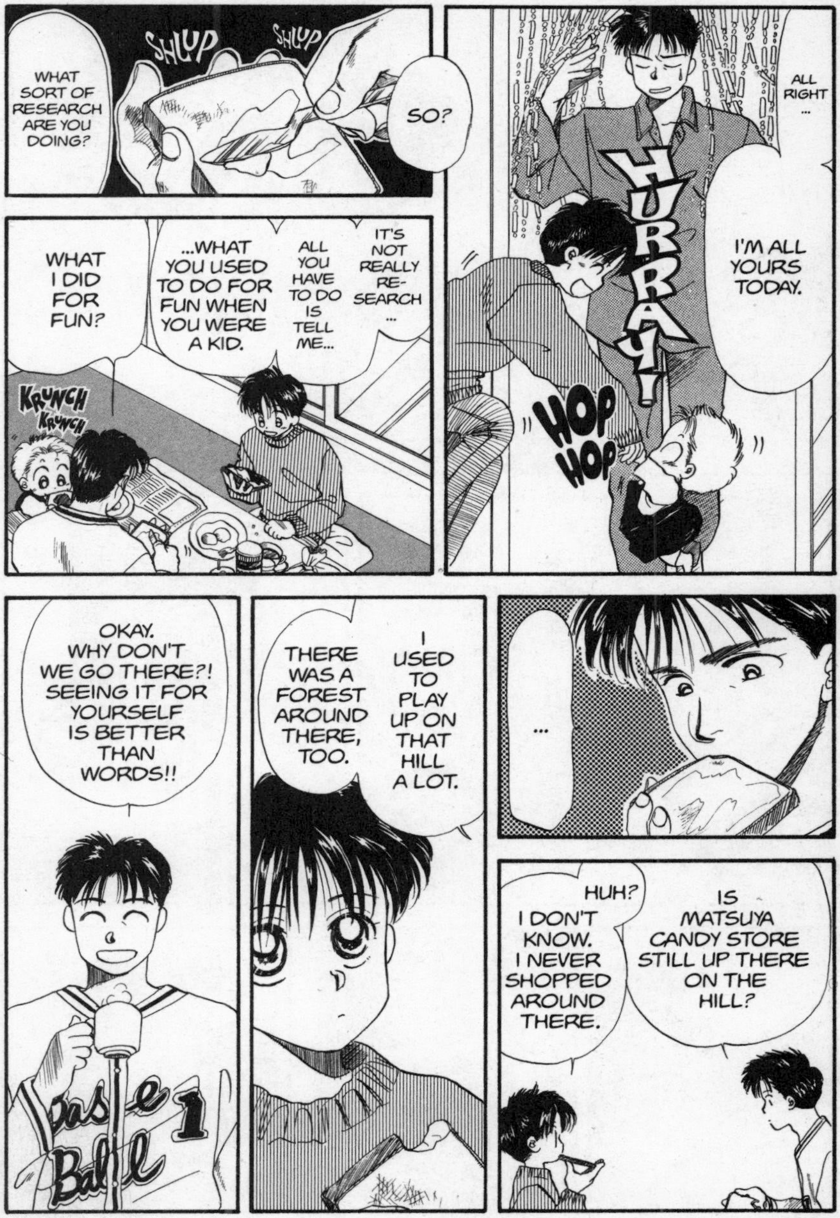
ALL RIGHT ...
I'M ALL YOURS TODAY.
HURRAY!
HOP HOP
SHLUP SHLUP
SO?
WHAT SORT OF RESEARCH ARE YOU DOING?
IT'S NOT REALLY RE-SEARCH ...
ALL YOU HAVE TO DO IS TELL ME...
...WHAT YOU USED TO DO FOR FUN WHEN YOU WERE A KID.
WHAT I DID FOR FUN?
KRUNCH KRUNCH
...
IS MATSUYA CANDY STORE STILL UP THERE ON THE HILL?
HUH? I DON'T KNOW. I NEVER SHOPPED AROUND THERE.
I USED TO PLAY UP ON THAT HILL A LOT.
THERE WAS A FOREST AROUND THERE, TOO.
OKAY. WHY DON'T WE GO THERE?! SEEING IT FOR YOURSELF IS BETTER THAN WORDS!!

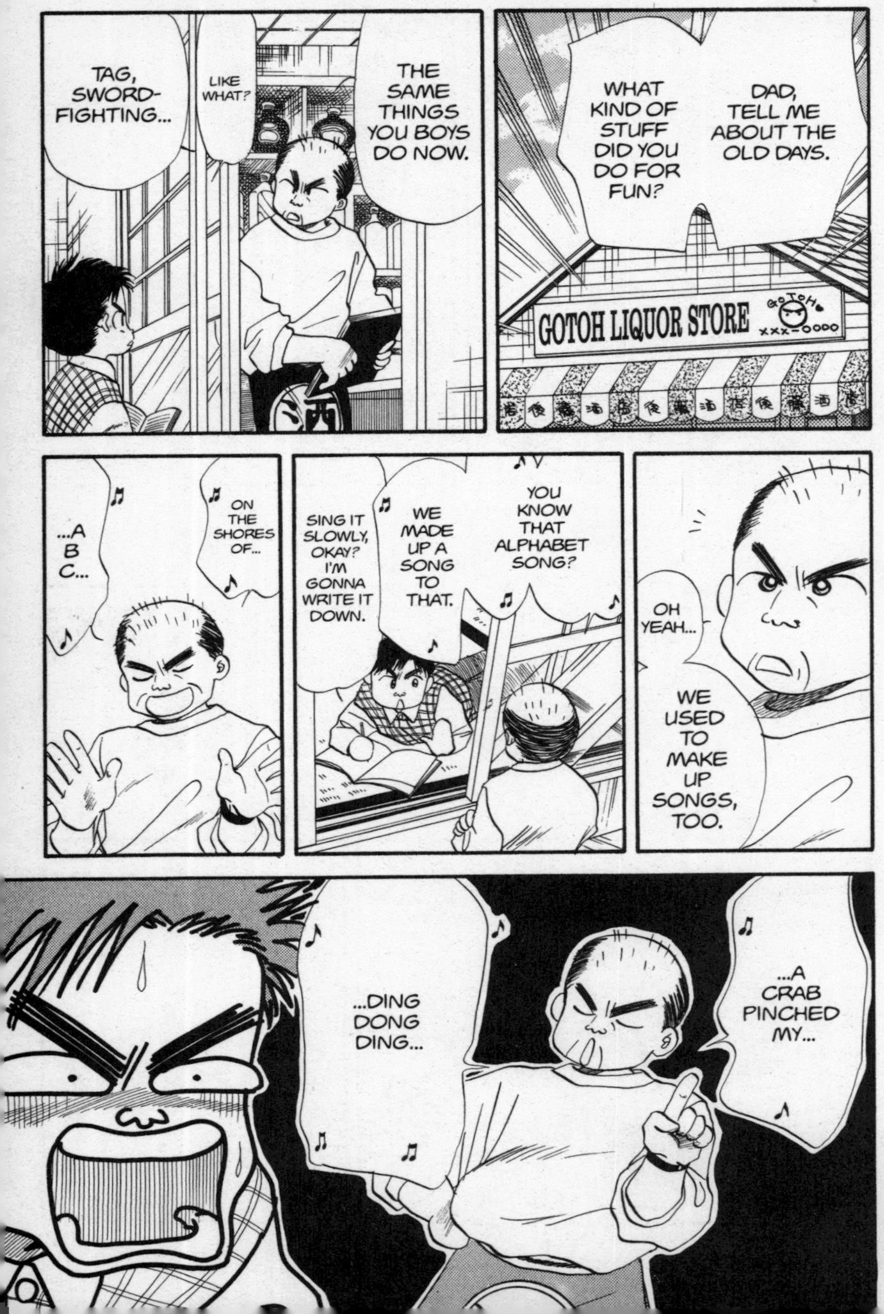
DAD, TELL ME ABOUT THE OLD DAYS.
WHAT KIND OF STUFF DID YOU DO FOR FUN?
GOTOH LIQUOR STORE
THE SAME THINGS YOU BOYS DO NOW.
LIKE WHAT?
TAG, SWORD-FIGHTING...
OH YEAH...
WE USED TO MAKE UP SONGS, TOO.
YOU KNOW THAT ALPHABET SONG?
WE MADE UP A SONG TO THAT.
SING IT SLOWLY, OKAY? I'M GONNA WRITE IT DOWN.
ON THE SHORES OF...
...A B C...
...A CRAB PINCHED MY...
...DING DONG DING...

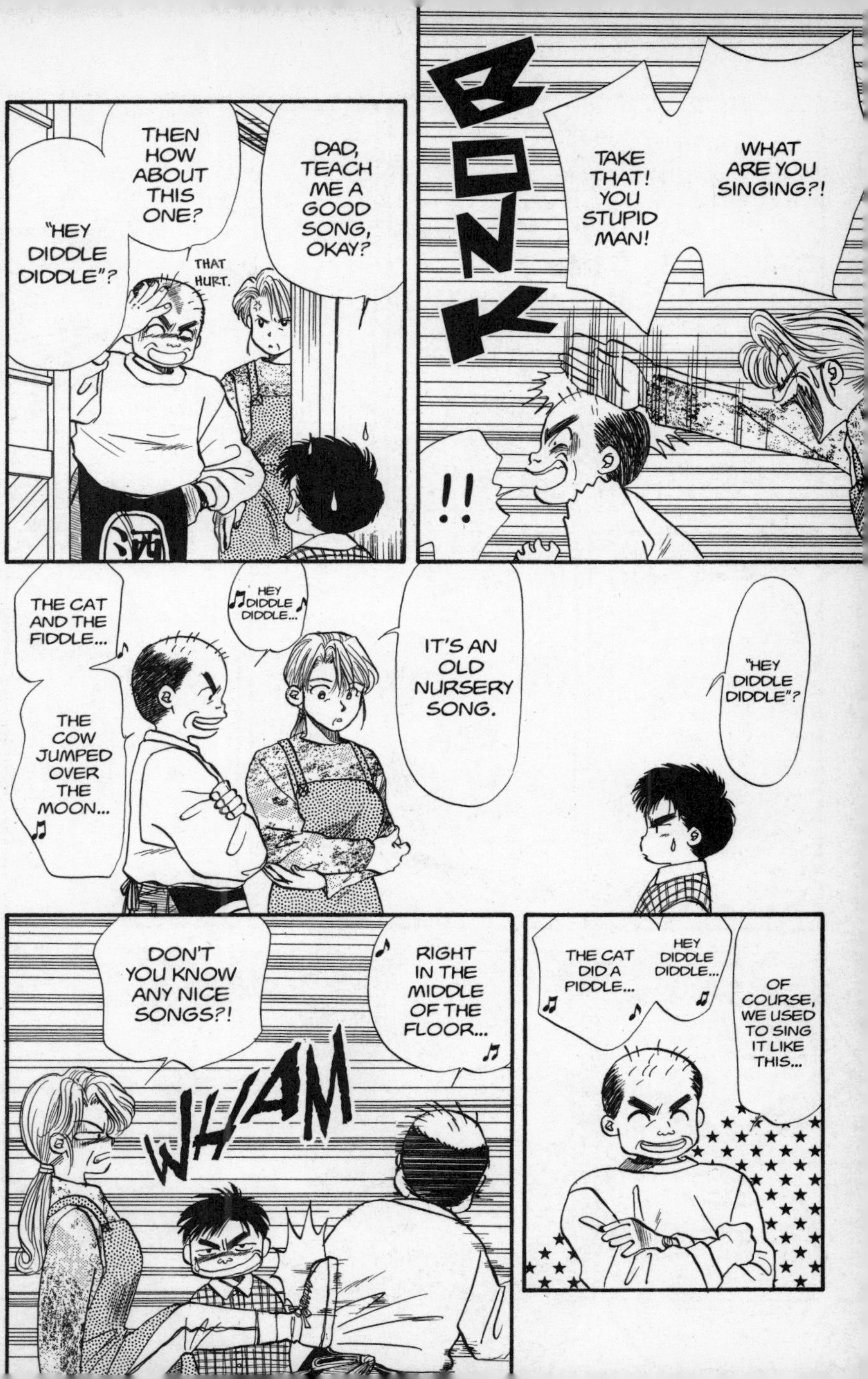
WHAT ARE YOU SINGING?!
TAKE THAT! YOU STUPID MAN!
BONK
!!
DAD, TEACH ME A GOOD SONG, OKAY?
THEN HOW ABOUT THIS ONE?
"HEY DIDDLE DIDDLE"?
THAT HURT.
"HEY DIDDLE DIDDLE"?
IT'S AN OLD NURSERY SONG.
HEY DIDDLE DIDDLE...
THE CAT AND THE FIDDLE...
THE COW JUMPED OVER THE MOON...
OF COURSE, WE USED TO SING IT LIKE THIS...
HEY DIDDLE DIDDLE...
THE CAT DID A PIDDLE...
RIGHT IN THE MIDDLE OF THE FLOOR...
DON'T YOU KNOW ANY NICE SONGS?!
WHAM

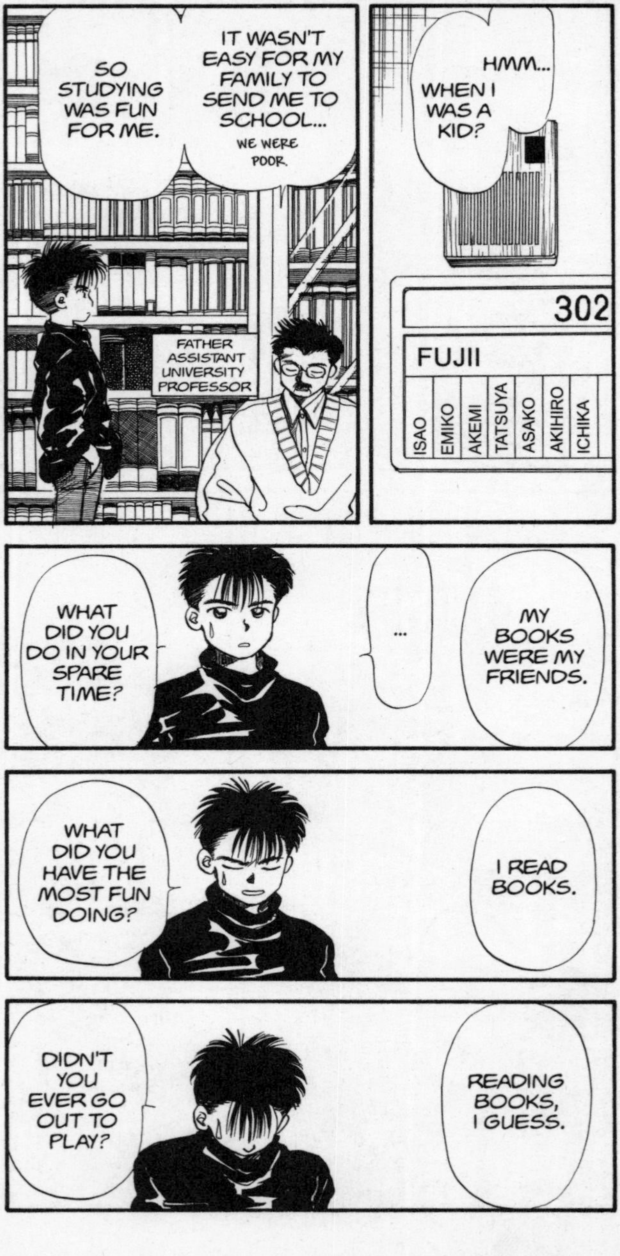
HMM... WHEN I WAS A KID?
302
FUJII
ISAO
EMIKO
AKEMI
TATSUYA
ASAKO
AKIHIRO
ICHIKA
IT WASN'T EASY FOR MY FAMILY TO SEND ME TO SCHOOL...
WE WERE POOR.
SO STUDYING WAS FUN FOR ME.
FATHER ASSISTANT UNIVERSITY PROFESSOR
MY BOOKS WERE MY FRIENDS.
...
WHAT DID YOU DO IN YOUR SPARE TIME?
I READ BOOKS.
WHAT DID YOU HAVE THE MOST FUN DOING?
READING BOOKS, I GUESS.
DIDN'T YOU EVER GO OUT TO PLAY?

Author's Note
Part 5
The Making of...

"Dumb, Flighty, and Selfish" is my award-winning story, and it is reprinted in this volume beginning on page 159. This is the one I drew on sketch paper. This anecdote is really famous. It's almost become a legend.

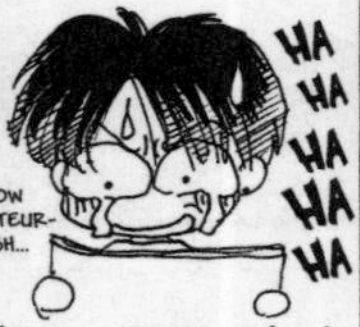
HA HA HA HA HA
HOW AMATEUR-ISH...

(This was my reaction when I looked at the manuscript recently.)

This is the piece I worked on non-stop until the day I left for Tokyo. I had to leave home at 6:00 a.m. and I worked on it until 2:00 a.m.

When I look at it now, I realize how bad it is. The people and backgrounds are bad. I drew the lines around the panels with a G pen with a worn tip.

High-quality paper? What's that? I was so ignorant. I didn't even have the money to buy screentone. You can tell all that at a glance. And what's more, what's Aki wearing at the end? A t-tulip?! What a laugh! There was no way to make any corrections. Sigh... Please read this and gain a little confidence, everyone.
How embarrassing!

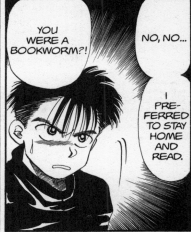

YOU WERE A BOOKWORM?!
NO, NO...
I PRE-FERRED TO STAY HOME AND READ.
ACTUALLY, THAT WAS MY NICKNAME.
GREAT!
KLAP
KLAP
CHEEP
CHEEP
AHA!
IT'S STILL THERE.
THAT'S THE SHOP?
THAT'S IT.
HOT
MATSUY
HELLO!
THIS BRINGS BACK MEMORIES.
AHH ...

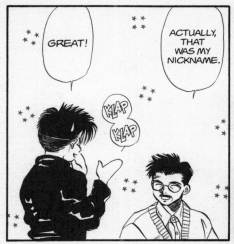

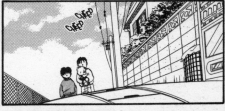

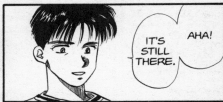

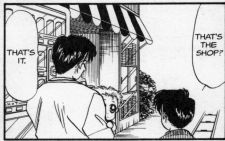

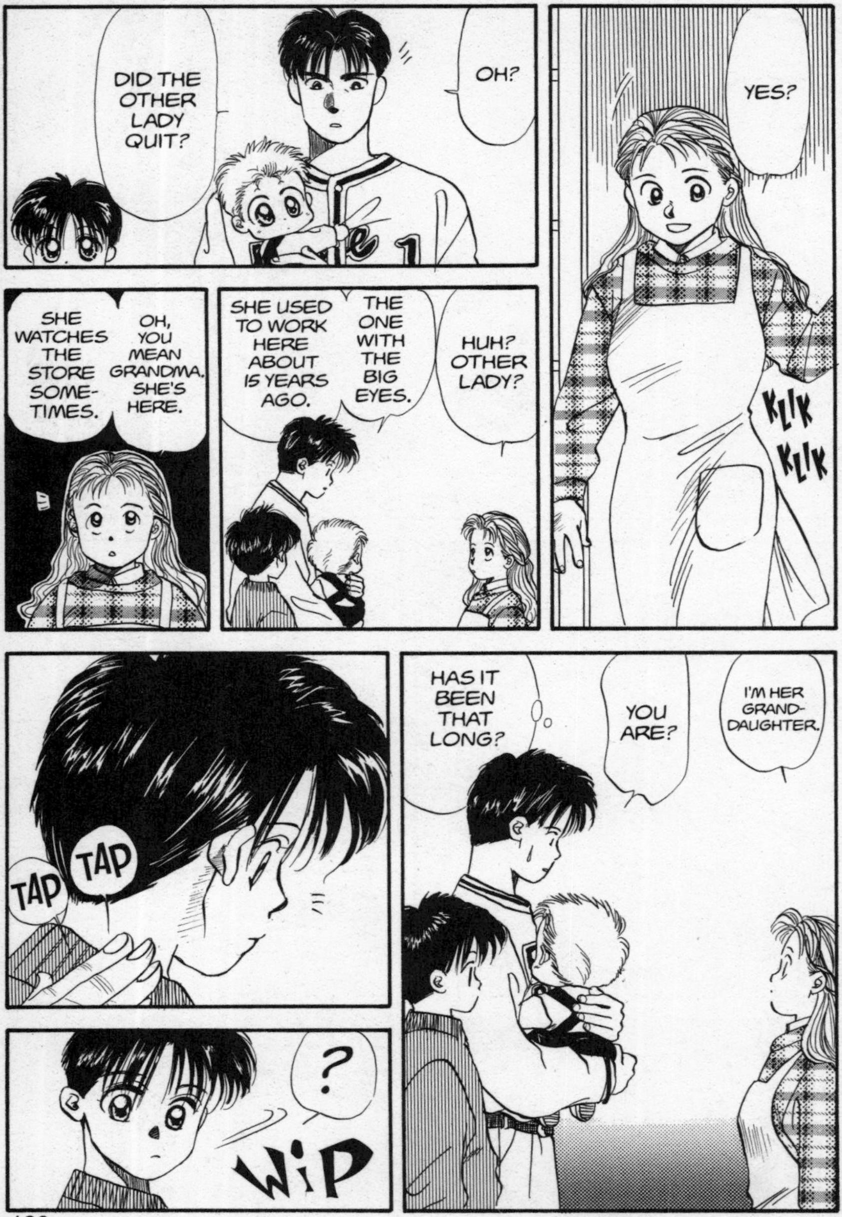
YES?
KLIK
KLIK
OH?
DID THE OTHER LADY QUIT?
HUH? OTHER LADY?
THE ONE WITH THE BIG EYES.
SHE USED TO WORK HERE ABOUT 15 YEARS AGO.
OH, YOU MEAN GRANDMA. SHE'S HERE.
SHE WATCHES THE STORE SOME-TIMES.
I'M HER GRAND-DAUGHTER.
YOU ARE?
HAS IT BEEN THAT LONG?
TAP
TAP
?
WiP

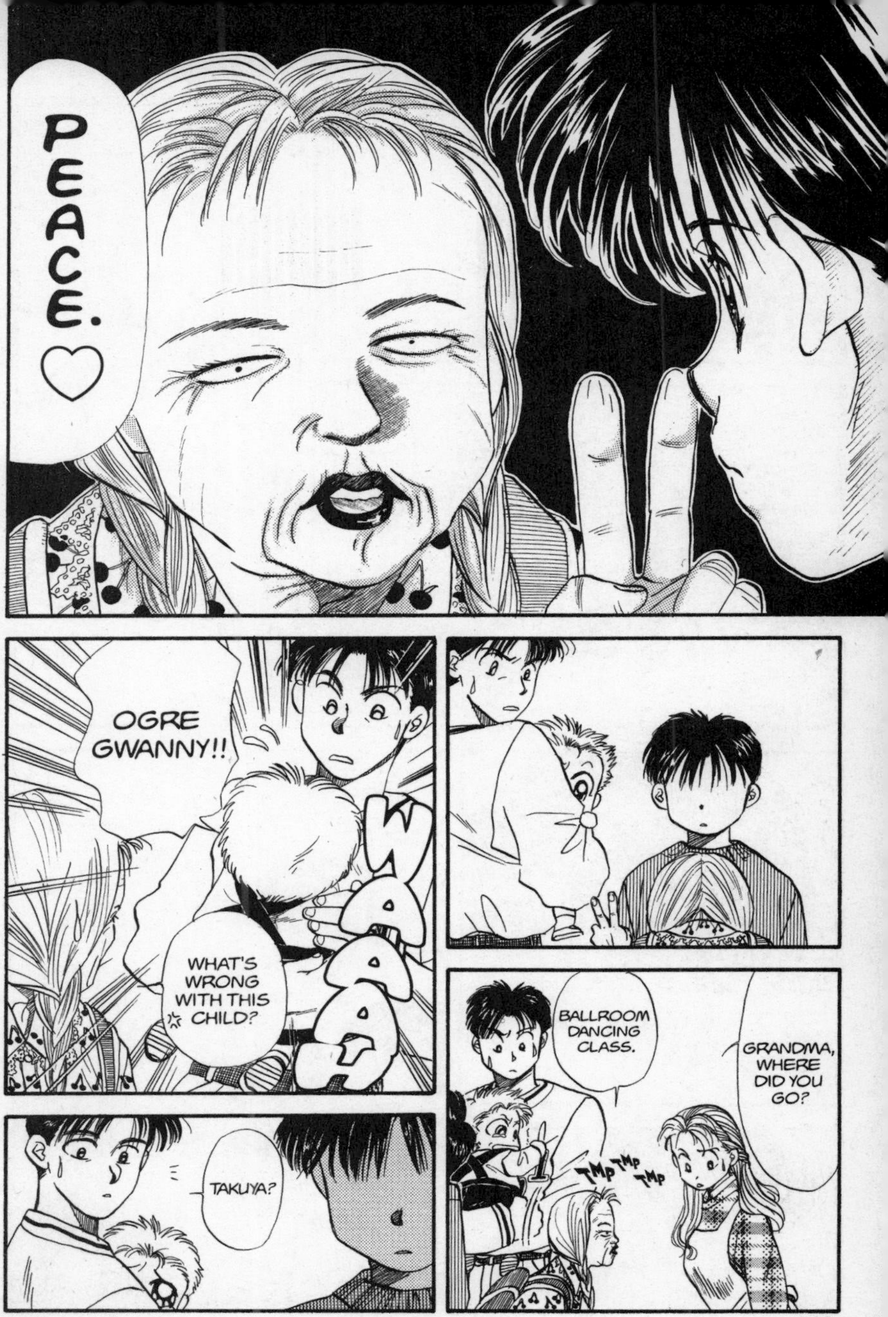
PEACE. ♥
OGRE GWANNY!!
WAAAH
WHAT'S WRONG WITH THIS CHILD?
GRANDMA, WHERE DID YOU GO?
BALLROOM DANCING CLASS.
TMP TMP TMP
TAKUYA?

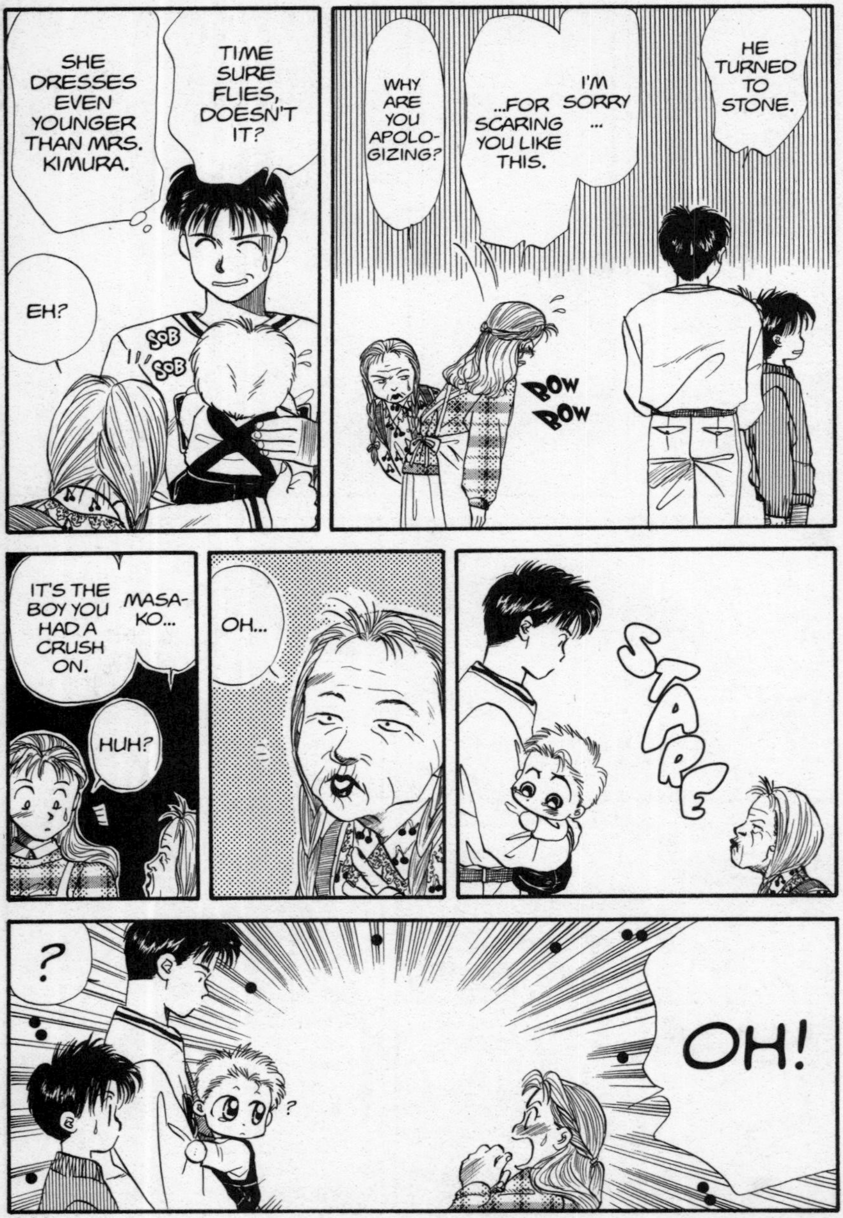
HE TURNED TO STONE.
I'M SORRY ...
...FOR SCARING YOU LIKE THIS.
WHY ARE YOU APOLOGIZING?
BOW BOW
TIME SURE FLIES, DOESN'T IT?
SHE DRESSES EVEN YOUNGER THAN MRS. KIMURA.
SOB SOB
EH?
STARE
OH...
MASAKO...
IT'S THE BOY YOU HAD A CRUSH ON.
HUH?
OH!
?
?

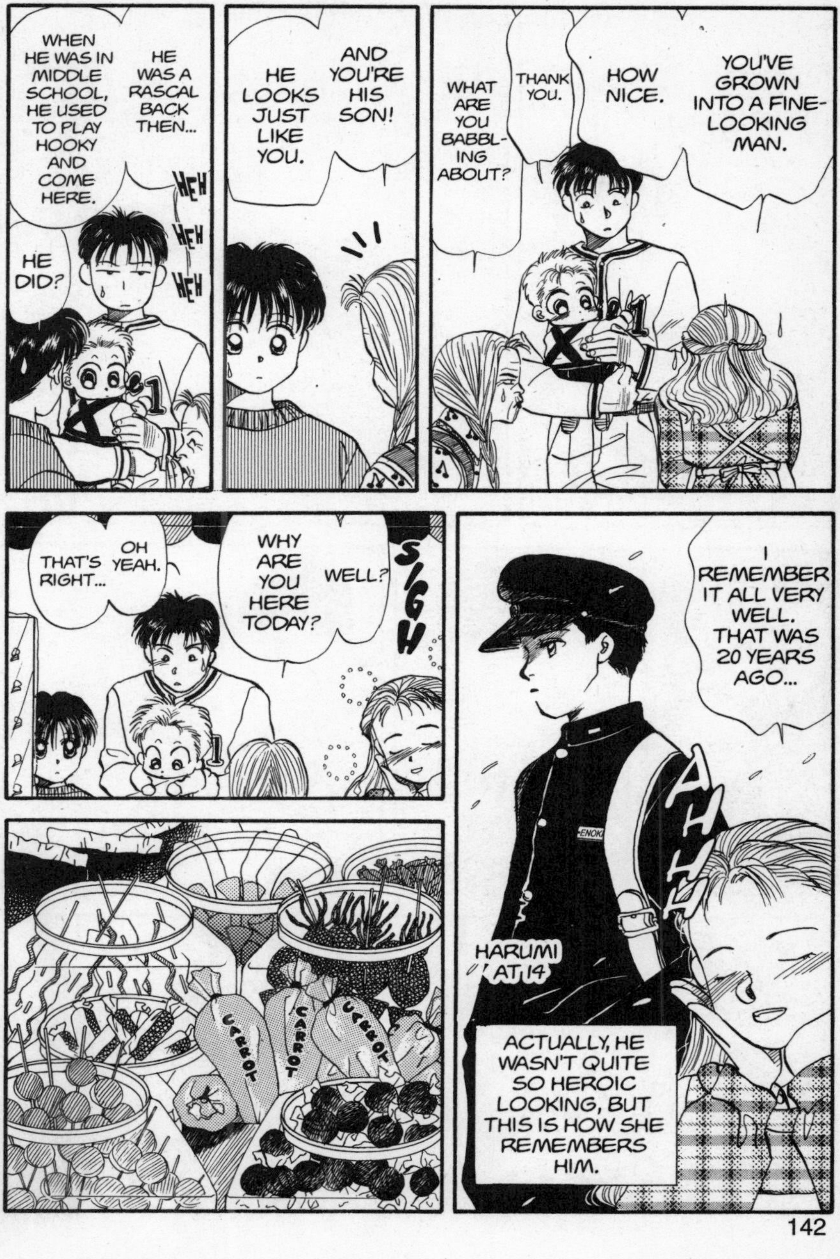
YOU'VE GROWN INTO A FINE-LOOKING MAN.
HOW NICE.
THANK YOU.
WHAT ARE YOU BABBL-ING ABOUT?
AND YOU'RE HIS SON!
HE LOOKS JUST LIKE YOU.
HE WAS A RASCAL BACK THEN...
WHEN HE WAS IN MIDDLE SCHOOL, HE USED TO PLAY HOOKY AND COME HERE.
HEH HEH HEH
HE DID?
I REMEMBER IT ALL VERY WELL. THAT WAS 20 YEARS AGO...
AHHH
ENOKI
HARUMI AT 14
ACTUALLY, HE WASN'T QUITE SO HEROIC LOOKING, BUT THIS IS HOW SHE REMEMBERS HIM.
WELL?
WHY ARE YOU HERE TODAY?
SIGH
OH YEAH.
THAT'S RIGHT...
CARROT
CARROT
CARROT

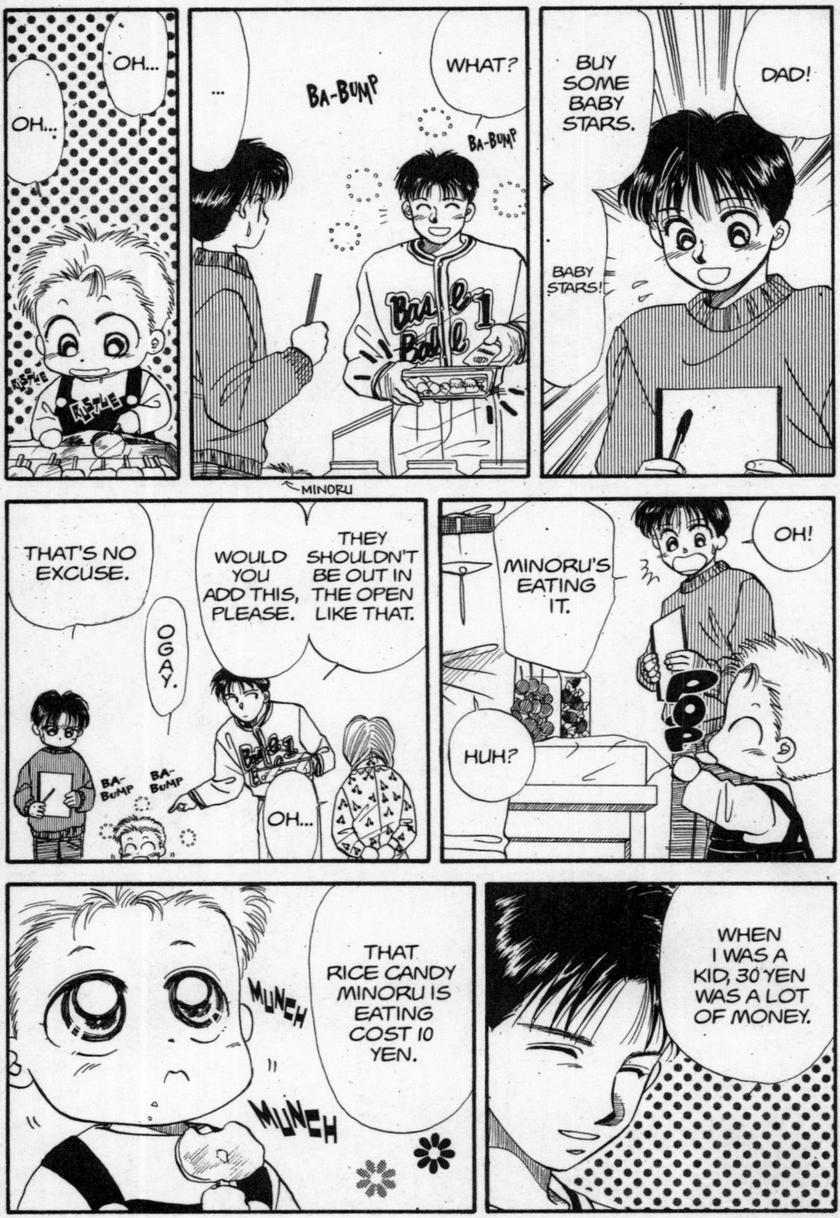
DAD!
BUY SOME BABY STARS.
BABY STARS!
WHAT?
BA-BUMP
BA-BUMP
...
MINORU
OH...
OH...
RUSTLE
RUSTLE
OH!
MINORU'S EATING IT.
POP
HUH?
THEY SHOULDN'T BE OUT IN THE OPEN LIKE THAT.
WOULD YOU ADD THIS, PLEASE.
THAT'S NO EXCUSE.
OGAY.
BA-BUMP
BA-BUMP
OH...
WHEN I WAS A KID, 30 YEN WAS A LOT OF MONEY.
THAT RICE CANDY MINORU IS EATING COST 10 YEN.
MUNCH
MUNCH

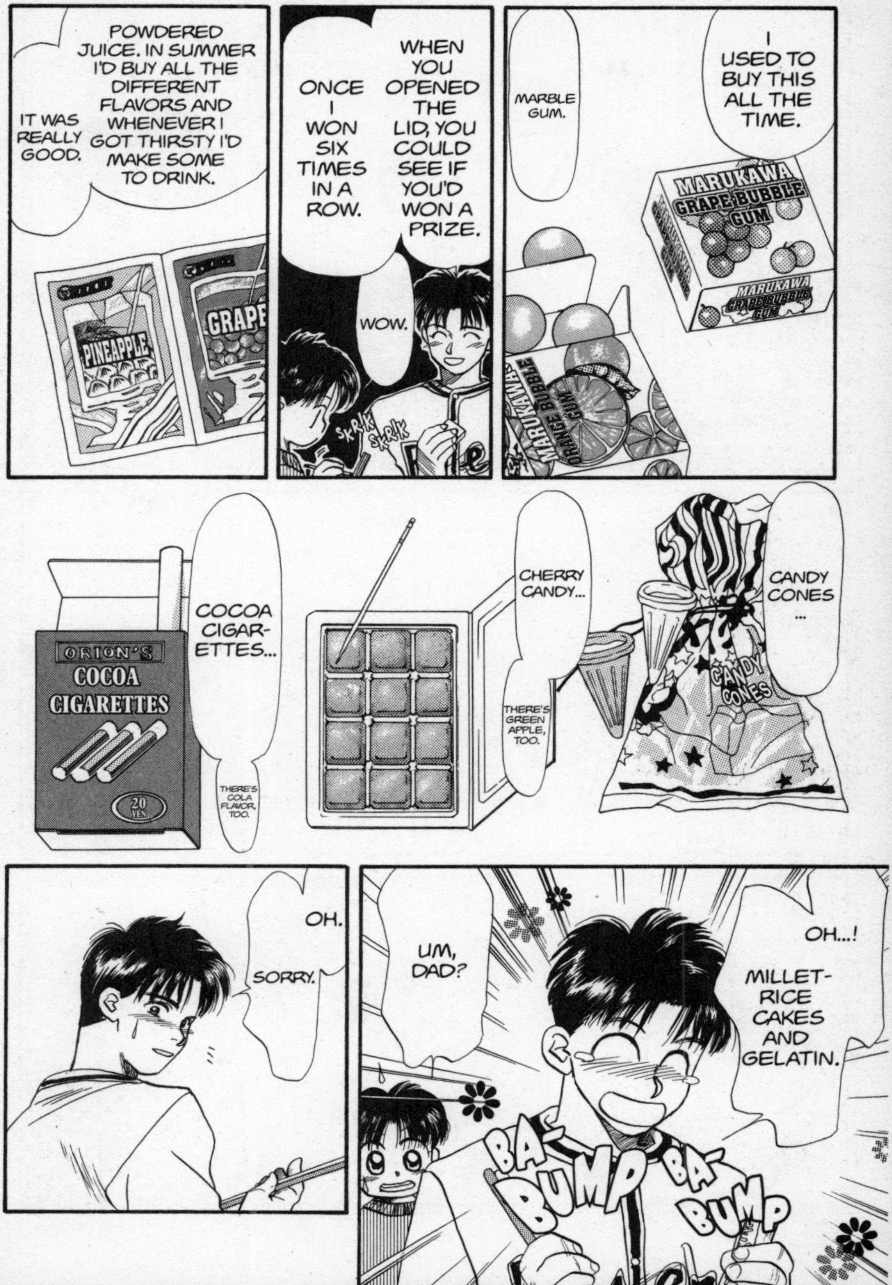
I USED TO BUY THIS ALL THE TIME.
MARBLE GUM.
MARUKAWA GRAPE BUBBLE GUM
MARUKAWA GRAPE BUBBLE GUM
MARUKAWA
ORANGE GUM
WHEN YOU OPENED THE LID, YOU COULD SEE IF YOU'D WON A PRIZE.
ONCE I WON SIX TIMES IN A ROW.
WOW.
SKR/K SKR/K
POWDERED JUICE. IN SUMMER I'D BUY ALL THE DIFFERENT FLAVORS AND WHENEVER I GOT THIRSTY I'D MAKE SOME TO DRINK.
IT WAS REALLY GOOD.
GRAPE
PINEAPPLE
CANDY CONES ...
CANDY CONES
CHERRY CANDY...
THERE'S GREEN APPLE, TOO.
COCOA CIGAR-ETTES...
THERE'S COLA FLAVOR, TOO.
ORION'S
COCOA CIGARETTES
20 YEN
OH...!
MILLET-RICE CAKES AND GELATIN.
UM, DAD?
BA-BUMP BA-BUMP
OH.
SORRY.

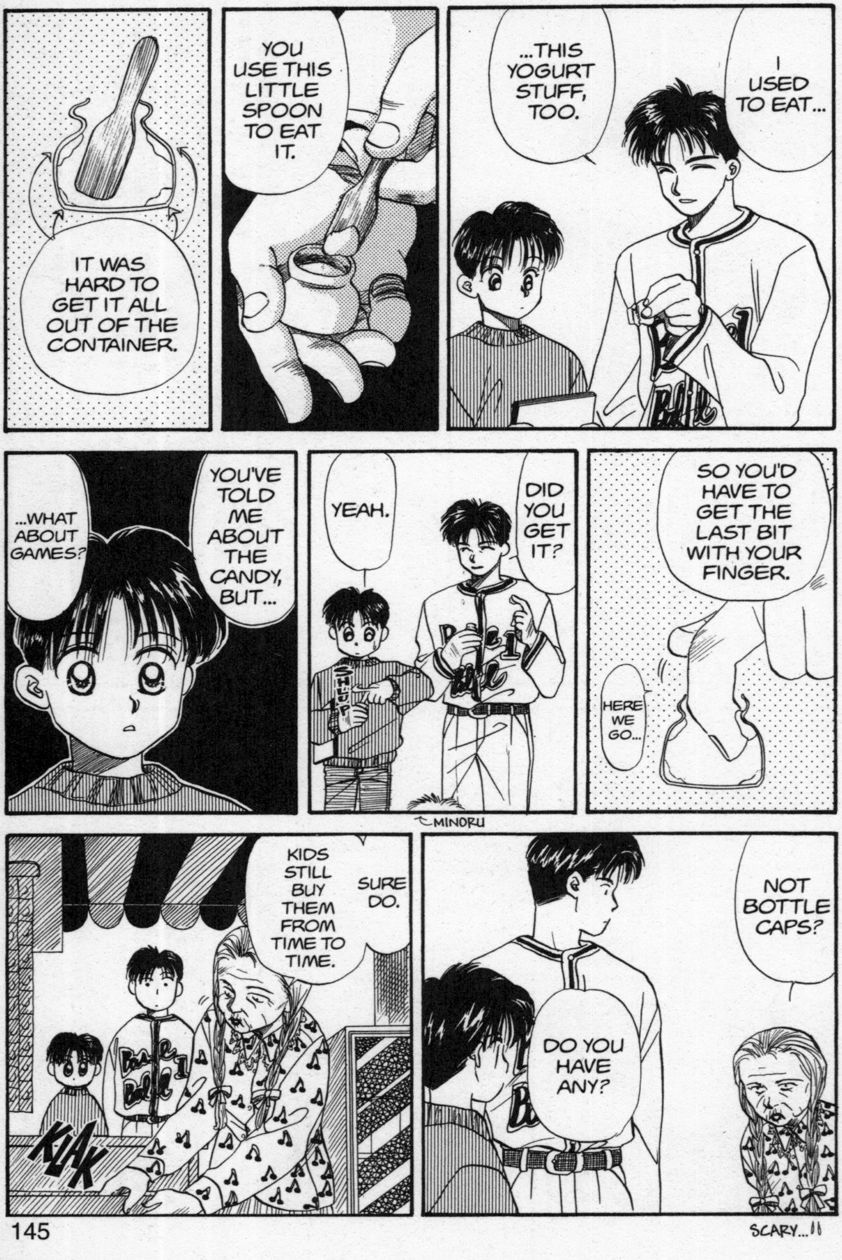
I USED TO EAT...
...THIS YOGURT STUFF, TOO.
YOU USE THIS LITTLE SPOON TO EAT IT.
IT WAS HARD TO GET IT ALL OUT OF THE CONTAINER.
SO YOU'D HAVE TO GET THE LAST BIT WITH YOUR FINGER.
HERE WE GO...
DID YOU GET IT?
YEAH.
SHLUP
MINORU
YOU'VE TOLD ME ABOUT THE CANDY, BUT...
...WHAT ABOUT GAMES?
NOT BOTTLE CAPS?
DO YOU HAVE ANY?
SCARY...!!
SURE DO.
KIDS STILL BUY THEM FROM TIME TO TIME.
KLAK

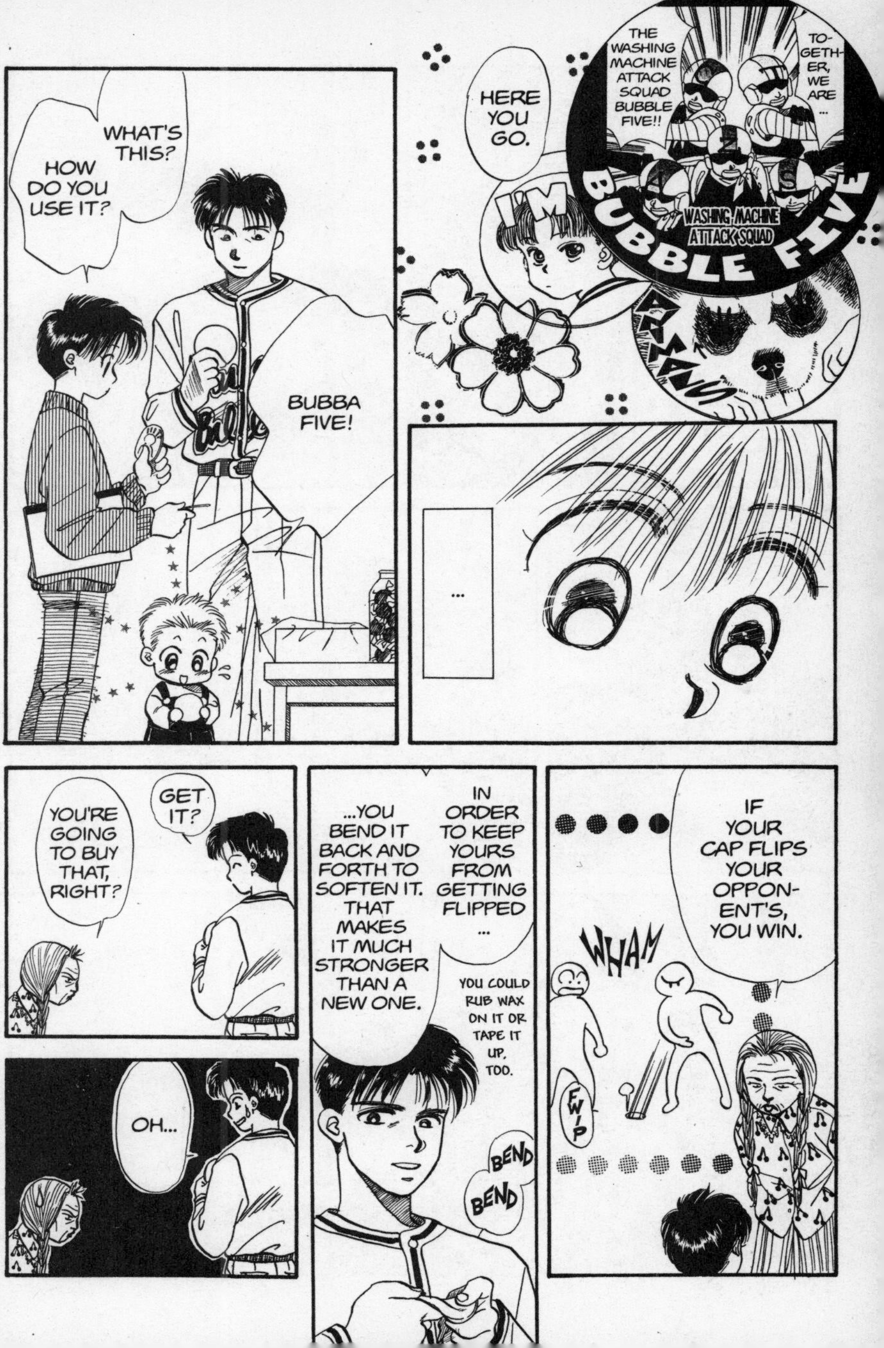
TO-GETH-ER, WE ARE ...
THE WASHING MACHINE ATTACK SQUAD BUBBLE FIVE!!
BUBBLE FIVE
WASHING MACHINE ATTACK SQUAD
HERE YOU GO.
I'M
...
WHAT'S THIS?
HOW DO YOU USE IT?
BUBBA FIVE!
IF YOUR CAP FLIPS YOUR OPPON-ENT'S, YOU WIN.
WHAM
FWIP
IN ORDER TO KEEP YOURS FROM GETTING FLIPPED ...
...YOU BEND IT BACK AND FORTH TO SOFTEN IT. THAT MAKES IT MUCH STRONGER THAN A NEW ONE.
YOU COULD RUB WAX ON IT OR TAPE IT UP, TOO.
BEND
BEND
GET IT?
YOU'RE GOING TO BUY THAT, RIGHT?
OH...

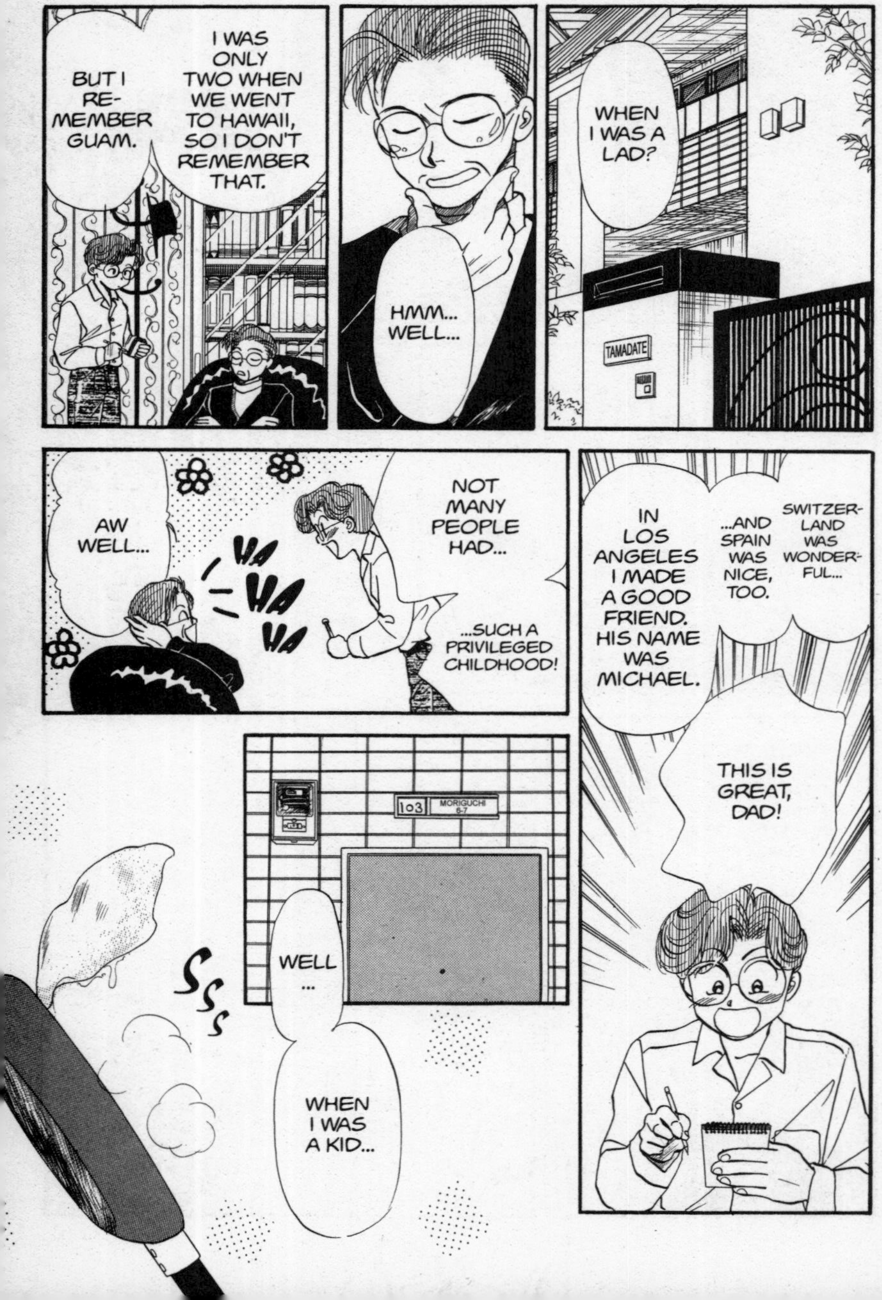

WHEN I WAS A LAD?
TAMADATE
HMM... WELL...
I WAS ONLY TWO WHEN WE WENT TO HAWAII, SO I DON'T REMEMBER THAT.
BUT I RE-MEMBER GUAM.
SWITZER-LAND WAS WONDER-FUL...
...AND SPAIN WAS NICE, TOO.
IN LOS ANGELES I MADE A GOOD FRIEND. HIS NAME WAS MICHAEL.
THIS IS GREAT, DAD!
NOT MANY PEOPLE HAD...
...SUCH A PRIVILEGED CHILDHOOD!
HA HA HA
AW WELL...
103
MORIGUCHI 6-7
WELL ...
WHEN I WAS A KID...
SSS

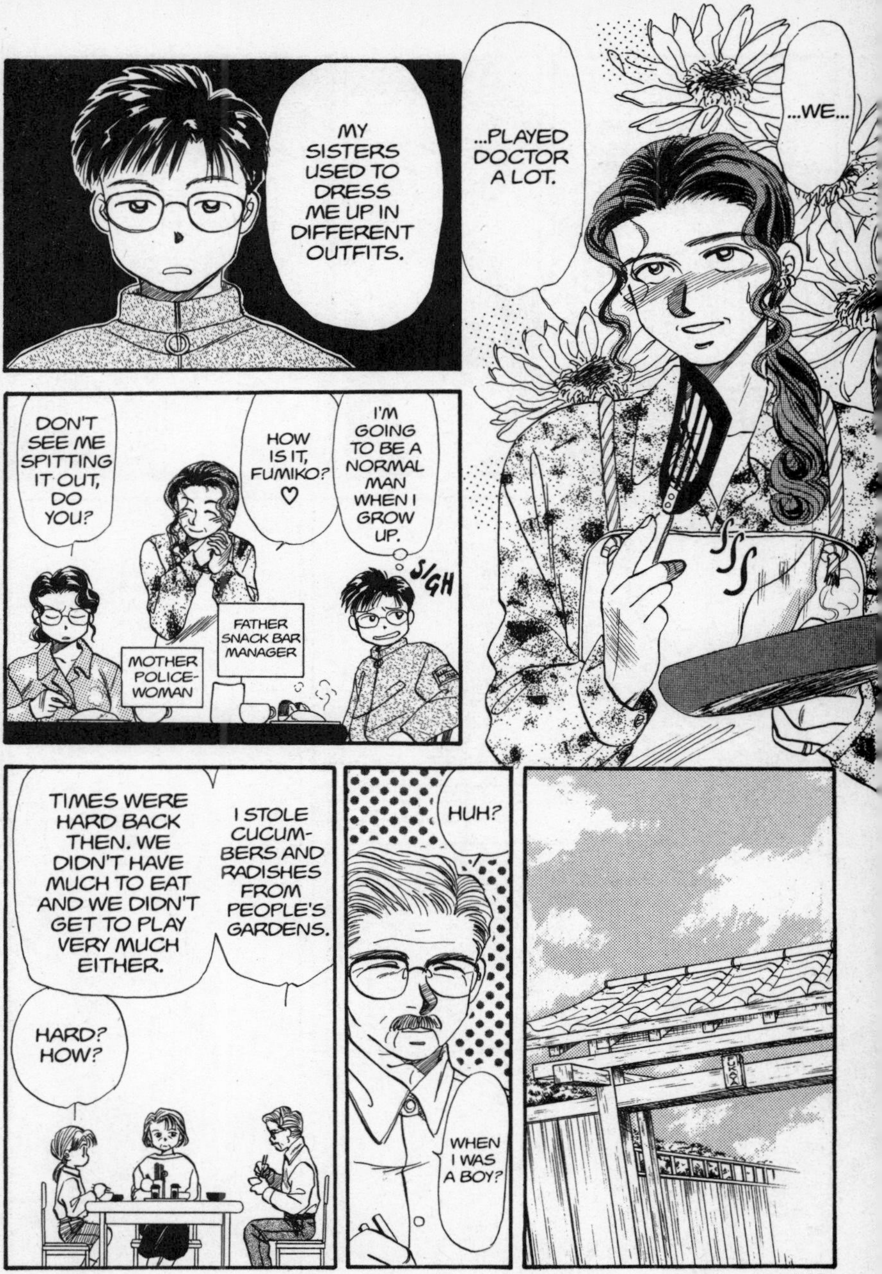
...WE...
...PLAYED DOCTOR A LOT.
MY SISTERS USED TO DRESS ME UP IN DIFFERENT OUTFITS.
I'M GOING TO BE A NORMAL MAN WHEN I GROW UP.
SIGH
HOW IS IT, FUMIKO? ♡
DON'T SEE ME SPITTING IT OUT, DO YOU?
FATHER SNACK BAR MANAGER
MOTHER POLICE-WOMAN
HUH?
WHEN I WAS A BOY?
I STOLE CUCUMBERS AND RADISHES FROM PEOPLE'S GARDENS.
TIMES WERE HARD BACK THEN. WE DIDN'T HAVE MUCH TO EAT AND WE DIDN'T GET TO PLAY VERY MUCH EITHER.
HARD? HOW?

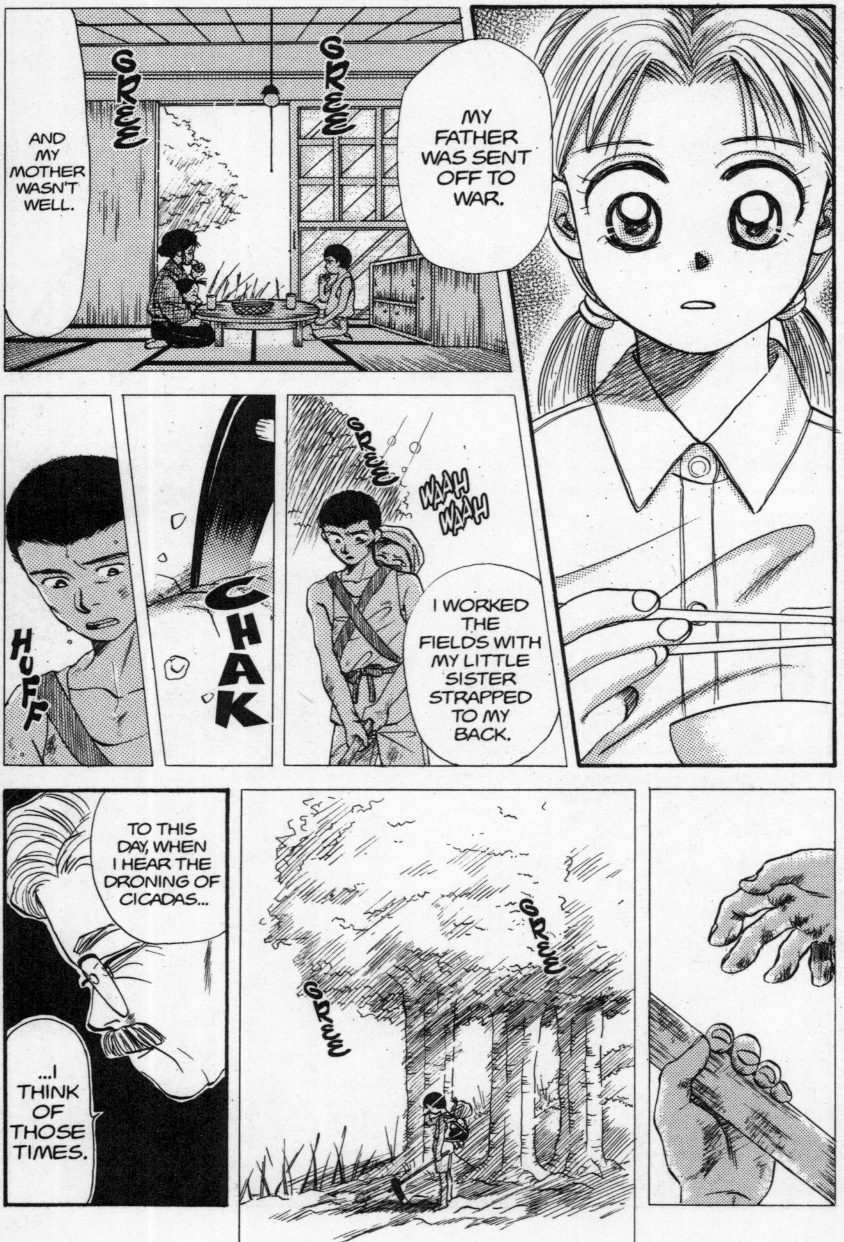
MY FATHER WAS SENT OFF TO WAR.
GREE
GREE
AND MY MOTHER WASN'T WELL.
GREW
WAAH WAAH
I WORKED THE FIELDS WITH MY LITTLE SISTER STRAPPED TO MY BACK.
CHAK
HUFF
GREW
GREW
TO THIS DAY, WHEN I HEAR THE DRONING OF CICADAS...
...I THINK OF THOSE TIMES.

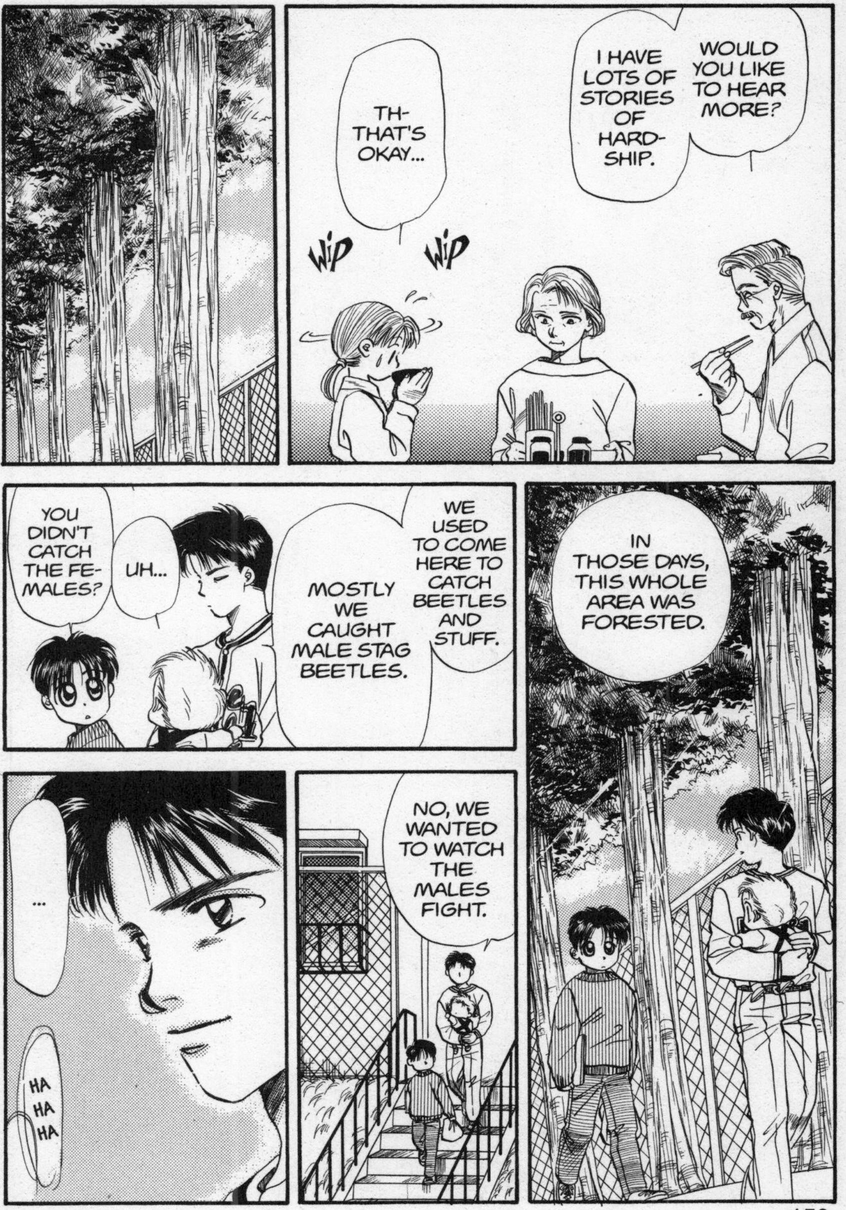
WOULD YOU LIKE TO HEAR MORE?
I HAVE LOTS OF STORIES OF HARD-SHIP.
TH- THAT'S OKAY...
WIP
WIP
IN THOSE DAYS, THIS WHOLE AREA WAS FORESTED.
WE USED TO COME HERE TO CATCH BEETLES AND STUFF.
MOSTLY WE CAUGHT MALE STAG BEETLES.
UH...
YOU DIDN'T CATCH THE FE-MALES?
NO, WE WANTED TO WATCH THE MALES FIGHT.
...
HA HA HA

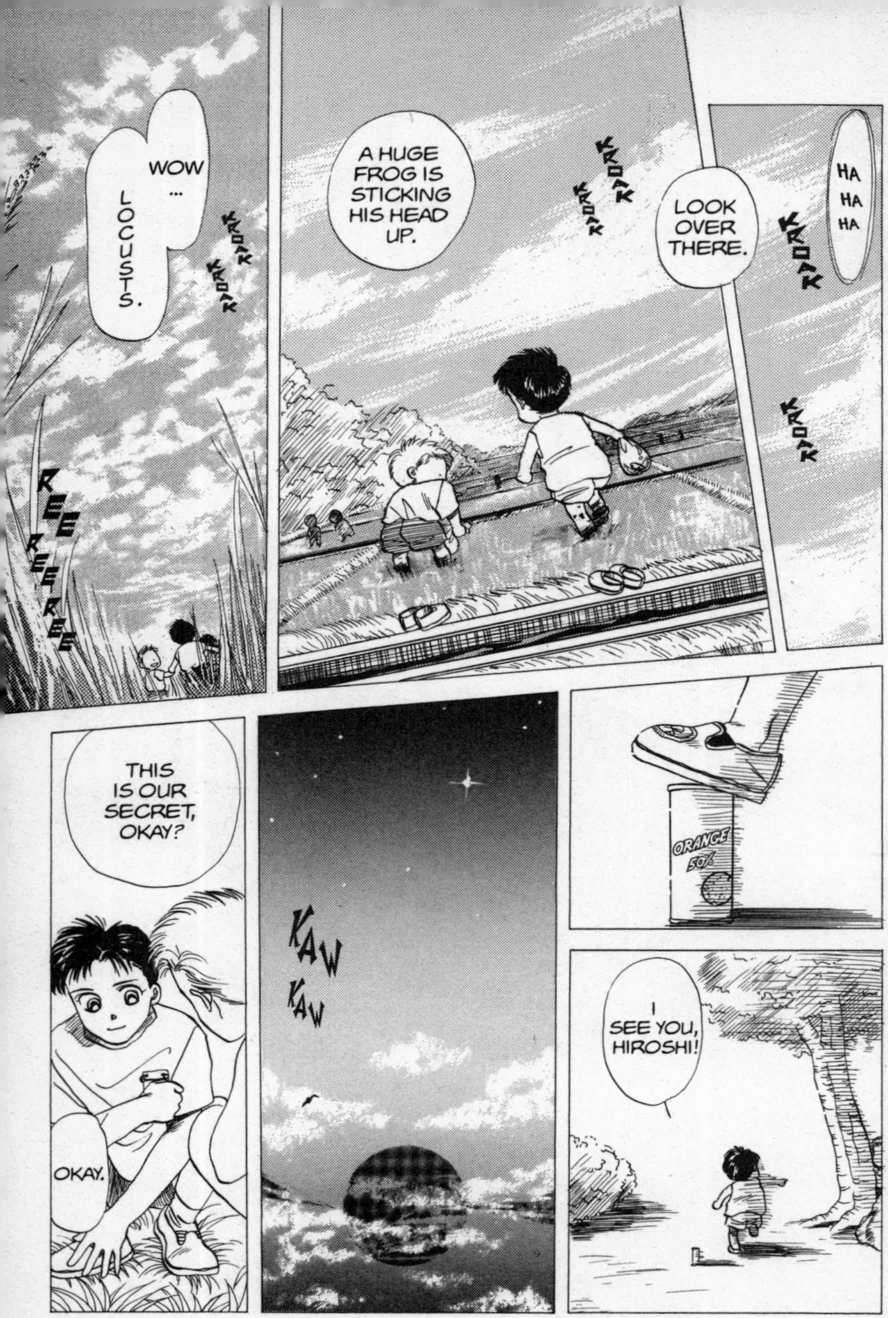
HA HA HA
KROAK
KROAK
LOOK OVER THERE.
KROAK KROAK
A HUGE FROG IS STICKING HIS HEAD UP.
KROAK KROAK
WOW ... LOCUSTS.
REE REE REE
ORANGE 50%
I SEE YOU, HIROSHI!
KAW KAW
THIS IS OUR SECRET, OKAY?
OKAY.

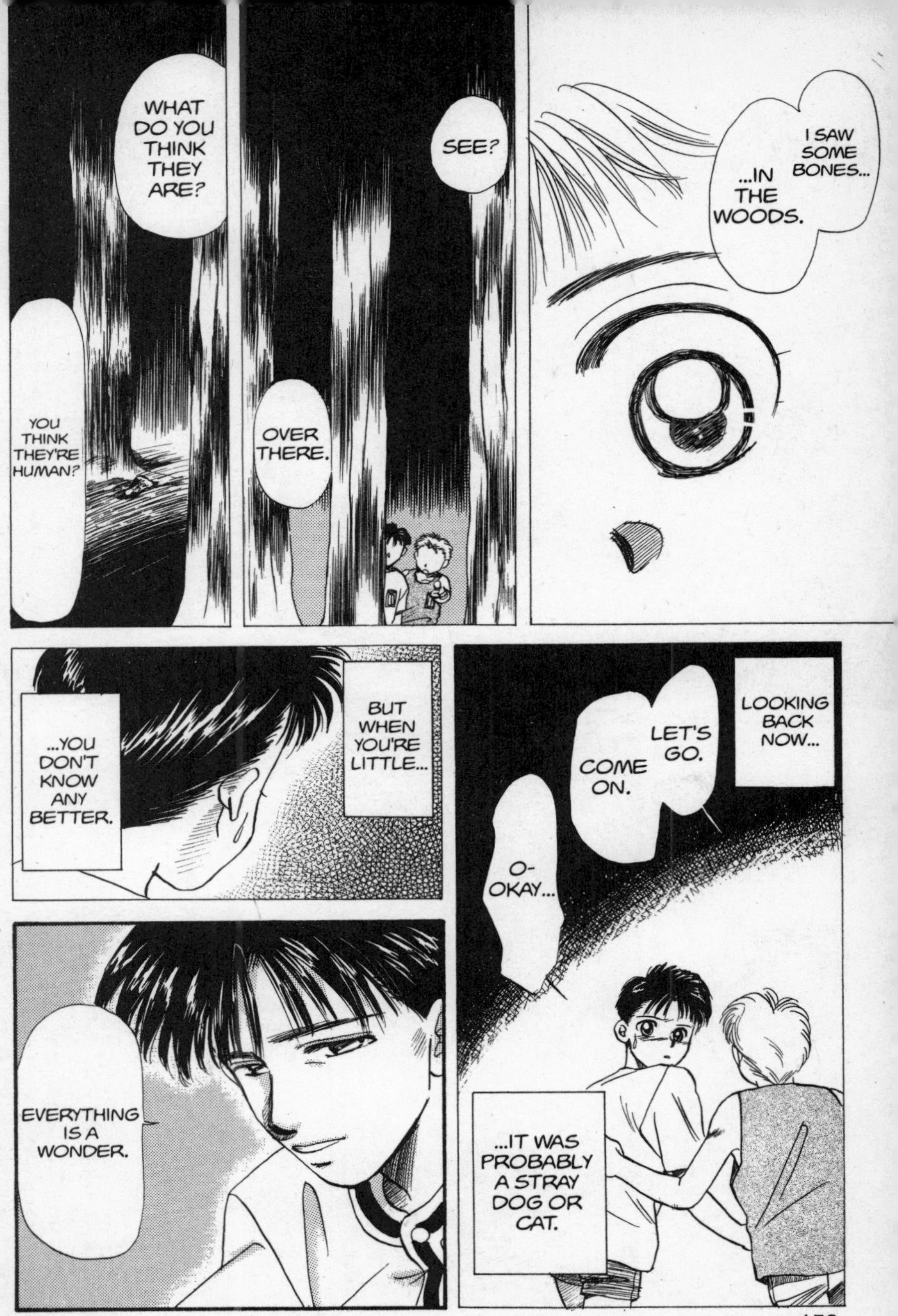
I SAW SOME BONES...
...IN THE WOODS.
SEE?
OVER THERE.
WHAT DO YOU THINK THEY ARE?
YOU THINK THEY'RE HUMAN?
LOOKING BACK NOW...
LET'S GO.
COME ON.
O-OKAY...
...IT WAS PROBABLY A STRAY DOG OR CAT.
BUT WHEN YOU'RE LITTLE...
...YOU DON'T KNOW ANY BETTER.
EVERYTHING IS A WONDER.

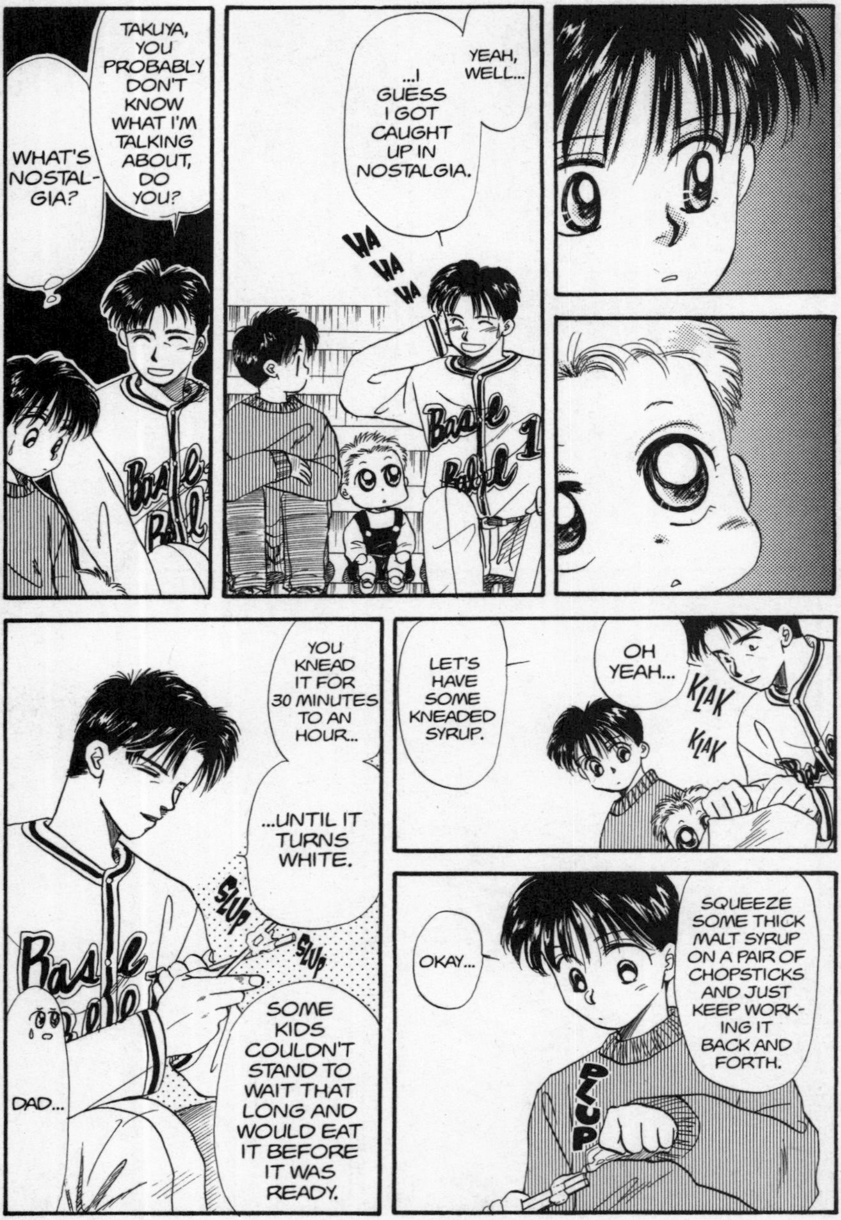
YEAH, WELL...
...I GUESS I GOT CAUGHT UP IN NOSTALGIA.
HA HA HA
TAKUYA, YOU PROBABLY DON'T KNOW WHAT I'M TALKING ABOUT, DO YOU?
WHAT'S NOSTAL-GIA?
OH YEAH...
KLAK
KLAK
LET'S HAVE SOME KNEADED SYRUP.
SQUEEZE SOME THICK MALT SYRUP ON A PAIR OF CHOPSTICKS AND JUST KEEP WORK-ING IT BACK AND FORTH.
OKAY...
PLUP
YOU KNEAD IT FOR 30 MINUTES TO AN HOUR...
...UNTIL IT TURNS WHITE.
SLUP
SLUP
SOME KIDS COULDN'T STAND TO WAIT THAT LONG AND WOULD EAT IT BEFORE IT WAS READY.
DAD...

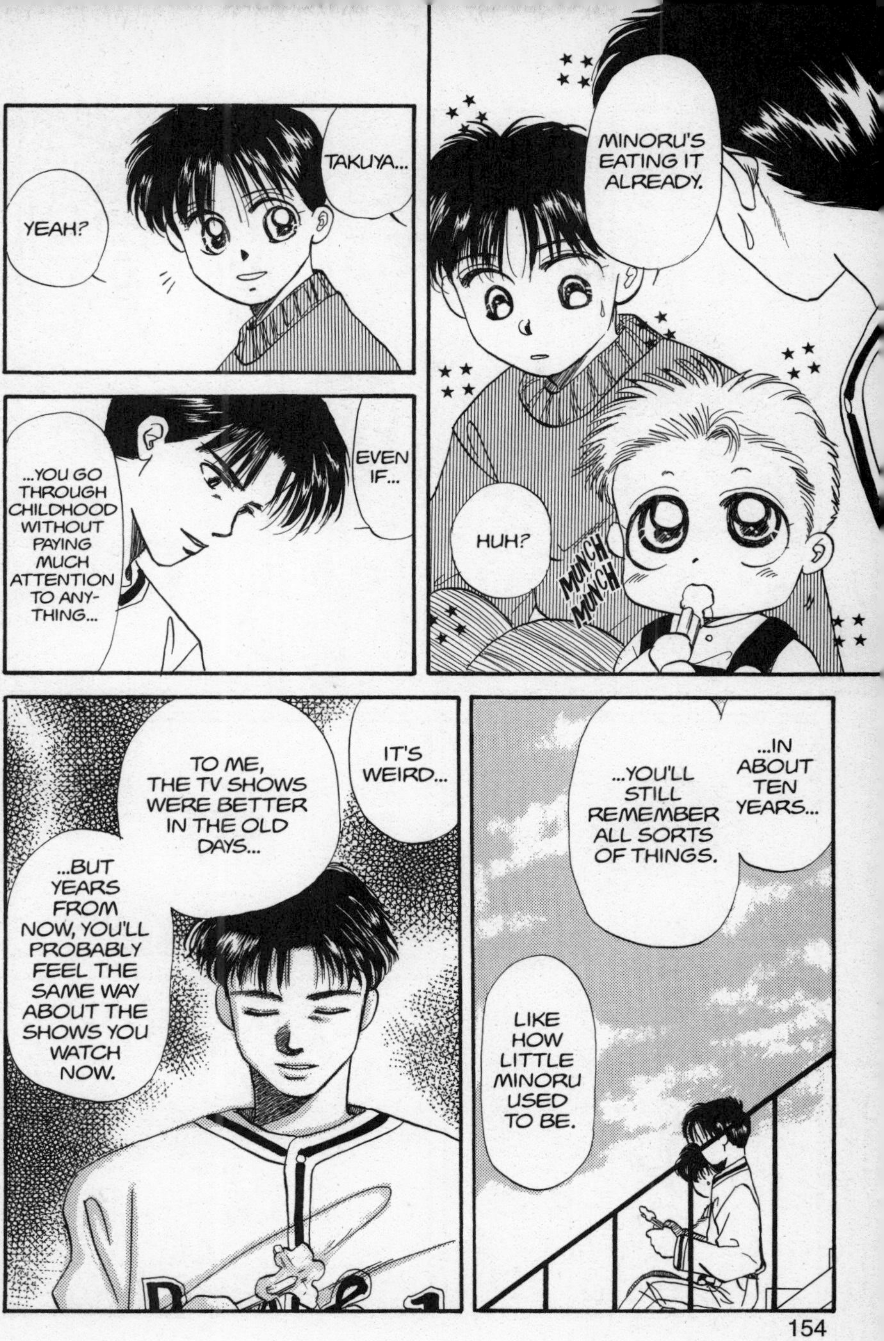
MINORU'S EATING IT ALREADY.
HUH?
MUNCH MUNCH
TAKUYA...
YEAH?
EVEN IF...
...YOU GO THROUGH CHILDHOOD WITHOUT PAYING MUCH ATTENTION TO ANY-THING...
...IN ABOUT TEN YEARS...
...YOU'LL STILL REMEMBER ALL SORTS OF THINGS.
LIKE HOW LITTLE MINORU USED TO BE.
IT'S WEIRD...
TO ME, THE TV SHOWS WERE BETTER IN THE OLD DAYS...
...BUT YEARS FROM NOW, YOU'LL PROBABLY FEEL THE SAME WAY ABOUT THE SHOWS YOU WATCH NOW.

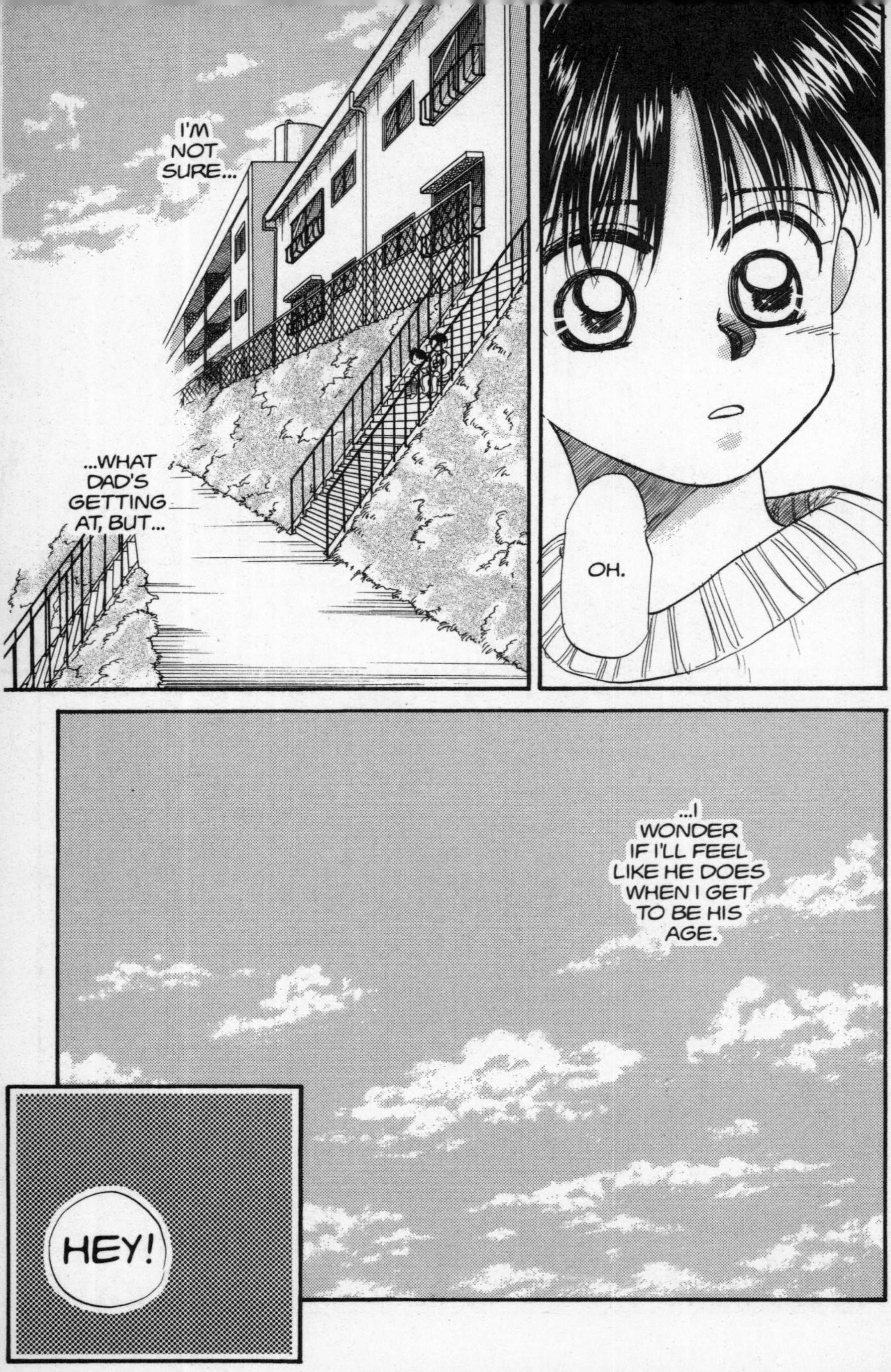
OH.
I'M NOT SURE...
...WHAT DAD'S GETTING AT, BUT...
...I WONDER IF I'LL FEEL LIKE HE DOES WHEN I GET TO BE HIS AGE.
HEY!

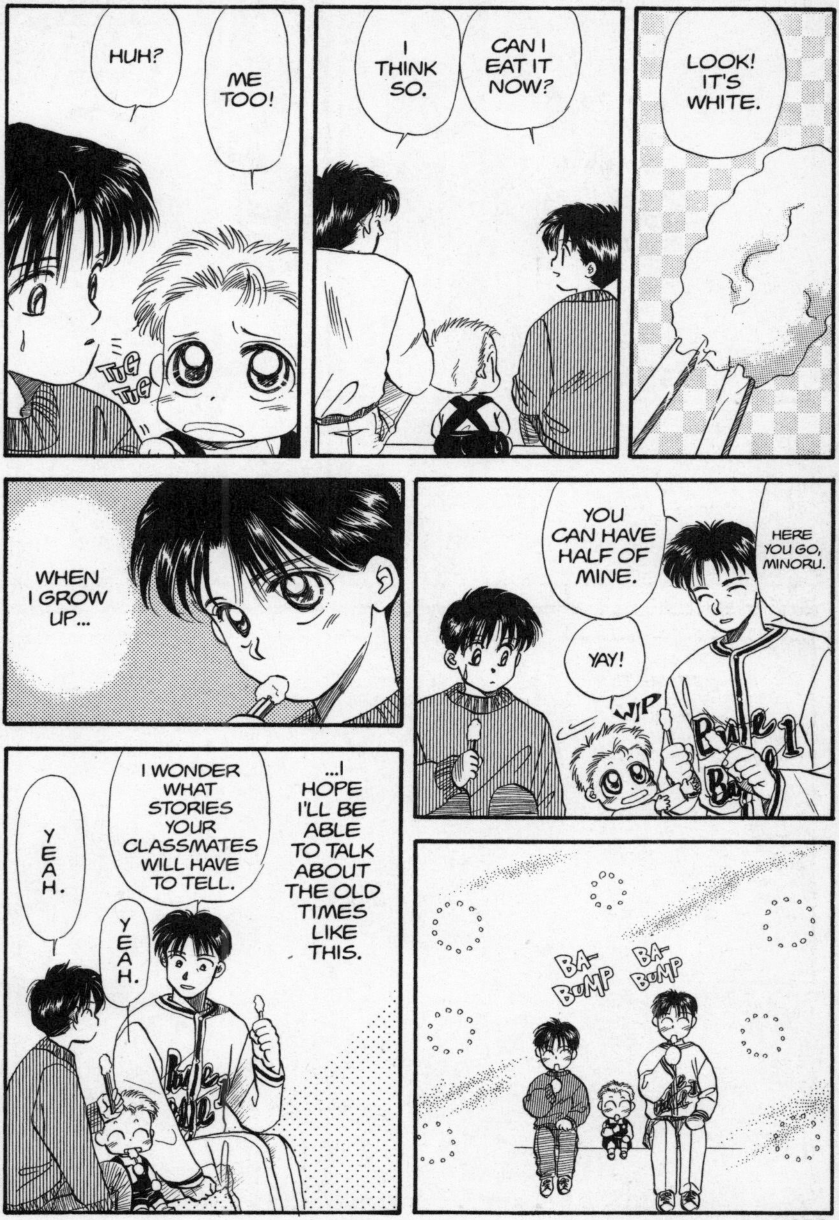
LOOK! IT'S WHITE.
CAN I EAT IT NOW?
I THINK SO.
ME TOO!
HUH?
TUG TUG
HERE YOU GO, MINORU.
YOU CAN HAVE HALF OF MINE.
YAY!
WIP
WHEN I GROW UP...
...I HOPE I'LL BE ABLE TO TALK ABOUT THE OLD TIMES LIKE THIS.
I WONDER WHAT STORIES YOUR CLASSMATES WILL HAVE TO TELL.
YEAH.
YEAH.
BA-BUMP
BA-BUMP

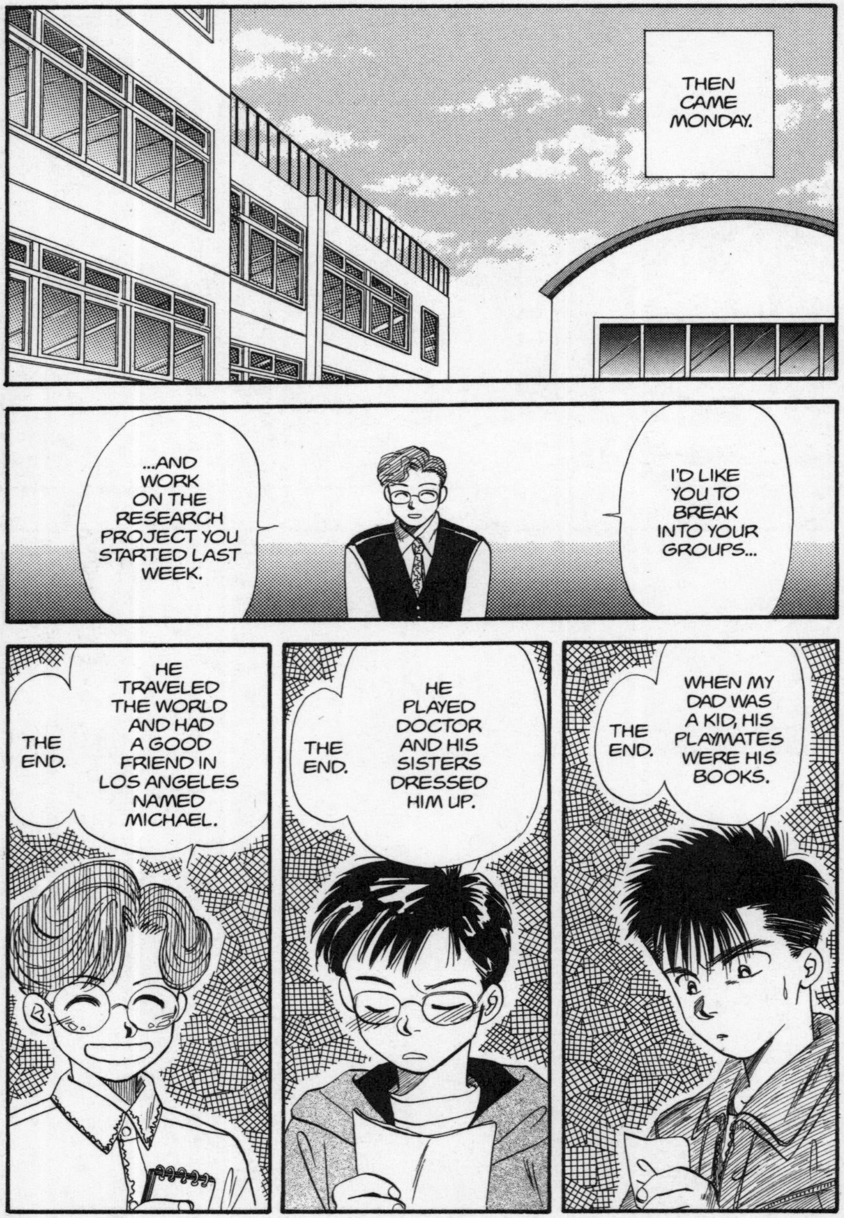
THEN CAME MONDAY.
I'D LIKE YOU TO BREAK INTO YOUR GROUPS...
...AND WORK ON THE RESEARCH PROJECT YOU STARTED LAST WEEK.
WHEN MY DAD WAS A KID, HIS PLAYMATES WERE HIS BOOKS.
THE END.
HE PLAYED DOCTOR AND HIS SISTERS DRESSED HIM UP.
THE END.
HE TRAVELED THE WORLD AND HAD A GOOD FRIEND IN LOS ANGELES NAMED MICHAEL.
THE END.

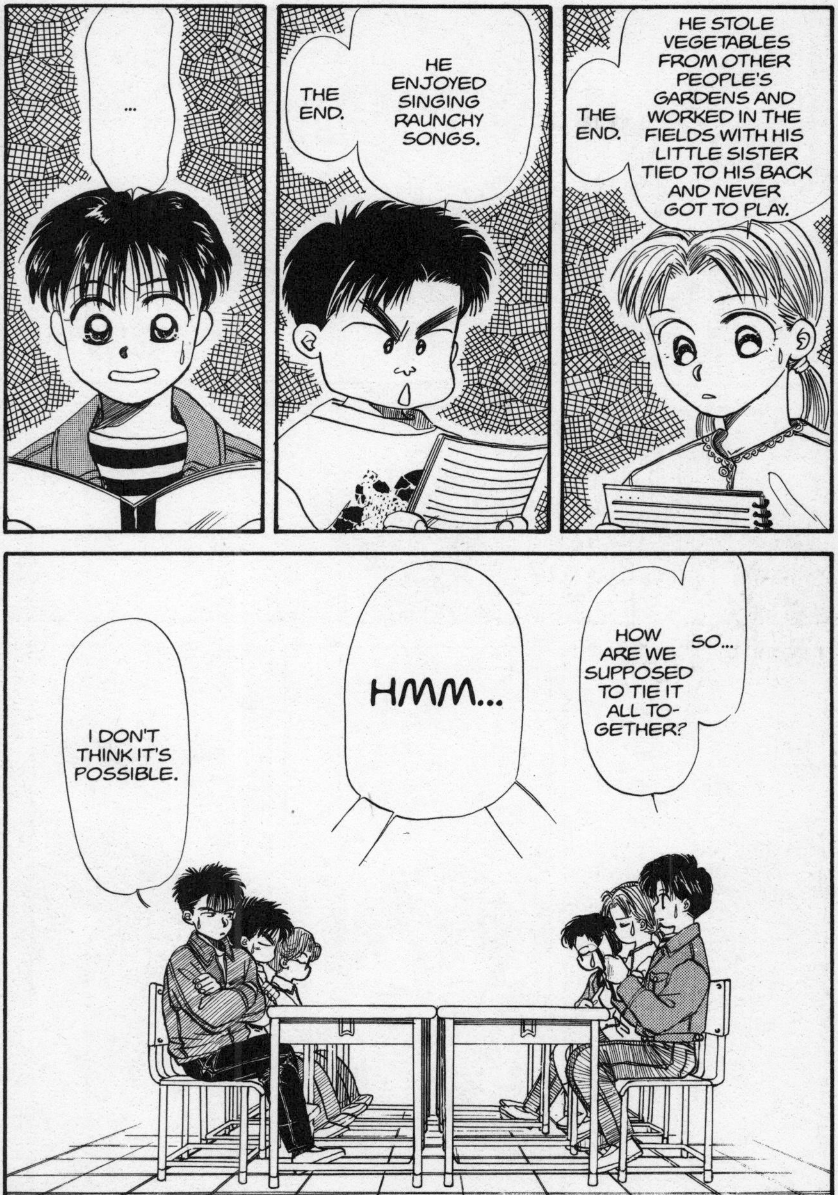
HE STOLE VEGETABLES FROM OTHER PEOPLE'S GARDENS AND WORKED IN THE FIELDS WITH HIS LITTLE SISTER TIED TO HIS BACK AND NEVER GOT TO PLAY.
THE END.
HE ENJOYED SINGING RAUNCHY SONGS.
THE END.
...
SO...
HOW ARE WE SUPPOSED TO TIE IT ALL TO-GETHER?
HMM...
I DON'T THINK IT'S POSSIBLE.

CHAPTER 32/THE END

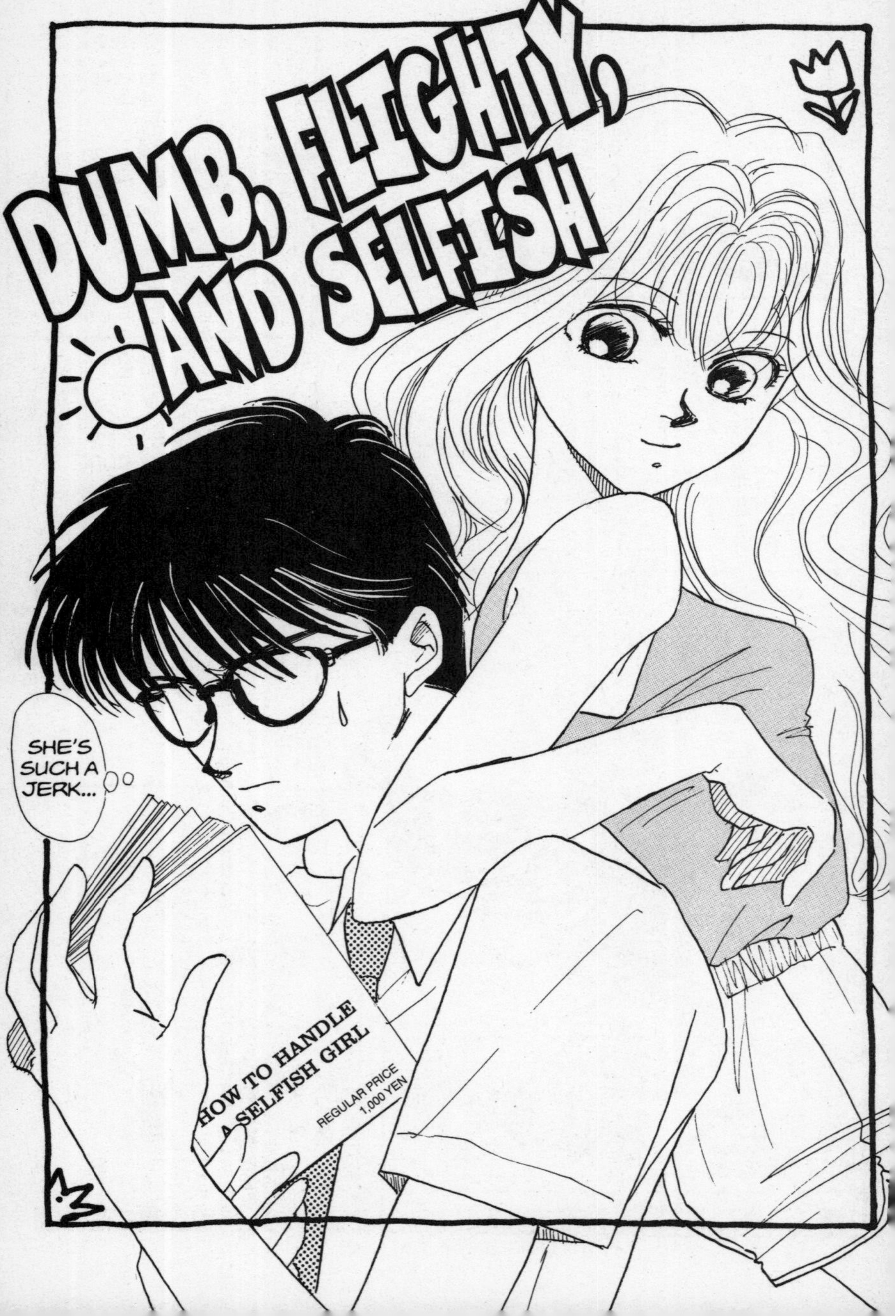
DUMB, FLIGHTY, AND SELFISH
SHE'S SUCH A JERK...
HOW TO HANDLE A SELFISH GIRL
REGULAR PRICE 1,000 YEN

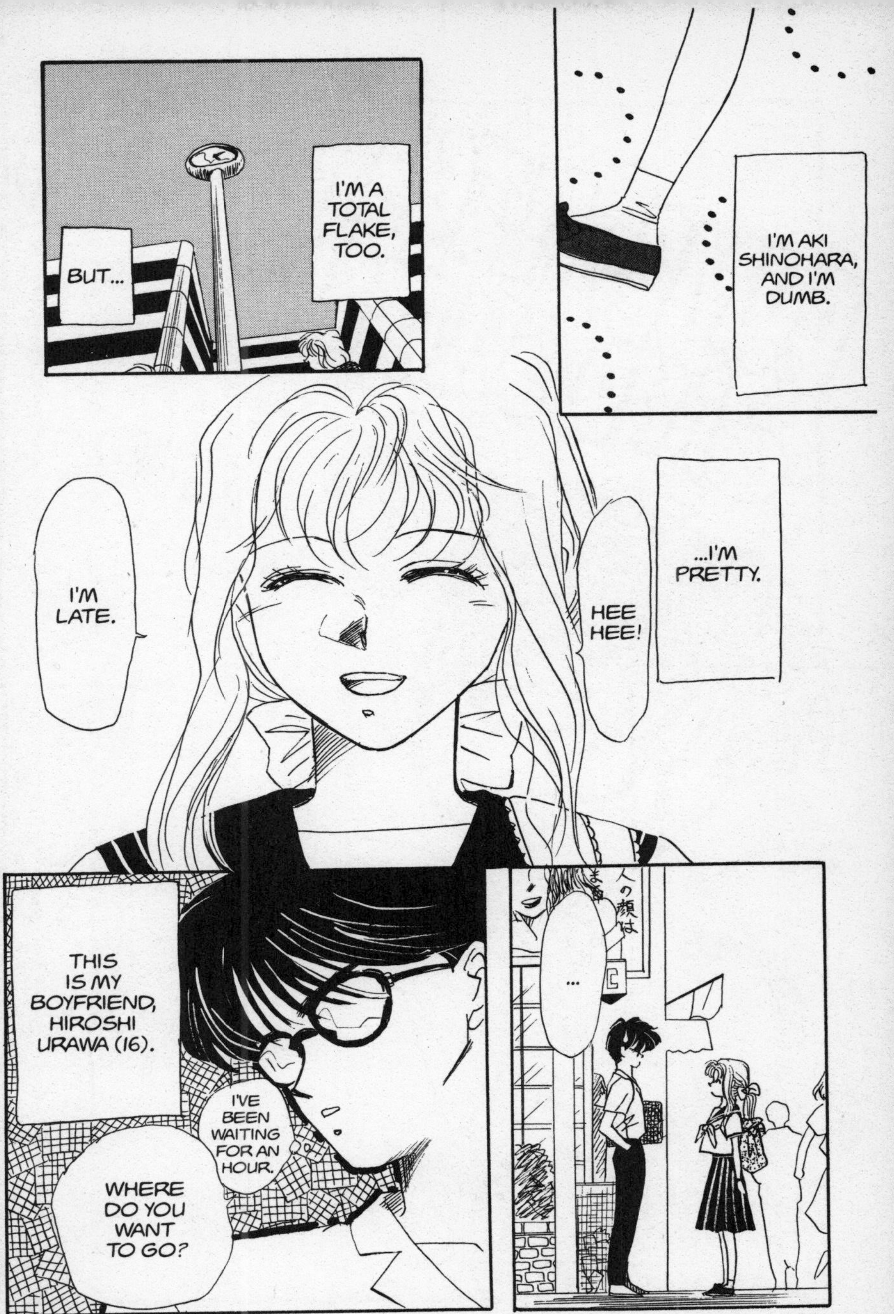
I'M AKI SHINOHARA, AND I'M DUMB.
I'M A TOTAL FLAKE, TOO.
BUT...
...I'M PRETTY.
HEE HEE!
I'M LATE.
人の顔は
...
THIS IS MY BOYFRIEND, HIROSHI URAWA (16).
I'VE BEEN WAITING FOR AN HOUR.
WHERE DO YOU WANT TO GO?

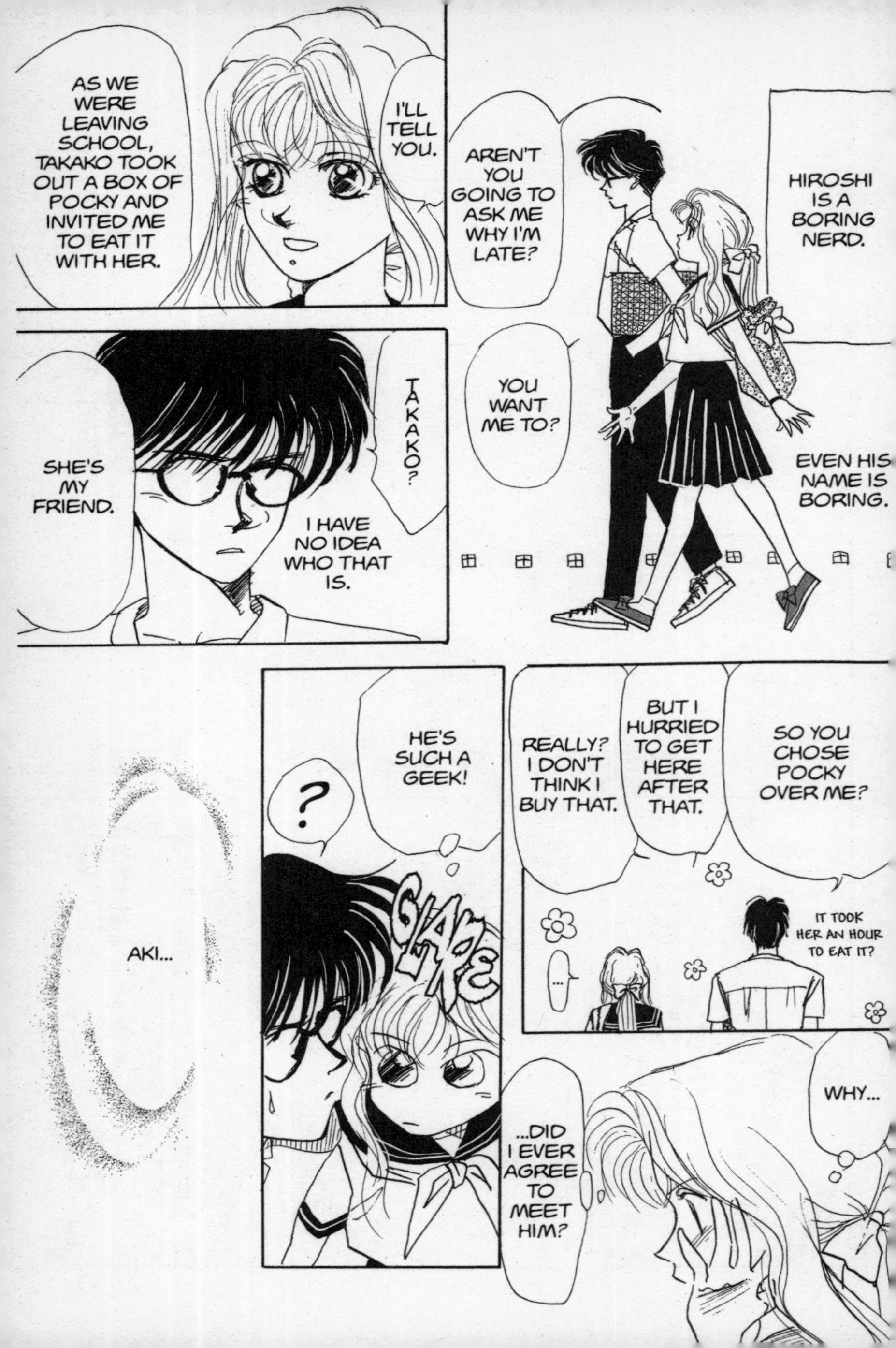
HIROSHI IS A BORING NERD.
AREN'T YOU GOING TO ASK ME WHY I'M LATE?
YOU WANT ME TO?
EVEN HIS NAME IS BORING.
I'LL TELL YOU.
AS WE WERE LEAVING SCHOOL, TAKAKO TOOK OUT A BOX OF POCKY AND INVITED ME TO EAT IT WITH HER.
TAKAKO?
I HAVE NO IDEA WHO THAT IS.
SHE'S MY FRIEND.
SO YOU CHOSE POCKY OVER ME?
BUT I HURRIED TO GET HERE AFTER THAT.
REALLY? I DON'T THINK I BUY THAT.
IT TOOK HER AN HOUR TO EAT IT?
...
WHY...
...DID I EVER AGREE TO MEET HIM?
HE'S SUCH A GEEK!
?
GLARE
AKI...

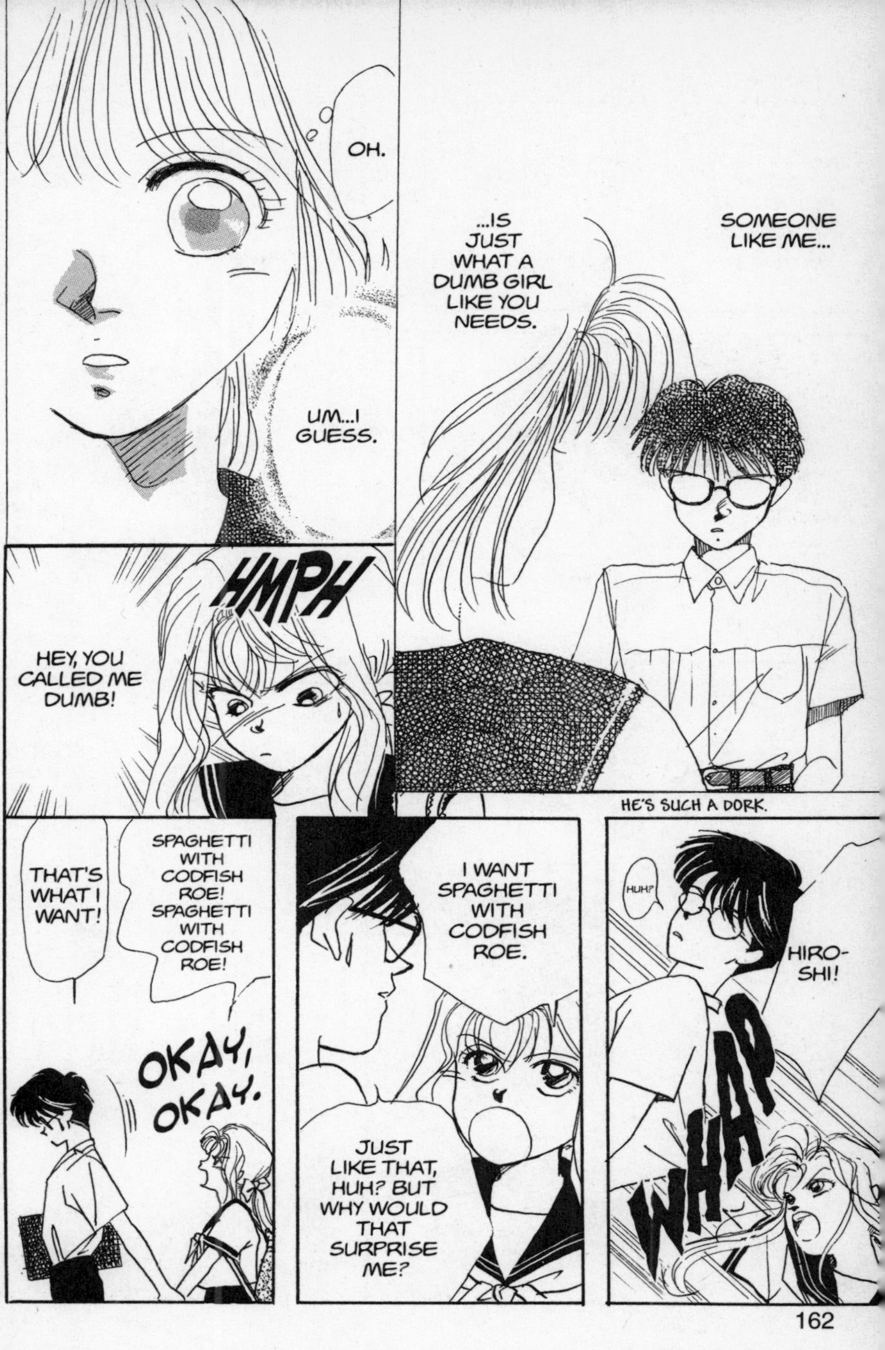
SOMEONE LIKE ME...
...IS JUST WHAT A DUMB GIRL LIKE YOU NEEDS.
OH.
UM...I GUESS.
HMPH
HEY, YOU CALLED ME DUMB!
HE'S SUCH A DORK.
HIRO-SHI!
HUH?
WHAP
I WANT SPAGHETTI WITH CODFISH ROE.
JUST LIKE THAT, HUH? BUT WHY WOULD THAT SURPRISE ME?
SPAGHETTI WITH CODFISH ROE! SPAGHETTI WITH CODFISH ROE!
THAT'S WHAT I WANT!
OKAY, OKAY.

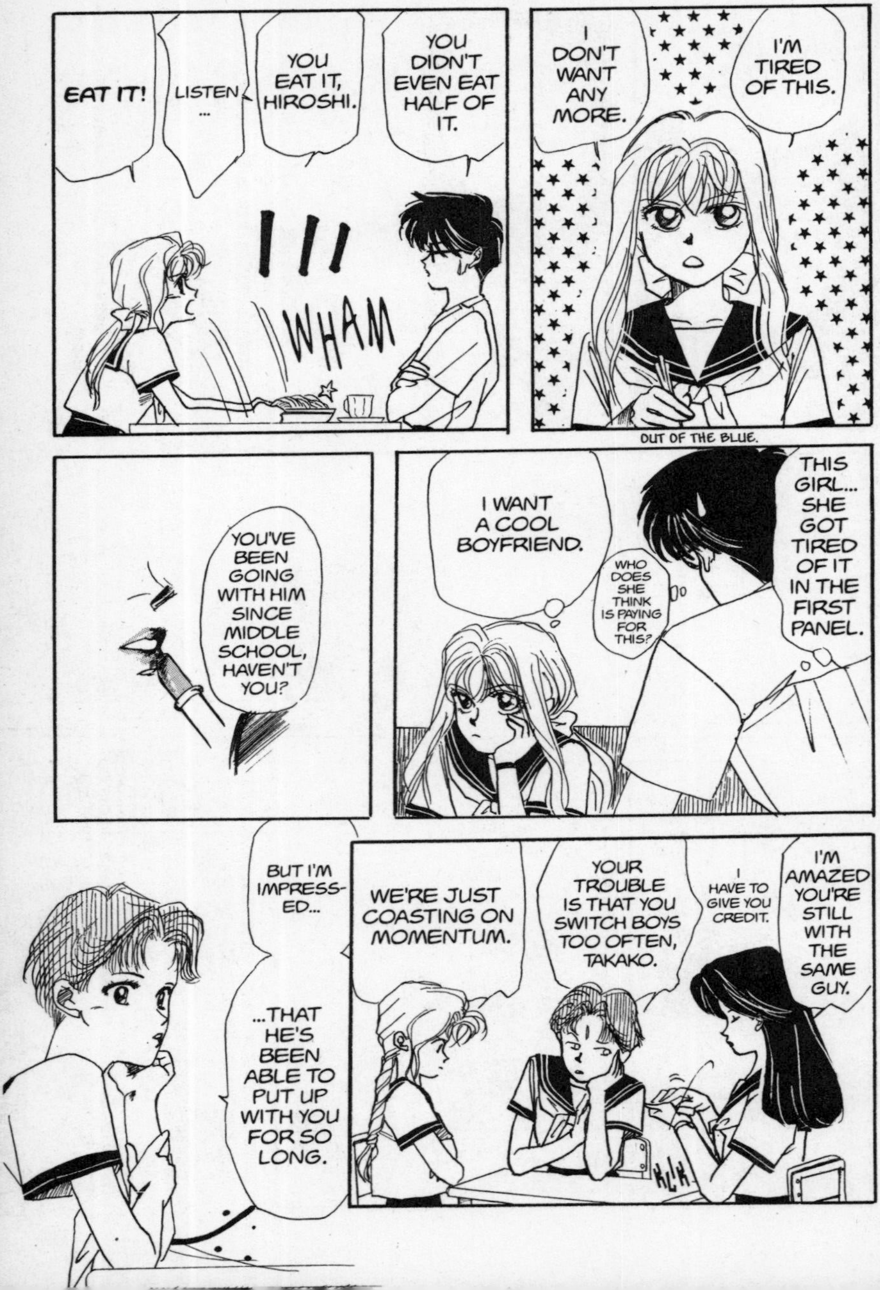
I'M TIRED OF THIS.
I DON'T WANT ANY MORE.
OUT OF THE BLUE.
YOU DIDN'T EVEN EAT HALF OF IT.
YOU EAT IT, HIROSHI.
LISTEN...
EAT IT!
WHAM
THIS GIRL... SHE GOT TIRED OF IT IN THE FIRST PANEL.
WHO DOES SHE THINK IS PAYING FOR THIS?
I WANT A COOL BOYFRIEND.
YOU'VE BEEN GOING WITH HIM SINCE MIDDLE SCHOOL, HAVEN'T YOU?
I'M AMAZED YOU'RE STILL WITH THE SAME GUY.
I HAVE TO GIVE YOU CREDIT.
YOUR TROUBLE IS THAT YOU SWITCH BOYS TOO OFTEN, TAKAKO.
WE'RE JUST COASTING ON MOMENTUM.
KLIK
BUT I'M IMPRESS-ED...
...THAT HE'S BEEN ABLE TO PUT UP WITH YOU FOR SO LONG.

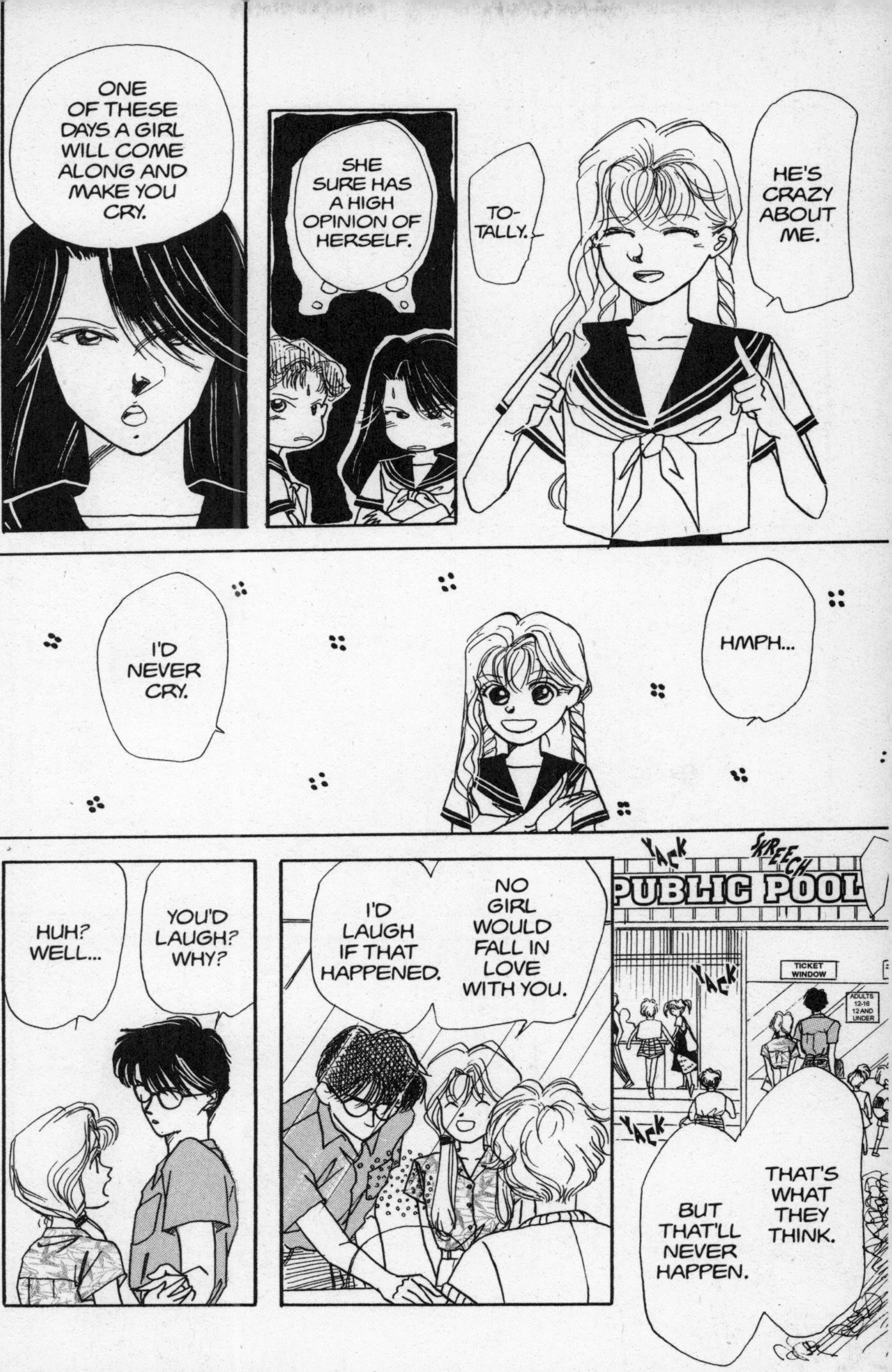
HE'S CRAZY ABOUT ME.
TO-TALLY.
SHE SURE HAS A HIGH OPINION OF HERSELF.
ONE OF THESE DAYS A GIRL WILL COME ALONG AND MAKE YOU CRY.
HMPH...
I'D NEVER CRY.
SKREECH
YACK
PUBLIC POOL
TICKET WINDOW
ADULTS 12-16 12 AND UNDER
YACK
YACK
THAT'S WHAT THEY THINK.
BUT THAT'LL NEVER HAPPEN.
NO GIRL WOULD FALL IN LOVE WITH YOU.
I'D LAUGH IF THAT HAPPENED.
YOU'D LAUGH? WHY?
HUH? WELL...

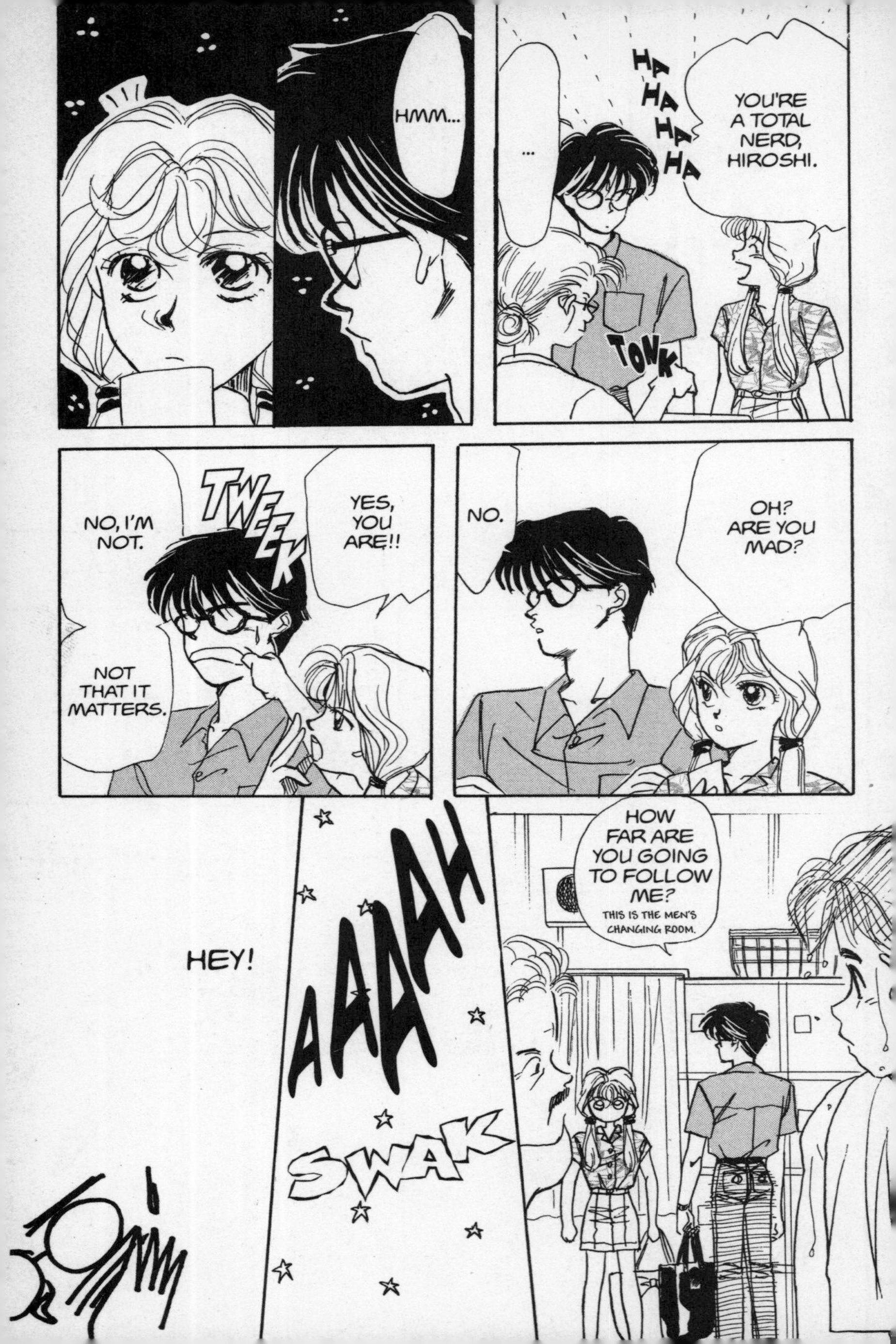
YOU'RE A TOTAL NERD, HIROSHI.
HA HA HA HA
...
TONK
HMM...
OH? ARE YOU MAD?
NO.
YES, YOU ARE!!
TWEEK
NO, I'M NOT.
NOT THAT IT MATTERS.
HOW FAR ARE YOU GOING TO FOLLOW ME?
THIS IS THE MEN'S CHANGING ROOM.
AAAAH
SWAK
HEY!

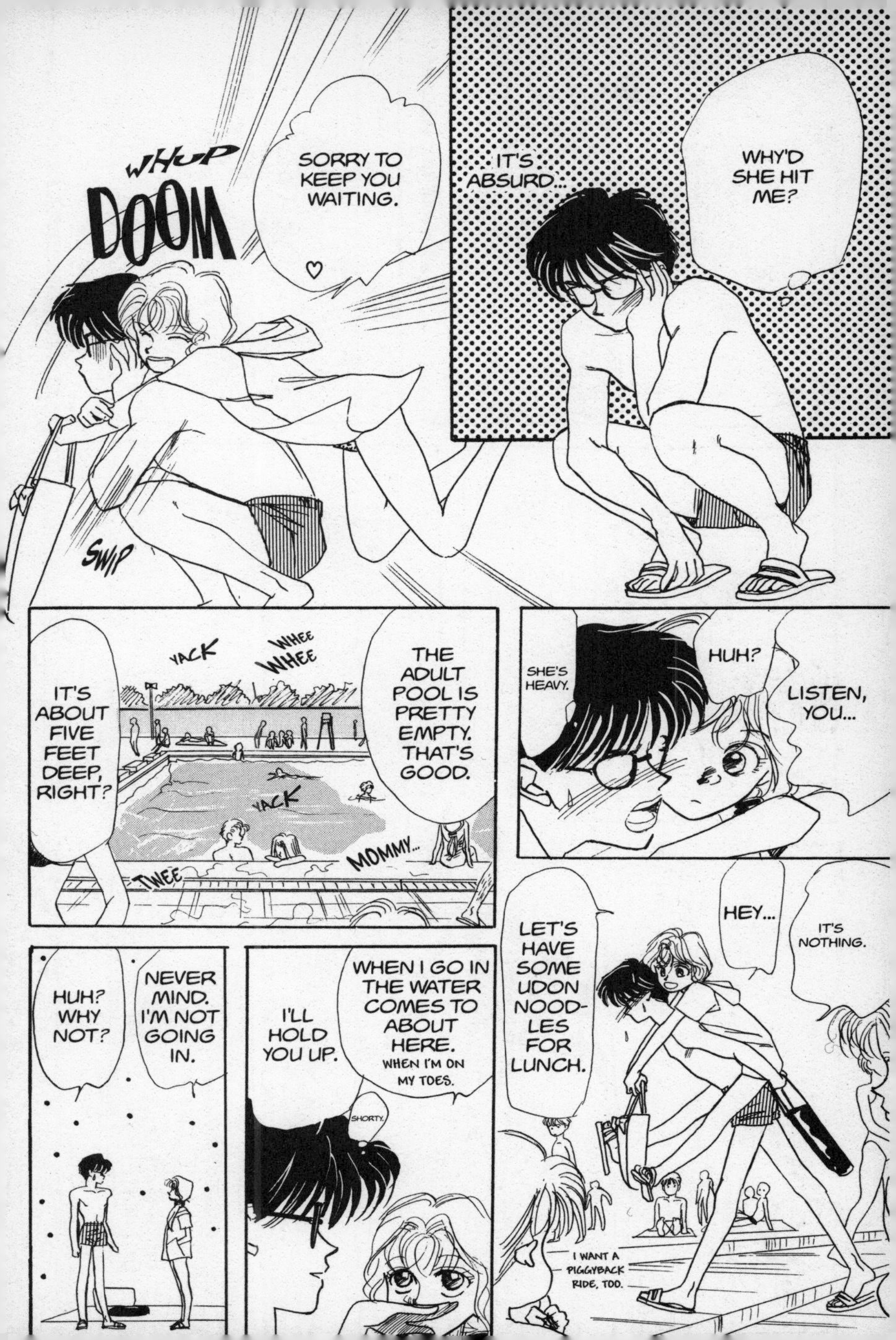
WHY'D SHE HIT ME?
IT'S ABSURD...
SORRY TO KEEP YOU WAITING. ♡
WHUP
DOOM
SWIP
HUH?
LISTEN, YOU...
SHE'S HEAVY.
THE ADULT POOL IS PRETTY EMPTY. THAT'S GOOD.
WHEE WHEE
YACK
IT'S ABOUT FIVE FEET DEEP, RIGHT?
YACK
MOMMY...
TWEE
IT'S NOTHING.
HEY...
LET'S HAVE SOME UDON NOODLES FOR LUNCH.
I WANT A PIGGYBACK RIDE, TOD.
WHEN I GO IN THE WATER COMES TO ABOUT HERE. WHEN I'M ON MY TOES.
I'LL HOLD YOU UP.
SHORTY.
NEVER MIND. I'M NOT GOING IN.
HUH? WHY NOT?

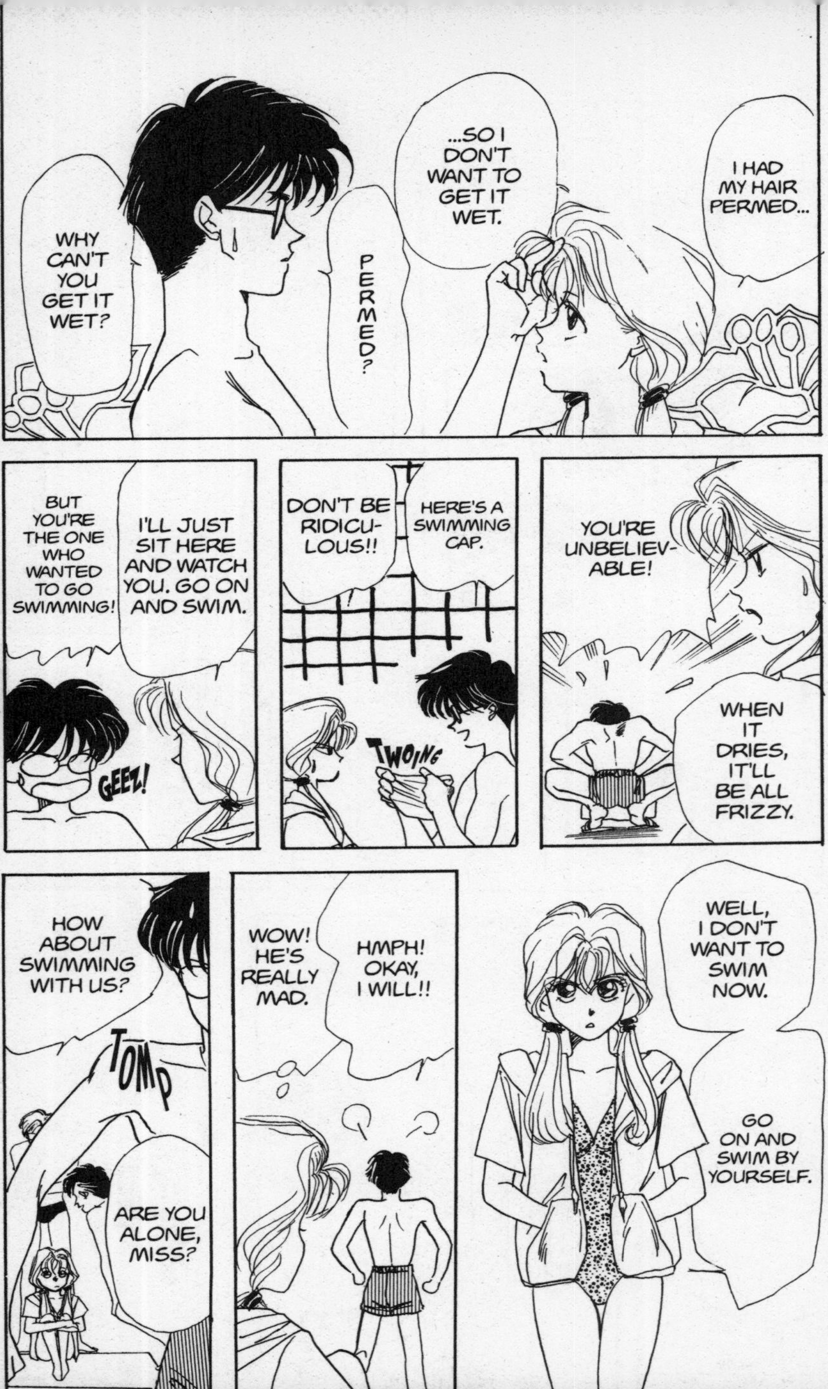
I HAD MY HAIR PERMED...
...SO I DON'T WANT TO GET IT WET.
PERMED?
WHY CAN'T YOU GET IT WET?
YOU'RE UNBELIEV-ABLE!
WHEN IT DRIES, IT'LL BE ALL FRIZZY.
HERE'S A SWIMMING CAP.
DON'T BE RIDICULOUS!!
TWOING
I'LL JUST SIT HERE AND WATCH YOU. GO ON AND SWIM.
BUT YOU'RE THE ONE WHO WANTED TO GO SWIMMING!
GEEZ!
WELL, I DON'T WANT TO SWIM NOW.
GO ON AND SWIM BY YOURSELF.
HMPH! OKAY, I WILL!!
WOW! HE'S REALLY MAD.
HOW ABOUT SWIMMING WITH US?
TOMP
ARE YOU ALONE, MISS?

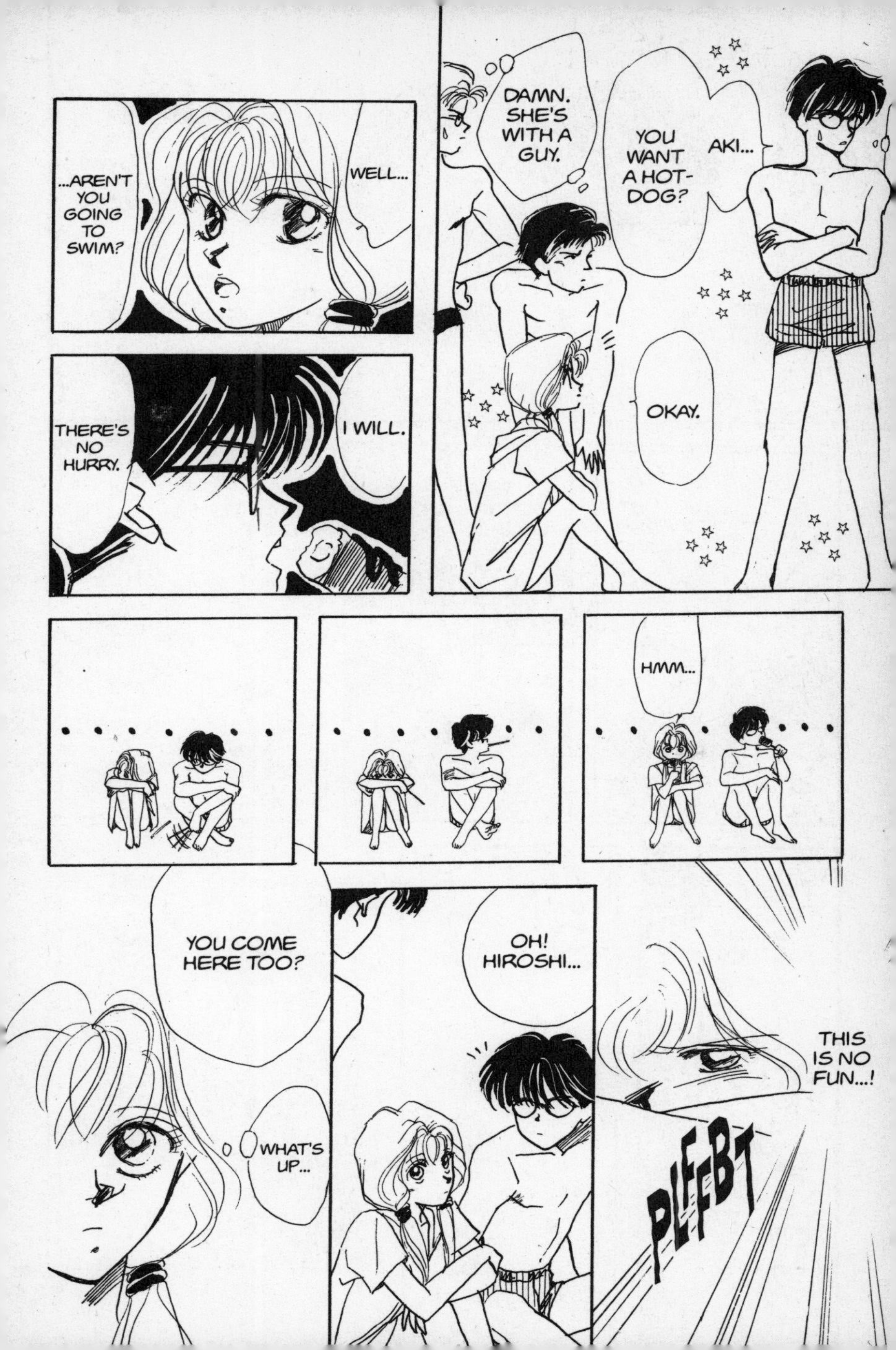
AKI...
YOU WANT A HOT-DOG?
DAMN. SHE'S WITH A GUY.
OKAY.
WELL...
...AREN'T YOU GOING TO SWIM?
I WILL.
THERE'S NO HURRY.
HMM...
THIS IS NO FUN...!
PLFFBT
OH! HIROSHI...
YOU COME HERE TOO?
WHAT'S UP...

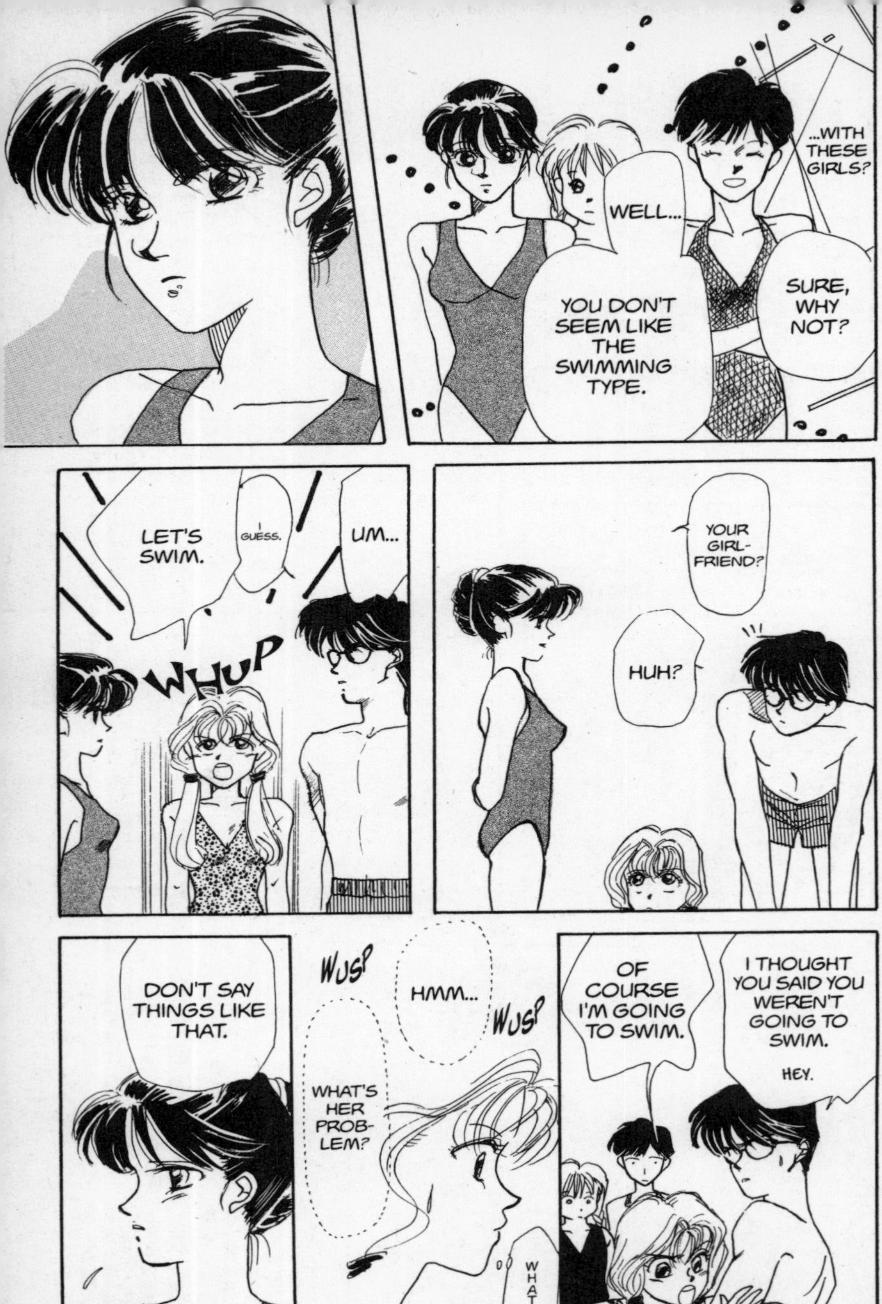
...WITH THESE GIRLS?
SURE, WHY NOT?
WELL...
YOU DON'T SEEM LIKE THE SWIMMING TYPE.
YOUR GIRL-FRIEND?
HUH?
UM...
I GUESS.
LET'S SWIM.
WHUP
I THOUGHT YOU SAID YOU WEREN'T GOING TO SWIM.
HEY.
OF COURSE I'M GOING TO SWIM.
WUSP
HMM...
WUSP
WHAT'S HER PROB-LEM?
WHAT?
DON'T SAY THINGS LIKE THAT.

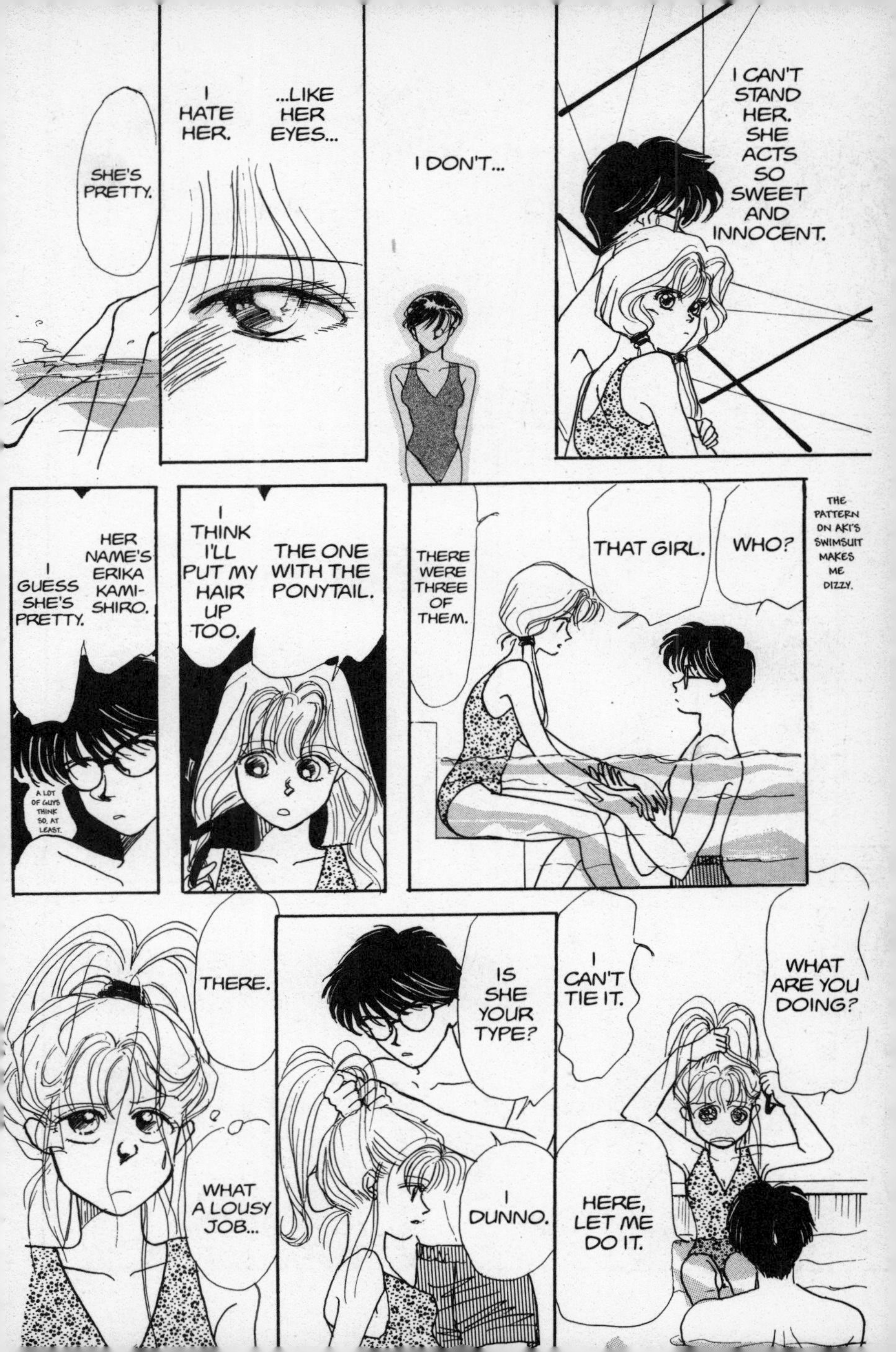
I CAN'T STAND HER. SHE ACTS SO SWEET AND INNOCENT.
I DON'T...
...LIKE HER EYES...
I HATE HER.
SHE'S PRETTY.
THE PATTERN ON AKI'S SWIMSUIT MAKES ME DIZZY.
WHO?
THAT GIRL.
THERE WERE THREE OF THEM.
THE ONE WITH THE PONYTAIL.
I THINK I'LL PUT MY HAIR UP TOO.
HER NAME'S ERIKA KAMI-SHIRO.
I GUESS SHE'S PRETTY.
A LOT OF GUYS THINK SO, AT LEAST.
WHAT ARE YOU DOING?
I CAN'T TIE IT.
HERE, LET ME DO IT.
IS SHE YOUR TYPE?
I DUNNO.
THERE.
WHAT A LOUSY JOB...

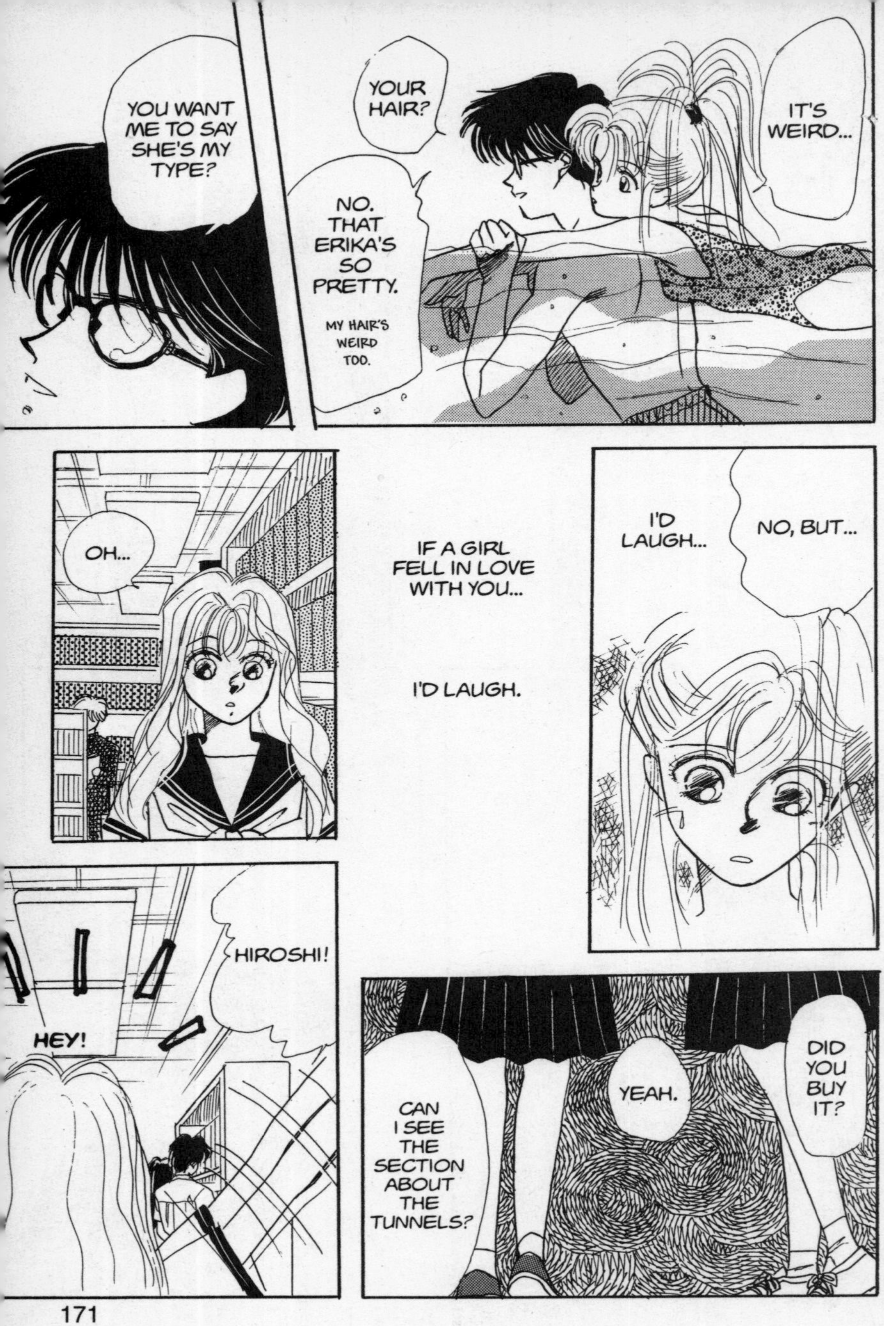

IT'S WEIRD...
YOUR HAIR?
NO. THAT ERIKA'S SO PRETTY.
MY HAIR'S WEIRD TOO.
YOU WANT ME TO SAY SHE'S MY TYPE?
NO, BUT...
I'D LAUGH...
IF A GIRL FELL IN LOVE WITH YOU...
I'D LAUGH.
OH...
DID YOU BUY IT?
YEAH.
CAN I SEE THE SECTION ABOUT THE TUNNELS?
HIROSHI!
HEY!

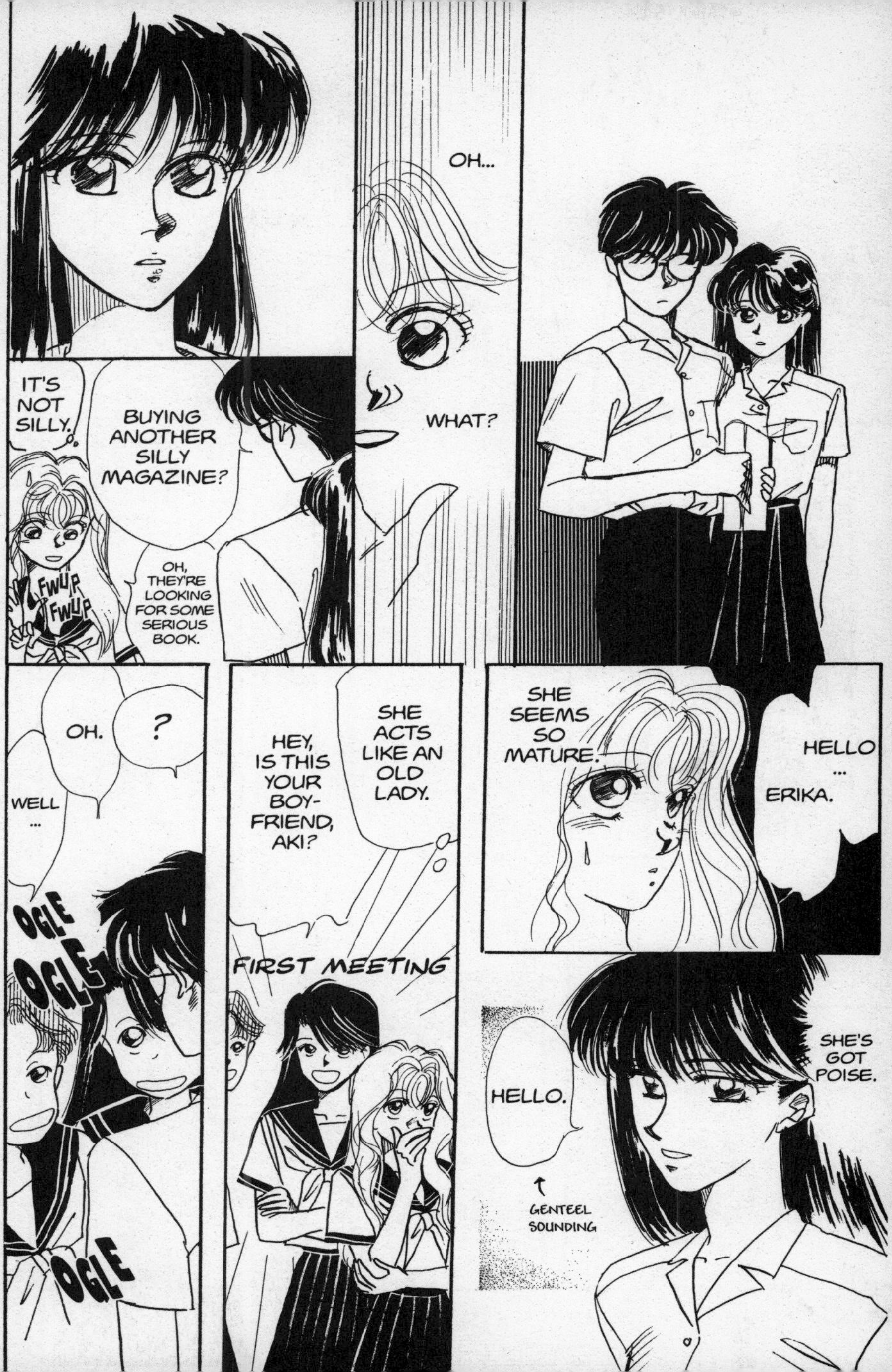

OH...
WHAT?
BUYING ANOTHER SILLY MAGAZINE?
IT'S NOT SILLY.
OH, THEY'RE LOOKING FOR SOME SERIOUS BOOK.
FWUP FWUP
HELLO ... ERIKA.
SHE SEEMS SO MATURE.
SHE'S GOT POISE.
HELLO.
GENTEEL SOUNDING
SHE ACTS LIKE AN OLD LADY.
HEY, IS THIS YOUR BOY-FRIEND, AKI?
FIRST MEETING
?
OH.
WELL ...
OGLE
OGLE
OGLE

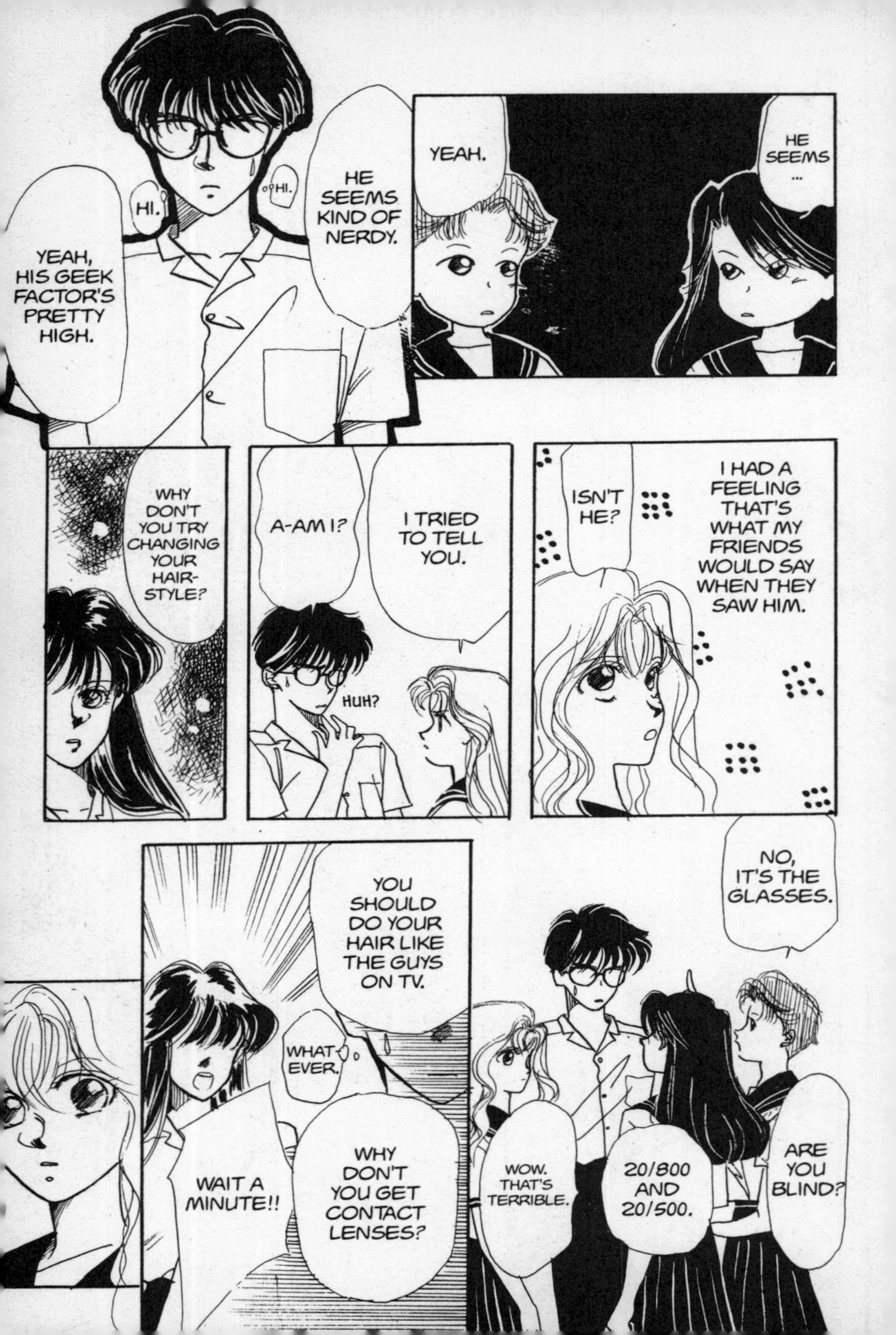
HE SEEMS ...
YEAH.
HE SEEMS KIND OF NERDY.
HI.
HI.
YEAH, HIS GEEK FACTOR'S PRETTY HIGH.
I HAD A FEELING THAT'S WHAT MY FRIENDS WOULD SAY WHEN THEY SAW HIM.
ISN'T HE?
I TRIED TO TELL YOU.
A-AM I?
HUH?
WHY DON'T YOU TRY CHANGING YOUR HAIR-STYLE?
NO, IT'S THE GLASSES.
ARE YOU BLIND?
20/800 AND 20/500.
WOW. THAT'S TERRIBLE.
YOU SHOULD DO YOUR HAIR LIKE THE GUYS ON TV.
WHAT-EVER.
WHY DON'T YOU GET CONTACT LENSES?
WAIT A MINUTE!!

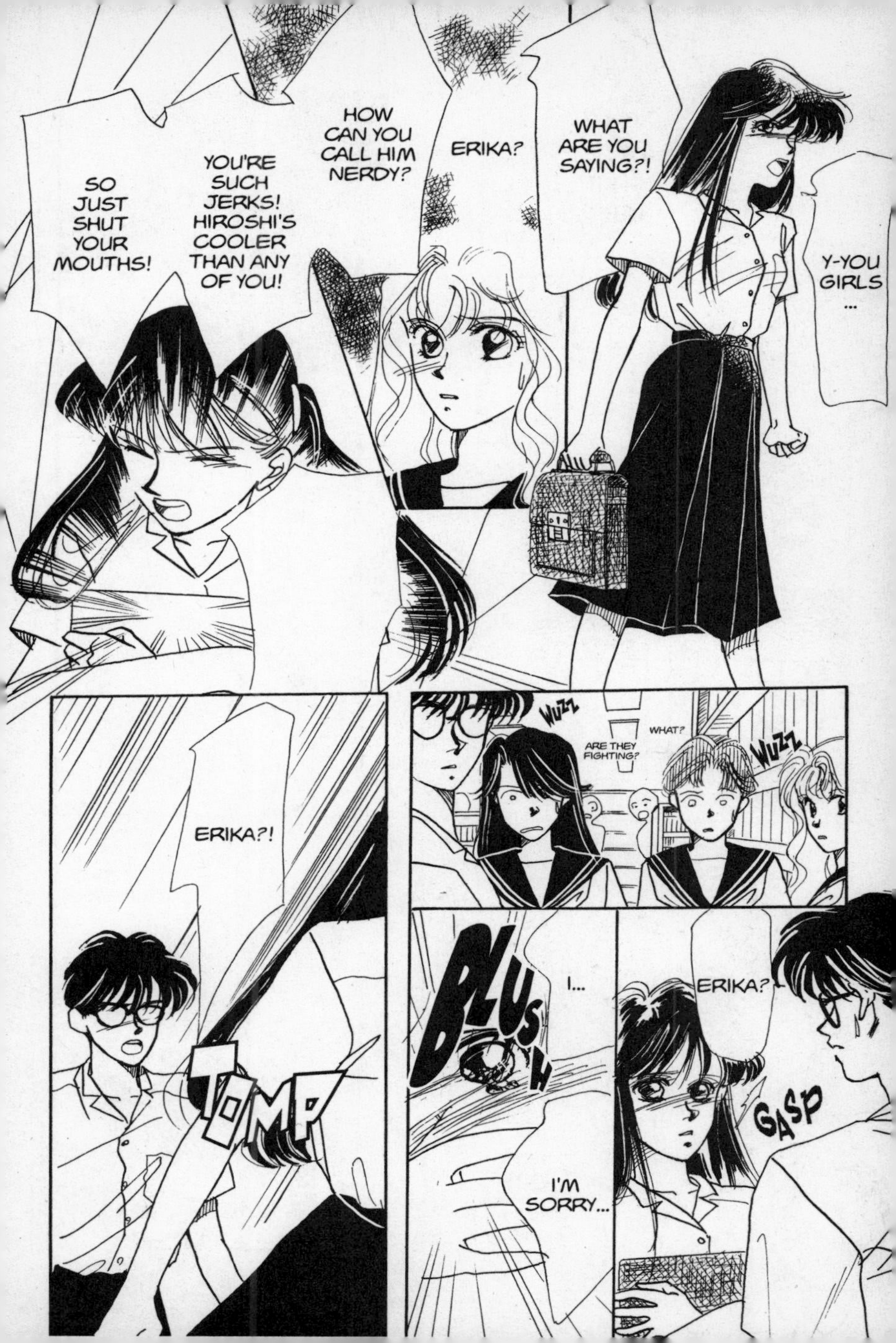
Y-YOU GIRLS ...
WHAT ARE YOU SAYING?!
ERIKA?
HOW CAN YOU CALL HIM NERDY?
YOU'RE SUCH JERKS! HIROSHI'S COOLER THAN ANY OF YOU!
SO JUST SHUT YOUR MOUTHS!
WUZZ
WHAT?
ARE THEY FIGHTING?
WUZZ
ERIKA?
GASP
BLUSH
I...
I'M SORRY...
ERIKA?!
TOMP

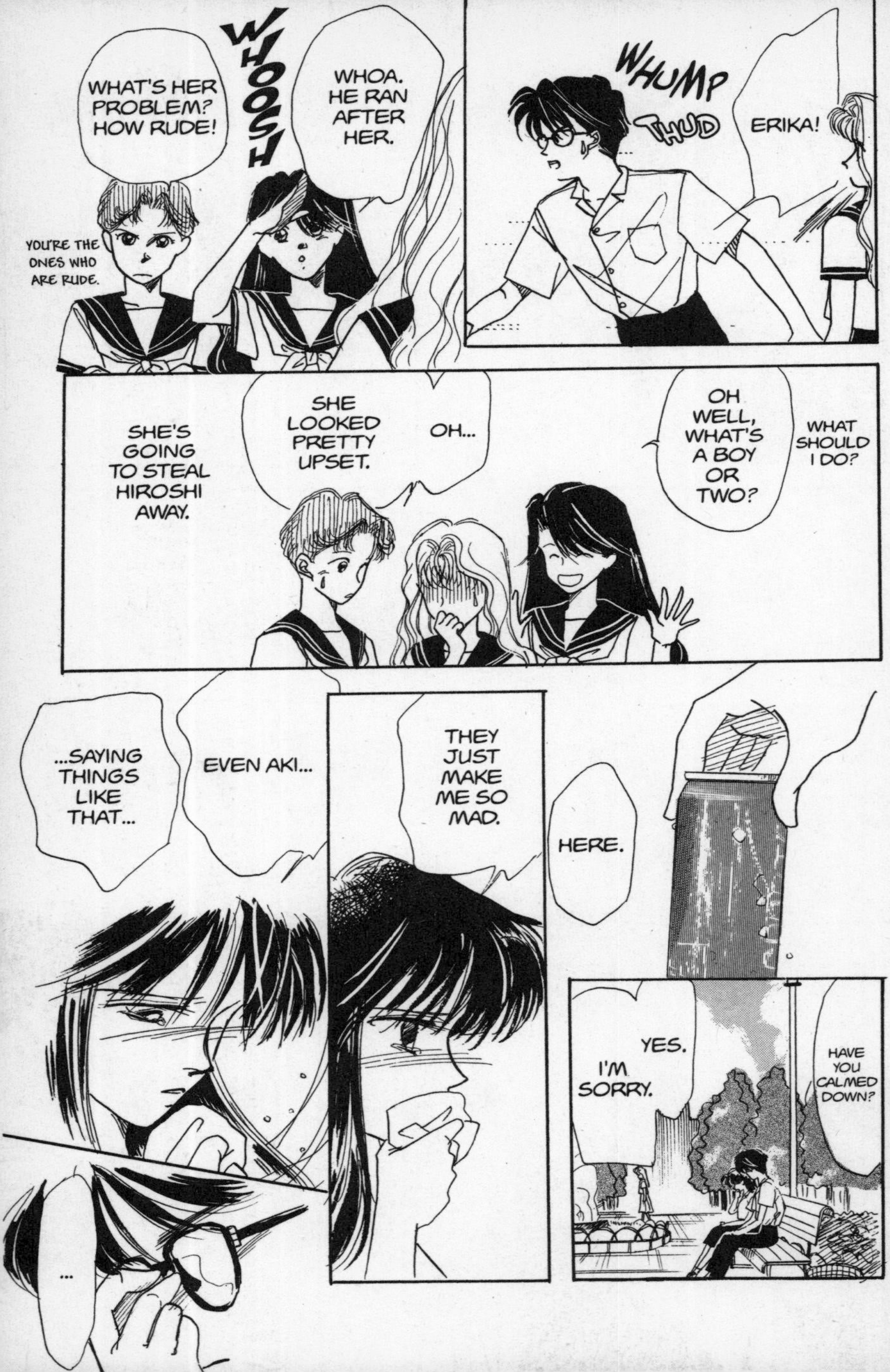
WHUMP
THUD
ERIKA!
WHOA. HE RAN AFTER HER.
WHOOSH
WHAT'S HER PROBLEM? HOW RUDE!
YOU'RE THE ONES WHO ARE RUDE.
WHAT SHOULD I DO?
OH WELL, WHAT'S A BOY OR TWO?
OH...
SHE LOOKED PRETTY UPSET.
SHE'S GOING TO STEAL HIROSHI AWAY.
HERE.
HAVE YOU CALMED DOWN?
YES.
I'M SORRY.
THEY JUST MAKE ME SO MAD.
EVEN AKI...
...SAYING THINGS LIKE THAT...
...

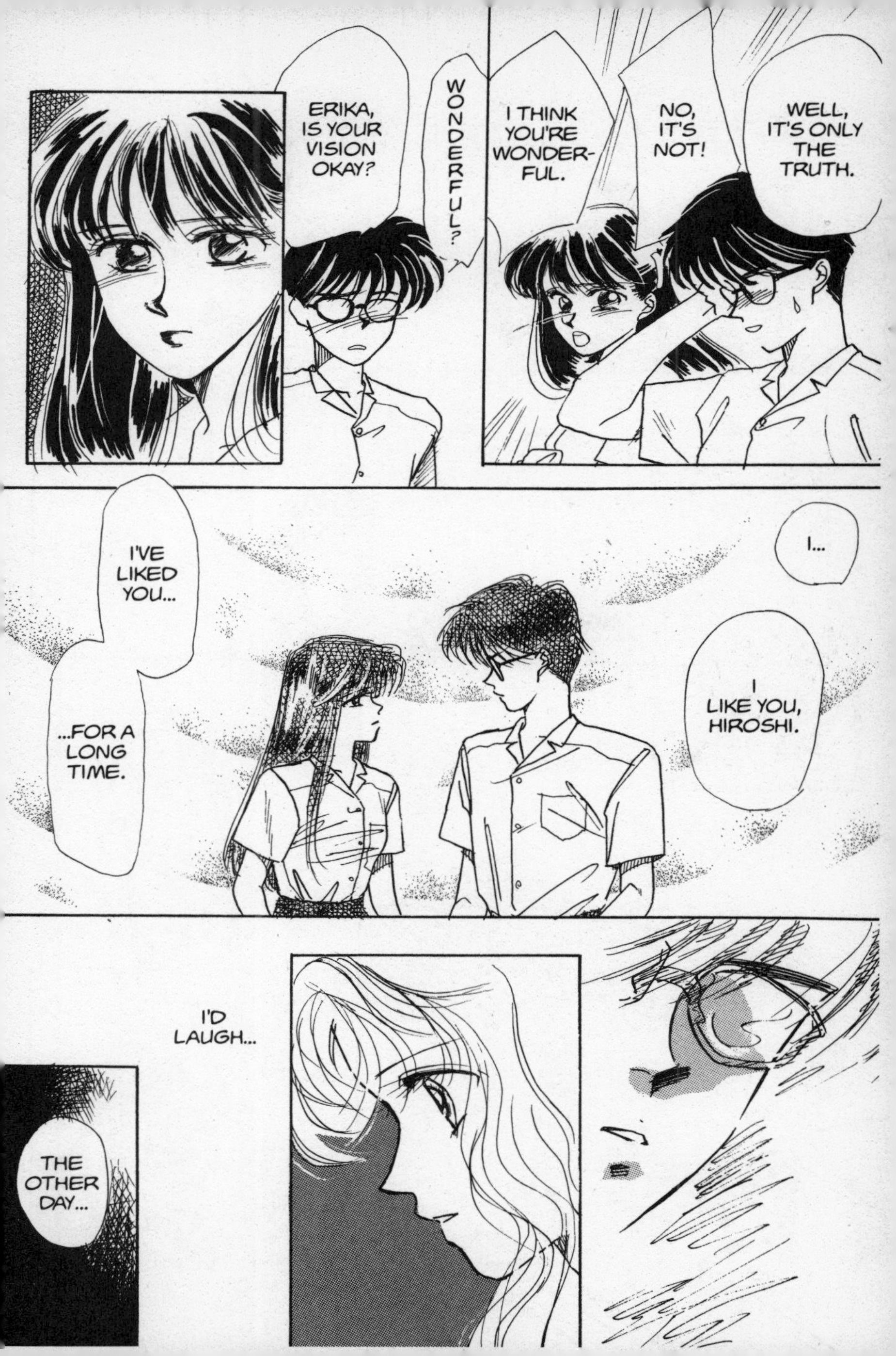
WELL, IT'S ONLY THE TRUTH.
NO, IT'S NOT!
I THINK YOU'RE WONDERFUL.
WONDERFUL?
ERIKA, IS YOUR VISION OKAY?
I...
I LIKE YOU, HIROSHI.
I'VE LIKED YOU...
...FOR A LONG TIME.
I'D LAUGH...
THE OTHER DAY...

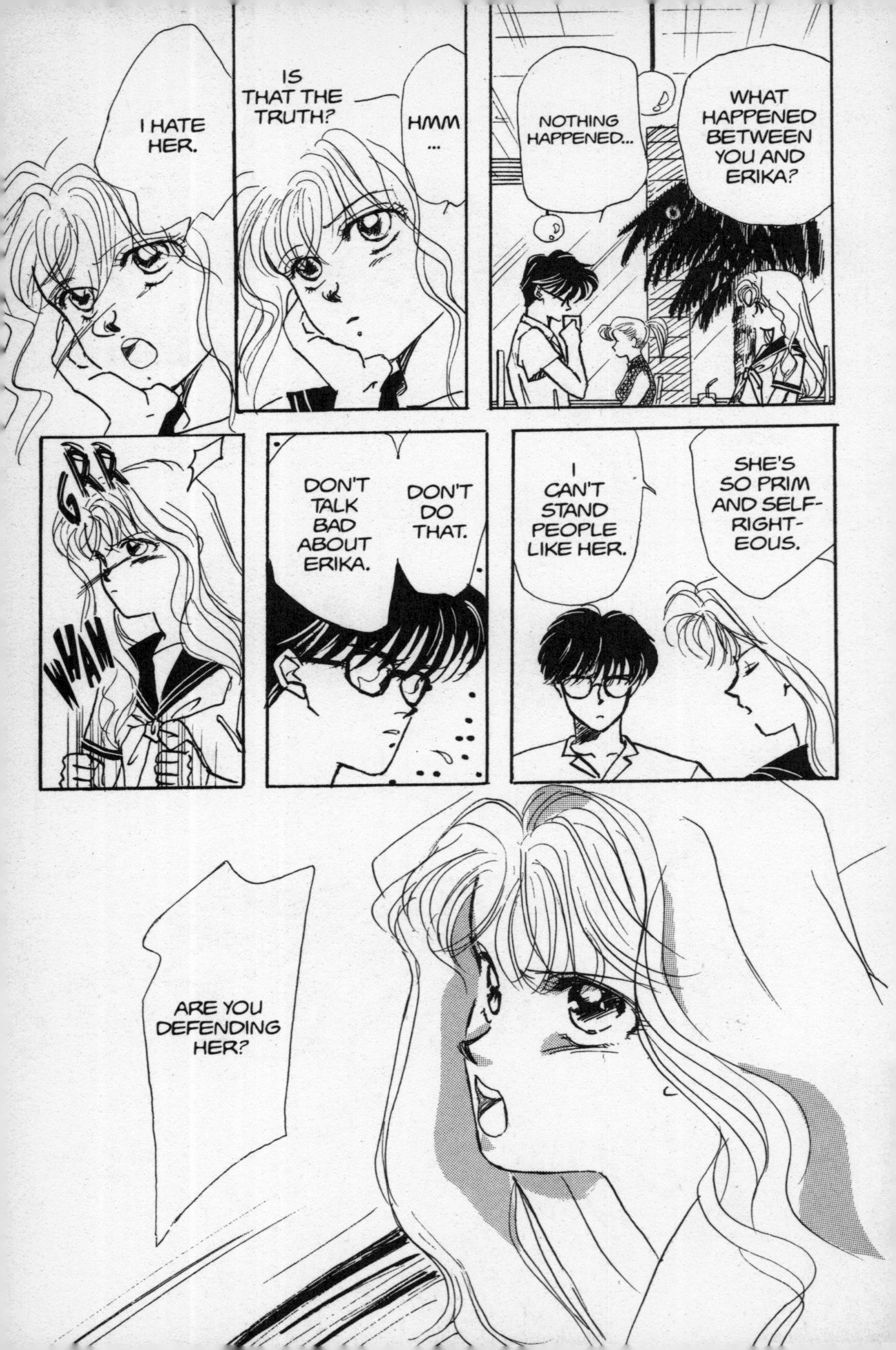
WHAT HAPPENED BETWEEN YOU AND ERIKA?
NOTHING HAPPENED...
HMM ...
IS THAT THE TRUTH?
I HATE HER.
SHE'S SO PRIM AND SELF-RIGHTEOUS.
I CAN'T STAND PEOPLE LIKE HER.
DON'T DO THAT.
DON'T TALK BAD ABOUT ERIKA.
GRR
WHAM
ARE YOU DEFENDING HER?

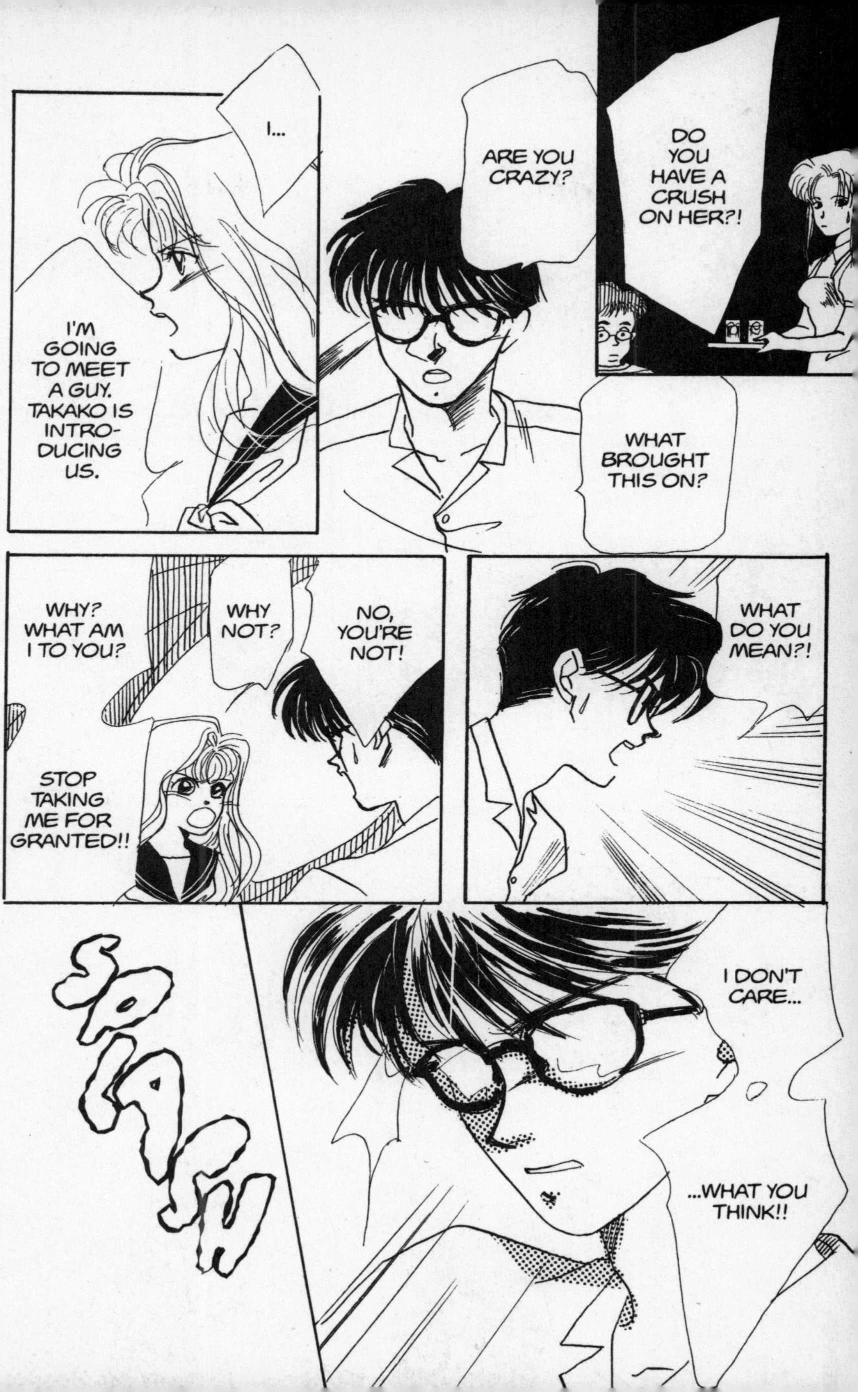
DO YOU HAVE A CRUSH ON HER?!
ARE YOU CRAZY?
WHAT BROUGHT THIS ON?
I...
I'M GOING TO MEET A GUY. TAKAKO IS INTRO-DUCING US.
WHAT DO YOU MEAN?!
NO, YOU'RE NOT!
WHY NOT?
WHY? WHAT AM I TO YOU?
STOP TAKING ME FOR GRANTED!!
I DON'T CARE...
...WHAT YOU THINK!!
SPLASH

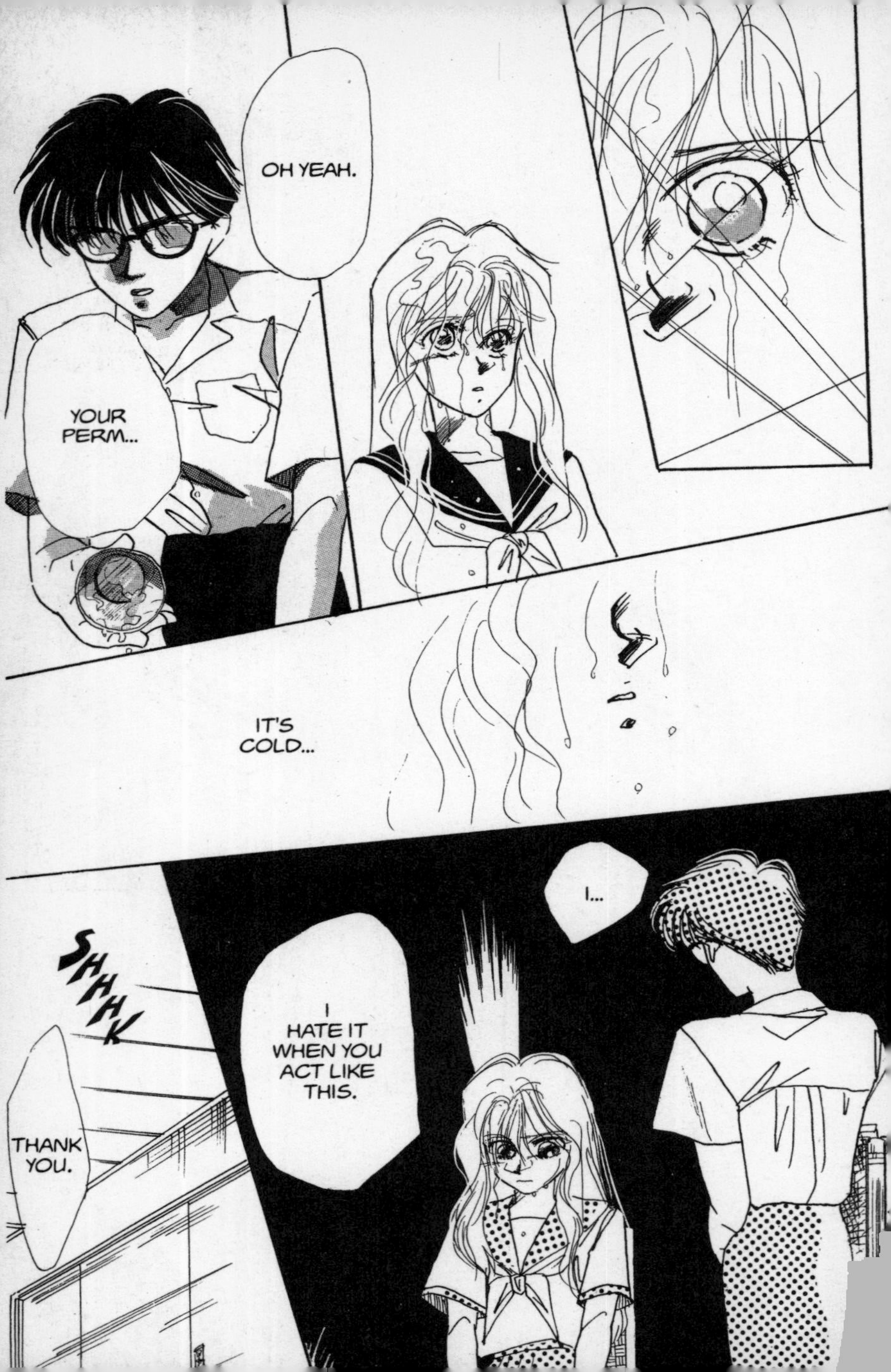
OH YEAH.
YOUR PERM...
IT'S COLD...
I...
I HATE IT WHEN YOU ACT LIKE THIS.
SHHHK
THANK YOU.

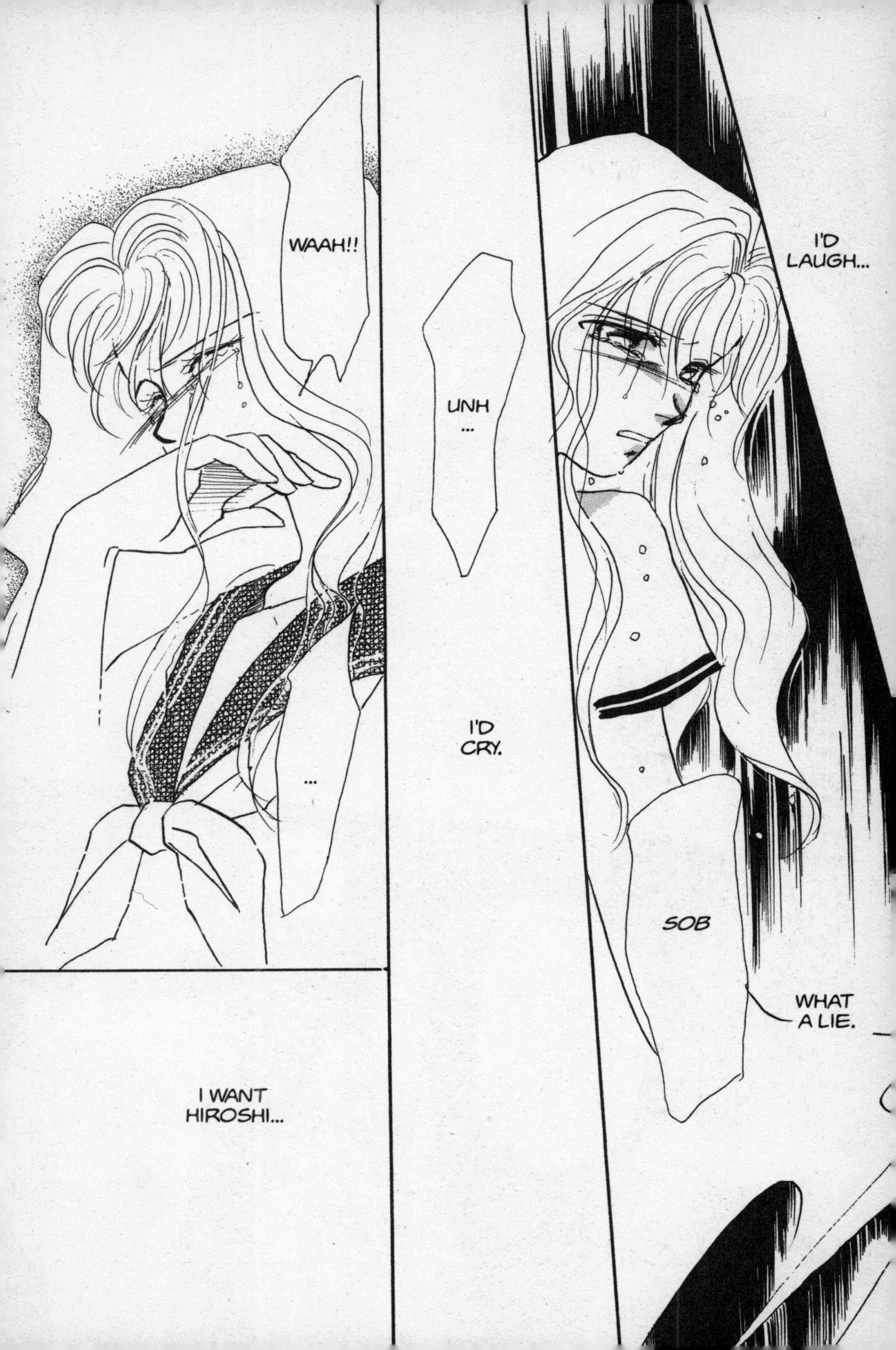
I'D LAUGH...
SOB
WHAT A LIE.
UNH ...
I'D CRY.
WAAH!!
...
I WANT HIROSHI...

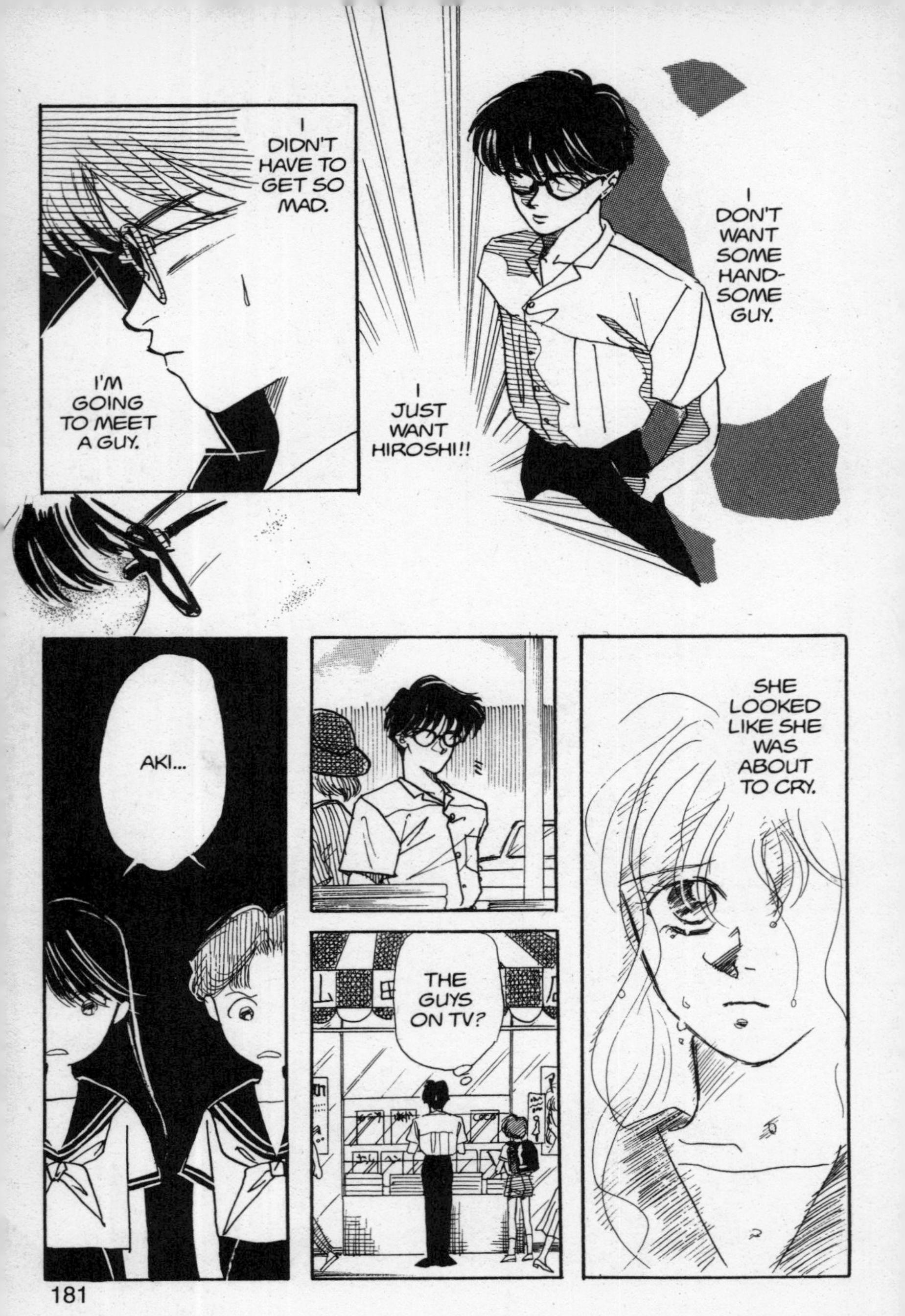
I DON'T WANT SOME HAND-SOME GUY.
I JUST WANT HIROSHI!!
I DIDN'T HAVE TO GET SO MAD.
I'M GOING TO MEET A GUY.
SHE LOOKED LIKE SHE WAS ABOUT TO CRY.
THE GUYS ON TV?
AKI...

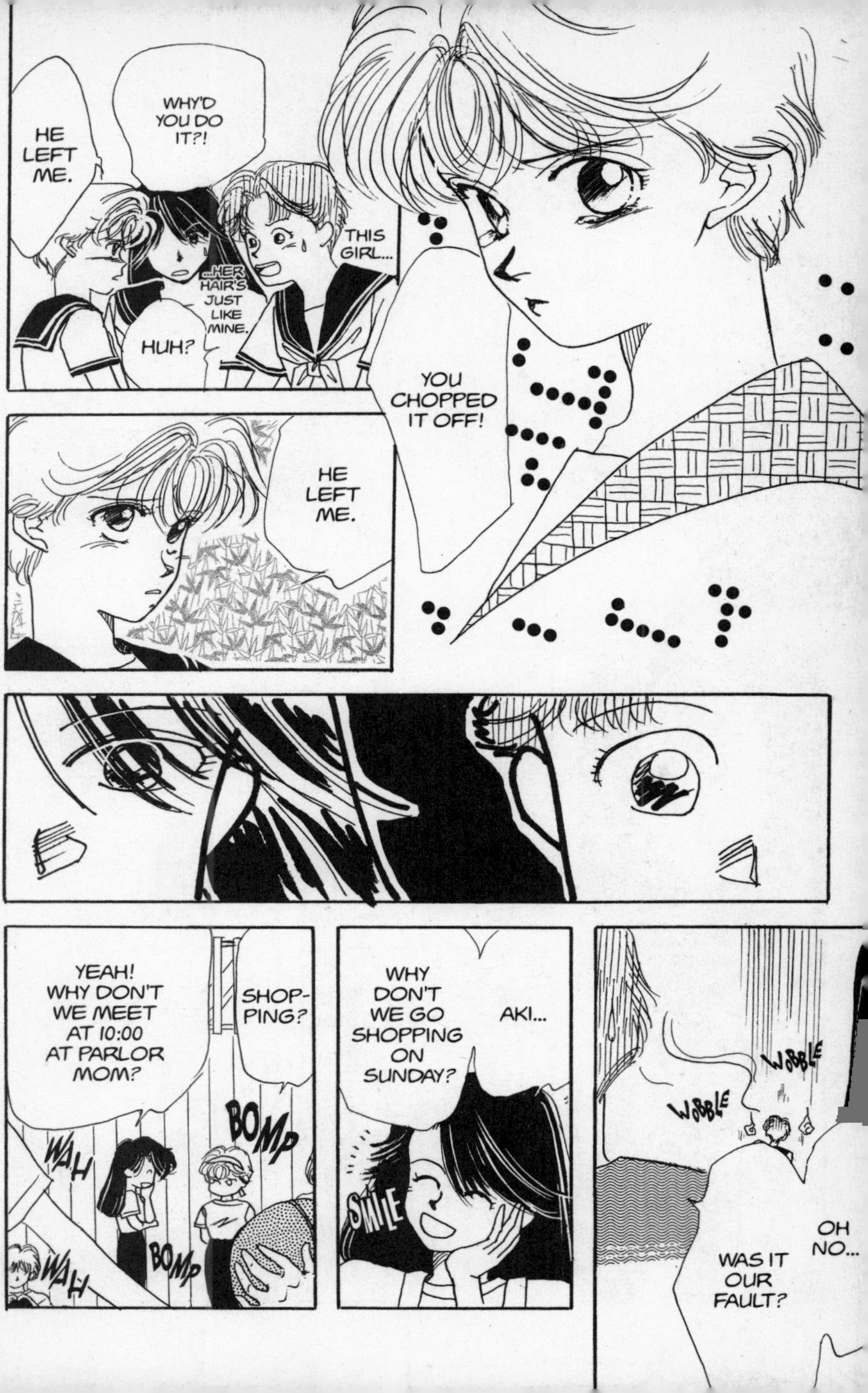
YOU CHOPPED IT OFF!
THIS GIRL...
WHY'D YOU DO IT?!
HE LEFT ME.
...HER HAIR'S JUST LIKE MINE.
HUH?
HE LEFT ME.
OH NO...
WAS IT OUR FAULT?
WOBBLE
WOBBLE
AKI...
WHY DON'T WE GO SHOPPING ON SUNDAY?
SMILE
SHOP-PING?
YEAH! WHY DON'T WE MEET AT 10:00 AT PARLOR MOM?
BOMP
BOMP
WAH
WAH

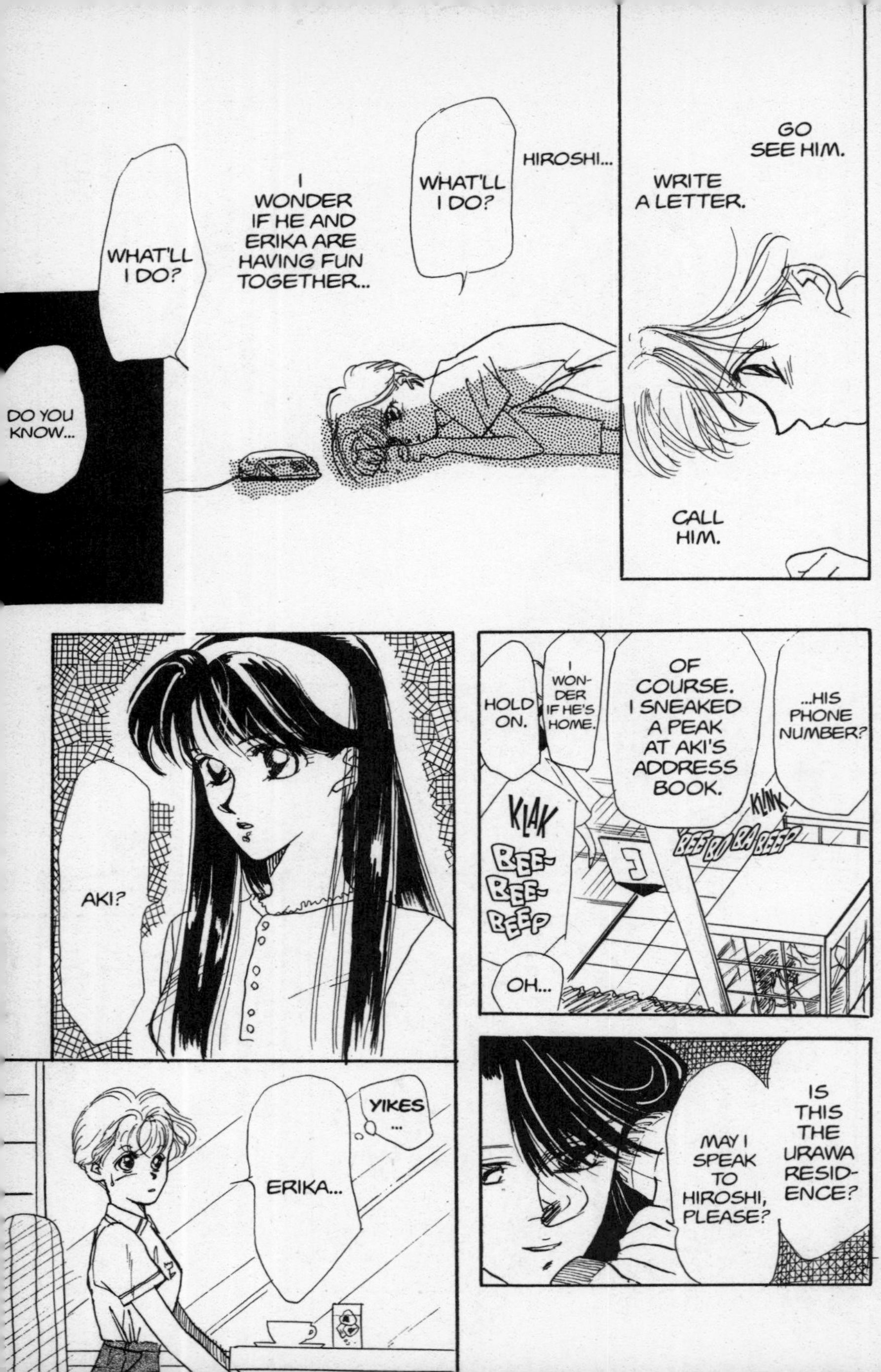

GO SEE HIM.
WRITE A LETTER.
CALL HIM.
HIROSHI...
WHAT'LL I DO?
I WONDER IF HE AND ERIKA ARE HAVING FUN TOGETHER...
WHAT'LL I DO?
DO YOU KNOW...
...HIS PHONE NUMBER?
OF COURSE. I SNEAKED A PEAK AT AKI'S ADDRESS BOOK.
I WONDER IF HE'S HOME.
HOLD ON.
KLINK
BEE BU BA BEEP
KLAK
BEE-BEE-BEEP
OH...
AKI?
IS THIS THE URAWA RESIDENCE?
MAY I SPEAK TO HIROSHI, PLEASE?
YIKES...
ERIKA...

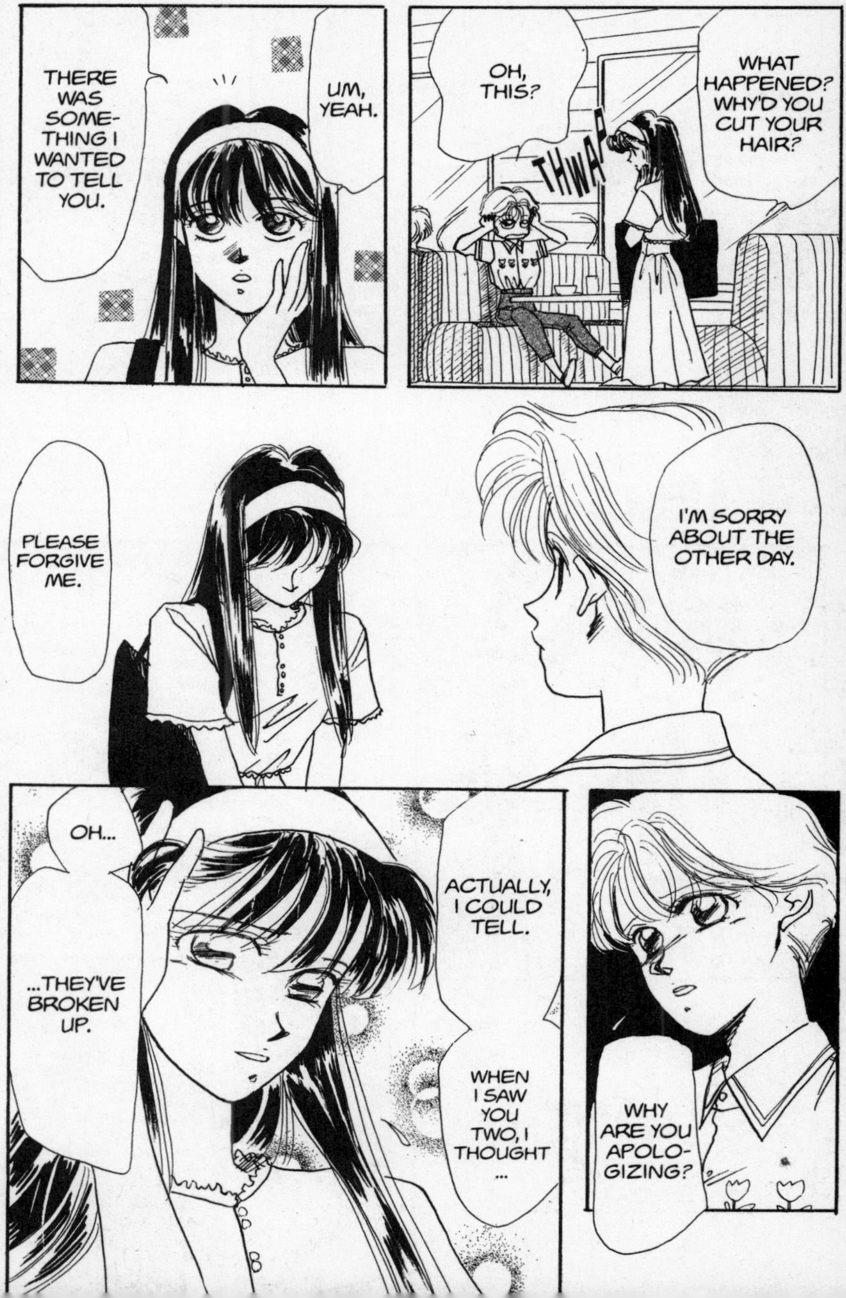
WHAT HAPPENED? WHY'D YOU CUT YOUR HAIR?
THWAP
OH, THIS?
UM, YEAH.
THERE WAS SOME-THING I WANTED TO TELL YOU.
I'M SORRY ABOUT THE OTHER DAY.
PLEASE FORGIVE ME.
WHY ARE YOU APOLO-GIZING?
ACTUALLY, I COULD TELL.
WHEN I SAW YOU TWO, I THOUGHT ...
OH...
...THEY'VE BROKEN UP.

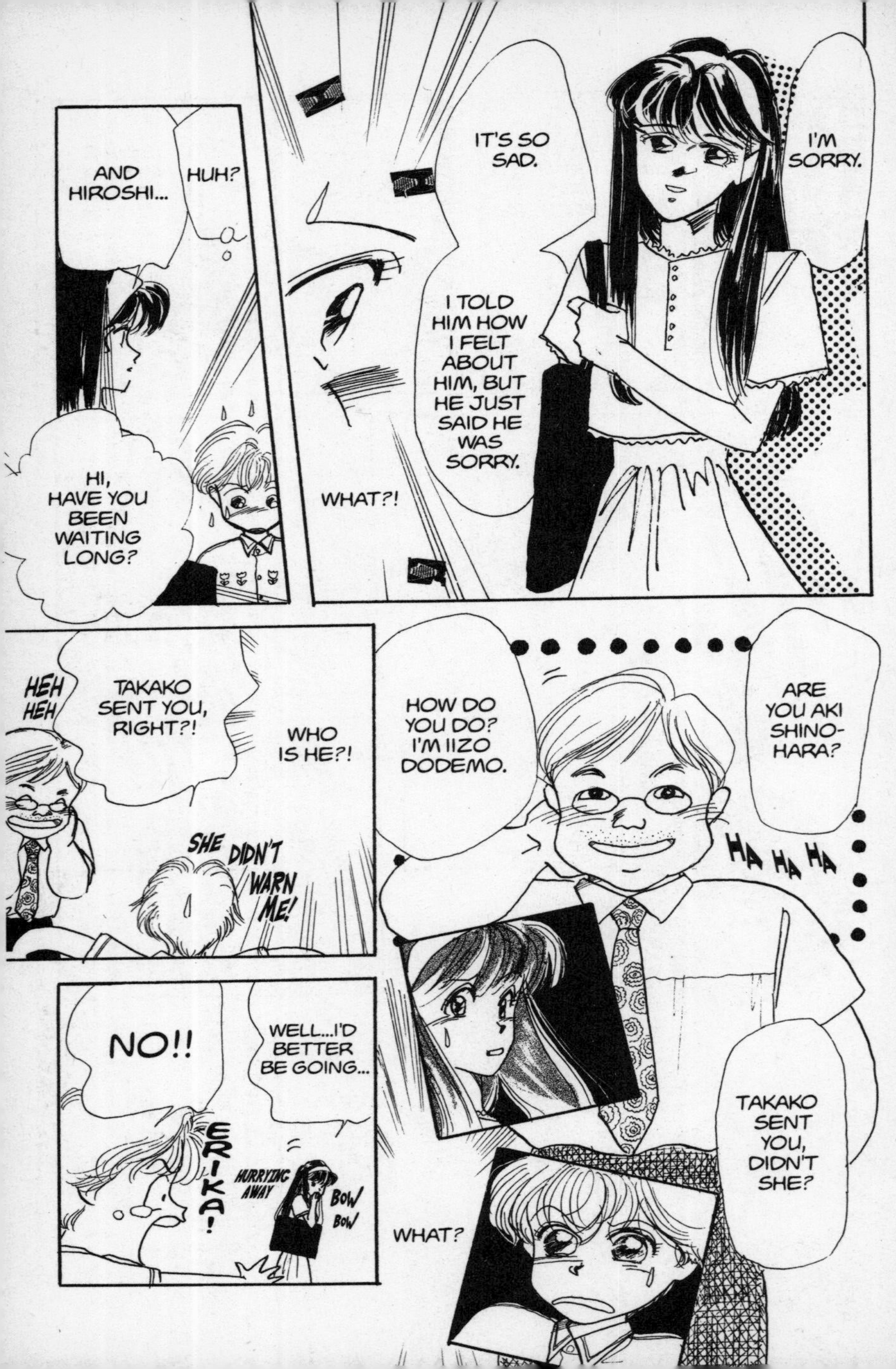
I'M SORRY.
IT'S SO SAD.
I TOLD HIM HOW I FELT ABOUT HIM, BUT HE JUST SAID HE WAS SORRY.
WHAT?!
HUH?
AND HIROSHI...
HI, HAVE YOU BEEN WAITING LONG?
ARE YOU AKI SHINO-HARA?
• • • • • • • • •
HOW DO YOU DO? I'M IIZO DODEMO.
HA HA HA
TAKAKO SENT YOU, DIDN'T SHE?
WHAT?
WHO IS HE?!
TAKAKO SENT YOU, RIGHT?!
HEH HEH
SHE DIDN'T WARN ME!
WELL...I'D BETTER BE GOING...
NO!!
ERIKA!
HURRYING AWAY
BOW BOW

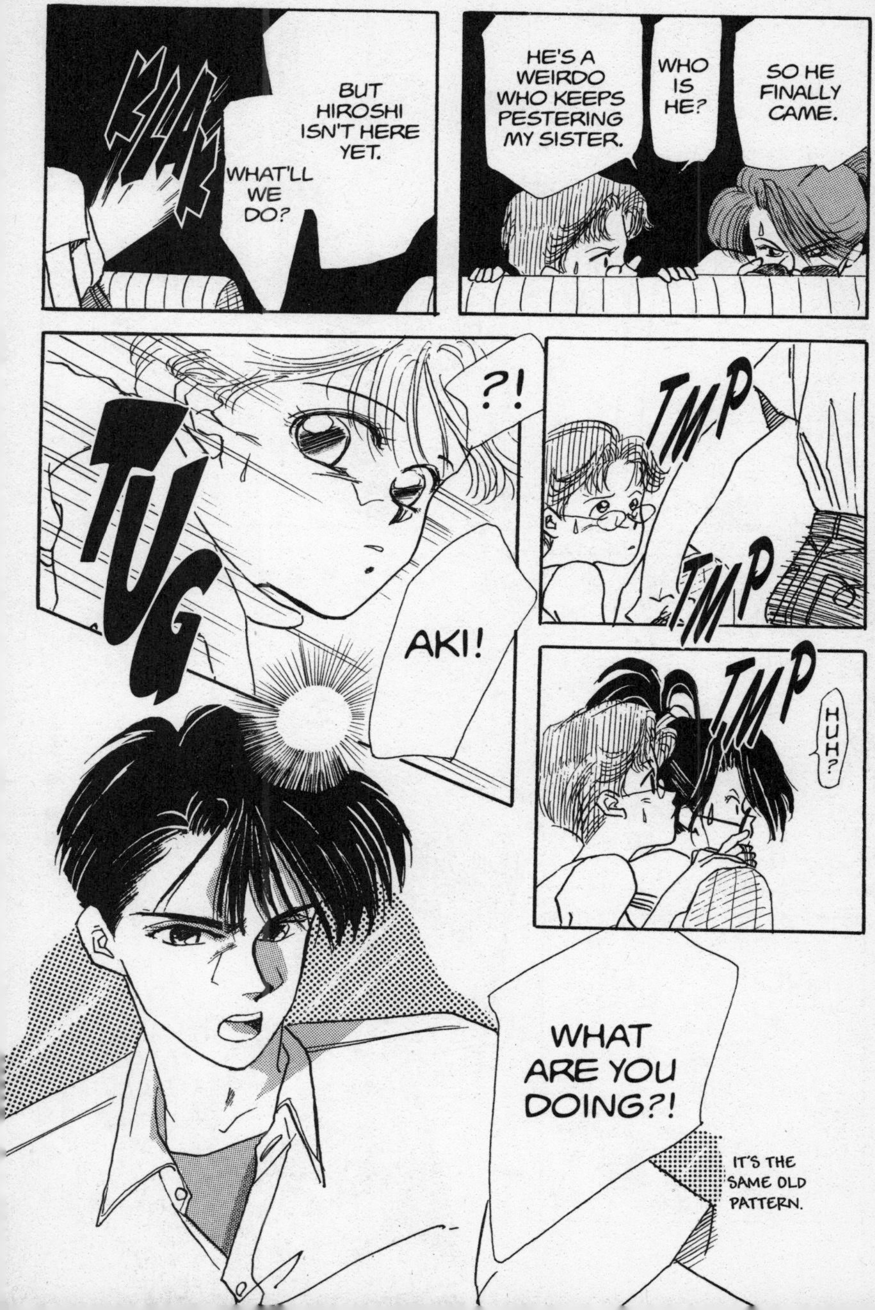
SO HE FINALLY CAME.
WHO IS HE?
HE'S A WEIRDO WHO KEEPS PESTERING MY SISTER.
BUT HIROSHI ISN'T HERE YET.
WHAT'LL WE DO?
TMP
TMP
TMP
HUH?
?!
TUG
AKI!
WHAT ARE YOU DOING?!
IT'S THE SAME OLD PATTERN.

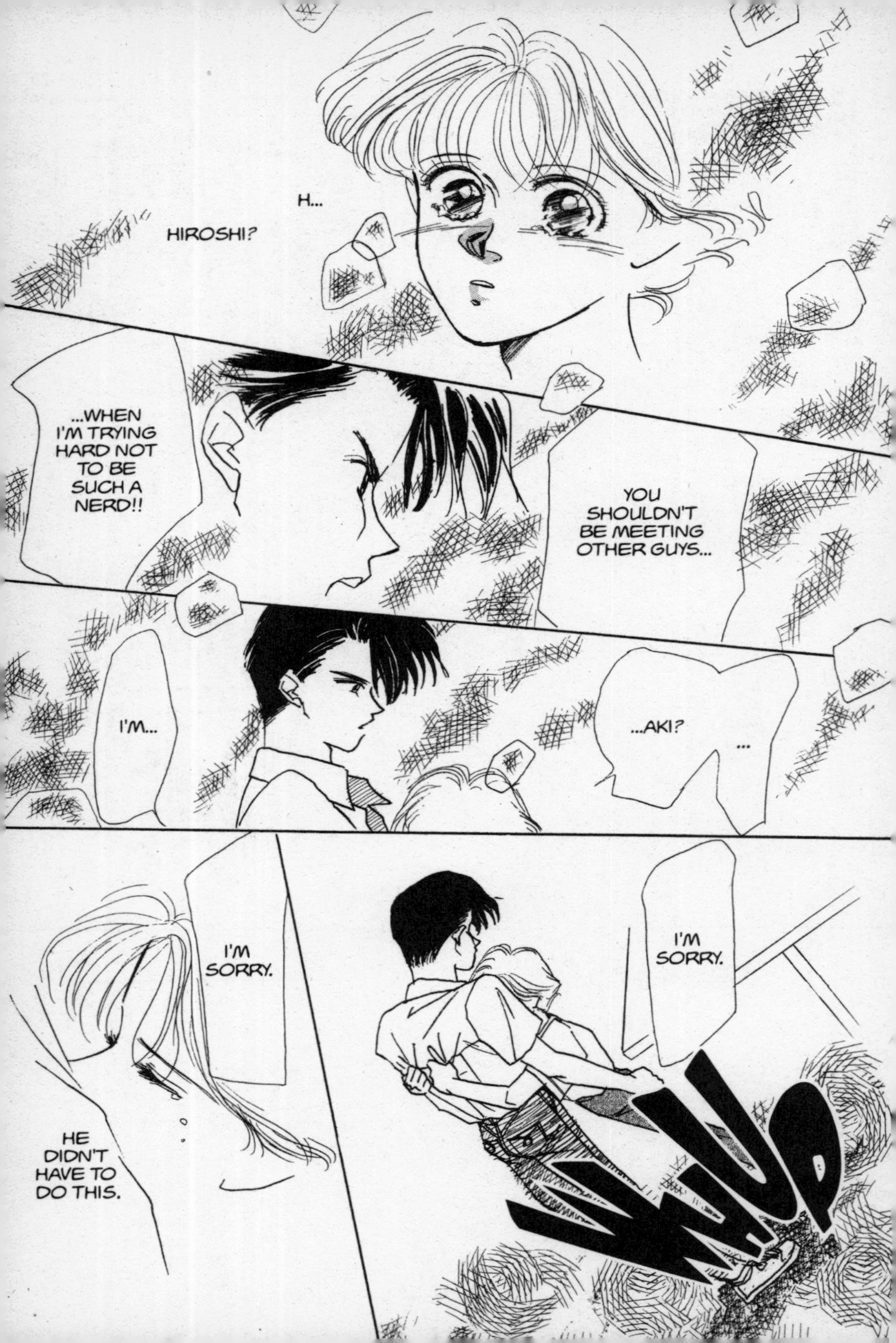
H...
HIROSHI?
YOU SHOULDN'T BE MEETING OTHER GUYS...
...WHEN I'M TRYING HARD NOT TO BE SUCH A NERD!!
...
...AKI?
I'M...
I'M SORRY.
WHUP
I'M SORRY.
HE DIDN'T HAVE TO DO THIS.

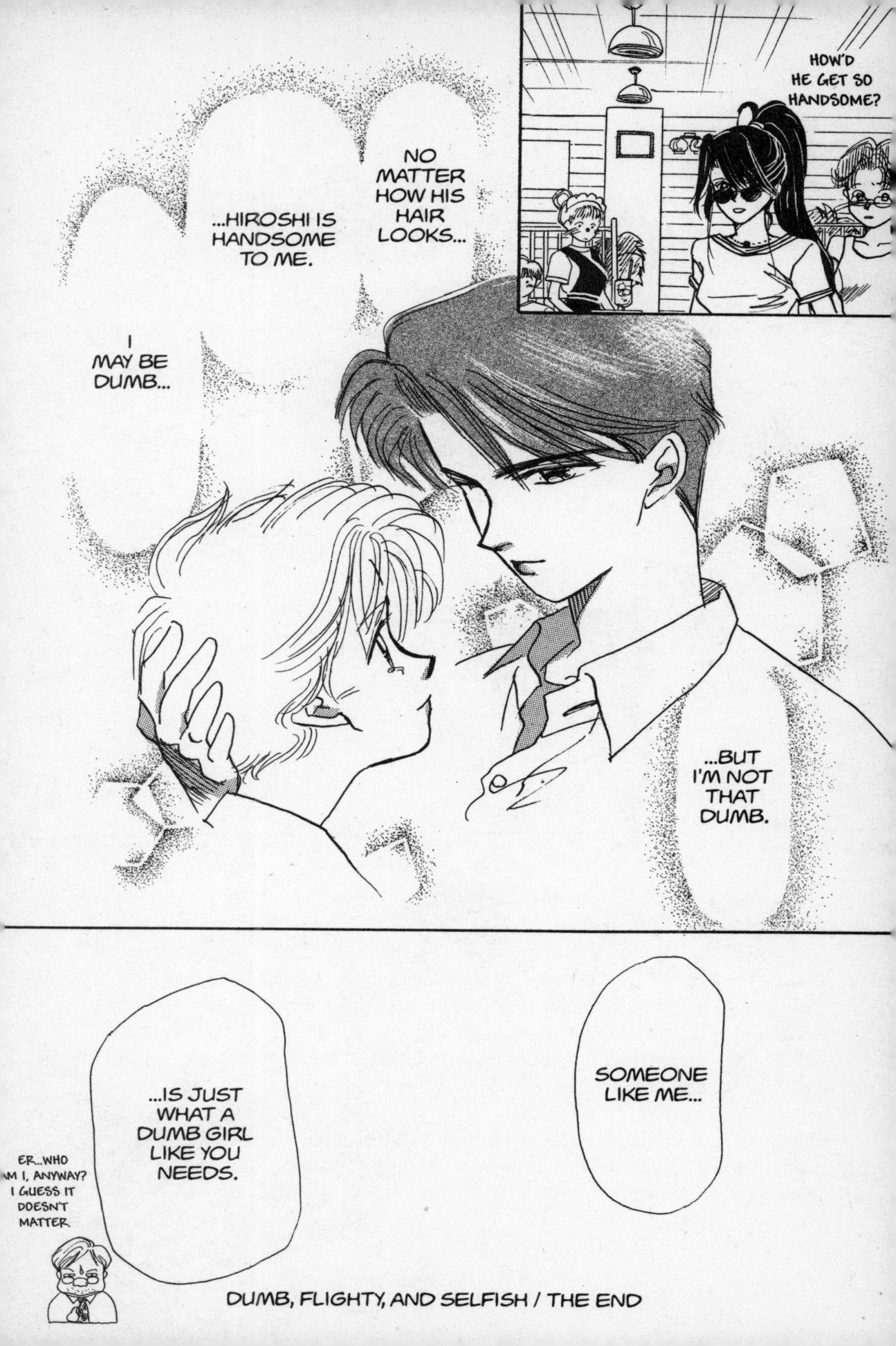
HOW'D HE GET SO HANDSOME?
NO MATTER HOW HIS HAIR LOOKS...
...HIROSHI IS HANDSOME TO ME.
I MAY BE DUMB...
...BUT I'M NOT THAT DUMB.
SOMEONE LIKE ME...
...IS JUST WHAT A DUMB GIRL LIKE YOU NEEDS.
ER...WHO AM I, ANYWAY? I GUESS IT DOESN'T MATTER.
DUMB, FLIGHTY, AND SELFISH / THE END

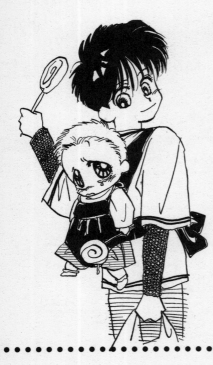

BABY & Me

Creator: Marimo Ragawa

SBM Title: *Baby & Me*

Date of Birth: September 21

Blood Type: B

Major Works: *Time Limit*, *Baby & Me*, *N.Y. N.Y.*, and *Shanimuni-Go* (Desperately—Go)

Marimo Ragawa first started submitting manga to a comic magazine when she was 12 years old. She kept up her submissions for four years, but to no avail. She decided to submit her work to the magazine *Hana to Yume*, where she received Top Prize in the Monthly Manga Contest as well as an honorable mention (Kasaku) in the magazine's Big Challenge contest. Her first manga was titled *Time Limit*. *Baby & Me* was honored with a Shogakukan Manga Award in 1995 and was spun off into an anime.

Ragawa's work showcases some very cute and expressive line work along with an incredible ability to depict complex emotions and relationships. Some of her other works include *N.Y. N.Y.* and the tennis manga *Shanimuni-Go*.

Ragawa has two brothers and two sisters.

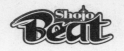

BABY & ME, Vol. 6
The Shojo Beat Manga Edition

Story & Art by
MARIMO RAGAWA

English Adaptation/Lance Caselman
Translation/JN Productions
Touch-up Art & Lettering/Mark Griffin
Design/Yuki Ameda
Editors/Pancha Diaz and Shaenon K. Garrity

Editor in Chief, Books/Alvin Lu
Editor in Chief, Magazines/Marc Weidenbaum
VP of Publishing Licensing/Rika Inouye
VP of Sales/Gonzalo Ferreyra
Sr. VP of Marketing/Liza Coppola
Publisher/Hyoe Narita

Akachan to Boku by Marimo Ragawa © Marimo Ragawa 1990. All rights reserved.
First published in Japan in 1993 by HAKUSENSHA, Inc., Tokyo. English language
translation rights in America and Canada arranged with HAKUSENSHA, Inc., Tokyo.
New and adapted artwork and text © 2008 VIZ Media, LLC. The stories, characters
and incidents mentioned in this publication are entirely fictional.

Printed in Canada

Published by VIZ Media, LLC
P.O. Box 77010
San Francisco, CA 94107

Shojo Beat Manga Edition
10 9 8 7 6 5 4 3 2 1
First printing, February 2008

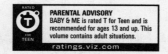

PARENTAL ADVISORY
BABY & ME is rated T for Teen and is
recommended for ages 13 and up. This
volume contains adult situations.
ratings.viz.com

store.viz.com

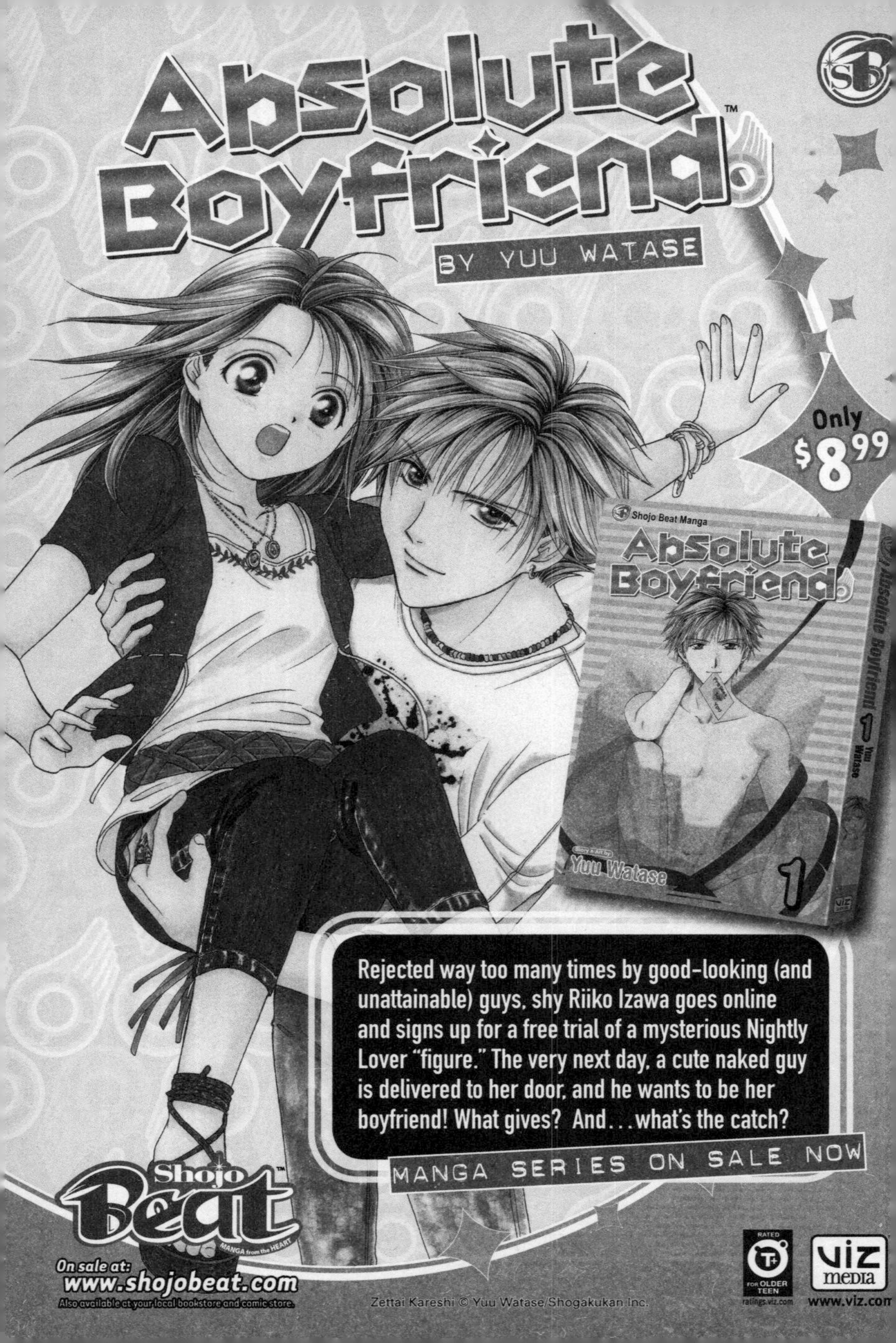
Absolute Boyfriend™
BY YUU WATASE
Only $8.99
Shojo Beat Manga
Absolute Boyfriend
Absolute Boyfriend 1 Yuu Watase
Story & Art by Yuu Watase
1
Rejected way too many times by good-looking (and unattainable) guys, shy Riiko Izawa goes online and signs up for a free trial of a mysterious Nightly Lover "figure." The very next day, a cute naked guy is delivered to her door, and he wants to be her boyfriend! What gives? And...what's the catch?
MANGA SERIES ON SALE NOW
Shojo Beat™
MANGA from the HEART
On sale at:
www.shojobeat.com
Also available at your local bookstore and comic store.
Zettai Kareshi © Yuu Watase/Shogakukan Inc.
RATED T+ FOR OLDER TEEN
ratings.viz.com
VIZ media
www.viz.com

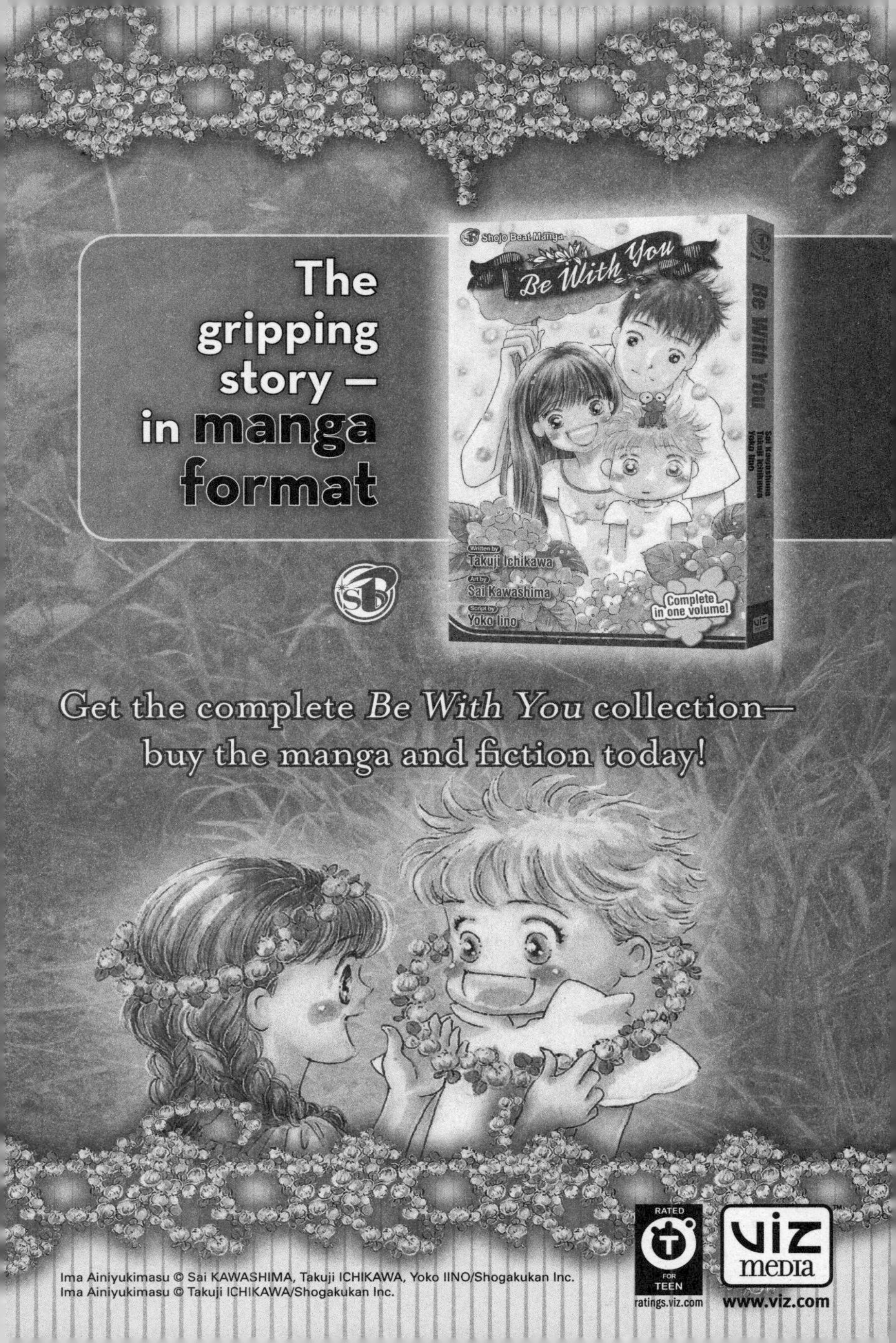
The gripping story — in manga format
Shojo Beat Manga
Be With You
Written by Takuji Ichikawa
Art by Sai Kawashima
Script by Yoko Iino
Complete in one volume!
Get the complete Be With You collection— buy the manga and fiction today!
Ima Ainiyukimasu © Sai KAWASHIMA, Takuji ICHIKAWA, Yoko IINO/Shogakukan Inc.
Ima Ainiyukimasu © Takuji ICHIKAWA/Shogakukan Inc.
RATED T FOR TEEN
ratings.viz.com
viz media
www.viz.com

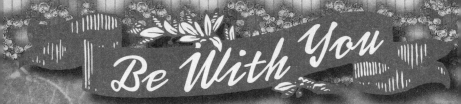
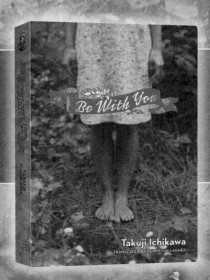

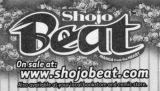

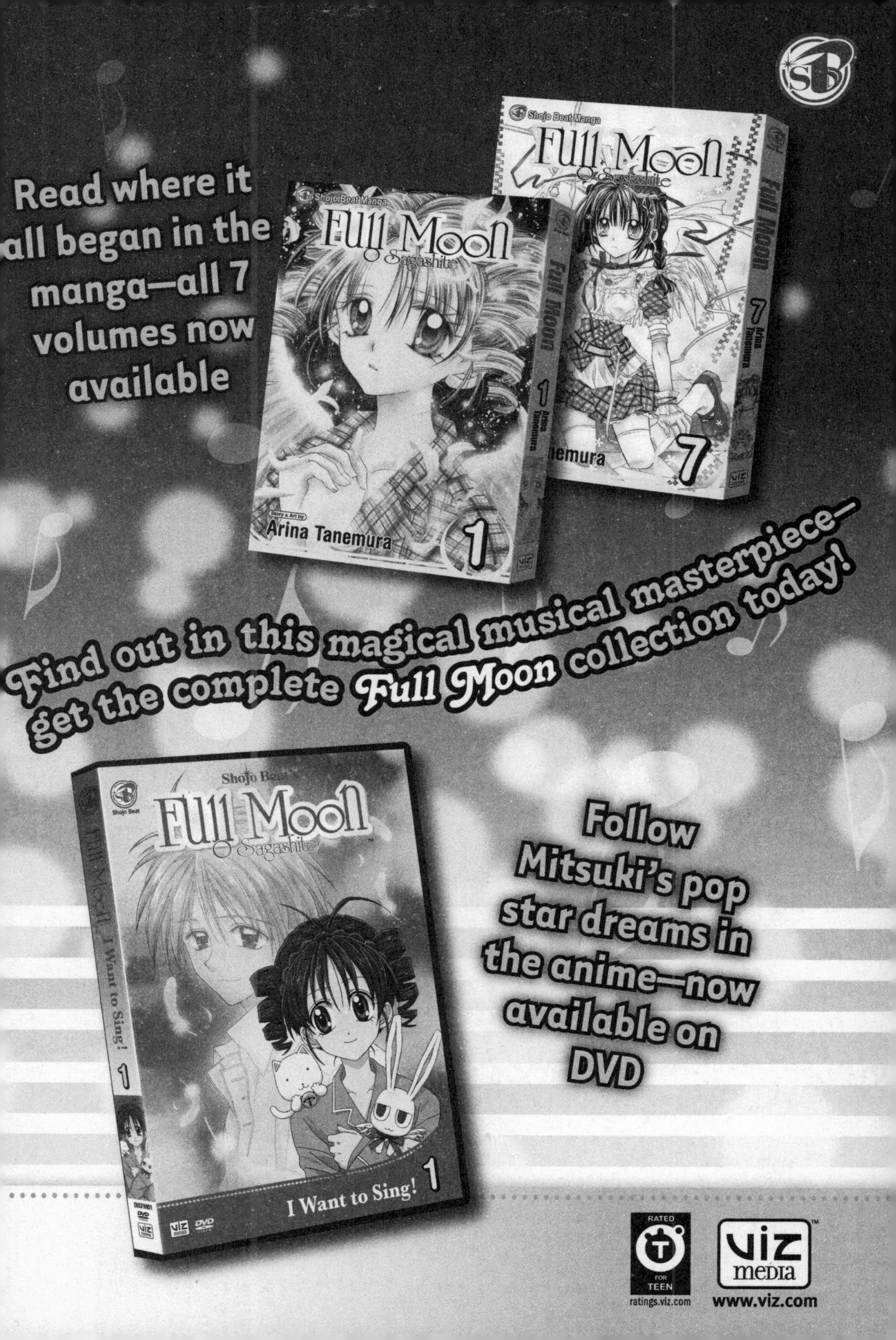
Read where it all began in the manga—all 7 volumes now available
Shojo Beat Manga
Full Moon O Sagashite
Story & Art by Arina Tanemura
1
7
Find out in this magical musical masterpiece—get the complete Full Moon collection today!
Shojo Beat
Full Moon O Sagashite
I Want to Sing! 1
Follow Mitsuki's pop star dreams in the anime—now available on DVD
RATED T FOR TEEN
ratings.viz.com
VIZ media
www.viz.com

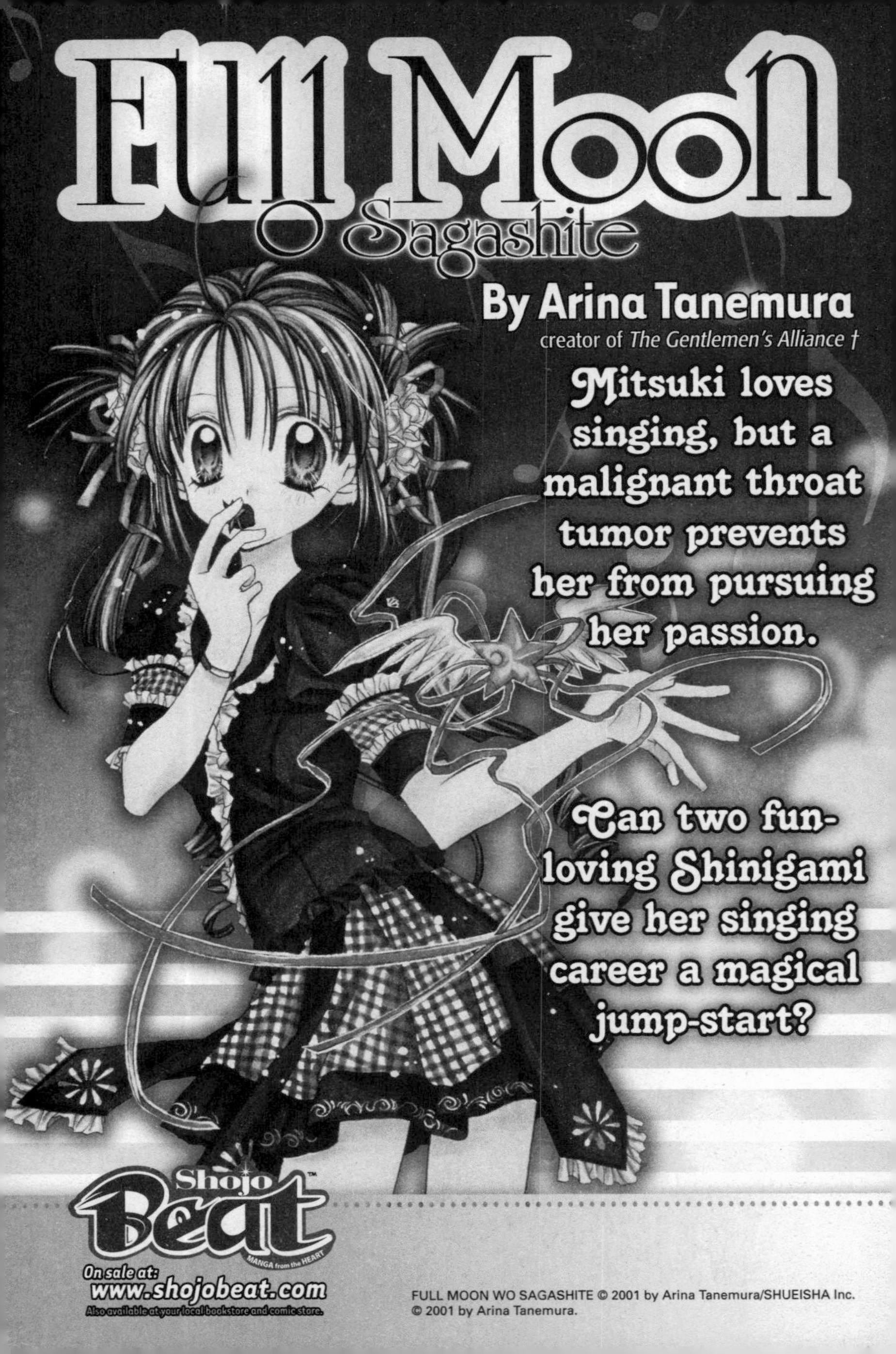

Full Moon
O Sagashite

By Arina Tanemura

creator of *The Gentlemen's Alliance †*

Mitsuki loves singing, but a malignant throat tumor prevents her from pursuing her passion.

Can two fun-loving Shinigami give her singing career a magical jump-start?

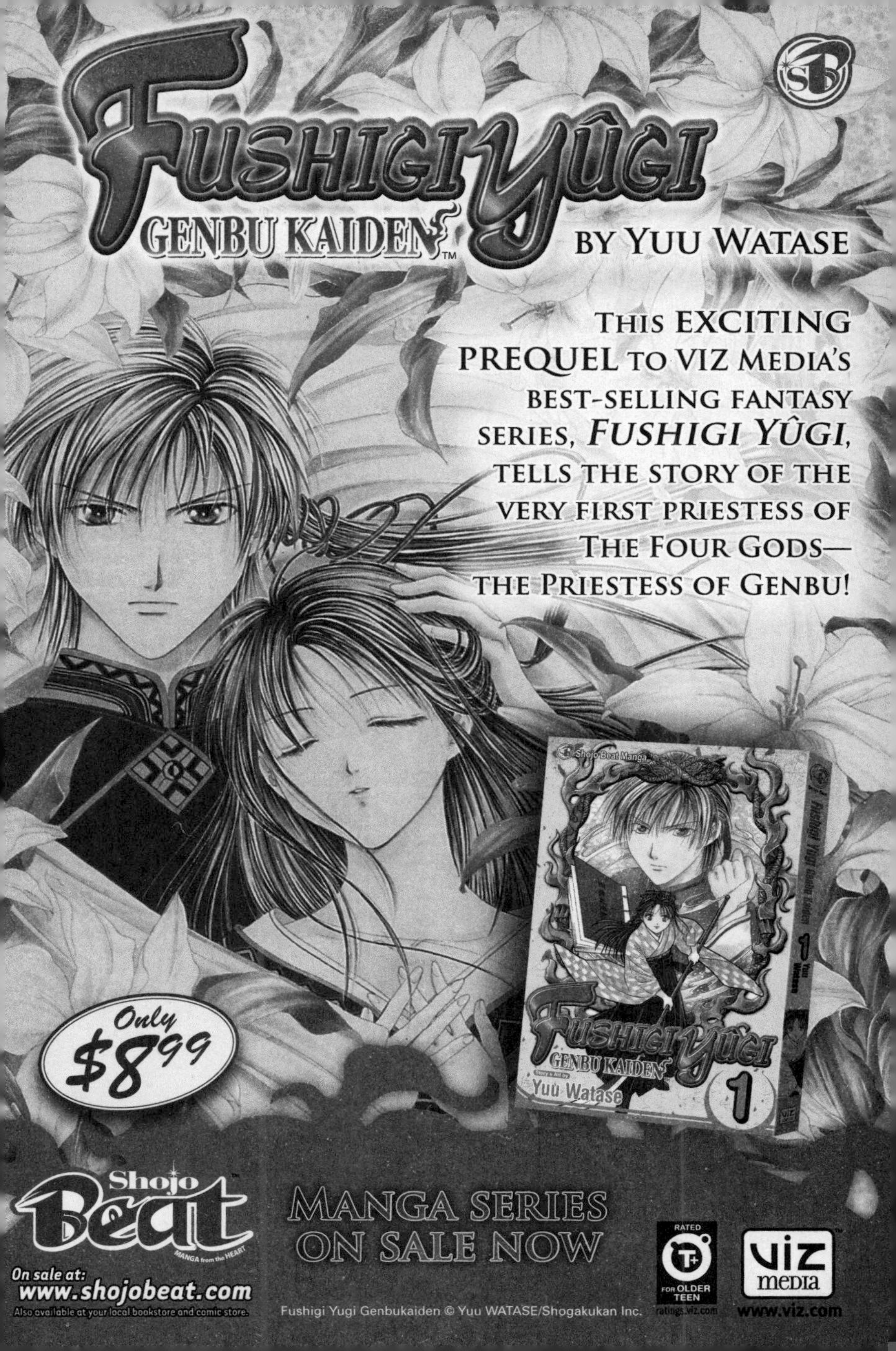

Fushigi Yûgi Genbu Kaiden™
by Yuu Watase
This exciting prequel to VIZ Media's best-selling fantasy series, Fushigi Yûgi, tells the story of the very first priestess of The Four Gods—the Priestess of Genbu!
Only $8.99
Shojo Beat Manga
Fushigi Yugi Genbu Kaiden
Story & Art by Yuu Watase
1
Shojo Beat™
MANGA from the HEART
On sale at:
www.shojobeat.com
Also available at your local bookstore and comic store.
MANGA SERIES ON SALE NOW
Fushigi Yugi Genbukaiden © Yuu WATASE/Shogakukan Inc.
RATED T+ FOR OLDER TEEN
ratings.viz.com
VIZ media
www.viz.com

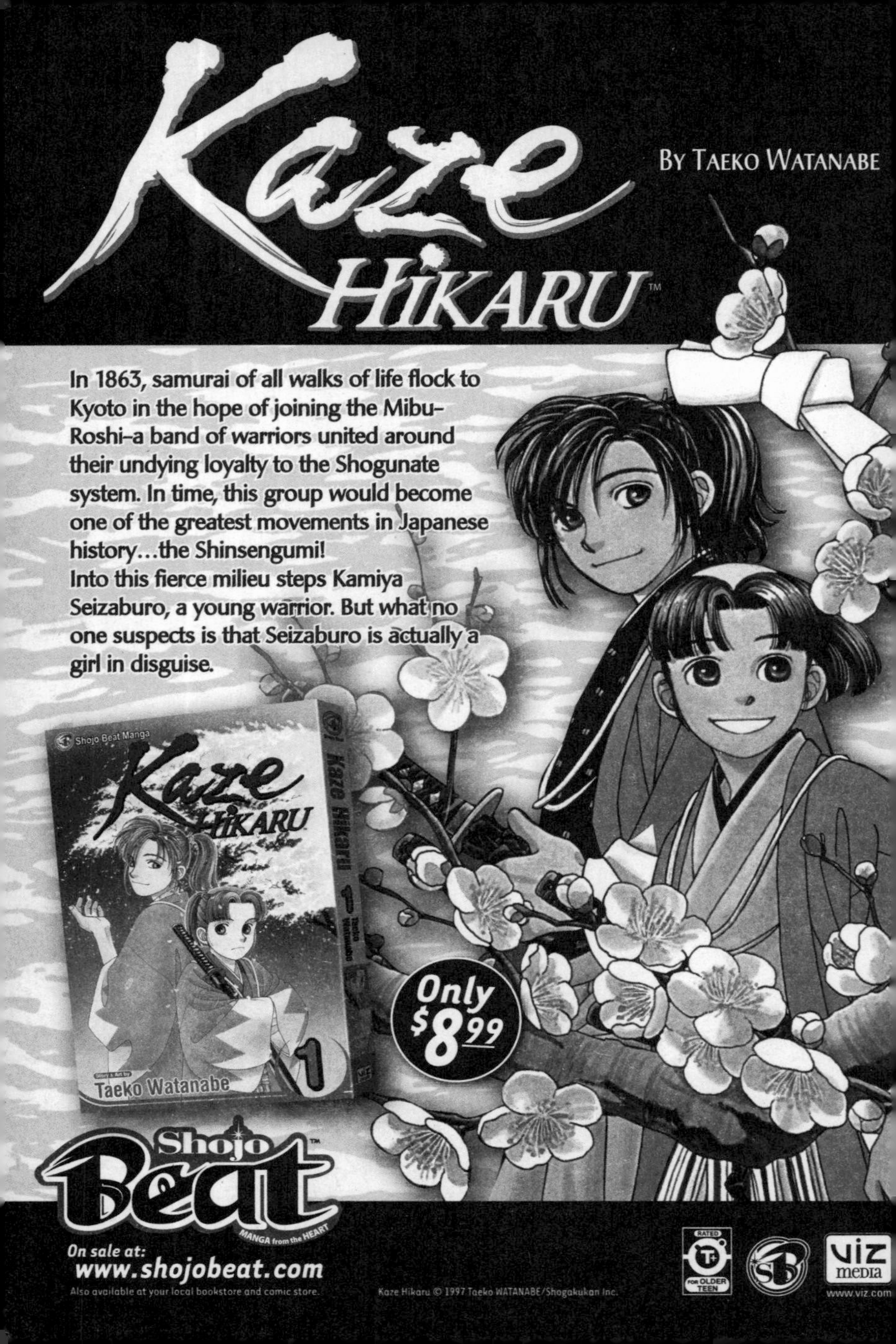

Kaze Hikaru™
By Taeko Watanabe
In 1863, samurai of all walks of life flock to Kyoto in the hope of joining the Mibu-Roshi–a band of warriors united around their undying loyalty to the Shogunate system. In time, this group would become one of the greatest movements in Japanese history…the Shinsengumi!
Into this fierce milieu steps Kamiya Seizaburo, a young warrior. But what no one suspects is that Seizaburo is actually a girl in disguise.
Shojo Beat Manga
Kaze Hikaru
1
Story & Art by
Taeko Watanabe
Only $8.99
Shojo Beat™
MANGA from the HEART
On sale at:
www.shojobeat.com
Also available at your local bookstore and comic store.
Kaze Hikaru © 1997 Taeko WATANABE/Shogakukan Inc.
RATED T+ FOR OLDER TEEN
viz media
www.viz.com

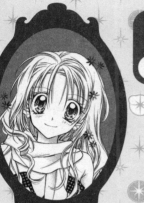
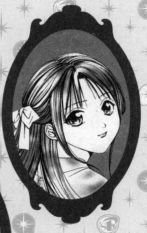

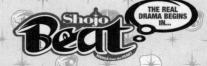

Shojo Beat™
MANGA from the HEART

12 GIANT issues for ONLY $34.99*

That's 51% OFF the cover price!

The Shojo Manga Authority

The most **ADDICTIVE** shojo manga stories from Japan **PLUS** unique editorial coverage on the arts, music, culture, fashion, and much more!

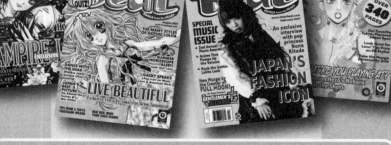

Subscribe NOW and become a member of the 🅢 Sub Club!

- **SAVE** 51% OFF the cover price
- **ALWAYS** get every issue
- **ACCESS** exclusive areas of www.shojobeat.com
- **FREE** members-only gifts several times a year

Strictly VIP!

3 EASY WAYS TO SUBSCRIBE!

1) Send in the subscription order form from this book **OR**
2) Log on to: www.shojobeat.com **OR**
3) Call 1-800-541-7876